ECONOMISTES AND THE REINVENTION OF EMPIRE

Exploring the myriad efforts to strengthen colonial empire that unfolded in response to France's imperial crisis in the second half of the eighteenth century, Pernille Røge examines how political economists, colonial administrators, planters, and entrepreneurs shaped the recalibration of empire in the Americas and in Africa alongside the intensification of the French Caribbean plantation complex. Emphasising the intellectual contributions of the Economistes (also known as the Physiocrats) to formulate a new colonial doctrine, the book highlights the advent of an imperial discourse of commercial liberalisation, free labour, agricultural development, and civilisation. With her careful documentation of the reciprocal impacts of economic ideas, colonial policy and practices, Røge also details key connections between Ancien Régime colonial innovation and the French Revolution's republican imperial agenda. The result is a novel perspective on the struggles to reinvent colonial empire in the final decades of the Ancien Régime and its influences on the French Revolution and beyond.

PERNILLE RØGE is Assistant Professor of History and convener of the Early Modern Worlds Initiative at the University of Pittsburgh. She is author of numerous articles and book chapters on the eighteenth-century French, Danish, and British colonial empires. She is also co-editor of *The Political Economy of Empire in the Early Modern World* (2013), with Sophus Reinert, and of the International Review of Social History's special issue on *Free and Unfree Labor in Atlantic and Indian Ocean Port Cities, 17th-19th Century* (2019), with Pepijn Brandon and Niklas Frykman.

NEW STUDIES IN EUROPEAN HISTORY

Edited by
PETER BALDWIN, University of California, Los Angeles
CHRISTOPHER CLARK, University of Cambridge
JAMES B. COLLINS, Georgetown University
MIA RODRÍGUEZ-SALGADO, London School of Economics and Political Science
LYNDAL ROPER, University of Oxford
TIMOTHY SNYDER, Yale University

The aim of this series in early modern and modern European history is to publish outstanding works of research, addressed to important themes across a wide geographical range, from southern and central Europe, to Scandinavia and Russia, from the time of the Renaissance to the present. As it develops the series will comprise focused works of wide contextual range and intellectual ambition.

A full list of titles published in the series can be found at:
www.cambridge.org/newstudiesineuropeanhistory

ECONOMISTES AND THE REINVENTION OF EMPIRE

France in the Americas and Africa,
c. 1750–1802

PERNILLE RØGE

University of Pittsburgh

CAMBRIDGE
UNIVERSITY PRESS

CAMBRIDGE
UNIVERSITY PRESS

University Printing House, Cambridge CB2 8BS, United Kingdom

One Liberty Plaza, 20th Floor, New York, NY 10006, USA

477 Williamstown Road, Port Melbourne, VIC 3207, Australia

314–321, 3rd Floor, Plot 3, Splendor Forum, Jasola District Centre,
New Delhi – 110025, India

79 Anson Road, #06–04/06, Singapore 079906

Cambridge University Press is part of the University of Cambridge.

It furthers the University's mission by disseminating knowledge in the pursuit of
education, learning, and research at the highest international levels of excellence.

www.cambridge.org
Information on this title: www.cambridge.org/9781108483131
DOI: 10.1017/9781108672900

First published 2019

Printed and bound in Great Britain by Clays Ltd, Elcograf S.p.A.

A catalogue record for this publication is available from the British Library.

ISBN 978-1-108-48313-1 Hardback

For Anders,
Oskar Emil and Otto

Contents

vii

Maps and Figures

Maps

Figures

Acknowledgements

This book has been long under way and is, like the history it narrates, shaped by numerous people, institutions, and places. It is therefore a privilege to be able to express my deep gratitude to all those who have supported me from its earliest inception to its completion. My first thanks go to Terence Murphy and Laurence Brown, my two undergraduate mentors at the American University of Paris, France. Terence Murphy's sharp wit drew me to Ancien Régime France and the French Revolution while Laurence Brown's passion for Caribbean history introduced me to a world of historical inquiry far beyond Europe. It was their classes that allowed me to see the contours of a possible research project on the eighteenth-century French colonial empire, just like it was their encouragements that led me to apply to the MPhil in Modern European History at the University of Cambridge.

As a graduate student in Cambridge, I was fortunate to have T.C.W. Blanning as my MPhil thesis advisor. His experienced hand and English humour guided me through my first year of graduate studies. Bernhard Fulda, Christopher Clark, Richard Evans, Hubertus Jahn, and Robert Tombs offered additional intellectual support. Maike Thier, Ruadhán Mac Cormaic, Kevin Quinlan, Jan Hennings, Jonathan Silverstein-Loeb, and Jonathan Goldberg helped me balance life as a budding historian. So did students, staff, and fellows at Queens' College, Cambridge, though no one more so than Louise Cowen, Adrien Vigier, Joseph Sandham, Miguel Ley Pineda, Natalie Evans, and Panagiotis Georgiadis. As my research interests moved towards imperial and intellectual history, I was blessed to have Richard Drayton as my supervisor and Emma Rothschild as my advisor. I could not have wished for a better team. Richard's intellectual creativity and his unrivalled ability to see the value of a rough research project, Emma's sharp eye, her kindness, and her profound knowledge of early modern France helped steer my doctoral dissertation towards completion. They taught me what it means to be a supportive mentor. I am forever in their debt.

As a Mellon Prize student at the Centre for History and Economics, Cambridge, I benefitted from insights and advice from Gareth Stedman Jones, William O'Reilly, Tim Harper, as well as the centre's students and fellows. Inga Huld Markan, my friend, my marathon partner! I was fortunate to enter my doctoral studies right as David Todd and Gabe Paquette finished theirs. Gabe's work inspired me to place my work within a larger transimperial framework. David read my drafts at various stages and offered invaluable comments at every turn. Conversations with Michael Sonenscher, Istvan Hunt, Christopher Bayly, Shruti Kapila, and Emma Spary helped further my project. Numerous doctoral students and research fellows at Cambridge inspired my work in direct and indirect ways. I profitted enormously from the reading group on French empires organised by David Todd and William Nelson that also included Anne-Isabel Richard, Isabel Noronha-DiVanna, Thomas Jones, and Tom Hopkins. Weekly seminars and workshops in World History, Modern European History, and the History of Political Thought allowed me to learn from Carrie Gibson, Elise Juzda Smith, Andrew Arsan, Tom Stammers, Catherine Bosley, Matthew Butler, Stefanie Gänger, Tom Neuhaus, Andrew Jarvis, Claire Levenson, Hester Vaizey, Jasper Heinzen, Michael Frisch, Victoria Harris, Emile Chabal, Dawn Dodds, Alois Maderspacher, David Motadel, Su Lin Lewis, D'Maris Coffman, and Jennifer Regan. Sophus Reinert shared my interest in the political economy of empire and collaborated with me on my first edited volume. When I defended my dissertation, Megan Vaughan and Keith Michael Baker offered fantastic advice on how to transform a PhD thesis into a book manuscript.

My doctoral research was supported by Det Obelske Familefond, the Arts and Humanities Research Council, UK, the Prince Consort Fund and the Ellen McArthur Fund at the University of Cambridge, and by the Centre for History and Economics, Cambridge. I was able to explore the Gustave Gimon Collection on French Political Economy at Stanford University as a visiting fellow in 2007. During this visit, I benefitted from my conversations with Keith Michael Baker, Dan Edelstein, Richard W. Lyman, and the history department's graduate students. Sarah Sussman helped me settle in. Nathalie and Ken Auerbach opened their home to me. During my numerous visits to French archives, Sofiane, Amine, and Zineb Bou-Salah always welcomed me with open arms. I am forever grateful to them. Archivists at the Archives nationales, the

Bibliothèque nationale, and the Ministère des affaires étrangères in Paris, the Archives départementales de la Gironde in Bordeaux, the Archives nationales d'outre-mer and the Musée Arbaud in Aix-en-Provence, the Archives départementales de la Martinique, the British National Archives in Kew, and librarians in Cambridge University Library's rare books room have helped me get to my requested sources and suggested new ones.

My visits to France allowed me to learn from numerous historians. Marcel Dorigny has supported this project since the first day I met him. Much of this book is in dialogue with his and Bernard Gainot's scholarship on the Société des amis des noirs and the French Revolution. Their encouragements have been vital to the evolution of this book. Allan Potofsky, François-Joseph Ruggiu, Paul Cohen, Bertie Mandelblatt, Loïc Charles, Paul Cheney, Cécile Vidal, Marie-Jeanne Rossignol, Pierre Singaravélou, and Manuel Covo were generous and insightful interlocutors as I developed my ideas. Right as I finished my doctoral research, Corpus Christi College, Cambridge, appointed me to a three-year college lectureship/research fellowship. My time at Corpus allowed me to start transforming my dissertation into a book. I am grateful to its fellows, staff, and history students. A special thanks to Keith Seffen, Sarah Fine, James Warren, Elizabeth Winter, Marina Fresca-Spada, Juliet Foster, Andrew Spencer, and Michael Sutherland whose company enriched my three years at Corpus.

In 2012, I moved to the University of Pittsburgh to take up an Assistant Professorship in History. My colleagues in the Department of History, and our graduate and undergraduate students, have provided me with a stimulating intellectual home to complete my research for this book and move it towards production. The European Studies Center awarded me a research grant to go to Martinique and Guadeloupe. In 2015, my chair, Lara Putnam, organized a manuscript workshop for me. I am grateful to her for her mentorship, and to everyone who participated in the workshop. A special thanks to Brett Rushforth, who came to Pitt and carefully engaged with my manuscript. Marcus Rediker, Rob Ruck, Niklas Frykman, Victoria Harms, Evelyn Rawski, Seymour Drescher, Holger Hoock, Gregor Thum, Mari Webel, Laura Gotkowitz, Molly Warsh, and Pepijn Brandon offered additional written comments and feedback. Amir Syed provided helpful comments on Chapter 4.

While at Pitt, I have also received advice and support from George Reid Andrews, Michel Gobat, Maurine Greenwald, Laurence Glasco, Bernard Hagerty, Lannie Hammond, Diego Holstein, Irina Livezeanu, Ruth Mostern, Raja Adal, Keisha N. Blain, Elizabeth Archibald, Jan

Musekamp, Carla Nappi, Tony Novosel, James Pickett, Scott Smith, John Stoner, Liann E. Tsoukas, Patrick Manning, Van Beck Hall, Janelle Greenberg, Allyson Delnore, Grace Tomcho, Kathy Gibson, Patty Landon, Zhaojin Zeng, Vincet Leung, Pinar Emiralioğlu, Ted Muller, Bill Chase, Jonathan Arac, Olivia Bloechl, Piotr Gwiazda, Emily Winerock, Emanuela Grama, Helen Wood, Adam Shear, Benno Weiner, Jamie Miller, Miriam Perez-Putnam, Michell Chresfield, Julia Guarneri, Molly Dennis-Estes, Alaina Roberts, David Luesink, Robert Bland, Katja Wezel, Urmi Willoughby, Madalina Veres, Katie Parker, Yevan Terrien, Patryk Reid, Abigail Owen, Elspeth Martini, Vanessa Mongey, Ryan Horne, Torsten Feys, Brian Shaev, Jessica Pickett, Christopher Drew Armstrong, Bruce Venarde, James Coleman, John Markoff, David Marshall, Anupama Jain, Michele Reid-Vazquez, Mrinalini Rajagopalan, Jennifer Waldron, Chloé Hogg, Chris Nygren, John Walsh III, Felix Germain, Todd Reeser, and Jotham Parsons.

As I was getting ready to submit my manuscript, Stuart Schwartz and Steven Pincus offered me an opportunity to share a draft of Chapter 3 at their Early Modern Empires Workshop at Yale University. Catherine Desbarats and Nicholas Dew allowed me to share a draft of the same chapter at their French Atlantic History Group at McGill University. I thank all participants at these two workshops for their wonderful comments and questions. Over the years, numerous colleagues in the field have helped me sharpen my ideas with their questions and observations – some at conferences, some through email correspondence. A special thanks to my co-panellists Alice Conklin, Jenna Nigro, and Bronwen McShea, whose research and comments allowed me to think about the history of French civilising missions in the longue durée. My co-panellists Christopher Hodson, Christopher Leslie Brown, and Gregory O'Malley helped me to think carefully about French activities in Senegambia. John Shovlin, Alexandre Dubé, Jeff Horn, William Doyle, Malick Ghachem, Rafe Blaufarb, and Laurie Wood offered comments or shared their work with me at important junctures. Sue Peabody, Christian Crouch, and Gillian Weiss gave good advice. Arad Gigi helped me in the archives. Michael Kwass and Michael Ledger Lomas provided generous feedback as I was making final revisions.

At Cambridge University Press several people helped me carry this project to completion. Michael Watson was patient and supportive, Liz Friend-Smith, Atifa Jiwa, Swati Kumari, and Holly Monteith lend their support at various stages. James B. Collins and two anonymous readers carefully read my manuscript. Their generous engagement with my work and invaluable feedback saved me from numerous mistakes and made the manuscript better. I am grateful to them all, and solely responsible for any remaining errors.

My greatest debt is to my extended family. Without their love and support I would not have finished this book. Inge Lise Jensen, Annich Michelle Bislev, Anne Kristine Helledi, Ewa Otulak, and Molly Warsh you are female power houses and a part of my family. My four goddesses – Lene, Mia, Laila, and Line – you spread sisterly laughter and support whenever I see you. My aunts and uncle, Aase, Magda, and Johan jumped on a plane to visit us in Pittsburgh. Mette, Jens Ole, Matias, Nanna, Ellen, Iben, Nikolai, Andreas, and Frida, you put a smile on my face. My grandparents, Inger and Børge, my uncle Niels Erik, and my father, Ole Jensen, I miss you and I look up to you. My family-in-law, Karen, Erik, Kristine, Søren, Andrea and Rebekka agreed to spend their summer holidays in Aix-en-Provence and Paris so that I could complete my research. My brothers, Jakob, Mads, and Peter keep me grounded with their humour and talents. Anders Jørgen has provided me with unconditional love since I was three. My mother, Birthe, is the strongest and wisest woman I know. The two of them have taught me to fight for my dreams, for my family, and to meet the world with an open mind. Anders Kloch Jeppesen, Oskar Emil, and Otto, you are my world. I dedicate this book to you.

Note on the Text

Throughout the text, I refer to the Secrétariat and Secrétaire d'État de la Marine during the Ancien Régime as the Ministry and the Minister of the Marine. Similarly, I refer to the Secrétariat and Secréetaire d'État des Affaires étrangères as the Ministry and Minister of Foreign Affairs. While researching this book, the Archives nationales d'outre-mer in Aix-en-Provence made the Correspondance à l'arrivée de la Martinique, Sous-série C8 and the archive on Personnel colonial ancien, Série E, XVIIe-XVIIIe available online. I have added their 'Référence Internet' for those documents in these two series that I consulted online but also preserved the archival reference.

Abbreviations

ADG	Archives départementales de la Gironde
ANOM	Archives nationales d'outre-mer, Aix-en-Provence
ANPMP	Archives nationales, Paris, Mirabeau Papers
AP	Archives Parlementaires de 1787 à 1860, French Revolution Digital Archive, University of Stanford. http://frda.stanford.edu
FM	Musée Arbaud, Aix-en-Provence, Fonds Mirabeau
MAE	Ministère des affaires étrangères, Paris
NAK	National Archives, Kew

Introduction

On 15 Messidor year V of the Revolutionary Calendar (3 July 1797), Citizen Talleyrand, known in his pre-revolutionary days as Charles Maurice de Talleyrand-Perigord, addressed the Institut National des Sciences et Arts in Paris on the 'advantages to be gained from new colonies in the current circumstances'.[1] To his listeners in the Institute, the intellectual power-house of the French Republic, 'current circumstances' was a recognisable shorthand for the cascade of events that had brought the Ancien Régime colonial empire to its knees. Metropolitan merchants' protected trade with the colonies had eroded as soon as authority collapsed and a chain of slave rebellions in Martinique, Guadeloupe, Guiana, and Saint-Domingue had jeopardised France's lucrative sugar and coffee industries. Then, in 1794, the combined forces of rebellion, warfare, and terror expedited the decree to abolish slavery throughout the French colonial empire, ushering in versions of republican rule in Saint-Domingue, Guiana, and Guadeloupe while pro-slavery planters on Martinique capitulated to British forces. By the time Talleyrand took to the podium, these cataclysmic events had nonetheless started to subside. Skilled at reading the winds, he therefore seized this opportune moment to advocate a new colonial doctrine for the French Republic.

Addressing the Institute as a member of its section on political econ-omy, and as a recent returnee from the United States, Talleyrand opened with the claim that men endowed with political foresight had long warned that the colonies in America would inevitably seek independence from their mother countries. Yet, he continued, European vice and mercantilist policies – '[t]hese pusillanimous doctrines that see a *loss* wherever a *gain* is made' – had accelerated the process and devastated

---

[1] Unless otherwise stated, all translations are my own. Charles Maurice de Talleyrand-Perigord, *Essai sur les avantages à retirer de colonies nouvelles dans les circonstances présents* (Paris: Baudouin, Imprimeur de l'Institut National, 1797).

and estranged the colonies. The Republic should therefore reject the old colonial strategies and embrace a just and kind approach that guaranteed free exchange and 'mutual enrichment'. He further promoted setting up new colonies with 'more natural, useful, and durable' ties to France, specifying that Egypt or 'a few settlements along the coast of Africa or on adjacent islands would be easy and fitting'. Africa, he contended, had a similar climate to that of the Americas and would allow for the production of American commodities on its soil. Since the decreed abolition of slavery had raised the need for a new system of cultivation, why not 'try such cultivation in the very region where the cultivators are born'? Regenerating the colonial system in such a manner, he emphasised, would beautifully complement the political achievements of revolutionary France.[2] All would be new. Or would it?

Some thirty years earlier, on a plot of land near the village of Rufisque in Senegal, a ship captain named Le Large was running his fingers through the topsoil to determine its fertility. Was this the right place for the colony and the cotton, indigo, sugar, and coffee plantations that the governor of Gorée, Jean-Georges, chevalier de Mesnager, was hoping to found? Le Large looked up. Cotton and indigo already grew around the village, cattle grazed and chickens and ducks waddled around. The air was fresh, the local fishing industry thrived, the dried fish was tasty, and the palm wine delicious, particularly when enjoyed cool. His sight fell on the local population. They looked healthy, large, and robust. Many were skilled farmers and fishermen and they seemed warmly disposed towards the French. He decided to report back that the plot was ideal for the founding of a new French colony.[3]

The terrain that Le Large reconnoitred belonged to the local ruler of Kayoor. The latter had offered it in tribute to de Mesnager after the governor had saved members of Kayoor's royal family from British slave traders. De Mesnager was now hoping to bring European settlers to Africa to found a colony that would compensate for the recent territorial losses France had incurred in the Americas in the Seven Years War. The moment was favourable, de Mesnager thought. The government had just abrogated the trade monopoly of the Compagnie des Indes in Africa and opened trade to all French traders – a policy in line with the latest fashion in

---

[2] Ibid., 3, 4, and 13.
[3] Report by Le Large, 14 September 1765, enclosed with a letter from de Mesnager to Choiseul, Gorée. Archives nationales d'outre-mer, Aix-en-Provence, France (hereafter ANOM), Sénégal et Côtes d'Afrique, Sous-série C⁶ (hereafter C⁶) 15, memo 56.

political economy. It was also in the throes of forming a new colony in Guiana and modifying trade policies with the Caribbean sugar islands as part of broad imperial reform. Le Large's expert knowledge of Senegambia, the governor hoped, would help whet the crown's interest in West African colonial expansion and inspire incoming settlers 'arriving with dreams of great fortunes'.[4]

Thirty-two years later, Talleyrand's proposal before the Institute came at a crucial moment in the Revolution. After the first calamitous years of rebellion and warfare, success on the battlefield had boosted French nationalist pride and transformed defensive warfare into a self-proclaimed mission to liberate Europe from the shackles of despotism. In addition to the abolition of slavery, the revolutionary government of the Convention had integrated the French colonies into the Republic as overseas departments in the Constitution of the year III (22 August 1795) and France was one year from sanctioning the invasion and colonisation of Egypt. Talleyrand's speech, therefore, seems to lend itself to a history in which French imperial innovation and resurrection took off during the later stages of the French Revolution. Yet his proposal, like so many others of the time, built on Ancien Régime experimentation, innovation, and reform.

Economistes and the Reinvention of Empire brings these connections between the First Republic's imperial agenda and Ancien Régime colonial innovation and reform into view. Tracing change in French colonial ideas, policy and practice, it explores multiple and often interlinked efforts to regenerate French imperial interests in the Americas and in Africa in the second half of the eighteenth century. As imperial warfare imperilled the crown's grip on colonial possessions in the Caribbean and on the North American continent, political economists, policy makers, stakeholders of colonial commerce, administrators, and local entrepreneurs on the ground participated in a wider struggle to reorganise and enhance French colonial commerce. Attention to their myriad efforts to shape the recalibration of empire during the last decades of the Ancien Régime allows us to contextualise the articulation of a republican imperial policy during the French Revolution in ways that get beyond the stale generalizations integral to the division between pre- and post-revolutionary France. It also allows us to broaden our understanding of the dynamics that drove colonial reform.

At the radical end of the Ancien Régime reformist spectrum were a group of political economists, known as the Economistes or the Physiocrates. From

---

[4] De Mesnager to Choiseul, undated, Gorée. ANOM C⁶ 15, memo 24.

the 1750s, this group elaborated a theoretical framework for a new mode of colonial empire in opposition to the body of commercial laws and attitudes that structured much of the existing French colonial system. Celebrating agriculture as the sole source of riches, they championed economic development over colonial exploitation, free international trade over monopoly trade, and free labour over slave labour. Later appropriated by revolutionaries during the Directory, their ideas were shaped not only by European intellectual circuits but also by policy makers and officials enmeshed in fractious and diverse colonial settings: an empire that was continually responding to, and occasionally even driving, efforts at top-down reform.

A core ambition of this book is to study how these attempts to reconstitute French empire in the Americas and in Africa developed in tandem with the better-studied push to strengthen the plantation complex in the Caribbean between the Seven Years War and the French Revolution. Within this story, the ambitions and perceptions of colonial entrepreneurs like Le Large and de Mesnager – as they sought to turn local land and labour into commodities and profit – proved decisive in shaping the colonial visions of political economists and metropolitan policy makers. In part for this reason, there is no single narrative arc of French imperial design, but rather multiple strands following distinct rhythms of change. With this polyphony in view, another core goal of this book is to examine how and why Talleyrand and his peers later adopted these elements of Ancien Régime colonial innovation for themselves as they set about fashioning a supposedly new imperial agenda for the First Republic.

Imperial Trajectories in the Second Half of the Eighteenth Century

The second half of the eighteenth century was an age of mammoth upheaval not only within the French imperial domains but across Europe's major colonial empires. In these decades, Britain rose as the prominent global power, yet warfare and competition crippled victor and losers alike. France lost its holdings up the Senegal River as well as its claims to colonial empire in India and on the North American mainland in the Seven Years War (1756–63) and was only able to secure the restoration of its sugar colonies in the Caribbean, a few trade stations in West Africa and India, and preservation of its Newfoundland fishery. Spain fared little better. Having joined the war on the side of the French in 1762, it was forced to cede Florida to Britain with the arrival of peace, prompting France to offer Louisiana to its ally in compensation. Britain could pride itself of territorial gains, yet the costs of war quickened its looming conflict with its thirteen colonies in North America and, once war broke out, saw it lose some of its earlier conquests. Over the years, the strains of rivalry and warfare among Europe's colonial empires generated a 'crisis of the anciens régimes' and a series of revolutions and independence movements in the Atlantic World, but also pan-European imperial reform as implicated powers strove to preserve their claims to colonies and markets.[5]

A key intellectual driver of reform was the growing attention paid to political economy. Whether one looks at Britain, France, Portugal, or Spain, this budding field 'galvanised a generation of reformers' looking to overhaul imperial relations and boost domestic prosperity. Proponents of often competing strands of political economy participated in attempts to recalibrate the characteristic features of what most scholars still refer to as Europe's mercantilist colonial systems.[6] Government officials with connections to the sprawling networks of merchants, traders, and economists readjusted tariff barriers and monopoly trade and scrutinised the obsession with a balance of commerce. During the 1760s, 1770s, and 1780s, first the Iberian and French colonial empires, and soon also the British, reorganised or abrogated the trade monopolies of chartered colonial companies and opened up sectors of colonial commerce to their merchants, while still looking to circumscribe colonies' access to international markets. In turn, the smaller maritime powers of the Dutch, Danes, and Swedes set out to enhance or develop their Caribbean free port systems in conjunction with a policy of neutrality to survive and profit from great power rivalry.[7]

---

[5] Jeremy Adelman, *Sovereignty and Revolution in the Iberian Atlantic* (Princeton, NJ: Princeton University Press, 2006), 5. On the Age of Revolution as an agent of imperial regeneration, see also his 'An Age of Imperial Revolutions', *The American Historical Review*, 113, 2 (2008), 319–40. On the global context of revolutions, see David Armitage and Sanjay Subrahmanyam (eds.), *The Age of Revolutions in Global Context, c. 1760–1840* (Basingstoke, UK: Palgrave Macmillan, 2010); on the French global context, see Suzanne Desan, Lynn Hunt, and William Max Nelson (eds.), *The French Revolution in Global Perspective* (Ithaca, NY: Cornell University Press, 2013).

[6] On political economy galvanicing reform, see Gabriel Paquette, *Enlightenment, Governance, and Reform in Spain and its Empire, 1759–1808* (Basingstoke, UK: Pagrave Macmillan, 2008), 2. On political economic theory and colonial empire more broadly, see Sophus Reinert and Pernille Røge (eds.), *The Political Economy of Empire in the Early Modern World* (London: Palgrave, 2013). For a critique of 'mercantilism', see Steven Pincus, 'Rethinking Mercantilism: Political Economy, the British Empire, and the Atlantic World in the Seventeenth and Eighteenth Centuries', *The William and Mary Quarterly*, 69, 1 (2012), 3–34, and Philip J. Stern and Carl Wennerlind (eds.), *Mercantilism Reimagined Political: Economy in Early Modern Britain and Its Empire* (Oxford: Oxford University Press, 2014).

[7] On Iberian imperial reform, see Adelman, *Sovereignty and Revolution*; Paquette, *Enlightenment, Governance, and Reform*. On French reform, see Jean Tarrade, *Le commerce colonial de la France à la fin de l'Ancien Régime. L'évolution du régime de 'l'Exclusif de 1763 à 1789*, 2 vols. (Paris: Presses universitaires de France, 1972). On Britain and its emulation of Bourbon reforms, see

For France, this broader moment of European imperial crisis and reform, pushed it to intensify its production of sugar and coffee for foreign markets. Boosting the French sugar and coffee business catered to French economic needs, but perpetuated endogenous problems particular to France and its colonies. In the eighteenth century, French colonial interests converged on the Caribbean plantation complex whose capital-intensive cash crop cultivation and forced labour system generated high profits for the metropole. Trailing British sugar production in the early 1700s, France became the world's greatest sugar producer in 1740 due to the rise of Saint-Domingue and soon also the biggest producer of coffee.[8] Yet the preservation of colonies in the Americas was inherently challenging in a region haunted by intermittent warfare, environmental disasters, epidemics, fraudulent colonial administrators, and often-distraught colonial populations. The quest to satisfy European consumers' appetites for sugar and coffee and French metropolitan merchants' ambitions to remain competitive on the world market further aggravated inherent instabilities. Seeking to drive up production, planters invested in technology, land, and ever-larger numbers of bonded labourers from Africa but fell into debt to colonial and metropolitan merchants along the way. Moreover, Saint-Domingue's privileged position within the French colonial system engendered intra-imperial frustrations because metropolitan merchants with an exclusive privilege to colonial markets – a system known as the Exclusif – preferred taking their manufactured goods, agricultural foodstuff, and African slaves to Saint-Domingue at the expense of other colonies.[9]

Tensions over provision, production, and debt in the French Caribbean colonies were compounded by anxieties produced by the use of African

---

Richard Drayton, *Nature's Government: Science, Imperial Britain, and the 'Improvement' of the World* (New Haven, CT: Yale University Press, 2000), 92. On the Dutch, Danes, and Swedes, see Han Jordaan and Victor Wilson, 'The Eighteenth-Century Danish, Dutch and Swedish Free Ports in the Northeastern Caribbean: Continuity and Change', in Gert Oostindie and Jessica V. Roitman, *Dutch Atlantic Connections, 1680–1800: Linking Empires, Bridging Borders* (Leiden: Brill, 2014), 275–308.

[8] On the French sugar and coffee economy, see Paul Butel, *L'économie française au XVIIIᵉ siècle* (Paris: Sedes, 1993), 114–15. On a definition of the plantation complex, see Philip D. Curtin, *The Rise and Fall of the Plantation Complex: Essays in Atlantic History*, 2nd edn. (Cambridge: Cambridge University Press, 1998), 10–13.

[9] On the ultimately ill-fated relationship between Ancien Régime France, its sugar economy, and nascent capitalism through the lens of a single plantation on Saint-Domingue, see Paul B. Cheney, *Cul de Sac: Patrimony, Capitalism, and Slavery in French Saint-Domingue* (Chicago: University of Chicago Press, 2017). On the growing prominence of Saint-Domingue at the expense of Guadeloupe and Martinique, see Tarrade, *Le commerce colonial*, i, 23. For an overview of Martinique and Guadeloupe's economic development, see Alain-Philippe Blérald, *Histoire économique de la Guadeloupe et de la Martinique du XVIIᵉ siècle à nos jours* (Paris: Karthala, 1986), Chapter 1.

slave labour. Colonial slavery was a brutal form of human exploitation, in which plantation owners and slave traders categorised African men, women, and children as commodities or cattle whose sole value stemmed from the labour that could be extracted from them. The demands for ever-higher numbers of slaves to maximise production generated a demographic imbalance in the colonies in which the enslaved population vastly out-numbered free whites. The latter constantly feared a violent reaction from African slaves, whose strategies of resistance took expression in both passive and aggressive forms. They also worried in ever-more racist tones about the rising population of free people of colour whose economic aspirations they found threatening to the colonies' social and racial hierarchies. Adding to these demographic concerns, slave owners increasingly faced moral headwinds as 'enlightened' sectors across the Atlantic World started portraying plantation slavery as incompatible with the moral fibre of civilised society.[10]

The French government was well aware of these mounting problems, yet the fiscal and financial benefits that it stood to make from its sugar colonies determined its response to them. It was not only merchants in French port cities or artisans producing goods for the plantations who chased the economic opportunities that the plantation complex fostered. Direct and indirect duties on colonial imports and exports bolstered state revenues and lined the pockets of receivers general and tax farmers, while state financiers and ministers reaped the benefits of private investments in colonial companies, sugar plantations, and sugar refineries. The quest for profits that drove the intensification of the plantation complex, however, was not confined to France. Several European states were willing to go to war to secure the colonial economies on which their domestic prosperity and consumer culture had come to rely. Excepting the 1720s, France was at war in every decade of the eighteenth century – often on numerous

---

[10] On the commodification of Africans during the transatlantic slave trade, see Marcus Rediker, *The Slave Ship: A Human History* (London: John Murray, 2007), and Stephanie E. Smallwood, *Saltwater Slavery: A Middle Passage from Africa to American Diaspora* (Cambridge, MA: Harvard University Press, 2008). On tensions between whites and free people of color, see Stewart R. King, *Blue Coat or Powdered Wig: Free People of Color in Pre-Revolutionary Saint Domingue* (Athens: University of Georgia Press, 2001). On the rise of anti-slavery in Atlantic and Global perspective, see David Brion Davis, *The Problem of Slavery in Western Culture* (Oxford: Oxford University Press, 1966), and Seymour Drescher, *Abolition: A History of Slavery and Antislavery* (New York: Cambridge University Press, 2009). On French anti-slavery, see Edward Derbyshire Seeber, *Anti-Slavery Opinion in France during the Second Half of the Eighteenth Century* (London: Oxford University Press, 1937); Jean Ehrard, *Lumière et Esclavage: L'Esclavage colonial et l'opinion publique en France au XVIIIᵉ siècle* (Bruxelle: André Versaille, 2008); and Madeleine Dobie, *Trading Places: Colonization and Slavery in Eighteenth-Century French Culture* (Ithaca, NY: Cornell University Press, 2010).

continents at once. Because it never found a sustainable way to finance these wars, the crown's ambitions to remain a leading power pushed it to teeter on the edge of bankruptcy as the eighteenth century unfolded. The expanded scene of conflict in the Spanish and then the Austrian Wars of Succession depleted state coffers while the costs of the Seven Years War and the American Revolution pushed the crown towards deluge.[11] With these latter wars, domestic, colonial, and trans-imperial tensions began to reinforce each other with alarming speed, threatening to render France's colonial empire in the Americas untenable within the existing French political and economic structures.

Economistes and the Rethinking of Colonial Empire

In an age of expanding public debate, none of this tumult went unnoticed. Since the seventeenth century, commentators had warned that France's political and social structures failed to respond adequately to the economic opportunities colonial and global commerce offered but also required to flourish. In the following century, an array of political economists of lesser or greater theoretical persuasion had turned their attention to the puzzle of how best to equip France to reap the benefits of colonial and global commerce. Among these were also the group of political economists with whom this book engages, a group co-founded by Victor Riqueti, marquis de Mirabeau and Doctor François Quesnay in the late 1750s and who later became known as the Physiocrats.[12]

The Physiocrats' critique of prevailing French colonial policies and practices, I argue in this book, embodied a radical rethinking of the under-pinnings of French relations with the Americas and Africa. Building on an

---

[11] On the financial burdens of warfare, see James C. Riley, *The Seven Years War and the Old Regime in France – The Economic and Financial Toll* (Princeton, NJ: Princeton University Press, 1986); on the fear of deluge, see Michael Sonenscher, *Before the Deluge – Public Debt, Inequality, and the Intellectual Origins of the French Revolution* (Princeton, NJ: Princeton University Press, 2007). The subject of the fiscal and financial problems leading to the French Revolution is discussed succinctly in Joël Félix, 'The Financial Origins of the French Revolution', in *The Origins of the French Revolution*, ed. Peter R. Campbell (Basingstoke, UK: Palgrave Macmillan, 2006), 35–62.

[12] On growing attention to commerce and agriculture, see Henry C. Clark, *Compass of Society: Commerce and Absolutism in Old-Regime France* (Lanham, MD: Lexington Books, 2007), and John Shovlin, *The Political Economy of Virtue: Luxury, Patriotism, and the Origins of the French Revolution* (Ithaca, NY: Cornell University Press, 2006). On the critique of Louis XIV's commercial policies, see Lionel Rothkrug, *Opposition to Louis XIV: The Political and Social Origins of the French Enlightenment* (Princeton, NJ: Princeton University Press, 1965). On the struggle to respond to expanding commercial opportunities and the rise of French economic thought, see Paul B. Cheney, *Revolutionary Commerce Globalization and the French Monarchy* (Cambridge, MA: Harvard University Press, 2010).

earlier generation of agrarian political economists, their economic doctrine rested on the notion that France was an agricultural monarchy whose failure to tend to the cultivation of land hindered its prosperity. In their view, agriculture was the sole source of riches. If allowed to thrive unfettered and in accordance with what they referred to as 'the natural order', a single land tax on the net product of agricultural production would be enough to alleviate the crown's financial problems and place the monarchy on a path to success. To the Physiocrats, the problem was that France's existing commercial laws impeded agricultural development. Labelling these laws the *système mercantile* years before Adam Smith baptised it the 'mercantile system', they castigated exclusive trade privileges, tariffs, and guilds as harmful to the general interests of the state.[13]

In the context of French colonial empire, the Physiocrats' critique of the mercantile system translated into damning attacks on the Exclusif and chartered colonial companies such as the French Compagnie des Indes. It also led to critiques of the institution of slavery and a reconceptualisation of colonies as 'overseas provinces'. Most in eighteenth-century France, including the Crown, viewed colonies as entities created to serve the economic development of the metropole. In contrast, the Physiocrats argued that the economic development of the metropole was best achieved if colonies enjoyed the same right to economic prosperity as French domestic provinces. According to Quesnay, colonies should be integrated into the metropole as overseas provinces and subjected to the same set of economic laws that he advocated for metropolitan France. This was a radical proposal at the time, not because colonies had never previously been depicted as provinces – Sicily, Sardinia, and Corsica were designated as *provinciae* of the Roman Empire – or because colonial integration was a new phenomenon.[14] The novelty of his proposition hinged on its

---

[13] On the Physiocrats' and Adam Smith's formulation and use of the concept of 'mercantile system', see Céline Spector, 'Le concept de mercantilism', *Revue de métaphysique et de morale* 39, 3 (2003), 289–309. Works that have informed my understanding of Physiocracy include Georges Weulersse, *Le mouvement physiocratique en France (de 1756 à 1770)*, 2 vols. (Paris: F. Alcan, 1910); Jean-Claude Perrot, *Une Histoire Intellectuelle de l'Economie Politique (XVIIᵉ–XVIIIᵉ siècle)* (Paris: Éditions de l'École des Hautes études en sciences sociales, 1992); Philippe Steiner, *La 'science nouvelle' de l'économie politique* (Paris: Presses Universitaires de France, 1998); Cathrine Larrère, *L'Invention de l'Économie au XVIIIᵉ siècle* (Paris: Presses Universitaires de France, 1992); Liana Vardi, *The Physiocrats and the World of the Enlightenment* (Cambridge: Cambridge University Press, 2012).

[14] On the Roman use and meanings of *provinciae*, see John Richardson, *The Language of Empire: Rome and the Idea of Empire from the Third Century B.C. to the Second Century A.D.* (Cambridge: Cambridge University Press, 2008), 11. On ideas of integration and assimilation in the early modern French colonial empire, see Saliha Belmessous, *Assimilation and Empire: Uniformity in French and British Colonies, 1541–1954* (Oxford: Oxford University Press, 2013), Part I.

assumption that the mutual prosperity of colonies and domestic provinces was best attained through the universal application of the same single and simple set of economic laws across the French colonial empire. This physiocratic reconceptualisation of colonies as overseas provinces, I argue in this book, served as an intellectual precursor to the recasting of colonies as 'overseas departments' in the Constitution of the year III.

Contemporaries of Quesnay usually depicted the doctor as the Physiocrats' principal leader and genius. While this may have been the case in terms of Physiocracy's domestic focus, the marquis de Mirabeau was the intellectual engine behind the doctrine's colonial stance. Mirabeau had developed a clear argument against the Exclusif before he started collaborating with Quesnay and had articulated a poignant critique of the use of African slave labour in his European best-seller, *L'Ami des hommes* (1756). Mirabeau's interest in colonies and slavery, as Michèle Duchet has noted, originated in the correspondence he maintained with his younger brother, Jean-Antoine Riqueti, chevalier de Mirabeau, during the latter's governorship of Guadeloupe in the 1750s. In the book, I analyse the ways in which *L'Ami des hommes* was a response to the chevalier de Mirabeau's abysmal portrayal of colonial life. I further consider how the marquis' ideas would subsequently influence Quesnay and the principal recruits to the physiocratic doctrine.[15] Although Mirabeau and Quesnay's earliest collaborator, Pierre-Paul Le Mercier de la Rivière, refrained from publicly attacking colonial slavery during his years as intendant of Martinique, key recruits such as the journalists Pierre Samuel Du Pont de Nemours, Abbé Nicolas Baudeau, and Abbé Pierre-Joseph-André Roubaud used the marquis de Mirabeau's initial critique to develop what they believed to be a more legitimate and rational form of colonial expansion. Mining a budding literature on the natural history of West Africa for commercial opportunities closer to home, they proposed relocating the production of sugar, coffee and other colonial cash crops to Africa where free local labourers could cultivate it with European encouragement. They coupled such suggestions with ideas of progress and 'civilisation', a concept coined by the marquis de Mirabeau and which would become integral to French imperialist discourse in the nineteenth and twentieth centuries.

Despite a recent increase in scholarly attention, the Physiocrats' ideas on colonial empire are not well known.[16] There is even a tendency to portray

---

[15] Michèle Duchet, *Anthropologie et histoire au siècle des Lumières*, 2nd edn. (Paris: Albin Michel, 1995), 161.

[16] There is still no single monograph on the colonial ideas of the Physiocrats except for André Labrouquère's dissertation, *Les idées coloniales des Physiocrates* (Paris: Presses Universitaires

the Physiocrats as early anti-colonialists. But like most men of letters in this period – including Denis Diderot who has been celebrated as an 'anti-imperialist' – the Physiocrats were not against colonial empire per se.[17] The body of physiocratic writings that discuss colonies, slavery, and empire contained an arsenal of suggestions on how to reconstitute the French relationship with its colonies. An amalgamation of their interventions – with their preference for free labour over slave labour, free trade over monopoly trade, and ideas of progress and 'civilisation' in Africa – could even sound like an early version of the vision promoted by liberalists who 'turned to empire' in the nineteenth century.[18] Such similarities between liberal imperialism and physiocratic colonial ideas should not be taken too far, of course. The Physiocrats were not 'liberals' in a political sense, but advocates of 'legal despotism', a term that contemporaries from Jean-Jacques Rousseau to Catherine the Great of Russia (mis)understood to offer an endorsement of despotic rule and top down reform, but which in actuality meant that if European despots agreed to rule in accordance

de France, 1927). Recent articles and book chapters include Alain Clément, '"Du bon et du mauvais usage des colonies": politique colonial et pensée économique française au XVIIIe siècle', *Cahiers D'Économie Politique* 56 (2009), 101–27; Dobie, *Trading Places*, Chapter 6; Marcel Dorigny, 'The Question of Slavery in the Physiocratic Texts: A Rereading of an Old Debate', in *Rethinking the Atlantic World: Europe and America in the Age of Democratic Revolutions*, ed. Manuela Albertone and Antonino De Francesco (London: Palgrave Macmillan, 2009), 147–62; and Caroline Oudin-Bastide and Philippe Steiner, *Calcul et Moral Coûts de l'esclavage et valeur de l'émancipation (XVIIIe–XIXe siècle)* (Paris: Albin Michel, 2015). My own research on this topic has appeared in Pernille Røge, '"La Clef de Commerce" – The Changing Role of Africa in France's Atlantic Empire c. 1760–1797', *History of European Ideas*, 34, special issue (2008), 431–43; Pernille Røge, 'The Question of Slavery in Physiocratic Political Economy', in *L'economia come linguaggio della politica nell'Europa del Settecento*, ed. Manuela Albertone (Milan: Feltrinelli, 2009), 149–69; Pernille Røge, 'A Natural Order of Empire: The Physiocratic Vision of Colonial France after the Seven Years' War', in *The Political Economy of Empire in the Early Modern World*, ed. Sophus Reinert and Pernille Røge (London: Palgrave, 2013), 32–52.

[17] Those who group the Physiocrats under anticolonialism include Claude Liauzu, *Histoire de l'anticolonialisme en France du XVIe siècle à nos jours* (Paris: Fayard/Pluriel, 2010), 43; Marcel Merle, 'L'Anticolonialisme', in *Le livre noir du colonialisme: XVIe–XXIe siècle: de l'extermination à la repentance*, ed. Marc Ferro (Paris: Robert Laffont, 2003), 815–61; and Sudipta Das, *Myths and Realities of French Imperialism in India, 1763–1783* (New York: Peter Lang, 1992), 28–29. The notion that Enlightenment thinkers were against colonial empire is articulated most clearly in Sankar Muthu, *Enlightenment against Empire* (Princeton, NJ: Princeton University Press, 2003), Chapter 3. Against this view, Christian Donath has argued that Abbé Raynal and Denis Diderot's *Histoire des deux Indes* embodied arguments in favour of an approach to colonial empire predicated on persuasion which later shaped Napoleon's military conquest of Egypt. See Christian Donath, 'Persuasion's Empire: French Imperial Reformism, 1763–1801', PhD dissertation, UC San Diego, 2012.

[18] On liberals and liberalism's turn to empire, see Jennifer Pitts, *A Turn to Empire: The Rise of Imperial Liberalism in Britain and France* (Princeton, NJ: Princeton University Press, 2005). On liberal imperialism in Europe, see Matthew Fitzpatrick (ed.), *Liberal Imperialism in Europe* (Basingstoke, UK: Palgrave Macmillan, 2012).

with Physiocracy (the term they used to describe their ideas and which means 'the rule of nature'), their regimes would constitute a legal form of despotism.[19]

The Physiocrats' rethinking of colonisation in the Americas and in Africa was profoundly at odds with the prevailing policies and practices that undergirded the French plantation complex. Though Ann Thomson and Madeleine Dobie have traced their ideas into Denis Diderot and Abbé Raynal's international bestseller, *Histoire philosophique et politique des établissements et du commerce des Européens dans les deux Indes* and eighteenth-century fiction, most statesmen, political economists, and commercial communities across France's maritime and urban regions of growth whose economies relied on the Exclusif and slave labour went out of their way to highlight the alleged flaws and misconceptions of the Physiocrats' colonial proposals as part of their wider attack on Physiocracy.[20] Despite such resistance, I argue in this book that aspects of the Physiocrats' colonial doctrine and vocabulary did come to resonate with some policy makers, officials, and colonial agents. In French colonies in the Americas and in West Africa, people on the ground who participated in reformist processes mapped new ideas and concepts, including physiocratic ones, onto colonial realities, though rarely in a manner that their original authors had intended, and always in combination with competing strands of political economy and in dialogue with the French crown's own attempts to ameliorate its colonial system from within its existing political and economic structures. In the book, I illuminate these resonances with particular attention to the Îles du Vent (Martinique, Guadeloupe, and their dependencies and also known as the Lesser Antilles) and French holdings in Senegambia to shed light on the sometimes tenuous and at other times observable relationship between intellectual innovation, colonial policy, and practices on the ground.

---

[19] This misunderstanding was clarified by the marquis de Mirabeau in his correspondence with Jean-Jacques Rousseau, in which he pointed out that 'le despotisme légal n'est autre chose que le despotisme de l'axiome: Deux et deux font quatre, appliqué au gouvernement des sociétés.' Cited in Louis de Loménie, *Les Mirabeau, Nouvelles Études sur La Société Française au XVIIIe siècle*, 5 vols. (Paris: E. Dentu, 1879–91), ii, 274. On the term 'legal despotism' and debates on its later historiographical variants 'enlightened absolutism' and 'enlightened despotism', see H. M. Scott (ed.), *Enlightened Absolutism: Reform and Reformers in Later Eighteenth-Century Europe* (London: Macmillan Education, 1990).

[20] Ann Thomson, 'Diderot, Roubaud; l'Esclavage', *Recherches sur Diderot et sur l'Encyclopédie*, 35 (2003), 73–93; Dobie, *Trading Places*. Contemporary critique of Physiocracy is illuminated in Gérard Klotz, Philippe Minard, and Arnaud Orain (eds.), *Les voies de la richesses? La physiocratie en question (1760–1850)* (Rennes: Presses Universitaires de Rennes, 2017).

French Colonies in the Americas and Africa

Possessions in the Caribbean and in West Africa were the main pivots around which concerns about the future of colonial empire turned in the second half of the eighteenth century. Along with Saint-Domingue, the Îles du Vent constituted France's most valuable theatres of sugar and coffee production while the French holdings in Senegambia were strategic locations for the protection of the French slave trade that supplied the sugar colonies with labour. Linking these areas to the development and circulation of alternative ideas and approaches to colonies, commerce, land, and labour, I examine in the book the ways in which colonial officials, independent entrepreneurs, and planters in the Îles du Vent and in Senegal partook in the rethinking of empire in this period. For Guadeloupe and Martinique, such an approach enables us to restore their critical role in the evolution of imperial reform between the Seven Years War and the French Revolution. In turn, a focus on Senegal reveals the ways in which French holdings in West Africa were not only sites for the transatlantic slave trade but also of colonial experimentation.

Guadeloupe and Martinique were some of France's oldest sugar colonies, whose relations to the metropole exacerbated in conjunction with the rise of Saint-Domingue. Tensions between them and domestic France rose exponentially when Guadeloupe capitulated to Britain in 1759 and Martinique did so in 1762. In the aftermath of Guadeloupe's surrender, the Crown scrambled to grant disgruntled white planters on Martinique and on Saint-Domingue metropolitan representation in the royal Council of Commerce on terms equal to French domestic provinces. The Council, as David Kammerling Smith has shown, was the central node within the 'communicative circuit' of metropolitan commercial lobbyists and policy makers that 'debated and negotiated economic affairs'. A seat within the Council, enabled planters to immediately respond to policy proposals, challenge commercial agendas of metropolitan ports, and shape colonial policy. Integral to that, the crown also established three Chambres mi-parties d'agriculture et de commerce in 1759 (two on Saint-Domingue and one on Martinique), in which colonial elites could deliberate on how best to attain local and colonial prosperity. Resonant with elements of the physiocratic view to eliminate colonial-metropolitan inequality and to encourage the development of agriculture throughout the colonial empire, the 1759 reform represented a shift in the crown's perspective on colonies towards an accommodation of planter interests and their right to prosperity.[21]

---

[21] This shift in attitude is more commonly dated to the transition from the Exclusif to the Exclusif mitigé in 1767. See, for instance, Guy Chaussinand-Nogaret, *Choiseul – naissance de la gauche* (Paris:

An analysis of the founding and activities of Martinique's *Chambre mi-partie d'agriculture et de commerce* discloses the ways in which Martinique's plantocracy used their position within what was now an intra-imperial communicative circuit to modify colonial policies and practices. Introduced to their commission by the intendant and Physiocrat-in-the-making, Le Mercier de la Rivière, members of the chamber dexterously appropriated some of the core tenets of Physiocracy when it served their interests, while unashamedly ignoring others. In the book, I show how the Chambre mi-partie d'agriculture et de commerce on Martinique – which transformed into the Chambre d'agriculture in 1763 and then the Assemblée coloniale in 1787 – came to serve as a midwife for a creole political economic discourse that sought reform in its own right – one that would eventually become a powerful and flexible tool with which to protect planter interests during the early stages of the French Revolution.

Scholars have paid relatively little attention to the contributions of the Îles du Vent to French imperial reform in the decades leading up to the Revolution. We are well aware of the importance of Martinique's first representative to Paris, Jean Dubuc, whom Étienne-François duc de Choiseul, Minister of the Marine from 1761 to 1766, appointed to the position of *premier commis* (a powerful position which usually entailed drafting a minister's policy proposals, instructions, and letters, filtering incoming correspondence, and keeping their assigned bureau in order) within the Ministry of the Marine of which French colonies were an administrative branch. Yet the Martinican side of this history – the extensive power not just of Jean Dubuc but also of the local Tribu des Dubucs, and the broader contributions of the island's white planter elite to the history of Ancien Régime centralisation, colonial integration, and innovation – is little known. One consequence of this is that we currently have an exaggerated picture of the political relevance of elite planters from the better-studied colony of Saint-Domingue in the same period. Focusing on the harder-pressed planters in the Îles du Vent helps balance this picture

Perrin, 1998), 212–13. On the emergence of this communicative circuit between 1700 and 1720, see David Kammerling Smith, 'Structuring Politics in Early Eighteenth-Century France: The Political Innovations of the French Council of Commerce', *The Journal of Modern History* 74, 3 (2002), 495. On the power of the Council of Commerce in the eighteenth century, see Philippe Minard, *La fortune du colbertisme: État et industrie dans la France des Lumières* (Paris: Fayard, 1998), 26. On the 1759 reform, see Jean Tarrade, 'L'administration coloniale en France à la fin de l'ancien régime: Projets de réforme', *Revue historique*, 229 (1963), 103–22, and Henri Joucla, *Le Conseil Supérieur des Colonies et ses Antécédents avec de nombreux documents inédits et notamment les procès-verbaux du comité colonial de l'assemblée constituante* (Paris: Les Editions du Monde Moderne, 1927), 20–23 and 38–43.

and nuance our understanding of the multipolarity of voices that propelled and challenged reform in the final decades of the Ancien Régime.[22]

Innovation, experimentation, and debates also animated French colonial activities in West Africa. Based on an assumed availability of cheap local labour and undeveloped fertile lands – and amidst their active participation in slave trading – colonial agents expanded French interests in the region in the aftermath of the Seven Years War, often in anticipation of a doomed French colonial future in the Americas. Local representatives of the Crown prepared to found colonies and develop cash crop cultivation on land opposite the island of Gorée and in negotiation with African rulers. Few generated more than ephemeral success and the French Ministry of the Marine deliberately sought to scale back experimentation. Only with the outbreak of the American Revolution did it become more amenable to these initiatives. At that juncture, commercial companies also began promoting French colonial expansion in West Africa, sometimes presenting their plans in a language of 'civilisation' and development. On the eve of the French Revolution, Stanislas de Boufflers, governor of Senegal, came closer than his predecessors in offering proof of a viable expansionist colonial project in West Africa, shipping cotton to France from his African plantations cultivated by labourers of unclear social status. While recent studies highlight how British, Danish, and Swedish colonial powers experimented with cash crop cultivation in West Africa alongside the transatlantic slave trade in the late-eighteenth century, French efforts in Senegambia and the context within which they took place remain largely unknown. This book reflects how the French participated in these experimental processes and in competition with other European powers, particularly the British.[23]

---

[22] On the evolution of the position of *premier commis*, see James Pritchard, *Louis XV's Navy 1748–1762: A Study of Organization and Administration* (Montreal: McGill-Queen's University Press, 1987), 29–33. Recent literature on the Saint-Domingue colonial elites include but is not confined to James E. McClellan, *Colonialism and Science: Saint Domingue in the Old Regime* (Baltimore: Johns Hopkins University Press, 1992); John D. Garrigus, *Before Haiti: Race and Citizenship in French Saint-Domingue* (Basingstoke, UK: Palgrave Macmillan, 2006); Charles Frostin, *Les révoltes blanches à Saint-Domingue aux XVIIe–XVIIIe siècles*, new edn. (Rennes: Presses Universitaires de Rennes, 2008); Malick Ghachem, *The Old Regime and the Haitian Revolution* (Cambridge: Cambridge University Press, 2012); Cheney, *Cul de Sac*.

[23] On Dutch, Swedish, and Danish efforts, see for instance Robin Law, Suzanne Schwarz, and Silke Strickrodt (eds.), *Western Africa: Commercial Agriculture, the Slave Trade and Slavery in Atlantic Africa* (Suffolk: James Currey, 2013); Daniel Hopkins, *Peter Thonning and Denmark's Guinea Commission: A Study in Nineteenth-Century African Colonial Geography* (Leiden: Brill, 2012), Part I; and Christopher Leslie Brown, *Moral Capital: Foundations of British Abolitionism* (Chapel Hill: University of North Carolina, 2006), Chapter 5. French proposals to expand into Africa in the second half of the eighteenth century are briefly mentioned in William B. Cohen, *The French Encounter with Africans White Response to Blacks, 1530–1880* (1980; repr., Bloomington:

The myriad efforts to expand French colonial interests in West Africa between the Seven Years War and the French Revolution disclose the diverse ways in which colonial innovation and experimentation intersected with the French Crown's ambition to strengthen its plantation complex in the Caribbean. Such multiplex and co-existing agendas are rarely captured in current interpretations of French colonial policy in these years. Recent studies underscore either a French 'no-territory policy' according to which the crown systematically refrained from investing in colonial expansion beyond the current cluster of islands and their contributory trade stations in India, West Africa, and South America or see in the same moment an embrace of 'Enlightenment colonialism'. Pushing the former, François-Joseph Ruggiu argues that in peace negotiations during the Seven Years War, the Crown – spearheaded by Choiseul – proved willing to sacrifice New France, Louisiana, trade up the Senegal River, and all but five trade stations in India (Pondicherry, Yanaon, Karikal, Mahé, and Chandernagor) to salvage its fishery off the coast of Canada and its Caribbean sugar colonies. Choiseul's rationale was that a small but extremely profitable colonial empire would stimulate the French economy, boost state coffers, and finance a strong navy to keep British pretentions to 'universal monarchy' in check.[24]

Another body of scholarship highlights the period after the Seven Years War as one in which growing interest in botany, agronomy, and scientific improvement stimulated French attempts to expand overseas. Scholars who focus on colonial experimentation on the ground – on Mauritius (formerly Ile de France) and Madagascar in the Indian Ocean and on French Guiana in South America – have portrayed the last three decades of the Ancien Régime as years of 'Enlightenment colonialism' and experimentation. Though most of these experiments enjoyed only minimal success – including the attempt to launch a slave-free colony at Kourou in French Guiana, Pierre Poivre's endeavours to advocate agricultural development on Ile de France by means of what he deemed a morally

---

Indiana University Press, 2003), 162–3; and Léonce Jore, *Les établissements français sur la côte occidentale d'Afrique de 1758à 1809* (Paris: publisher, 1964), 355.

[24] Ruggiu develops this interpretation in two publications, one on India and one on Canada. See François-Joseph Ruggiu, 'India and the Reshaping of the French colonial Policy', *Itinerario*, 35, 2 (2011), 25–43, and François-Joseph Ruggiu, 'Falling into Oblivion? Canada and the French Monarchy, 1759–1783', in *Revisiting 1759: The Conquest of Canada in Historical Perspective*, ed. Phillip Buckner and John G. Reid (Toronto: University of Toronto Press, 2012), 69–94. On the broader context for French imperial policy in these years, see Carl Ludwig Lokke, *France and the Colonial Question: A study of contemporary French opinion 1763–1801* (New York: Columbia University Press, 1932), and Pierre Boulle's unpublished dissertation, 'The French Colonies and the Reform of Their Administration during and following the Seven Years War', PhD dissertation, University of California, Berkeley, 1968.

sound labour system, or the comte de Maudave's initiative to establish a slave-free colony on Madagascar – they do not easily align with the 'no-territory' thesis.[25]

As my book shows, any opposition between 'Enlightenment colonialism' and a 'no-territory policy' is nonetheless illusory. Several and sometimes opposing policies and practices were deployed to maintain French colonial dominance on a global scale between the Seven Years War and the French Revolution (and surely also in other periods). The sheer number of ministers, governors, and intendants who cycled through the Ministry of the Marine as they fell in and out of favour at court ensured the co-existence of various approaches to colonial management and reform. Most officials ruled the colonies in accordance with prevailing norms and formal policies, of course, but they could also deviate from more conventional paths depending on their personal economic interests, interpretation of local opportunities, relationships to the Crown, and commitment to new intellectual trends. The same could be said for the many semi-private colonial agents whose business activities received government protection in exchange for their willingness to shoulder parts of the financial costs of empire. In tandem with a 'no-territory policy' that catered to the Caribbean plantation complex in the last four decades of the Ancien Régime, multiple colonial actors forged ahead with alternative paths to empire in pursuit of new markets and profits.

The French Revolution and the Tale of Two Colonial Empires

The numerous possible approaches to French colonial empire debated and explored during the last four decades of the Bourbon monarchy enabled a comprehensive recalibration of imperial ambitions once the French Revolution threw the plantation complex in the Americas into jeopardy.

---

[25] The term 'Enlightenment colonialism' stems from Megan Vaughan, *Creating the Creole Island: Slavery in Eighteenth-Century Mauritius* (Durham, NC: Duke University Press, 2005), 65. On the French Guiana project, see Emma Rothschild, 'A Horrible Tragedy in the French Atlantic', *Past & Present*, 192, 1 (2006), 67–108; Christopher Hodson, *The Acadian Diaspora: An Eighteenth-Century History* (Oxford: Oxford University Press, 2012), Chapter 3; Marion F. Godfroy, *Kourou, 1763: Le dernier rêve de l'Amérique française* (Paris: Vendémiaire, 2011). On Pierre Poivre see Vaughan, *Creating the Creole Island*, and Richard H. Grove, *Green Imperialism Colonial Expansion, Tropical Island Edens and the Origins of Environmentalism, 1600–1860* (Cambridge: Cambridge University Press, 1995), 168–263. On Madagascar, see Jean Meyer, Jean Tarrade, Annie Rey-Goldzeiguer, and Jacques Thobie, *Histoire de La France Coloniale Des origines à 1914*, 2 vols. (Paris: Armand Colin Éditeur, 1991), i, 222–5. On science and the eighteenth-century French colonial empire, see James McClellan III and François Regourd, *The Colonial Machine French Science and Overseas Expansion in the Old Regime* (Turnhout, Belgium: Brepols International, 2012).

I trace these continuities with respect to the ways in which revolutionaries set out to transform metropolitan relations with the Americas and Africa. As I show, members of France's first abolitionist society, the Société des amis des noirs (founded in 1788), were the first to initiate thoroughgoing reform. Like the Physiocrats, the *amis des noirs* promoted free labour over slave labour, a liberalisation of colonial commerce, and the spread of civilisation in Africa through the creation of new agricultural colonies. As the escalation of widespread slave revolt in the French Caribbean and revolutionary warfare in Europe and in the Americas endangered the preservation of the plantation complex, numerous policy makers followed in the *amis des noirs*'s footsteps. They hastened to integrate colonies into the metropole as 'overseas departments' equal to the newly reorganized metropolitan departments. In so doing, they injected political content into what had been a physiocratic suggestion to integrate domestic and overseas provinces under one law predicated primarily on an economic rationale. They also began promoting the creation of new slave-free colonies in Africa. Rather than breaking with Ancien Régime trends, they thus appropriated and expanded existing strands of imperial thought and experimentation as they set about articulating a French republican imperial agenda.

By casting the revolutionary decade as a crescendo of longer-term efforts to reinvent the French colonial empire, *Economistes and the Reinvention of Empire* complicates narratives that see this period as a cradle for France's 'imperial renaissance' in the nineteenth century.[26] In such literature, the Revolution stands as the birthplace of a liberal and republican imperial ideology that recast French imperial orientations, particularly with respect to Africa and the Americas. In their study of France's first and second abolitionist societies – the Société des amis des noirs and the Société des amis des noirs et des colonies – Marcel Dorigny and Bernard Gainot, for instance, note the ambitions of these two societies to create 'new colonies' and bring 'civilisation' to Africa through commercial exchange and agricultural development. And though they insist on particularly the Société des amis des noirs's emphasis on colonisation without territorial conquest, they identify within the second society an evolving imperialist agenda directed towards Africa that included 'the premises of the future colonial empire of the nineteenth century'. Gainot has also depicted the Constitution of the year III that declared Martinique, Guadeloupe, Réunion, and French Guiana overseas departments of the French Republic as the point of

---

[26] The notion of an 'imperial renaissance' is from Jean Martin, *L'empire renaissant (1789–1871)* (Paris: Persée, 1987).

departure for the long process of integration and departmentalisation of these *vieilles colonies* (old colonies) that culminated in the establishment of the Départements et territoires d'outre-mer (DOM-TOM) in 1946 and which still characterises France's relationship with these territories. In a similar manner, Jennifer E. Sessions and Alice L. Conklin highlight the importance of the legacies of the revolutionary and Napoleonic decades – and particularly the Egyptian expedition – to France's subsequent conquest of Algeria and civilising mission in West Africa. These scholars are right to argue that the Revolution and Napoleonic period helped pave the way for later imperial developments. But as I show, when successive French regimes tapped into the French Revolution for ideas and approaches of empire to justify their colonial relationship with the Caribbean and expansionist activities in Africa, they simultaneously connected with Ancien Régime innovation, experimentation, and reform.[27]

By showing how the French Revolution consolidated earlier processes of imperial innovation, this book also softens the emphasis on a rupture between the pre- and post-revolutionary period and between France's so-called first and second colonial empires. In histories of French colonialism, France's 'first' colonial empire appears as an early modern empire anchored in the Americas, worked by predominantly African slave labour, and undergirded by metropolitan exclusive trade privileges, while the 'second' colonial empire is cast as an empire that slowly integrated its older colonies into the metropole while embracing an expansionist policy towards the continents of Africa and Asia underpinned by a *mission civilisatrice* and military conquest. This tale of two empires is further corroborated with a narrative of decline, rupture, and rebirth associated with domestic regime changes. In this vein, the decline of the 'first' colonial empire began with the Seven Years War, when France lost Canada and India to Britain and gave Louisiana to Spain, and culminated in the revolutionary and Napoleonic periods with the temporary collapse of the

[27] Marcel Dorigny and Bernard Gainot, *La société des amis des noirs, 1788–1799: Contribution à l'histoire de l'abolition de l'esclavage* (Paris: UNESCO, 1998), 36–39 and 313. See also Yves Benot, *La Révolution française et la fin des colonies 1789–1794*, 2nd edn. (Paris: La Découverte, 2004), 194–5. Marcel Dorigny, 'La Société des Amis des noirs et les projets de colonisation en Afrique', *Annales historiques de la Révolution française*, 293–4 (1993), 421–9; Marcel Dorigny, 'Intégration républicaine des colonies et projets de colonisation de l'Afrique: civiliser pour émanciper?', in *Grégoire et la cause des noirs (1789–1831)*, ed. Yves Bénot and Marcel Dorigny (Paris: Société française d'histoire d'Outre-mer, 2005), 89–105. Alice L. Conklin, *A Mission to Civilize: the Republican Idea of Empire in France and West Africa, 1895–1930* (Stanford: Stanford University Press, 1997), 17–19; Jennifer E. Sessions, *By Sword and Plow: France and the Conquest of Algeria* (Ithaca, NY: Cornell University Press, 2011), 6–7. On the Revolution and the DOM-TOM, see Bernard Gainot, 'La naissance des départements d'Outre-Mer La loi du 1er janvier 1798', *Revue historique des Mascareignes*, 1 (1998), 51–74.

slave-driven plantation complex and the independence of Saint-Domingue
in 1804 (Haiti). The rise of the 'second' colonial empire, in turn, is
tentatively dated to the French Revolution, after which the second empire
was consolidated in a series of steps, spanning the invasion of Algeria in
1830, the second abolition of slavery in 1848, the gradual integration and
assimilation of Martinique, Guadeloupe, French Guiana, and La Réunion
into the metropole, and the Third Republic's espousal of the *mission
civilisatrice* in the 1880s, which carried France deep into Africa.[28]

Decline, rupture, and rebirth form a part of the history of French
colonialism, yet they only reveal one side of the story. The other side is
that of continuity. In his *Old Regime and the Haitian Revolution*, Malick
Ghachem teases out how a set of 'strategic ethics' to safeguard and control
the colony of Saint-Domingue during the French Revolution was rooted in
the decrees of the seventeenth-century Code Noir that structured religious
and racial relations in the colonies. Ghachem thereby detects a continuation of the old within the new. Similarly, David Todd has identified
a return of the Exclusif in the first half of the nineteenth century. In
their separate ways, both scholars explore the lingering impacts of well-
established Ancien Régime policies and practices in the revolutionary and
post-revolutionary periods.[29] Additional continuities come into view,
I argue, when we focus on processes to reinvent French colonial relations
with the Americas and Africa during the last decades of the Ancien Régime
and their influences on republican imperialism in the revolutionary period
and beyond.

Identifying continuities and reappearances of colonial ideas, policies,
and practices across the *longue durée* enables us to suspend the linearity

---

[28] Committed to such a narrative, comprehensive histories of French colonialism see the years between
1789 and 1830 as the crucial dates for closure and departure. The first two volumes of the six-volume
L'aventure coloniale de la France reveal precisely this logic. Volume 1 is Philippe Haudrère, *L'empire
des rois (1500–1789)* (Paris: Persée, 1997), which ends with the Revolution. Volume 2 is Martin,
L'empire renaissant, which ascribes the rise of the second empire to this period. Similarly, the multi-
authored study *Histoire de la France coloniale: des origines à 1914* (followed by *Histoire de la France
coloniale, 1914–1990*) divides the period around the dates 'origins to 1763' and '1763–1830', stressing
the period 1789–1830 as the collapse of the first colonial empire and 1830 as the departure for
the second. Jean Meyer, Jean Tarrade, Annie Rey-Goldzeiguer, and Jacques Thobie, *Histoire de la
France coloniale*. Pierre Pluchon and Denise Bouche's *Histoire de la colonisation française* repeats this
division, providing 1815 as the key date for the end of the first colonial empire. Pierre Pluchon,
L'histoire de la colonisation française, I: Le premier empire colonial: des origines à la restauration (Paris:
Fayard, 1991). For a condensed version of this narrative of two empires and their rise and fall see
Gérard Gabriel Marion, 'L'outre-mer français: de la domination à la reconnaissance', *Pouvoirs*, 113
(2005), 233–40.
[29] Ghachem, *The Old Regime and the Haitian Revolution*; David Todd, 'A French Imperial Meridian,
1814–1870', *Past & Present*, 210, 1 (2011), 155–86.

ingrained in the narrative of a 'first' colonial empire's rise and decline, a revolutionary rupture, and the rise of a 'second' colonial empire in the nineteenth and twentieth centuries. In its place, a focus on innovation and continuity alongside moments of rupture allows for a polyrhythmic history that exposes ways in which prevailing modes of colonial empire overlapped and interlocked with experimentation and change. Dominant colonial policies and practices always co-existed with, and responded to, novel and competing ideas and approaches on the ground that followed different logics and that might appear only momentarily or perhaps grow in force right at the moment when previously dominant policies were falling out of favour. My book seeks to accommodate these intertwined processes in all their complexity.

Connecting Ideas, Policies, and Practices

Embracing a polyrhythmic narrative brings questions in its trail: What gave birth to innovative processes when they occurred? How were they received? Why did some triumph at a given time and others not? Why did some resurface years later with reinvigorated force? I explore these questions through the lens of political economy in the period between the Seven Years War and the rise of Napoleon. Their answers, I show, lie neither within a single archive nor in a narrow European intellectual history of colonial ideas but through a combination of miscellaneous sources and historical methodological approaches associated with intellectual history and with the history of French colonial policy and practice. I am guided by David N. Livingstone's insistence that for ideas to gain force, they 'must resonate with their environments or they [cannot] find expression, secure agreement, or mobilize followers'. Moreover, as Shruti Kapila observes, sometimes there were 'significant ruptures in the meaning, content, and use' of ideas as they circulated through different locales.[30] While paying attention to these spatial factors, I try to remain sensitive to the broader historical transformations that characterise the period under investigation. The world looked very different in 1756 than it did in 1802. The Seven Years War, the American Revolution, and the French and

---

[30] David N. Livingstone, *Putting Science in Its Place: Geographies of Scientific Knowledge* (Chicago: University of Chicago Press, 2003), 7. Shruti Kapila, 'Global Intellectual History and the Indian Political', in *Rethinking Modern European Intellectual History*, ed. Darrin M. McMahon and Samuel Moyn (Oxford: Oxford University Press, 2014), 254. For discussions on the avenues opened up by the global turn in intellectual history, see Samuel Moyn and Andrew Sartori (eds.), *Global Intellectual History* (New York: Columbia University Press, 2013).

Haitian Revolutions subverted traditional political, economic, social, and cultural norms and geopolitical configurations. In the process, they shifted the parameters of innovation and historical possibility.

My interest in the connections between ideas, policy, and practice in the context of innovation and reform leads to sources that were generated through the fragile networks of communication between private and official colonial agents. These authors were not primarily focused on arguments about political economy, let alone theory, even when they sometimes echoed strands of contemporary thought. Instead, they were typically concerned with how to survive and profit from the French colonial empire. In addition, moving from the pages of published treatises to archival sources uncovers a reality that never adhered to an ideal type enclosed French colonial empire, but reflects the diversity of competing interest groups pertaining to it. French colonies were part of an empire but simultaneously rubbed up against, or were fully integrated into, other regional networks and communities. Respecting these local realities means exploring ideas as they appeared, transformed, disappeared, and reappeared within the broader transatlantic framework of colonial and regional life.

Keeping this in sight, the foundation of *Economistes and the Reinvention of Empire*'s reinterpretation rests on a close scrutiny of miscellaneous sources. Alongside published treatises of political economy, I use archival depositories of past colonial and commercial policies and practices to gain insights about eighteenth-century political economic ideas in action. I draw heavily on the Fonds des colonies, Sous-séries C6 on Africa, Sous-série C7 on Guadeloupe, and Sous-série C8 on Martinique, and the Collection Moreau de Saint-Méry Sous-série F3 located in Aix-en-Provence; letters of correspondence between the Mirabeau brothers, held at Musée Arbaud in Aix-en-Provence; papers from Bordeaux's Chambre de commerce in the Archives départementales de la Gironde; the Archives du Ministère des Affaires Etrangères in Paris, and papers on the British occupation of Martinique at the National Archives in Kew. I combine these archival materials with eighteenth-century journals, legal documents, and printed administrative directives and reports.

The structure of the book is largely chronological. It begins on the eve of the Seven Years War and ends with the rise of Napoleon, layering the argument with attention to developments in France, the Îles du Vent, and Senegal in between. Chapter 1 provides a historical context for the intellectual and reformist processes that the Seven Years War set in motion. It uses the governorship of chevalier de Mirabeau on Guadeloupe as a window onto the growing crisis of the Ancien Régime colonial empire and then shifts to the war itself to analyse how the Crown and stakeholders of empire struggled to negotiate the future of the French colonies. Chapter 2 explores the Physiocrats' articulation of a new theoretic framework for colonial empire. Chapter 3 studies the founding of the Chambre mi-partie d'agriculture et de commerce on Martinique and the unintended consequences that this reform produced. Chapter 4 explores how French government officials, semi-private commercial companies, and independent colonial agents discussed opportunities for colonial empire in Senegal and strove to test the feasibility of territorial expansion and cash crop cultivation in this region. Chapter 5 connects the processes of innovation and reform explored in the book's first four chapters with the formulation of a republican imperial agenda during the French Revolution. The conclusion surveys how some of the innovative processes detailed in the five main chapters filtered through to the post-Napoleonic period and conditioned subsequent French imperial expansion in uneven and surprising ways.

CHAPTER I

A Colonial Empire in Crisis

On the eve of the Seven Years War, the French governor of Guadeloupe, Jean-Antoine Riqueti, chevalier de Mirabeau, sent a series of letters to the Ministry of the Marine, warning the administration of the impending disasters facing its Caribbean colonies. Mirabeau had arrived in the Îles du Vent in late 1753 and spent his first five months reconnoitring local sites. Along the way, he had steadily formed his verdict on the future of France's colonies in the region. To him, the perfidious behaviour of the free white population, the brutality of colonial slavery, the failure of French commerce adequately to provision the islands, and the prevalence of contraband trade steadily undermined French control of the colonies. Without their immediate remedy, Guadeloupe would 'collapse from weakness into the hands of our enemies'.[1] Delineating the fragilities of the French colonial empire in his official correspondence with the Crown, Mirabeau tactfully identified only those exterior to the centre of power. Yet, in letters to his older brother, the political economist and co-founder of Physiocracy Victor Riqueti, marquis de Mirabeau, he singled out a much more formidable culprit. As he said, '[m]onarchs will be little flattered to possess entire Kingdoms at a distance of two thousand *lieues* if they did not immediately see a considerable profit from taxation'. In another letter he merely sighed 'Versailles, Versailles, the source of our evils'.[2]

Despite the gloomy warnings from Mirabeau and other officials stationed in the colonies, Versailles did little to redress the inherent weaknesses of its colonial empire prior to the Seven Years War. Only when war broke out in 1756 and a string of French colonial possessions capitulated to the British Navy did a languid colonial administration jump into action.

---

[1] Letters of concern include Mirabeau to Antoine-Louis Rouillé, Martinique, 8 May 1754, ANOM, C⁷ᴬ17, f. 54; Mirabeau to Rouillé, Martinique, 7 June 1754, ANOM C⁷ᴬ 17, f. 58; Mirabeau to Rouillé, Guadeloupe, 30 July 1754, ANOM C⁷ᴬ 17, f. 63. The quotation is from 30 July 1754.
[2] Chevalier de Mirabeau (hereinafter CM) to marquis de Mirabeau (hereinafter MM), 10 January 1754 and 24 January 1754, Musée Arbaud, Aix-en-Provence, Fonds Mirabeau (hereinafter FM), vol. 23.

Against the backdrop of the peace negotiations that stripped France of its claims to empire in India and on the North American mainland, government officials and stakeholders of colonial commerce embarked on a thorough inspection of the French colonial economy and its component parts. A clamour of voices within the French Ministries of the Marine and of Foreign Affairs offered up competing perspectives on how to salvage and enhance colonial commerce, epitomising the intertwined processes of colonial defeat, reform, and innovation. Beyond the well-known result of generating a French colonial policy centred on an intensification of the Caribbean plantation complex, policy makers and colonial officials also weighed alternative paths to empire. Two of these included strands that are central to this book: the view that liberal economic ties and mutual prosperity should undergird metropolitan–colonial relations and the suggestion that colonial expansion in West Africa could negate the impact of French colonial losses in the Americas.

To situate these wartime deliberations over the future of the French colonial empire within their historical context, I first consider chevalier de Mirabeau's portrayal of the Îles du Vent between 1753 and 1755. This cluster of islands, composed of Martinique, Guadeloupe, St Lucia, Dominica, and Grenada, was subject to unique socio-economic and geopolitical circumstances, yet the difficulties pertaining to their daily existence capture effectively the multiple and multi-layered metropolitan and colonial tensions that weakened France's grip on its American colonies in the mid eighteenth century. Mirabeau's correspondence explains in harrowing detail how brutality and violence, racial hierarchies, and a quest for profits combined to produce a volatile atmosphere in the Îles du Vent. Furthermore, it introduces many of the colonial and metropolitan communities whose involvement in the restructuring of the French colonial system runs like a thread through this book. A unique quality of Mirabeau's correspondence is also that it helps us anchor physiocratic colonial ideas in the imperial realities from which they partly emerged. While the chevalier was stationed in Guadeloupe, he and his brother exchanged close to a hundred letters. The governor's complaints about the soft underbelly of the French colonial system would profoundly influence the marquis's outlook on the French colonial empire and his subsequent economic writings on how to move beyond it. In this way, attention to Jean-Antoine's governorship offers a window onto the intricate problems facing France and its colonies on the eve of the Seven Years War and sets the scene for the diplomatic, intellectual, and practical activities that developed in response to them.

Mirabeau and the Ancien Régime Colonial Empire

When Mirabeau took up the governorship of Guadeloupe in 1753, the French colonial empire was already a well-established assemblage of territories across the globe. Stretching from Canada and Louisiana on the North American mainland to the trade stations in Bengal and on the Coromandel and Malabar coasts, it included in between the Newfoundland fisheries, the sugar islands in the Caribbean, the colony of Guiana in South America, the slave factories on the coast of West Africa, and the Mascarene Islands east of the Cape of Good Hope. These territories had accumulated over centuries, initially due to the entrepreneurial efforts of independent fishermen, buccaneers, and explorers and, from the seventeenth century, with more direct encouragement from the Crown.[3]

Increased royal involvement was fuelled by the Crown's ambition to make France self-sufficient in the supply of exotic goods, boost domestic industry, and outrival neighbouring powers on land and at sea. Central architects of early French colonial policy, such as Cardinal Richelieu under Louis XIII and Jean-Baptiste Colbert under Louis XIV, saw colonies as a means to enrich the state, increase fiscal revenue to finance warfare, and meet the costs of building up an efficient and centralised bureaucratic state. As Grand Maître de la navigation et du commerce, Richelieu pioneered official naval and colonial developments, but his untimely death in 1642 precluded a full execution of his plans. When Louis XIV appointed Jean-Baptiste Colbert Intendant of Finances in 1661 and Minister of the Marine in 1669, Colbert continued Richelieu's projects for overseas expansion.[4]

With his eyes jealously fixed on the maritime successes of the Dutch and the English, Colbert enlarged the navy and merchant fleets. Initially, he also parcelled out colonial responsibility to chartered companies modelled on the Vereenigde Oostindische Compagnie and the English East India Company. In 1664, he put the Compagnie française des Indes occidentales in control of French colonial holdings west of the Cape of Good Hope and the Compagnie française des Indes orientales of territories east of the Cape. Although enjoying the support of the powerful lobby of financiers whose backing animated the policies of the French monarchical state, these pseudo-private companies largely failed as instruments of commercial

---

[3] On early French empire building, see Frederick Quinn, *The French Overseas Empire* (Westport, CT: Praeger, 2000), Chapter 1.

[4] Alan James, 'The Development of French Naval Policy in the Seventeenth Century: Richelieu's Early Aims and Ambitions', *French History*, 12 (1998), 384–402, 384, and Franklin Charles Palm, 'Mercantilism as a Factor in Richelieu's Policy of National Interests', *Political Science Quarterly*, 4 (1924), 650–64.

gain, though less so as weapons of war. When both companies ran into trouble, French forts down the coast of West Africa and colonies east of the Cape of Good Hope remained in the hands of a series of reorganised East India Companies, whereas possessions in the Americas were folded into the royal administration. In 1674, the Crown purchased Saint-Christopher, Martinique, Guadeloupe, and Tortuga from the Compagnie des Indes occidentales (whose main private shareholder was Louis XIV) and added them to a royal administration that already included Canada.[5]

Over the next decades, Colbert and his successors clothed Crown colonies in an administration resembling that of the French domestic provinces. As representatives of the Crown, a governor-general oversaw their military protection and an intendant tended to their civil and fiscal administration. Several of the colonies also received colonial councils moulded after the French *parlements* and known initially as sovereign councils and, from 1703, as superior councils. Unlike in the metropole, colonial councils did not have to register laws for the latter to be binding, and the balance of power between government branches in the colonies steadily gravitated towards the governor-general and the intendant, while the councils evolved into senior appellate courts and increasingly represented the economic and social interests of the white colonial elites.[6]

Jean-Antoine de Mirabeau took up the governorship of the Îles du Vent to serve within this administrative framework. The second son of a well-respected aristocratic family from Aix-en-Provence (whose famous members included not only the governor and the political economist but also Victor's son, Honoré Gabriel Riqueti, comte de Mirabeau, who obtained a prominent role during the early stage of the French Revolution), Jean-Antoine had left home at the age of twelve, when his father had him admitted into the order of the Knights of Malta (in 1730). That same year, he joined the French galley corps. In 1746, he participated in the failed attempt to retake Louisbourg. It was while recovering from the wounds

---

[5] On Colbert's West and East India policies, see Stewart L. Mims, *Colbert's West India Policy* (New Haven, CT: Yale University Press, 1912), and Glenn J. Ames, *Colbert, Mercantilism, and the French Quest for Asian Trade* (DeKalb: Northern Illinois University Press, 1996). On his ties to the world of finance, see Daniel Dessert and Jean-Louis Journel, 'Le lobby Colbert: un royaume ou une affaire de famille?', *Annales. Economies, sociétés, civilisation*, 30, 6 (1975), 1303–36, and, more broadly, Daniel Dessert, *Argent, pouvoir et société au grand siècle* (Paris: Fayard, 1984). On the integral role of colonial companies in French colonial expansion, see J. Chailley-Bert, *Les compagnies de colonisation sous l'ancien régime* (Paris, 1898); on companies as weapons of war, see Jeff Horn, *Economic Development in Early Modern France: The Privilege of Liberty, 1650–1820* (Cambridge: Cambridge University Press, 2015), 118.

[6] James Pritchard, *In Search of Empire: The French in the Americas, 1670–1730* (Cambridge: Cambridge University Press, 2004), 247.

inflicted upon him in battle that he began to find the administration of the Marine in need of reform. He accepted the governorship of Guadeloupe in the hope that it would lead him next to the governorship of Saint-Domingue, and then to that of Canada, before elevating him to the highest office within the Ministry of the Marine.[7]

Belonging to the military nobility, Mirabeau communicated strong views on the shortcomings of colonial management to his superiors, including memoranda on how to solve widespread contraband trade and government corruption. Reading his official correspondence alongside letters to his brother further discloses the bewilderments, disappointments, and joys that animated this reformer. Detailing the countless problems with which he believed the colonial system was marred, his letters are replete with descriptions of crooked planters followed by lamentations of their commercial captivity at the hands of voracious metropolitan merchants. They linger on the horrors of African enslavement in the colonies only to segue into disparaging statements on racial intermarriage. They ardently castigate the greedy and careless culture of Versailles but seek to rationalise the corruption of colonial officials. They reveal, in short, as much about the norms and values of the man who composed them as they do about the social, political, and economic circumstances that enfeebled the American colonies and metropolitan control of them.

A New World

When Mirabeau entered the port of Basse-Terre in December 1753, he debarked in some of France's oldest sugar colonies. Situated in the eastern corner of the Caribbean ocean, Martinique had a population of 77,787 people in 1753, 12,210 of whom were whites, 64,038 slaves, 385 maroons, and 1,154 free people of colour. Guadeloupe counted 9,172 free people in 1753, of whom some were people of colour, though we have no exact data (in 1731, there were 1,180 free people of colour on the island). It counted

---

[7] On Mirabeau's political aspirations, see Loménie, *Les Mirabeau*, i, 145–8. Two recent studies have paid attention to his colonial administration. See Pernille Røge, '"Legal Despotism" and Enlightened Reform in the Îles du Vent: The Colonial Governments of Chevalier de Mirabeau and Mercier de la Rivière, 1754–1764', in *Enlightened Reform in Southern Europe and Its Atlantic Colonies, c. 1750–1830*, ed. Gabriel Paquette (Farnham, UK: Ashgate, 2009), 167–82, and Loïc Charles and Paul Cheney, 'The Colonial Machine Dismantled: Knowledge and Empire in the French Atlantic', *Past and Present*, 219, 1 (2013), 127–63. On career trajectories within the Ministry of the Marine, see Alexandre Dubé, 'Making a Career out of the Atlantic: Louisiana's Plume', in *Louisiana: Crossroads of the Atlantic World*, ed. Cécile Vidal (Philadelphia: University of Pennsylvania Press, 2014), 44–67.

41,026 slaves and 501 maroons. Collectively, the two islands had approximately 700 sugar plantations – 331 on Guadeloupe and 374 on Martinique – and produced 457,441 *quintaux* of sugar (or 22,500 tonnes).[8] Aside from its substantially larger population of slaves, Martinique enjoyed the added advantage of being the administrative and commercial centre of the Îles du Vent, with Fort-Royal as the administrative capital and Saint-Pierre as the main commercial hub of the entire cluster of islands (see Map 1.1). In contrast, Basse-Terre, the chief urban centre on Guadeloupe, assisted only local needs.

In the first half of the eighteenth century, Martinique's and Guadeloupe's sugar production continued to expand (although the number of sugar plantations vacillated), yet the rapid ascent of Saint-Domingue in these years contributed to a sense of decline on both islands. Cultivation on Saint-Domingue had taken off only at the turn of the eighteenth century, and the island had a much larger arable surface. By the 1740s, it produced twice as much sugar as the Îles du Vent (43,000 tonnes) and already had a much larger population since metropolitan slave traders and merchants brought slaves and provisions more regularly. As many as 172,000 slaves lived on Saint-Domingue in 1755, a number which had increased to 480,000 in 1790. Similarly, its white population counted approximately 18,000 in 1750 and went up to 30,800 in 1790, while its population of free people of colour saw a greater increase from approximately 3,400 in 1750 to 27,000 in 1789.[9]

The economic and political disparities that characterised the mid eighteenth-century French Caribbean plantation complex coloured Mirabeau's perception of the colonial system and his role within it. Like many visitors before and after him, he marvelled at the wealth the plantation complex could produce but regarded with suspicion its power to challenge established hierarchies. He found Guadeloupe at once a 'promised land' of immense fertility and a terrifying nest of 'rascality', where the ordered society of Europe had given way to disorder and honour and virtue to vice and deceit.[10] To him, the vehicle behind this paradoxical situation was the sugar plantation and the

---

[8] Plantation statistics are from 1752; see Blérald, *Histoire économique*, Table 1, 23 and Table 2, 28. On demographic data for Martinique, see Léo Elisabeth, *La société martiniquaise aux XVIIᵉ et XVIIIᵉ siècles 1664–1789* (Paris: Karthala, 2003), 29. On Guadeloupe, see Lucien Abénon, *La Guadeloupe de 1671 à 1759 – Étude politique, économique et sociale*, 2 vols. (Paris: L'Harmattan, 1987), ii, 9, 24, 62, and 72.

[9] On Saint-Domingue's sugar production vis-à-vis Guadeloupe and Martinique, see Paul Butel, *Histoire des Antilles françaises XVIIᵉ-XXᵉ siècle* (Paris: Perrin, 2007), 119. Population numbers for Saint-Domingue are from Frostin, *Les révoltes blanches*, 30, 79, 162, and 185.

[10] CM to MM, 24 December 1753, FM, vol. 23.

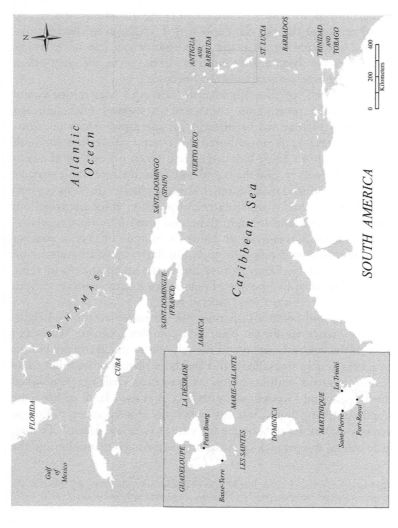

Map 1.1 Eighteenth-century Caribbean Sea
Source: Courtesy Anders Kloch Jeppesen

wealth, manners, and misery that it fostered. Its ability to elevate commoners to the highest level of society was particularly baffling. Explaining this phenomenon to his older brother, he noted that, '[i]f a prince came here and he only wished to plant coffee whereas his footman planted sugar, his footman would soon think himself superior to the prince'. As a result, 'the vilest part of white humanity [*l'humanité blanche*] considers itself above a peer of France in Paris', while they also 'all see themselves as equals'.[11]

The egalitarian attitude that Mirabeau described only applied among the plantocracy; colonial society was anything but egalitarian. Many Europeans who migrated to the colonies never managed to amass a fortune but lived out their days in poverty. Over time, they became known as the *petits blancs*, the 'small whites', in contrast to the successful *grands blancs*. Mindful of the unevenness of white colonial society, Mirabeau balanced his disdain for white colonists by a deeper sympathy for the European poor, acknowledging that they came with a naive faith in the possibility of enrichment but found in the colonies 'a new and more pressing misery' which merely pushed them towards 'roguery'.[12]

Mirabeau's often tepid portrayal of whites in the colonies, whether rich or poor, tended to reflect views within the colonial administration as well. The Crown had long struggled to attract what it considered 'good' settlers to its colonies, but unfounded fears of underpopulation precluded migration. Periodically, authorities tried to recruit with various degrees of force the most exposed members of the populace to journey overseas, but most were eager to return to the mother country once their labour contracts ran out. France, the most populous country in Europe with 25 million inhabitants, sent only 51,000 people to America between 1608 and 1760, compared to Britain's 722,000 people between 1607 and 1780.[13]

As the plantation economy in the Caribbean developed, growing labour demands therefore accelerated the introduction of African slave labour. Following the example of its Portuguese, Spanish, English, and Dutch neighbours, the French Crown sanctioned a trade in African slaves in the 1630s and supported the establishment of slave trading forts along the coast of West Africa to supply labour to the New World. From Saint-Louis and Gorée in Senegal, and soon also from the Bight of Benin and West Central Africa, the Compagnie française des Indes orientales and licensed individual merchants purchased slaves (as well as gold, cattle, ivory, beeswax,

---

[11] CM to MM, 24 January 1754, FM, vol. 23.   [12] CM to MM, 7 May 1754, FM, vol. 23.
[13] On total numbers, see Ida Altman and James Horn (eds.), *'To Make America': European Emigration in the Early Modern Period* (Berkeley: University of California Press, 1991), 3.

hides, and the valuable gum arabic also known as gum acacia or gum Senegal) from African merchants in exchange for European commodities. By the time Mirabeau became governor, French slave traders had shipped more than 420,000 slaves to the French Caribbean colonies, earning West Africa the label 'annexe-des-Antilles'. Unlike on the American mainland, the French sugar colonies in the Caribbean therefore quickly caught up with British population patterns in this region, reaching parity around 1750 (approximately 330,000 in each case).[14]

The influx of Africans into the Americas partly solved the issue of labour but ensured that racial inequality and unregulated violence suffused French colonial culture. A toiler himself, Mirabeau decried how racial slavery fostered an excessive degree of violence in the colonies and led to the devaluation of work. In his view, the daily vision of African slaves cutting sugarcane, working the mills, cooking, cleaning, and nursing bequeathed whites with 'the idea that the whiteness of their skin should exempt them from work'. White children in the colonies were corrupted from birth, he wrote to his older brother, first through the 'milk they suck[ed]' from their African wet nurses, and then by being surrounded by fearful slaves throughout their upbringing which taught them to be vain, lazy, and violent.[15] Racial violence was rarely punished, he further observed, since there was a 'custom of neglecting to punish the murder of Negroes' on the island. In his view, not a single day passed without a European rogue or his offspring murdering a slave, often due to fights over 'dishonourable Negro women' (*infames négresses*). Even when slaves on rare occasions managed to escape bondage through manumission – entering the community of free people of colour – discrimination and injustice haunted their existence because the skin colour of the freed slave always reminded 'him of his position'.[16]

[14] On French entry into the slave trade, see Christopher L. Miller, *The French Atlantic Triangle: Literature and Culture of the Slave Trade* (Durham, NC: Duke University Press, 2008), 19. On the broader European context, see Robin Blackburn, *The Making of New World Slavery from the Baroque to the Modern 1492–1800* (London: Verso, 1997). On trade with Africa, see Philip D. Curtin, *Economic Change in Precolonial Africa: Senegambia in the Era of the Slave Trade* (Madison: University of Wisconsin Press, 1975), 215–16. On estimates of slave imports to the French Caribbean, see Voyages: The Trans-Atlantic Slave Trade Database, ww.slavevoyages.org. On the comparison with Britain, see François Crouzet, *La guerre économique franco-anglaise au XVIIIe siècle* (Paris: Fayard, 2008), 107.

[15] On lazy whites and wet nursing, see MC to MM, Martinique, 7 May 1754, FM, vol. 23.

[16] Mirabeau on skin colour and work, see MC to MM, Guadeloupe, 10 January 1754, FM, vol. 23; on slave murder going unpunished, see CM to MM, Guadeloupe, 24 December 1754, FM, vol. 24; on free men of colour, see CM to MM, Guadeloupe, 11 August 1754. FM, vol. 23. On women, slavery, and sexual relations, see Bernard Moitt, *Women and Slavery in the French Antilles 1635–1848* (Bloomington: Indiana University Press, 2001), 99–100.

Mirabeau's vexation over the evils of racial slavery was genuine, yet his critique also reflects the racialised views that helped sustain this institution. More than once, he echoed a hardened discourse of race that characterised the mid eighteenth-century French colonies and which stood in contrast to the more relaxed views scholars have pointed to in the previous century.[17] It was not only when making references to 'dishonourable' black women or when discussing wet nursing that he disclosed a bias. In reference to a man of colour who had murdered another man, he explained that the offender was 'a vile mulatto, child of the most detestable debauchery, a kind of monster composed of the rascality of the two colours'.[18] Such views on interracial relations and 'dishonourable' women were widespread in the discourse of white elites and Mirabeau was far from immune to it.[19] Nevertheless, he mostly expressed a sincere compassion for the colonies' enslaved and coloured populations and frequently condemned the legal culture that helped sustain injustices.

The Colonial Legal Culture

The legal system of the French Antilles had evolved in combination with the rise of the plantation complex. French colonies followed the Coutume de Paris, a set of regulations based on customary laws in the Paris region. The Coutume du Paris, however, had no articles on slavery. In fact, a slave touching French territory customarily was granted immediate freedom, even though this 'freedom principle' was strongly restricted in conjunction with the intensification of plantation slavery. In the colonies, the Coutume de Paris was therefore initially accompanied by local ordinances on the management of slaves drawn up by colonial superior councils. With time, the Crown merged these ordinances into the Code Noir that codified legal relations between planters and slaves and suppressed religious practices other than Roman Catholicism. Applied in the French Caribbean sugar islands between 1685 and 1687, in French Guiana in 1704, in Réunion in 1723, and in Louisiana in 1724, the Code Noir supposedly protected slaves

---

[17] On the rise of racialised views in the French colonies, see Guillaume Aubert, '"The Blood of France": Race and Purity of Blood in the French Atlantic World', *The William and Mary Quarterly*, 61, 3 (2004), 439–78, 477; and Mélanie Lamotte, 'Colour Prejudice in the Early Modern French Atlantic World', in D'Maris Coffman, Adrian Leonard, and William O'Reilly (eds.), *The Atlantic World* (London: Routledge, 2015), 151–71.

[18] CM to MM, Guadeloupe, 24 December 1754, FM, vol. 23.

[19] On views of sexual relations between women of colour and white men, see Doris Garraway, *The Libertine Colony: Creolization in the Early French Caribbean* (Durham, NC: Duke University Press, 2005), Chapter 4.

and free men from each other, but most often served to help plantation owners, governors, and intendants police a race and slave-based society.[20] This was clear from the Code Noir's legislation on violence, which stipulated that a slave who struck his master should be punished by death, whereas the murdering of a slave should be punished 'according to the circumstances of the atrocity'. Unsurprisingly, 'circumstances' usually let the perpetrator off the hook.[21]

The parameters within which colonial officials could mete out punishments against whites who mistreated their slaves were therefore narrow, not only in a legal sense but also culturally. Deeply attuned to these restrictions, Mirabeau periodically deliberated over the problem of how best to police planter brutality. In one letter, he challenged his older brother to tell him if he could think of a legal code and a government 'fitting such a country'. The marquis de Mirabeau, who had never set foot in the colonies, responded with genuine surprise when learning about the level of racial violence in the colonies – 'what you tell me about creoles' cruelty towards the poor slaves is unbelievable' – and found 'it is impossible that such a barbarous society will not one day be subjected to divine wrath and human vengeance'. The marquis insisted that murder merited hanging regardless of the victim's social status or skin colour, thus giving voice to a common view that murder of one of the King's subjects was an affront to the King's authority. The political economist even encouraged his younger brother to bring the issue to the attention of the Minister of the Marine and ask, 'if it is the intention of the King' to tolerate such behaviour or whether he should restore 'the force of law and the nerve of society'.[22]

Though tormented by colonial violence, the governor refrained from following his brother's advice. Privately, he agreed about the horrors of slavery. Having spent years in the galley corps, where oarsmen were often enslaved Turks or Frenchmen condemned to penal servitude (the *forçats*),

---

[20] On the application of the Coutume de Paris in the French Antilles, see Edith Géraud-Llorca, 'La Coutume de paris outre-mer: l'habitation antillaise sous l'Ancien Régime', *Revue historique de droit français et étranger*, 60 (1982), 207–59. On the freedom principle, see Sue Peabody, *'There Are No Slaves in France': The Political Culture of Race and Slavery in the Ancien Régime* (New York: Oxford University Press, 1996), and Pierre Pluchon, *Nègres et Juifs au XVIII* siècle: Le racisme au siècle des Lumières* (Paris: Tallandier, 1984). On the creation of the *Code Noir* see Vernon Valentine Palmer, 'Essai sur les origines et les auteurs du Code Noir', *Revue Internationale de droit comparé* 50, 1 (1998), 111–40, and Brett Rushforth, *Bonds of Alliance Indigenous and Atlantic Slaveries in New France* (Chapel Hill: University of North Carolina Press, 2012), 122–34.

[21] Louis Sala-Molins, *Le Code Noir ou le calvaire de Canaan*, 2nd edn. (Paris: Presses Universitaires de France, 2003), 176.

[22] MM to CM, Paris, 9 December 1754, FM, vol. 23. And MM to CM, Paris, 22 February 1755. FM, vol. 23.

he revealed that he found plantation slavery in the Îles du Vent much harsher than 'white slavery' due to 'injustices attached to skin colour'. He even suggested that African slavery in the colonies could easily be abolished, though he admitted that it was hard to believe that anyone would 'take the steps to implement it'.[23] Nevertheless, the governor remained mute about the widespread maltreatment of Africans and their descendants in his official correspondence, nor did he advocate for abolition. Instead, he informed the Minister of the Marine without a sign of discomfiture that Guadeloupe needed an additional 30,000 slaves. Responsible for the daily management and prosperity of a sugar colony, he simply could not adopt his older brother's resolute response to slave murder. The loose patrolling of whites in the colonies, he explained to his brother, had accustomed the white population to do as they saw fit and made it dangerous for a governor suddenly 'to oppose them too strongly'. If white colonial society was policed rigorously – if they were punished for murdering or torturing slaves – they might rise in revolt or try to court the English. Thus, to the chevalier de Mirabeau, an effort to restore order and the force of law in the Îles du Vent was a recipe in its own right for the loss of these colonies.[24]

Local Despotism and Corruption

Obstacles to imperial control were not confined to an unruly populace but extended to the colonial administration itself. As delegates of the monarch, governors and intendants in the colonies were furnished with instructions from the Ministry of the Marine's Bureau of Colonies (the Bureau des colonies established in 1710), overseen by the minister, the *premier commis,* and assistant clerks. Yet oceanic distance left the powers of colonial officials relatively unchecked. The central administration received complaints from all corners of the empire about the despotism of colonial officials. In 1765, the local plantocracy scolded the governor of Martinique, François Louis de Salinas, marquis de la Mothe-Fénelon, for his 'acts of despotism'. On the island of Gorée off of Senegal, the French governor, Charles Hippolyte Boniface, was similarly criticised for his 'despotic disposition' in 1773. Mirabeau described how legislation drawn up by the King's Council was only executed if the local governor approved it: 'here', he told his brother,

---

[23] MC to MM, Guadeloupe, 10 January 1754, FM, vol. 23. On galley slavery see Paul Walden Bamford, 'The Procurement of Oarsmen for French Galleys, 1660–1748', *The American Historical Review*, 65, 1 (1959), 31–48.

[24] CM to MM, Guadeloupe, 11 August 1754. FM, vol. 23.

'governors are the real sovereigns'. Of his own power, he noted that he was 'feared like six provosts' and admitted how easy it would be to abuse his powers.[25]

Local protest against colonial officials' exploitation of power was a commonplace. Like in the Paris *parlement* where denunciations of ministerial despotism challenged the sovereignty of the Crown, so accusations of despotic rule in the colonies served to undermine local governor-generals or intendants. More often than not, accusations rang true but they were also mechanisms through which colonial elites could eliminate local officials who sought to police abuses. In most cases, complaints ended with a change in the local administration but rarely expeditiously. Months could pass between the issuing of complaints from the colonies, to its reception in France, to a subsequent issuing of an official discharge. While the Ministry of the Marine had a hard time implementing its policies within domestic France, oceanic distance diluted the voice of authority exponentially.[26] The Crown therefore used well-known mechanisms of state surveillance to counterbalance the weakening of central authority in the colonies. More than once, Mirabeau disclosed that he felt surrounded by spies from Versailles 'who wanted to know everything about everything' and who 'manipulate court as they s[aw] fit', thereby opening up new avenues for abuse.[27]

Alongside the abuse of power, Mirabeau was also deeply concerned about the widespread use of bribery. Still, his private letters disclose some of the causes that fostered it. He tirelessly complained about the lack of economic opportunity through honest means that the Îles du Vent offered a colonial official compared to Saint-Domingue. As governor of Guadeloupe, Mirabeau received 12,000 livres tournois annually and

---

[25] On Fénelon's behaviour, see 'Avis émis par la chambre d'agriculture de la Martinique sur l'administration de Fénelon', 1765, ANOM C^{8A} 67, pièce 380. On Boniface's behaviour, see 'Report', Gorée, 1773, ANOM C^6 16, pièce 8. On Mirabeau's views on administrative despotism, see CM to MM, 10 January 1754, FM, vol. 23; CM to MM, 24 January 1754, FM, vol. 23 and CM to MM, 22 March 1754, FM, vol. 23. On the colonial office, see Marie Houllemare, 'Le bureau des colonies et ses commis', in *La liasse et la plume: Les bureaux du secrétaiat d'État de la Marine*, ed. Jörg Ulbert et Sylviane Llinares (Rennes: Presses Universitaires de Rennes, 2017), 99–109.

[26] Tensions between the Ministry of the Marine, Crown representatives, and local populations had a long lineage and served as obstacles to reform in domestic France as much as in the colonies. See Eugene L. Asher, *The Resistance to the Maritime Classes: The Survival of Feudalism in France of Colbert* (Berkeley: University of California Press, 1960). On the overseas context, see Kenneth J. Banks, *Chasing Empire across the Sea: Communications and the State in the French Atlantic, 1713–1763* (Montreal: McGill-Queen's University Press, 2006), Chapter 7.

[27] MC to MM, Guadeloupe, 24 January 1754, FM, vol. 23; MC to MM, Martinique 7 May 1754, FM, vol. 23. On the secret collection of information as part of state building, see Jacob Soll, *The Information Master: Jean-Baptiste Colbert's Secret State Intelligence System* (Ann Arbor: University of Michigan Press, 2009).

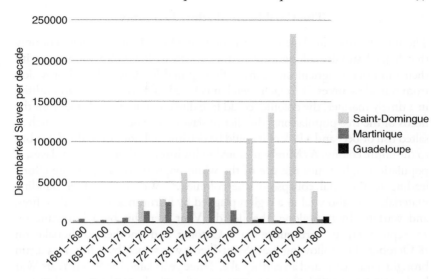

Figure 1.1 French slave trade estimates to Martinique, Guadeloupe and Saint-Domingue, 1680–1800
Source: *Voyages: The Trans-Atlantic Slave Trade Database*, www.slavevoyages.com

collected a bonus for each slave French traders brought to the island. Compared to a seamstress in Paris, who with full employment could earn anywhere between 60 and 270 livres annually in the eighteenth century, his salary was enormous.[28] However, a governorship came with considerable expenses (including a duty to maintain a proper dinner table for guests), just like the discrepancy in economic opportunities among officials in the sugar islands was real enough.[29] Saint-Domingue received the majority of the slaves furnished by French slave traders (see Figure 1.1), whereas Guadeloupe, which imported slaves from Martinique prior to the reforms of 1763, received many of its slaves through the illicit intra-Caribbean slave trade. Officials in the Îles du Vent were instructed to suppress the illegal trade but often ignored their orders, in part because of bribes and their own opportunities to make a profit but also because they agreed that the colonies needed more slaves than those French slave traders provided. Such attitudes helped sustain the plantation complex in the Îles du Vent, but not metropolitan control of it.

---

[28] Clare Haru Crowston, *Fabricating Women: The Seamstresses of Old Regime France, 1675–1791* (Durham, NC: Duke University Press, 2001), 91–3.
[29] MC to MM, Martinique, 22 March 1754, FM, vol. 23.

The Caribbean Shadow Economy

The inter-Caribbean slave trade was only one branch of the illicit economy that helped sustain colonisation in the Americas. Plantation colonies, with their mono-crop agriculture, constantly required food, wood, and provision from outside sources. If French merchants failed to deliver such commodities in a timely manner, the colonies could face dire consequences. Aside from the needs of the free populations, the diet of slaves was based on imports such as salted fish or beef and a lack of it could be detrimental not just to the slaves but to the entire colony. As Mirabeau noted to his brother about starving slaves, 'a population eight times the size of the white population can provoke efforts leading to the total collapse of the colonies'.[30] Wood and other building materials were also vital in a region plagued by hurricanes, earthquakes, fires, and warfare. In 1751 alone, the Îles du Vent were hit by a hurricane on 22 September, an earthquake on 1 October and another earthquake on 18 October. The following year, Saint-Pierre was struck by a fire. 1753 again brought a hurricane and an earthquake. Three years later, the Seven Years War broke out. As a part of a broader economy of survival, small *pirogues* therefore crossed like busy water bugs among French, English, Dutch, and Danish Caribbean islands loaded with sugar, cotton, indigo, slaves, food, and building materials to be exchanged in secluded creeks and habours.[31]

Like in France where colonial commerce produced its own problems with contraband trade, people in the colonies participated in the illicit trade at a high risk. If caught, a *colon* trading with foreigners would face the confiscation of his vessel, its cargo, a fine of 1,000 livres, and three years in the galleys.[32] Though he applied this punishment on several occasions, Mirabeau did not think that it took the realities of empire into account. In letters to the Crown,

---

[30] CM to MM, Guadeloupe, 27 October 1754. F.M. vol. 24.

[31] For a list of natural disasters hitting the Îles du Vent between 1642 and 1792, see Gérard Gabriel Marion, *L'administration des finances en Martinique 1679–1790* (Paris: L'Harmattan, 2000), 115–17. There is a considerable literature on the Caribbean shadow economy. For a succinct introduction, see Wim Klooster, 'Inter-Imperial Smuggling in the Americas, 1600–1800', in *Atlantic History: Latent Structures and Intellectual Currents, 1500–1830*, ed. Bernard Bailyn and Patricia L. Denault (Cambridge, MA: Harvard University Press, 2009), 141–80. On how hurricanes and inter-Caribbean illicit trade contributed to a sense of regional community, see Stuart B. Schwartz, *Sea of Storms: A History of Hurricanes in the Greater Caribbean from Columbus to Katrina* (Princeton, NJ: Princeton University Press, 2015), and Ernesto Bassi, *An Aqueous Territory: Sailor Geographies and New Granada's Transimperial Greater Caribbean World* (Durham, NC: Duke University Press, 2016), Chapter 1.

[32] *Lettres patentes du Roy en forme d'édit, Concernant le Commerce estranger aux Isles & Colonies de l'Amérique*. Fontainebleau, October 1727 (Paris: Imprimerie Royale, 1727), Article 1. On the domestic side, see Michael Kwass, *Contraband: Louis Mandrin and the Making of a Global Underground* (Cambridge, MA: Harvard University Press, 2014).

he pointed out that the Îles du Vent saw far fewer metropolitan ships than did Saint-Domingue. People were therefore more easily pushed into the world of crime. Though the Îles du Vent could arm ships to go to Louisiana or Canada to purchase essentials such as lumber, flour, horses, or fish in exchange for rum and molasses – by-products of sugar that the metropole had no interest in – Mirabeau informed the Ministry of the Marine that colonists who obtained a permit merely used it 'as a pretext to trade with New England'.[33]

Through the illicit trade, foreigners could thus syphon off a sizeable portion of the profits that the metropole stood to make from its sugar islands. Scholars have calculated that contraband trade in the colonies swallowed between 38 per cent and 48 per cent of overall production. Given that the Îles du Vent were poorly provisioned by France compared to Saint-Domingue, the percentage might have been even higher on these islands. In Mirabeau's estimate, two-thirds of Guadeloupe's production went to foreigners but as he explained to Versailles, it was impossible to prevent since one 'could not deracinate an evil rooted in the real needs of the local population'. Why else, he charged on a different occasion, would they run the risk of 'being condemned to the galleys', particularly since goods at Sint Eustatius, the Dutch free port from which the French on Guadeloupe often obtained their supplies, were as expensive as those provisioned by French commerce? For people in the colonies as much as for large parts of the population in France who tried to keep starvation at bay through poaching or smuggling, the economy of survival dictated a precarious existence at the edges of the Ancien Régime legal system.[34]

Debt and Commissionnaires

The high cost of goods provided by French merchants was one of the by-products of the Exclusif that would preoccupy the Mirabeau brothers as well as Mirabeau *fils*. But while father and son would discuss it with a view to the cost of commodities in both the metropole and in the colonies, Jean-Antoine concentrated on the ways in which high prices in the colonies led not just to contraband trade but also to the augmentation

---

[33] Mirabeau to Rouillé, 7 June 1754, ANOM C[7A] 17, f. 58.

[34] On the level of contraband trade according to scholars, see Butel, *L'économie française*, 116–17. Tarrade, *Le commerce colonial*, i, 111. Mirabeau's estimate, Mirabeau to Rouillé, Martinique, 7 June 1754. ANOM C[7A] 17, f. 58; on trade with Sint Eustatius, see Mirabeau to Machault, Guadeloupe 30 July 1754, ANOM C[7A] 17, f. 63. On theft and smuggling among the poor in France, see Olwen H. Hufton, *The Poor of Eighteenth-Century France, 1750–1789* (Oxford: Clarendon Press, 1974), Chapters 9 and 10.

of planter debt. Most planters had become indebted the moment they acquired a plantation due to colonial inheritance law. Modelled after the Coutume de Paris, it prescribed that at the death of a plantation owner, his or her assets should be shared equally among immediate descendants. To ensure continued production, one of the heirs would therefore take over the plantation and its slaves, against a commitment to reimburse his or her siblings of their share. For the plantation owner, starting out in debt quickly led to more debt. It also bound the owner to the *commissionnaires* at Saint-Pierre, the only ones in the colonies with ready specie.

Commissionnaires were at the centre of the colonial-metropolitan commercial nexus. Overseeing the sale of planters' colonial produce to the metropole in exchange for a commission, many were also agents of larger metropolitan merchant houses. When a planter purchased or inherited a plantation, he immediately began to rely on a *commissionnaire* to purchase food for slaves and goods for his household, but also to pay local taxes which the *commissionnaire* would do in return for an exclusive right to oversee the sale of his customer's crops. Operating in ways similar to intermediaries of the eighteenth-century French wine trade, the *commissionnaire* would charge a fee for all of these transactions he undertook. Mirabeau estimated that planters on Guadeloupe incurred a loss of up to 20 per cent when buying or selling commodities to *commissionnaires*. Guadeloupe 'moans in the chains of the *commissionaires* of St Pierre', he told the Crown, though he also recognised that planters never paid their debts. As with much else, he stressed that if the problem of debt remained unresolved, the colony would 'decline and finally fall from weakness into the hands of our enemies'.[35]

Planter debt, in fact, was a Gordian knot seemingly impossible to cut. The lack of specie in the islands was one cause of it. The colonial legal system was another. Although it placed nearly all planters in debt from the moment they acquired a plantation, it also protected them from ever truly facing the consequences. Like areas in France where it was forbidden to seize work implements such as plough teams to force a payment of the *tailles*, the Code Noir stipulated that creditors could not seize the debtors' plantation slaves as a form of payment. Protected from the expropriation of their slaves, planters had very little incentive to pay their creditors. As one scholar points out, this situation 'impeded the development of production' and fuelled 'a latent state of crisis beneath the seeming prosperity of the

[35] u to Rouillé, 7 June 1754, ANOM C⁷ᴬ 17, f. 58 and 30 July 1754, ANOM C⁷ᴬ 17, f. 63. On *commissionnaires*, see also Marion, *L'administration des finances en Martinique*, 70–75. On the intermediaries in the French wine trade, see Thomas Brennan, *Burgundy to Champagne: The Wine Trade in Early Modern France* (Baltimore: Johns Hopkins University Press, 1997).

age'.[36] It was not only a volatile colonial population, corruption and abuse of power, fraud, and illicit trade that undermined the French grip on its mid eighteenth-century colonies in the Îles du Vent, so did the legal system and the colonial debts it produced. Creditors, whether in the colonies or in the metropole, raged against planters' refusal to honour their debts, all the while continuing to pour their capital into the sugar islands in pursuit of profits.

The Riches of Empire

There were, indeed, profits to be made. French international commerce grew exponentially in the eighteenth century and much of this was fuelled by exports to the colonies and the re-exportation of French sugar and coffee to foreign markets. Compared to Britain, France's main rival, French international commerce was half that of Britain's in 1716–20 but had surpassed it by 25 per cent on the eve of the French Revolution.[37] Domestically produced goods such as wine, textiles, and other merchandise formed a part of French exports, but more and more of it came proportionally from the colonies. According to François Crouzet, 34 per cent of total French exportation was produced in the colonies in 1716, a number which increased to 39 per cent in 1756 and to 59 per cent in 1787. The value of French imported produce from its colonies in 1751–5 was 67 million livres compared to England's 39 million livres. This number increased to a staggering 219 million livres in 1786–90 compared to England's 83 million livres.[38] Despite the many flaws in the French colonial system, the plantation complex was a highly profitable enterprise.

The most immediate beneficiaries of France's colonial commerce were the string of port cities along the French Atlantic and Mediterranean coasts. Calais, Dieppe, Le Havre, Rouen, Honfleur, St Malo, Morlaix, Brest, Nantes, La Rochelle, Bordeaux, Bayonne, and Sète received the right to trade with the French colonies in the Letters Patent of 1717. In these ports, French raw and manufactured goods exported to the colonies were exempt from duties and taxes, unlike all foreign goods (excepting salt beef used in slave diets). Re-export of colonial commodities from Calais,

---

[36] Géraud-Lloca, 'La Coutume de Paris outre-mer', 231. On the issue of planter debt see also Caroline Oudin-Bastide, *Travail, capitalisme et société esclavagiste: Guadeloupe, Martinique (XVIIᵉ–XIXᵉ siècle)* (Paris: Édition La Découverte, 2005), 40. On the collection of debt and the inability to seize work implements in France, see James B. Collins, *The State in Early Modern France*, 2nd edn. (Cambridge: Cambridge University Press, 2009), 22.

[37] Butel, *L'économie française*, 81. [38] Crouzet, *La guerre économique*, 277 and 114.

Dieppe, Le Havre, Rouen, Honfleur, La Rochelle, Bordeaux, Bayonne and Sète to European markets were exempt of all duties and taxes except for a general tax of three per cent and, in Brittany, the import-export duty known as the 'droits de prévôté'. The Letters Patent of 1717 also forbid any direct trade between the colonies and foreign countries, a decision that was repeated in the Letters Patent of 1727.[39] Known as the Exclusif, these commercial dictates cemented domestic port cities' exclusive right to colonial markets. They ensured, as Mirabeau underlined to his older brother, that metropolitan merchants considered colonies to be the 'farms of French commerce' (des fermes du commerce de France).[40]

As French colonial commerce increased in the eighteenth century, the political and economic power of French Atlantic ports grew proportionately. Bordeaux, the main port for the direct trade with the Antilles, became a formidable regional capital. From here, French wine, flour, and textiles were loaded onto ships headed for the French Antilles; upon their return they brought raw sugar, coffee, cocoa, indigo, and cotton. A third of these goods were preserved for domestic consumption while two-thirds of French sugar and coffee were reloaded onto foreign ships who carried them off to Northern European markets.[41] Nantes, the key port for the French slave trade, was another port animated by the colonies. Of the 3,291 documented slave voyages from France in the eighteenth century, 1,431 began in Nantes (compared to 435 in La Rochelle, 396 in Le Havre, 385 from Bordeaux, 207 from Saint-Malo, 135 from Lorient, and 123 from Honfleur).[42] La Rochelle, in turn, was the main centre of trade with Canada; Lorient was the key port for trade with the East Indies. Privileging specific ports and merchant communities with distinct trades was a typical feature of Ancien Régime France. The Crown happily handed out partial monopolies in exchange for a guaranteed state income.

With such a set-up, individual merchants could make fortunes in the colonial trades albeit at a high risk. A study of eighteenth-century patterns of private investment shows that of all foreign trades, the branch that guaranteed the highest profit involved direct trade with the West Indies.

---

[39] Letters Patentes du Roy, Portant Règlement pour le Commerce des Colonies Franoises. Du mois d'Avril 1717. Registrées en Parlement (Paris: Imprimerie Royale, 1717). Tarrade, Le commerce colonial, i, 90. On how ports and their hinterlands profited from colonial expansion, see Richard Drayton, 'The Globalisation of France: Provincial Cities and French Expansion c. 1500–1800', History of European Ideas, 34, 4 (2008), 424–30.

[40] CM to MM, 27 October 1754. FM, vol. 24. See also CM to MM, Guadeloupe, 10 January 1754. FM, vol. 23.

[41] On Bordeaux, see Éric Saugera, Bordeaux port négrier XVIIe–XIXe siècles (Paris: Karthala, 1995).

[42] Voyages: The Trans-Atlantic Slave Trade Database, www.slavevoyages.org.

The mean profit rate of this trade per completed voyage was 25 per cent. If it included slave trading, it reached 30 per cent. The slave trade alone generated a mean profit of only 15 per cent, while trade with the East Indies generated a profit of 18 per cent. Although long-distance trade generally came with a high profit, it could take years before a ship was back in port. Hurricanes, piracy, and disease also produced a high risk of failure. Merchants, therefore, preferred diversifying their investments. For instance, the outfitter from Nantes, Espivent de La Villeboisnet, invested in ninety voyages from 1764 to 1791, out of which eleven were privateering voyages, twenty-eight slave trade voyages, twenty-three direct West Indies voyages, eighteen fishing voyages, and ten miscellaneous voyages, including two to the Indian Ocean. Based on these commercial strategies, a merchant could expect an average annual profit of 6 per cent (a conservative estimate), a solid percentage compared to many investment opportunities within France. In France, the maximum legal rate of interest was 5 per cent. French public bonds, such as the Rentes sur l'Hôtel de Ville de Paris, had an internal rate of return that varied between 4.8 per cent and 6.5 per cent from 1746 to 1792. The internal rate of return on land investment was between 3.5 and 4.5 per cent. Though history is full of examples of merchants ruined by intrinsic hazards of colonial commerce, commercial involvement in the empire was therefore generally a lucrative affair, though increasingly also a competitive one.[43]

Throughout the eighteenth century, port merchants fought hard to guard their exclusive privilege to colonial markets. They vied for protection against foreign competition but also against neighbouring ports within France. This embrace of protection and commercial privilege was intertwined with their strong support for what they referred to as the 'liberty of commerce', an elusive concept which definition was much debated in these years. French chambers of commerce throughout the realm often used it to speak against 'la maxime de M. Colbert' and Colbert's support of privileged commercial companies. Though this captured poorly the views of Colbert – who used companies to penetrate long-distance markets but generally proclaimed himself to be against 'that which got in the way of commerce which should be extremely free' – ports' conception of liberty entailed a strong opposition to state intervention when it came to duties and taxes on goods that they traded or to companies with an exclusive right

---

[43] Guillaume Daudin, 'Profitability of Slave and Long-Distance Trading in Context: The Case of Eighteenth-Century France', *The Journal of Economic History*, 64 (2004), 144–71, 146, and 153–5. On commercial ruin, see Paul Butel, *Les négociants bordelais: l'Europe et les Iles au XVIIIe siècle* (Paris: Aubier, 1974), 110.

to trade with a colony. They easily combined such a stand with their quest for state protection, for instance in the form of a military presence along the African coast, financial encouragements in the form of premiums, or when seeking help to keep foreigners from trading in the colonies. Such understanding of liberty was not particular to metropolitan merchants engaged in colonial commerce, but could also be found in the French textile industry for instance.[44] It stood in sharp contrast to views in the French colonies, where planters found that metropolitan ports' exclusive 'liberty' to their markets prohibited their own 'liberty' to trade with foreigners.

Profits and the Crown

The Crown served as the principal arbiter of the tense relations that burdened French colonial commerce; it was, however, far from a neutral one. Its physical frame was the Chateau of Versailles, where the King, his ministers, his council, and hundreds of hopeful lobbyists exchanged nods and words in the pursuit of power. Paris operated as a political, intellectual and financial centre, where public opinion formed and obtained ever-greater levels of influence. It was in Paris and at Versailles that the marquis de Mirabeau laboured to help his brother advance up the ladder of the Ministry of the Marine while refashioning himself as a political economist. It was also here that decisions on colonial appointments, legislation, and military protection were made. For the financially unstable government, these decisions were first and foremost tailored to help replenish state coffers through direct and indirect taxes on colonial production and trade. Court intrigue, however, usually determined who was in charge of the decision-making process and for how long, just like the personal economic interests of such decision makers would further influence official views.

The Crown considered colonies to be generators of fiscal income. The Domaine d'Occident, part of the Ferme Générale, collected a tax on all incoming sugar as well as other colonial commodities. Further duties fell on sugar for the domestic market as it made its way to the consumer,

---

[44] On French chambers against 'la maxime de M. Colbert', see Jean Tarrade, 'Liberté du commerce, individualisme et État. Les conceptions des négociants français au XVIIIᵉ siècle', *Cahiers d'économie politique/Papers in Political Economy* 27/28 (1996), 175–91, 178, and 180–81. On Colbert's views, see E. Levasseur, *Histoire du commerce de la France* (Paris: Librairie Nouvelle de Droit et de Jurisprudence, 1911), 296. For parallel debates within the French textile industry, see Minard, *La fortune du Colbertisme*. On liberty and privilege within French economic sectors more generally, see Horn, *Economic Development in Early Modern France*.

sometimes elevating its cost with more than 50 per cent. As Jan de Vries has noted, while the growth in production caused relative prices of colonial goods to decline, 'rising fiscal charges on their consumption did much to hide this from consumers'. The French Crown, like its British and Dutch counterparts, skilfully adapted its fiscal regime to the new realities that consumption helped produce.[45] Though he could hardly say so in his official letters, Mirabeau considered the Crown's view of colonies as a vehicle for fiscal income a direct impediment to successful colonial reform. As he told his brother with regret: 'in France one makes commerce serve finance when instead one should let finance serve and assist commerce'. Stating the irony of such pursuit, he declared with stoic distance that 'the father of all masters is gold and wealth is the father of all forms of slavery'.[46]

Court intrigue, political favouritism, and economic manoeuvring dictated who oversaw fiscal, financial, naval, foreign, or military matters – all government branches that bore on colonial policy. The rise and fall of particular policies could therefore be immediately dependent on the rise and fall of political careers, fortunes, and misfortunes as well as on the personal economic and political interests of people temporarily in charge. No one would come to know this better than Mirabeau himself. Half way through his governorship of Guadeloupe, his aspirations to one day become Minister of the Marine eroded when Antoine-Louis Rouillé, whose patronage Mirabeau enjoyed, moved from the Marine to the Ministry of Foreign Affair. The new minister, Jean-Baptiste de Machault d'Arnouville, former Controller General of Finance, did not know Mirabeau, who consequently fell out of favour due to the machinations of Arnaud de la Porte, chief clerk of the Marine (*premier commis*).

De la Porte, in fact, perfectly embodied the intertwined nature of public and private interests that suffused the French monarchical state and undergirded colonial policy. As *premier commis*, he handled the Minister of the Marine's colonial correspondence and often wrote up instructions to newly appointed governors and intendants. De la Porte also had a knack for exploiting his position for personal gain. He secured his brother the intendancy of Saint-Domingue in 1751 alongside a position for his son

---

[45] On French taxes on sugar, see Robert Louis Stein, *The French Sugar Business in the Eighteenth Century* (Baton Rouge: Louisiana State University Press, 1988), 159–60. On consumption, see Jan de Vries, *The Industrious Revolution: Consumer Behavior and the Household Economy, 1650 to the Present* (Cambridge: Cambridge University Press, 2008), 164.

[46] On finance, see CM to MM, 27 October 1754. FM, Vol. 24. On Richelieu, Colbert and gold as the father of masters, see CM to MM, 11 August 1754. FM, vol. 23.

within the Ministry of the Marine. He built up a fortune through
the acquisition of tax farming rights on fur at Lake Nipigon in Canada,
five-sixths of the fishery of Baie de Brador, and investments in Saint-
Domingue.[47] Mirabeau, who often barked at bureaucrats, suspected as
much. He told his older brother that de la Porte's brother treated his
intendancy on Saint-Domingue as a cash cow. With time, the hamstring-
ing of Mirabeau's political aspirations pushed him to portray the *premier
commis*, who pretended to be a friend of the Mirabeau brothers, as a
corrupt deceitful officer of the pen. Drawing parallels between his own
situation and the rivalry that poisoned relations within French Catholic
groups, he noted that 'the friendship of a man of the pen with a man of the
military is not and never will be but what that of a Jesuit is to a Jansenist'.[48]

Looming Crisis and Collapse

In the two years that Jean-Antoine de Mirabeau resided in Guadeloupe
he produced a deplorable picture of the Caribbean plantation complex
which horrific features were only rivalled by his portrayal of the colonies'
central administration. Ultimately, the metropolitan and colonial structures and attitudes that he described made him certain that France's days in
the New World were numbered. It was part of his commission to alert the
government to the many causes that might lead to the loss or collapse of
a colony, yet he and his peers in other colonies – whether because of the
fragile lines of communication across the Atlantic, the ever-growing
French bureaucracy, or neglect – often felt that they were speaking into
a void. Depending on the disposition of the official, negligence on the part
of the Crown could prove fruitful. As one scholar has shown, in French
colonial New Orleans, innovation, adaptation, and self-determination in
the hands of a 'rogue' colonial officer sometimes helped build or sustain
the French colonial empire. Yet to officials striving to play by the rules,
Versailles' long silences crippled their ability to effectively govern the
colonies.[49]

---

[47] Later his son became Minister of the Marine during the French Revolution, albeit only for three
days. On de la Porte see Pritchard, *Louis XV's Navy*, 26; and Donald J. Horton, 'Laporte de Lalanne,
Jean de', in *Dictionary of Canadian Biography*, vol. 3 (Toronto: University of Toronto/Université
Laval, 2003), www.biographi.ca/en/bio/laporte_de_lalanne_jean_de_3E.html.

[48] CM to MM, 8 June 1754. FM, 23. On friendship CM to MM, 24 December 1754, FM, 23.

[49] On lack of communication, Banks, *Chasing Empire*, 190. On 'rogue' administrators, Shannon
Lee Dawdy, *Building the Devil's Empire French Colonial New Orleans* (Chicago: University of
Chicago Press, 2009), 233.

Mirabeau's indefatigable attempts to draw attention to the weaknesses of the Îles du Vent in general, and Guadeloupe in particular, generated frustration over time. Many of the issues he listed in his official correspondence to the Ministry of the Marine received no response from his superiors. Neither did his suggestions on how to ameliorate matters. He had proposed moving Guadeloupe's principal port, Basse-Terre, to Petit Bourg to better check contraband trade. He had also asked the Crown to ensure that French slave traders sold their slaves and provisions directly to Guadeloupe, rather than through Saint-Pierre on Martinique, where *commissionaires* controlled and inflated prices. When Machault took over from Rouillé in the middle of Mirabeau's administration, Mirabeau painstakingly listed all his previous requests hoping for answers. None of his pleadings carried fruit. Disgruntled, he told his brother that '[w]e write ten letters about the same thing often without receiving a single response'. The political economist did his best to help his brother, passing on messages to high-powered people and informing him of court politics. Little did it help. When the governor finally received a reply from the Ministry of the Marine towards the end of his stay, he told his older brother with biting sarcasm: 'This letter, which is the only one in a year responding to seven of mine, informs me that contraband is an offence against French commerce; *belle nouvelle*'.[50]

Since his royal interlocutors remained mute, the governor's private letters brimmed with complaints of imminent colonial collapse. Soon, his brother started chiming in. In one letter, the political economist responded that some people in the metropole believed that the colonies in the New World would secede from Europe in fifty years, while he himself believed it would happen sooner. In his subsequent reply, the governor cautioned that colonies on the American mainland and those in the Caribbean should not be conflated. Both were on the verge of secession, he agreed, but for different reasons. New England had grain, flour, and wood, and even a budding manufacture. It was therefore on a trajectory towards independence. This was not the case in the sugar islands. A sugar colony's subsistence was fragile, which kept it dependent but only on 'the nation that would provision it the best and protect it the most'.

---

[50] On moving the port, Mirabeau to Rouillé, Martinique, 8 May 1754. ANOM C⁷ᴬ 17 and Guadeloupe 30 July 1754, ANOM C⁷ᴬ 17. On creating direct trade, Mirabeau to Machault, Guadeloupe 30 July 1754, ANOM C⁷ᴬ 17. On repeating concerns, Mirabeau to Machault, Guadeloupe 16 October 1754, ANOM C⁷ᴬ 17. On a lack of replies, see CM to MM, 7 May 1754, FM, vol. 23. On finally receiving a response, see CM to MM, Guadeloupe, 24 December 1754, FM, vol. 23.

Guadeloupe was close to collapse and Martinique was not far behind, he said, and local inhabitants on both islands preferred the English. With impressive foresight, Jean-Antoine ensured his brother that the region 'is close, very close to a revolution if order is not re-established, and the next war will teach us this'.[51]

Warfare and the Negotiation of Empire

Revolutions in the New World, we now know, were decades away. War, in contrast, was just around the corner; within a few years, Mirabeau's perspicacious remarks on the impending loss of the Îles du Vent started to unfold. Shortly after the Seven Years War erupted in North America and spread across the globe, numerous French territories overseas surrendered to the British. In March 1757 the British captured Chandernagor in India. In July they took Louisbourg and Île Royale in New France, and the following year the Senegalese possessions in Africa. In May 1759, Guadeloupe surrendered after short-lived resistance. Four months later, Québec did the same, and in September 1760 all of New France was in British hands. By 1762, Dominica, Grenada, St Lucia, Tobago, St Vincent, and Martinique had also come under British occupation. Of its main Caribbean colonies, France was only able to hang on to Saint-Domingue against which Britain never organised a serious attack.

Local officials condemned the surrender of the Îles du Vent to the enemy and scolded inhabitants for their 'unfaithful' behaviour. In his report to Versailles, the new governor-general of the Îles du Vent, Louis-Charles Le Vassor de la Touche, unequivocally blamed Martinique's defeat on the local population's lack of patriotism and 'the bad example of Guadeloupe'.[52] The intendant of the Îles du Vent, Le Mercier de la Rivière, agreed, describing the free local inhabitants as 'arrogant, presumptuous, greedy, infatuated with liberty, and consequently an enemy of all authority'. But unlike Le Vassor de la Touche, Le Mercier tempered his critique. As if privy to Mirabeau's many complaint – a not impossible proposal given that the two had been in touch via Mirabeau's older brother, Victor, about Jean-Antoine's private affairs in the Îles du Vent in 1758 – he emphasised that while Martinique's inhabitants were disloyal, the metropole carried some of the blame since it had neglected this colony

---

[51] For the marquis de Mirabeau's predictions, see MM to CM, Paris, 26 September 1754, FM, vol. 23; for the chevalier de Mirabeau's response see CM to MM, Guadeloupe, 24 December 1754. FM, vol. 23.

[52] Le Vassor de la Touche to Choiseul, 14 May 1762, ANOM C^{8A} 64, pièce 16–27bis.

'for a very long time'.[53] Ignoring critical voices prior to the war, the Crown was now forced to tackle the weaknesses of its colonial empire if it were to save any of it.

The first official steps in that direction occurred during negotiations for peace. On the French side, these were carried out under the aegis of Étienne-François, duc de Choiseul. Entering office as Minister of the Marine on 6 April 1761, Choiseul was one of the most influential figures in French colonial affairs since Colbert. His ambition to revive France's global power and his tendency to seek specialist opinion before making decisions made him an outstanding conductor of peace negotiations and the dynamo for colonial reform in subsequent years. Acquainted with prominent figures within the enlightened sector (including the older Mirabeau brother), he skilfully exploited public opinion for political ends.[54]

Choiseul's engineering of a domestic debate on empire on the heels of the first round of peace negotiations exemplifies such cunning. It also reveals that he already at this point was aiming to preserve the French plantation complex and its necessary territorial components but would accept British rule in Canada. In spring 1761, when negotiations commenced, Choiseul notified his British counterpart that France expected the return of Guadeloupe, Marie-Galante, and Gorée in exchange for Minorca but was willing to relinquish Canada, though not Cape Breton or its fishing rights off Newfoundland. Britain rejected these terms, insisting that France cede Canada, Cape Breton, and its fishing rights in the Gulf of St Lawrence as well as Senegal and Gorée in West Africa. When Choiseul rebuffed British demands, negotiations collapsed.[55] To justify the continuation of war to the public (and to blame Britain for the failure of negotiations), Choiseul published a *Mémoire historique sur la négociation*, documenting the diplomatic exchanges between the two courts.

The publication of the *Mémoire* prompted a plethora of responses from chambers of commerce in French port cities and directors of the

---

[53] 'Le Mercier de la Rivière, Mémoire sur la prise de la Martinique, contenant les détails demandés par Monsieur le duc De Choiseul', 5 August 1762, N 212, ANOM C⁸ᴬ 64, f. 123. On Le Mercier's connections to Jean-Antoine, see CM to MM, Brest, 4 August 1758, FM, vol. 24 and MM to CM, 39 August 1758, FM, vol. 24.

[54] On Choiseul's colonial administration, see Eugène Daubigny, *Choiseul et la France d'outre-mer après le traité de Paris: étude sur la politique coloniale au XVIIIᵉ siècle, avec un appendice sur les origines de la question de Terre-Neuve* (Paris: Hachette, 1892); on his broader career, see Chaussinand-Nogaret, *Choiseul*.

[55] Daniel Baugh, *The Global Seven Years War 1754–1763: Britain and France in a Great Power Contest* (New York: Longman, 2011), 563 and 538.

Compagnie des Indes. All of them strove to safeguard the branch of colonial commerce in which they were invested. Their reports, in turn, generated a flood of internal memoranda. Among the perspectives that emerged, those on Canada, Senegal, and the Îles du Vent proved crucial to the immediate and long-term future of the French colonial empire. All three cases exposed the Crown's determination to salvage its lucrative plantation complex in the French Caribbean. The debate on Canada highlights how this could happen at the expense of France's century-old commitment to the American mainland. Discussions on Senegal and the Îles du Vent confirm such preferences, but they also disclose how the administration was weighing the possibility of forging a new colonial empire in Africa and seeking to rethink its ties to the Caribbean.

Sacrificing Canada

It is often said that no tears were shed over the loss of Canada, a view that owes its tenacity to Voltaire's reference to the ruinous war over a few acres of snow. These powerful words, of course, do not capture the Crown's long relationship with New France. Canada was of strategic importance to the French colonial presence in North America even if it were a financial liability for the state. To supporters of Canada within the central administration, royal outlays formed a necessary part of the costs of protecting France's colonial commerce. Canada prevented Britain from acquiring 'universal empire' in America, and with that control over all trade of the New World. Losing it could be irreparably harmful to French interests. Furthermore, the colony accounted for less than 10 per cent of the Ministry of the Marine's annual outlays and Île Royale for less than 5 per cent. Still, at no point was Canada generating a profit that surpassed state expenses.[56]

During negotiations for peace, several of France's commercial sectors played up Canada's economic pull. No one tried harder to convince the government of the considerable profits to be made from Canada than the Chambre de commerce d'Aunis, representing the merchants of La Rochelle. Once Choiseul's *Mémoire* was in circulation, the chamber immediately contacted the ports of Marseilles, Nantes, Saint-Malo,

---

[56] On Canada and Île Royale's financial contributions, see Catherine M. Desbarats, 'France in North America: The Net Burden of Empire during the First Half of the Eighteenth Century', *French History*, 11 (2007), 1, 24, and 19, and Albert Duchêne, *Histoire des finances coloniales de la France* (Paris: Payot, 1938), 108. On Canada's supporters, see John Shovlin, 'Selling American Empire on the Eve of the Seven Years War: The French Propaganda Campaign of 1755–1756', *Past and Present*, 206 (2010), 122–49, 128–9.

Dunkerque, Bayonne, Le Havre, Bordeaux, and Montpellier to garner support for its campaign to retain Canada. Its members informed their peers that they were shocked to learn about 'the sacrifice that our monarch has been prepared to make of Canada to arrive at a peace with the court of London'. To reverse the King's willingness to relinquish Canada, La Rochelle had therefore prepared a memorandum for Versailles in the hope that they could 'demonstrate the infinite importance of this colony'.[57]

Numerous ports offered La Rochelle their assistance. Some proposed to write a memorandum to the central administration; others set out to contact their deputy in the Council of Commerce in Paris and ask him to lobby alongside the deputy of La Rochelle. The Chambre de commerce de Guienne, representing the merchants of Bordeaux whose share in the Canada trade was considerable, wrote to Choiseul underlining that 'we do not all wish for peace, if it will cost us the cession of Canada'. To strengthen its case, it supplied the government with trade statistics, pointing out that in times of peace, sixty vessels yearly went to Canada charged with wine, *eau-de-vie*, and other luxurious goods, generating a profit of 2 million livres. Another 150 vessels went to fish for cod, training 10,000–12,000 sailors. On their return, they would bring seal oil or carry wood to the sugar islands in exchange for rum and molasses. The Bordeaux merchants further asserted that Canada could become the ideal setting for the cultivation of tobacco. It could also help France expand its navy through the cultivation of hemp, a better exploitation of Canadian wood, and the training of sailors for the Marine, thus providing France with all the means to rebuild its colonial empire and prepare for a future war against Britain. In contrast, if France ceded Canada to Britain, the latter would have no enemy to fear on the North American continent and its fleet would be free to concentrate on capturing the French sugar islands in the next war.[58]

La Rochelle and Bordeaux's eagerness to drum up support for Canada was predictable given their direct involvement in this trade. However, both ports omitted to mention the numerous bankruptcies trade with Canada had fostered over the years and many of which even involved the Crown itself. In the wars France fought against Great Britain between 1688 and 1763, the government contracted merchant ships to send supplies to Canada,

---

[57] Chambre de commerce d'Aunis to Chambre de commerce de Marseille, La Rochelle, 10 November 1761. *Rapport de l'archiviste de la Province de Québec (1924–5)* (Ls-A. Proulx Imprimeur de sa Majesté le Roi, 1925), 202–3.

[58] Letter to M. le duc de Choiseul, 22 December 1761, Bordeaux, Archives départementales de la Gironde (ADG), Chambre du commerce de Guienne (C) 4246. See also *Rapport de l'archiviste de la Province de Québec*, 223–5.

Newfoundland, Acadia, and Louisburg but tried to defer payments for as long as possible. As J. F. Bosher has shown, the Jewish merchant from Bordeaux, David Gradis, who claimed 299,000 livres from the Ministry of the Marine after the War of the Austrian Succession, felt 'hampered a good deal' by the Crown's reluctance to pay. In the middle of the Seven Years War, Gradis claimed another 2.7 million livres, and informed the government that he was on the verge of bankruptcy. The profits to be made from Canada that Bordeaux described in its plea to the Crown therefore appeared idealistic at best.[59]

Based on Canada's association with bankruptcy, it is unsurprising to see some members of the French maritime community swerve in their commitment to the North American mainland. Merchants in the port of Nantes, the main port of the slave trade, told their colleagues in La Rochelle that 'Canada was the cause of war' and that the minister was probably already fully aware of its importance and might feel insulted by the ports' joint lobbying. As Nantes' rebuff discloses, metropolitan port cities acting as one united commercial front could easily and swiftly disaggregate into the particular interests that they each represented. Because French possessions in Senegal were also in danger, Nantes was careful to spend whatever goodwill it enjoyed with the Crown on its own sphere of interest. Besides, the port was right about the minister's sensitivities. When Marseilles wrote in support of La Rochelle, Choiseul responded with a severe scolding, commanding the port to stay out of an affair that did not concern it and to stop associating with other chambers without official authorisation.[60]

In the broader scheme of things, supporters of France's oldest settler colony stood little chance. Being on the losing side in the war, the Crown had to make territorial sacrifices overseas. Despite Bordeaux and La Rochelle's fervent attempts to convince the Crown of Canada's geostrategic and economic importance, Choiseul decided that giving up Canada was a low price to pay compared to the alternative losses France would have to make in the Caribbean and in West Africa. As François-Joseph Ruggiu

---

[59] For David Gradis's quote and the problem of bankruptcies associated with the trade to Canada, see J. F. Bosher, 'Success and Failure in Trade to New France, 1660–1760', *French Historical Studies*, 15, 3 (1988), 444–61, 451.

[60] On La Rochelle's and Bordeaux's links to Canada, see Dale Miquelon, 'Canada's Place in the French Imperial Economy: An Eighteenth-Century Overview', *French Historical Studies*, 15, 3 (1988), 432–43, 437. For Nantes' rebuff, see Chambre de commerce de Nantes to Chambre de commerce d'Aunis. Nantes, 16 November 1761, in *Rapport de l'archiviste de la Province de Québec*, 207. For Choiseul's response, see Choiseul to the Chambre de commerce in Marseille, 4 January 1762. Ibid., 206–7.

notes, Choiseul's decision thus gestured towards a 'no-territory' policy, the essence of which would be to mould the French colonial empire into a small but lucrative colonial empire centred on the Caribbean which would stimulate the French economy, replenish state coffers, and pay for a strong navy. In line with such logic, the loss of Canada – this country of meagre profits and a cause of war – was a blessing in disguise.[61]

The Senegalese Possessions

Unlike Canada, French Senegalese possessions in Africa were central to the prosperity of France's Caribbean sugar islands due to their strategic role in the slave trade. Britain had captured the Senegalese possessions early in the war for this very reason, in accordance with a rationale developed by a former associate of Britain's Royal Africa Company, Malachy Postlethwayt. In his *Importance of the African Expedition Considered* (1758), Postlethwayt argued that trade with Africa drove French commercial success since it underpinned the French plantation complex in the Americas which, in turn, was the life and spirit of its commerce with Europe. Therefore, 'if *England* strikes at the root of the *French African trade*, she, of course, cuts off the very stamina of the enemies' trade and navigation to *Europe* as well as *America*'.[62] Following Postlethwayt's plan expeditiously, the British occupied Saint-Louis, the main centre of France's holdings in Senegal, on 1 May 1758. The French Compagnie des Indes, who had committed numerous ships to the French war efforts, had requested military assistance from the Crown to defend its African possessions prior to the attack, but had been met with a polite refusal because the government had no available ships.[63]

Strained resources notwithstanding, the Crown fought hard to regain its holdings in Senegal once peace negotiations commenced. An internal memorandum within the Ministry of Foreign Affairs presented clearly and

---

[61] Ruggiu, 'Falling into Oblivion?', 69–94.

[62] Malachy Postlethwayt, *The Importance of the African Expedition Considered: with Copies of the Memorials, as Drawn up Originally, and Presented to the Ministry; to induce them to take Possession of the French Forts and Settlements in the River Senegal, as well as all other on the Coast of Africa* (London: C. Say, 1758), ii.

[63] Internal note to Monsieur Silhouette, Versailles, 8 October 1758, Ministère des affaires étrangères, Paris (hereinafter MAE), Archives Diplomatiques (hereinafter AD), Afrique 10, f. 146. And Paris, 6 October 1758, MAE, AD, Afrique 10, f. 138. On these negotiations, see also André Delcourt, *La France et les établissements français au Sénégal entre 1713 et 1763* (Dakar: IFAN, 1952), 81–7; Pierre H. Boulle, 'Eighteenth-Century French Policies towards Senegal: The Ministry of Choiseul', *Canadian Journal of African Studies*, 4 (1970), 305–20.

comprehensively what a potential loss or preservation of Senegal might
mean. According to its author, who unfortunately remained anonymous,
giving up Senegal would not critically hurt French trade. As he said, the
Compagnie des Indes currently obtained 800 to 900 slaves per year from
this region and some gold. Due to its monopoly, it was able to buy slaves
at a price of 50 livres per captive. Yet African merchants increasingly
preferred to bypass Senegal and trade with the British on the Gambia
River where competition was left open and prices were as high as 300 livres.
Furthermore, the French-Senegalese trade in gum was declining. France
had once furnished all of Europe with gum, but the British and the Dutch
were encroaching on the company's monopoly. Since the conquest, prices
had soared, and it would take the company at least three years before prices
would return to their pre-war level. For these reasons, the author argued,
France should not hesitate to give up Senegal, if the British instead would
allow the French to build a fort at Anamabou (in present-day Ghana)
where the slave trade was abundant and guarantee French right to trade
freely in competition with other European powers on the Gold Coast.[64]

The other scenario was to keep Senegal. Should it be restored to France,
the internal memorandum stated that the only way to make it profitable
again would be through considerable reform. The government would need
to abolish the monopoly of the Compagnie des Indes, place the holdings
directly under the Crown, and open trade to all French merchants. Were
that to be done, the author argued, Senegal could ultimately compensate
entirely for French losses in the New World if the French turned to
commercial agriculture. Detailing how this might happen, the memorandum broke with the conventional view that Africa was chiefly a source of
slaves for the Antilles:

> One could also try to benefit from this country by means of agriculture. The
> Senegalese territory is good and well-watered by rivers and streams. Wild
> indigo is very common and grows as high as four to five feet. One can easily
> plant cacao, sugar cane, tobacco, coffee, and cotton and the country is
> settled by free negroes whom, through encouragement, can be brought to
> clear the land, without using enslaved negroes who can too easily escape into
> the forest. The population of this type of people will multiply because of the
> surplus of agricultural production. With time, white, creole, or European
> cultivators will also establish themselves here and when that happens this
> colony can become of some consequence and largely compensate us for
> losses we have incurred elsewhere.

[64] 'Côte d'Afrique', June 1761, MAE, AD, Afrique 10, f. 156.

This remarkable suggestion was the first time that someone within the Crown administration considered relocating the cash crop cultivation of the Americas to Africa to compensate for French colonial losses in the New World. The proposal to cultivate cash crops in Africa was nothing new. Some of these crops were indigenous to West Africa, as the author noted, and African populations cultivated them for local markets. The English Royal African Company had tried to establish indigo plantations on the Upper Guinea coast in the late seventeenth century using its own grometto slaves as labourers. The Dutch West India Company had endeavoured to cultivate cotton on the Gold Coast as early as the 1650s and added experiments with sugar and indigo in the early eighteenth century, again using slave labour.[65] Yet none of these experiments had shared the above report's emphasis on using free local labour, a testimony to the rising concerns over the cost of labour required by the Caribbean plantation complex. The use of free labour to cultivate American crops in Africa would be integral to abolitionist propaganda in the following decades. Humanitarian concerns, however, were nowhere to be found in this author's report who instead underlined that free labour was a more manageable labour system in an area pregnant with opportunities for escape.

Despite the potential the author of the memorandum saw in the transferral of sugar, coffee, cotton, and indigo production to Africa, he seemed in no hurry to capitalise on Senegal's agricultural opportunities. In his view, the Crown's immediate aim should be to guarantee an influx of slaves to the Caribbean colonies. The area in which he did seek reform regarded the Compagnie des Indes. Encouraging the Crown to abolish the company's monopoly and open trade in Africa from Cape Blanc to the Cape of Good Hope to all French merchants, he further proposed to have two frigates patrol the African coast and recommended the construction of forts at Anamabou, Petit Popo, Loango, and the Rade de Cabinde (on the stretch from present-day Ghana to Angola) where the slave trade was most active. Although considering opportunities to cultivate the coveted staples of the Americas in Africa by deploying free local labourers – a model that could potentially render the slave trade, slavery, and the high cost of protecting colonies in the Americas redundant – his immediate focus was

---

[65] On the English attempt, see Colleen E. Kriger, '"Our indico designe" Planting & processing indigo for export, Upper Guinea Coast, 1684–1702', in Robin Law, Suzanne Schwarz, and Silke Strickrodt (eds.), *Western Africa: Commercial Agriculture, the Slave Trade and Slavery in Atlantic Africa* (Suffolk: James Currey, 2013), 98–115, 112. On the Dutch attempt, see Robin Law, '"There's nothing grows in the West Indies but will grow here": Dutch and English projects of plantation agriculture on the Gold Coast, 1650-1780s' in ibid., 116–37, 120–22.

on ways to boost the French slave trade to the Caribbean, leaving it in the hands of the minister to decide if a relocation of colonial empire to Africa was even desirable.

The Compagnie des Indes participated in these early discussions and tried to counter internal voices critical of its monopoly. Its directors suggested that France do its best to maintain Senegal and pointed particularly to the abundance of gold and slaves in the region. Yet they too wished to see the Senegalese holdings transferred to the Crown, stating that the company had been charged with these possessions by the government against its will. Its shareholders had therefore suffered vast expenses because they had had to shoulder this costly administrative burden. All the directors hoped to maintain was the company's exclusive right to trade in slaves and to sell licences to independent merchants. In other words, they hoped to preserve those privileges that generated a profit and transfer expenses associated with the Senegalese administration to the Crown.[66]

With Spain joining the war on the side of the French on 10 December 1761, these discussions receded momentarily but resumed with renewed force once peace negotiations recommenced in April 1762. By then, the administration had discovered Malachy Postlethwayt's *The Importance of the African Expedition Considered* and was alarmed by its content. To those who wished to retain Senegal, it revealed Britain's design to become 'the universal monarchy of commerce and of the seas'. Repeating Postlethwayt's arguments, a report to the minister underlined that Africa was the real key to French commercial success. If the British managed to hold on to Senegal, they would 'strike the most gruesome blow against French agriculture, manufacture, and navigation'.[67]

Choiseul wholly understood the importance of the French Africa trade to domestic prosperity but remained uncertain about Senegal's role within it. As negotiations entered their final stages, he drew up a list of twenty questions to Jean-Augustin Accaron, the *premier commis* of the colonial administration, requesting how many men it would take to maintain the concession, how reliant it was on assistance from France, whether it was threatened by the British or the local populations, how valuable it was to the slave trade, how much gold and gum France could expect to get from it, and what types of domestically produced commodities France was exporting to Senegal. Accaron responded that while Senegal was important, the small island of Gorée rather than Senegal was the more important

---

[66] 'Memoire touchant le Sénégal', 3 July 1761. MAE, AD, Afrique 10, f. 164.
[67] 'Considératios sur le commerces d'Affrique', 13 October 1762, ANOM C⁶ 14.

concession to preserve, because of its role in protecting the slave trade.[68] With France being pressed at negotiations, Accaron thus sealed the fate of the French possessions in Senegal. In the Treaty of Paris, concluded on 10 February 1763, France gave up its territorial claims to Senegal but saved its slave trading. Article X specified that 'His Britannick Majesty shall restore to France the island of Gorée in the condition it was in when conquered' whereas France would cede to Britain 'the river Senegal, with the forts and factories of St Lewis, Podor, and Galam, and with all the rights and dependencies of the said river Senegal'.[69]

Upon the restoration of peace, the Crown followed the advice of the anonymous author and took direct charge of the remaining French possessions in Africa. It also opened the slave trade to all French merchants and embarked on the dissolution of the Compagnie des Indes. Did this signal a commitment to a no-territory policy? Evidence within the Ministries of Foreign Affairs and of the Marine suggests that there was at least no unanimous endorsement of such a policy. A letter from the Controller General of Finance, Henri Léonard Jean-Baptiste Bertin, to Louis-Jules Mancini-Mazarini, duc de Nivernais, Minister of State (both of whom happened to be protectors of the Mirabeau brothers) reveals that French diplomats had deliberately ensured that the Treaty of Paris was silent about Juda (Whydah) on the Gold Coast and the trading stations of Rufisque, Portudal, Joal, and Albreda in Senegambia to furnish the French Crown with the means to steadily reclaim its African holdings.[70] An exchange between Choiseul and the French botanist, Michel Adanson, further indicates an ongoing interest in West African territorial expansion. While it is doubtful that Choiseul were supportive of this plan, Adanson stressed that the preservation of Gorée would allow France 'to have a foot on the coast' in order to take possession of territory on the mainland 'the moment it be[came] advantageous to do so'.[71] As we shall see in Chapter 4, attempts to reclaim the Senegalese territories began with the very first governor that the Crown sent to Gorée after the war.

---

[68] 'Instruction relative au Mémoire sur la concession du Senegal', 30 October 1762, ANOM C⁶ 14.

[69] 'Treaty of Paris', The Avalon Project at Yale Law School, http://avalon.law.yale.edu/18th_century/paris763.asp.

[70] 'Copie de la lettre de M. le controlleur-général à M. le duc de Nivernois', 20 October 1762, MAE, AD, Afrique 10.

[71] Michel Adanson, 'Pièce instructives concernant l'Ile gore', May and June 1763, ANOM C⁶ 15.

Martinique and the Îles du Vent

Alongside deliberations over the degree to which possessions in Senegal were paramount to the French plantation complex, the Crown also weighed its future in the Îles du Vent. It was clear that Guadeloupe and Martinique had not been able to keep up with Saint-Domingue but remained valuable producers of sugar and coffee. The question was whether the preservation of these islands was critical rather than merely valuable to a successful future of France's international sugar business. To assess the importance of the Îles du Vent, and Martinique in particular, Choiseul therefore asked Le Mercier de la Rivière who had just returned to France after the British capture of Martinique to clarify what the monarchy would stand to gain from their preservation.

Le Mercier, whose reputation as a talented political economist was already rising, reciprocated with a reply that filled an impressive eighty-five handwritten pages and read more like a piece of political economic theory than a government report.[72] In his publication of the report that Le Mercier crafted, historian L. P. May argued that it helped convince Choiseul of the need to retain Martinique and Guadeloupe rather than Canada.[73] However, as shown above, Choiseul was already willing to give up Canada in 1761. The importance of Le Mercier's memorandum, therefore, does not concern Canada. Instead, it lies with Le Mercier's persuasive argument for a liberalisation of the Exclusif and the need to acknowledge that colonial and metropolitan prosperity were inextricably linked and could mutually reinforce each other – arguments not only dear to Le Mercier the administrator, but also to Le Mercier the *économistes*.

Like chevalier de Mirabeau before him, Le Mercier indicated that there were deep structural problems within the French colonial system that stifled the economic progress of the Îles du Vent. He conveyed that Martinique had lost a fourth of its sugar plantations prior to the outbreak of conflict without seeing a corresponding increase in the production of cotton, coffee, or cocoa. In his view, the reasons for this were four-fold: Martinique's disastrous inheritance law, the shortage and high price of slaves from Africa, the high price of French goods, and the weight of expenses associated with the plantation complex. In spite of these problems, the Îles de Vent had still been able to generate profits. Le Mercier

---

[72] Le Mercier de la Rivière, 'Mémoire sur la Martinique' (1762), ANOM C⁸ᴬ 64.

[73] L. P. May (ed), *Le Mercier de la Rivière (1719–1801) Mémoires et Textes inédits sur le gouvernement économique des Antilles avec un commentaire et des notes de L. Ph. May* (Paris: Éditions du Centre National de la Recherche Scientifique, 1978), 1.

estimated that French commerce introduced goods to the Îles de Vent to the value of 24 million *argent des îles* and that the islands exported to France goods to the value of 26 million *argent des îles*, stimulating a trade worth 50 million *argent des îles*. Commerce between France and Martinique alone was estimated at 30 million, the equivalent of 20 million *argent de France*.

Le Mercier also pointed out that Martinique posed a commercial threat to the English, Danish, Dutch, and Spanish Caribbean islands and could become a central entrepôt for trade in the region due to its excellent port. Until the occupation, the island had significantly upset English commerce during the war by serving as a base for French privateering. It was also 'the key to the Gulf' and therefore not only of immense value to France, but also to Spain with whom France had formed the *pacte de famille* in 1761. If it remained in British hands, it would directly threaten Spanish America. Worse, Britain would be able to underbid French sugar on Northern European markets, since Saint-Domingue in Le Mercier's estimate did not produce enough sugar to outperform British sugar production single-handedly. Despite the less than perfect economic and political state of the island, Martinique was therefore of foremost importance to the overall success of French colonial commerce.

If permitted to reach its best possible state, Le Mercier continued, Martinique's economic forecast could become even brighter. A third of Martinique remained uncultivated and to bring such barren land under cultivation, the population would have to increase. In his estimate, Martinique would be able to sustain twice its current enslaved population which he overestimated at 80,000 slaves prior to the war (there were 66,263 slaves in 1755) and three times its white population which he correctly put at approximately 12,000 prior to the war. Martinique could also have a flourishing commerce, particularly if allowed to continue its trade with the Spanish in the Gulf as well as with neutral islands in the region and with the British at Sint Eustatius. Surely aware that he entered contested waters proposing foreign trade in the colonies, he underlined that such commerce could be done using rum and molasses as currency and in which French commerce had little interest.

Upon his overview of pre-war realities and future economic opportunities, Le Mercier returned to his four courses of colonial decline and how to eradicate them. On the issue of inheritance, he insisted that the law that required a father to divide the land equally among his heirs should be replaced by a law which gave the oldest son or daughter everything the maintenance of a plantation required. Remaining assets could be divided equally between other heirs. The shortage and high price of slaves could be solved by exempting the slave trade and all the goods used in this trade from tariffs and taxes, even when such goods were produced in England. Le Mercier also echoed the view that the monopoly of the Compagnie des Indes should be dissolved and the slave trade opened to all merchants in France and in the colonies. Regarding the two remaining issues – the elevated price of French goods and the high cost of production – these had their solution in commercial liberalisation as well. The high price of French goods, he argued, was caused by the excessive cost of French navigation. Sailors and building materials were more expensive in France than in England or in the Dutch Republic. To cover such costs, merchants raised the price of goods in the colonies, which increased the cost of colonial production. If France lowered tariffs on the French trade with Northern Europe, the region from which France received its naval stores, the cost of French shipping would fall, and so would the cost of French goods and, hence, colonial production.

Le Mercier even went so far as to suggest that a redressing of the above problems through a liberalisation of trade would ameliorate the planters' fraught relationship with the metropole. To him, a reduction in prices would help diminish contraband trade and turn plantation owners into loyal subjects. As he noted: 'to lower the price of French manufactured goods on Martinique will be, so to speak, to provide France with a new property title to this colony, an even more sacred title since it will be founded on the plantation owners' interest in rendering it valuable'. Offering an early rendition of what would soon become a characteristic physiocratic argument, Le Mercier de la Rivière insisted that France should no longer ignore the interests of its planters overseas because they directly influenced metropolitan interests – the two, in fact, were inseparable.

Although he was asked to speak on the topic of the Îles du Vent, Le Mercier could not refrain from sharing his views on the general plan for French colonial commerce either. Acknowledging that free trade would be unrealistic given the political system of European imperial powers, he suggested that a free trade in goods that French commerce could not easily supply would be a great advantage to the colonies, and ultimately also to the metropole. He particularly encouraged a trade agreement with England. Taking a stab at the Exclusif and what the Physiocrats would soon refer to as the 'mercantile system', he stressed that always aiming to export more to a people than import from them was 'a pernicious and false system which sooner or later will push others to stop trading with us altogether'. To him, the prohibitive French commercial laws were the real reason why Martinique, Guadeloupe, Grenada, Saint-Domingue, Québec, and Louisburg still had not reached their full potential:

> If our general plan had been established on such a base, this is to say on the abundance of the production of our islands and our domestic land and on the liberty of commerce with England, our colonies today would have been well populated and rich in production, our countryside covered with plantation owners, our manufacture would have multiplied proportionately and our commerce would have been a hundred times richer and more extensive; it would have been sustainable because it would pertain to our land and be cemented by the shared interests between us and our rivals.

Instead, France had followed a plan that had led it to lose 'almost all its colonies, Canada, and its establishments in India'.[74]

Thus, while furnishing Choiseul with direct answers to his questions regarding the value of Martinique, Le Mercier simultaneously delivered a biting critique of the Exclusif, identifying the ways in which he believed it to be undermining not just the economic potential of the Îles du Vent but also that of the French colonial empire in general. He further gave an unambiguous lecture about the ways in which French and French colonial prosperity was attainable alongside the growing prosperity of competitors, a view that clashed with conventional economic wisdom. Though the Crown was reluctant to adopt such views, many of Le Mercier's reformist ideas resonated not only with the Physiocrats whose colonial ideas developed against the backdrop of the mid-century French imperial crisis. They also aligned with some of the views of the Martinican plantocracy (as we shall see in Chapter 3), pointing to the interlaced and multi-sited web of eighteenth-century intellectual exchange.

The Spoils of War

As the debates on Canada, Senegal, and the Îles du Vent reflect, port merchants and colonial investors who had sunk their capital into France's colonial commerce, bureaucrats within the Ministries of the Marine and of Foreign Affairs, and high-powered government officials in France and in the colonies vigorously scrutinised the future of the French colonial empire during peace negations between France and Britain. In the process, several advocated the need for colonial reform, though few agreed on what such reform should entail. Directors of the French Compagnie des Indes pushed for a commercial privilege that freed it from the administrative expenses

---

[74] Le Mercier de la Rivière, 'Mémoire sur la Martinique' (1762), ANOM C[8A] 64.

with which the Crown had saddled the company. Pulling in another direction, port merchants and voices within the colonial administration lobbied for an abrogation of the company's privileges and an opening of trade to all French merchants. The intendant of Martinique went further championing free trade with the British, finding that a liberalisation of trade coupled with a recognition of the sugar islands' right to prosperity would boost profits and safeguard French sovereignty in its remaining American colonies. Should this project fail, other voices had started to contemplate the possibility of reorienting French expansionist efforts towards Africa.

It was, of course, not up to France alone to decide which colonies to keep and which to give up. In Britain, a pamphlet war on the values of Canada and Guadeloupe had raged since 1760 and was reopened upon its capture of Martinique. Two main issues dominated this debate. The first was whether it would be worthwhile retaining Canada and building a vast American empire at the risk of seeing the American colonies demand independence. The second was whether Guadeloupe would become a threat to the Jamaica sugar planters.[75] In the end, this argument (made by Jamaican planters fearing competition from Guadeloupe) won the day. Retaining Canada, it was pointed out, would not prevent a later capture of Guadeloupe and Martinique. In the words of one pamphleteer: 'If we have "an Universal Empire on the Continent of North America", we can take the sugar islands when we will'.[76] Britain therefore agreed to restore Martinique, Guadeloupe, Marie-Galante, La Désirade, and St Lucia to France. French fishermen were also able to enjoy 'the liberty of fishing and drying on a part of the coasts of the island of Newfoundland ... and the liberty of fishing in the gulph [sic] of St. Lawrence'.[77] France, moreover, ceded Louisiana to Spain to compensate for the Spanish loss of Florida to the British. French territorial empire on the North American mainland was over.

The reduced French colonial empire centred on the Caribbean plantation complex would serve French commerce brilliantly until the French Revolution. As the Ancien Régime was about to crumble, France

---

[75] William L. Grant, 'Canada versus Guadeloupe: An Episode of the Seven Years' War', *The American Historical Review*, 17 (1912), 735–43, 738. See also Helen Dewar, 'Canada or Guadeloupe? French and British Perceptions of Empire, 1760–1763', *Canadian Historical Review*, 91, 4 (2010), 637–60. On the British side of the war, see P. J. Marshall, *The Making and Unmaking of Empires: Britain, India, and America c. 1750–1783* (Oxford: Oxford University Press, 2005), Chapter 3.

[76] Quoted in Grant, 'Canada versus Guadeloupe', 740.

[77] Article V and VIII in 'Treaty of Paris', The Avalon Project at Yale Law School, http://avalon .law.yale.edu/18th_century/paris763.asp.

re-exported 60,000 tonnes of sugar to foreign markets annually compared to Britain's 16,000, thus winning what François Crouzet calls the Anglo-French 'sugar war'. Britain compensated by relying on its domestic consumers whose relative wealth vis-à-vis French domestic consumers enabled them to purchase six times as much sugar as their French counterparts.[78] To fuel French primacy on continental European sugar markets, French slave traders carried approximately 576,000 captives from Africa to the Americas between 1763 and 1790, 491,000 of whom made it to the Americas alive.[79] The Crown's continued reliance on slavery and the Exclusif, however, also certified continued volatility within the French colonial empire. Few were more receptive to the vulnerability of the French Caribbean plantation complex than an emerging group of political economists tied to two of the most insightful colonial administrators in these years – the chevalier de Mirabeau and Le Mercier de la Rivière. Known first as the *économistes* and from 1768 as the Physiocrats, this group responded to the crisis of colonial empire with a vision that was not altogether different from some of the novel ideas that had surfaced within the colonial administration during negotiations for peace. It is to their ideas that the book now turns.

---

[78] Crouzet, *La guerre économique*, 119 and 126.
[79] *Voyages: The Trans-Atlantic Slave Trade Database*, www.slavevoyages.org.

CHAPTER 2

Empire beyond the Mercantile System

In my view, the art of colonies is still in its most imbecile infancy.[1]
Marquis de Mirabeau, *L'ami des hommes* (1756)

[C]olonial commerce ... today is the bone of contention between nations striving to abduct from each other the exclusive means to enrich their merchants.[2]
Marquis de Mirabeau, *Philosophie rurale* (1763)

During the imperial debacle of the Seven Years War, Victor de Riqueti, marquis de Mirabeau, and Doctor François Quesnay busied themselves developing a science of political economy that they and their fellow *économistes* would later refer to as Physiocracy (Physiocratie). Working from within the walls of Versailles, where the doctor served as first physician in ordinary to the King, and keeping abreast with affairs in Paris, their economic doctrine was crafted to remedy the Crown's dire financial situation and place the monarchy on a path to prosperity and peaceful coexistence. In their view, the tools with which to attain these goals included a privileging of agricultural development over industry, a liberalisation of trade and labour, and thorough-going fiscal reform. Together with the expanding cadre of writers who joined them, they set out to determine the forms of international and colonial relations that would enable their domestic ambitions. The result was a radical response to the colonial problems that the Mirabeau brothers had discussed so vividly during Jean-Antoine's tenure in the Îles du Vent. Proposing a dismantlement of the Exclusif and its underlying premise that colonies were subservient to the interests of the metropole, they argued that

---

Sections of this chapter replicate material I published in Røge, 'La Clef de Commerce'; Røge, 'The Question of Slavery in Physiocratic Political Economy'; and Røge, 'A Natural Order of Empire'.
[1] Victor Riqueti, marquis de Mirabeau, *L'Ami des hommes*, 3 vols. (Avion, 1756), iii, 293.
[2] Victor Riqueti, marquis de Mirabeau, *Philosophie rurale, ou économie générale et politique de l'agriculture, réduite à l'ordre immuable des loix physiques et morales, qui assurent la prospérité des empires* (Amsterdam: Chez les libraires associés, 1763), iii, 195.

colonies should be seen as 'oversees provinces' equal to provinces in France. Several among them were also outspoken critics of colonial slavery, a stance they coupled with a proposal to relocate the cultivation of sugar, coffee, cotton, indigo, and tobacco to Africa. Tied to an understanding of how to spread 'civilisation', the Physiocrats' colonial ideas combined to form a powerful rethinking of France's colonial interests in the Americas and in Africa.

The development and maturation of their reform programme was undergirded by intellectual compromise and interaction with the political, economic, and social concerns of the mid eighteenth-century French monarchy. An analysis of their repertory of ideas captures not only an original response to the French colonial crisis, but also the difficulties associated with the production of alternative paths to French economic development and the tenacious influences of prevailing norms and practices. Not all Physiocrats had the same response to colonial empire, nor did they all adhere blindly to the economic theories and topical preferences of François Quesnay, who was celebrated and reviled as their intellectual leader. Seeking to expose the internal developments of the physiocratic colonial doctrine as much as its subsequent influences, I analyse in this chapter the particular contributions of key members and the ways in which their ideas evolved in response to the writings of other intellectual elites and broader geopolitical shifts.

Mirabeau's pioneering role in advancing a vision of empire beyond slavery and monopoly trade becomes clear in a close reading of his writings on colonies in *L'Ami des hommes* (*The Friend of Man*, or *Treatise on Population*), which he published prior to his collaboration with Quesnay. The core elements of the physiocratic colonial doctrine represented a compromise between Mirabeau's interests in perfecting what he referred to as the 'art of colonies' and Quesnay's doctrinaire analysis of the domestic French economy. As recruits such as Baudeau, Du Pont de Nemours, and Roubaud joined the co-founders of Physiocracy, they expanded Quesnay and Mirabeau's core colonial ideas, adding a critique of slavery rooted in economic calculation and a rethinking of French colonial activities in Africa. Although the Physiocrats' popularity declined in the final years of the Bourbon monarchy, their ideas on colonial empire lived on in the writings of their contemporaries and gained new relevance once the French Revolution erupted.

Political Economy in Eighteenth-Century France

The search to equip France to reap the benefits of a world increasingly shaped by overseas trade and rivalry formed a crucial context for the advancement of eighteenth-century economic thought. Both Mirabeau and Quesnay belonged to a fast-expanding cohort of writers and philosophically minded administrators who saw in political economy a panacea for Europe's fierce jealousy of trade and its corollary of injurious political and financial impacts. The growing public debt contracted by the French Crown to defend its European and colonial interests and its constant rivalry with Britain propelled *philosophes,* government officials, and commercial and financial elites to interrogate legal, economic, and political features of Europe and its colonial empires in pursuit of a formula for peaceful international success. Though political economic recipes for reform had been debated since the seventeenth century, the acceleration of imperial competition across the globe broadened the pool of participants in the eighteenth century.[3]

In France, discussions received a boost in 1748 when Charles-Louis de Secondat, Baron de la Brède de Montesquieu, published his *L'Esprit des Lois*. In it, he brought to the fore questions about modern slavery, the value of the Exclusif, and the civilising qualities of commerce, all of which he linked to cultural relativism and a theory of climate. Many of Montesquieu's ideas were taken up in the *Encyclopédie*, the multi-authored work edited by Denis Diderot and Jean le Rond d'Alembert and published from 1751.[4] Itself a vehicle for the furthering of political economic debates, the *Encyclopédie* included numerous entries written by leading economic thinkers caught up in the swirling vortex of power. François Véron de Forbonnais, soon to be named *inspecteur general des Monnaies*, wrote entries such as 'colonies', 'commerce', 'concurrence', 'change', and 'espace' in 1753. Anne-Robert Turgot, who would become Minister of the Marine in 1774 and Controller General of Finance until 1776, penned 'foires' and 'fondations'. Quesnay, who at the time was known as the esteemed doctor to Madame de Pompadour, Louis XV's mistress, authored 'fermiers' in 1756 and 'grains' in 1757. All these entries were not mere definitions but specific interventions in the broader upswell in debates on the need for reform.[5]

---

[3] On the development of French economic thought against the backdrop of global European rivalry, see Cheney, *Revolutionary Commerce*. On the expansion of interest in political economy beyond a small intellectual elite in the second half of the eighteenth century, see John Shovlin, *The Political Economy of Virtue*. On the European context, see Sophus A. Reinert, *Translating Empire Emulation and the Origins of Political Economy* (Cambridge, MA: Harvard University Press, 2011).

[4] Louis de Jaucourt's entry on 'slavery' in the *Encyclopédie*, for instance, was taken directly from *L'Esprit des Lois*. See Ehrard, *Lumière et Esclavage*, 169.

[5] Steiner, *La 'science nouvelle'*, 9–17. On contributors to the *Encyclopédie*, see Frank A. Kafker and Serena L. Kafker, *The Encyclopedists as Individuals: A Biographical Dictionary of the Authors of the Encyclopédie* (Oxford: Oxford University Press, 1988).

Overlapping with the Encyclopédistes, the circle surrounding Vincent de Gournay (*intendant du commerce* from 1751 to 1758) also contributed to the vibrancy of political economic debates. Gournay was an international trader (*négociant*) from the Atlantic Port of Saint-Malo who nourished a keen interest in the insights of English economic thinkers such as Joshua Gee, Charles Davenant, Josiah Child, and Joshua Tucker. Striving to introduce their ideas to a French audience in the hope that it would help France rival English international commerce, Gournay enlisted a cluster of bright men to translate and interpret foreign texts, including Abbé Coyer, Duhamel de Monceau, Butel-Dumont, Jean-Baptiste Secondat de Montesquieu (son of Charles), Abbé Morellet, and Encyclopédistes such as Turgot and Forbonnais. Collectively, the group translated over forty publications on matters economic. Proponents of what Simone Meysonnier terms a 'libéralisme égalitaire', a precursor to economic liberalism, these authors promoted freer trade, though never unequivocally. On the topic of colonial commerce, most remained firm supporters of the Exclusif and few engaged critically with France's use of African slave labour. On these matters, the Physiocrats were the first economists to take a radical stand.[6]

Mirabeau and the Art of Colonies

In the world that Mirabeau and Quesnay inhabited, Quesnay was always seen as the pioneer of Physiocracy. Although Mirabeau's role as a co-founder was acknowledged, followers and critics alike found the physiocratic doctrine to be based on the economic principles that Quesnay had developed in his encyclopaedic entries 'grains' and 'fermiers'. Scholars have since complicated this picture and ascribed particularly the social dimension of the doctrine to Mirabeau's influences.[7] With respect to physiocratic colonial ideas, there is no doubt that the marquis was the more original thinker. Prior to his collaboration with Quesnay, and on the heels of his long discussions with his brother in Guadeloupe, Mirabeau published *L'Ami des hommes* in 1756, in which he included a commentary on colonisation. The work became an instant best seller across Europe, reaching no fewer than twenty editions, and catapulted Mirabeau into intellectual

---

[6] On a 'libéralisme égalitaire', see Simone Meysonnier, *La balance et l'horloge. La genèse de la pensée libérale en France au XVIIIe siècle* (Paris: Edition de la Passion, 1989), 179–80.

[7] Mirabeau's contributions to the development of Physiocracy's domestic focus is clearly developed in Elizabeth Fox-Genovese, *The Origins of Physiocracy: Economic Revolution and Social Order in Eighteenth-Century France* (Ithaca, NY: Cornell University Press, 1976).

stardom.[8] Though Mirabeau disavowed many of his own ideas upon his collaboration with Quesnay, his early views on colonies and slavery were picked up not just by later physiocratic political economists, but also by advocates of colonial reform during the French Revolution, including his son Honoré Gabriel Riqueti, comte de Mirabeau, one of the founding members of the Société des amis des noirs.

The main thrust of *L'Ami des hommes* was that France should tend to its population through agricultural development and free trade. In Mirabeau's view, it was particularly the French nobility's abandonment of their pastoral duties in the French countryside and the government's lack of interest in agriculture that needed redressing. As the title of the book indicated, these criticisms formed a part of Mirabeau's broader concern with social and economic prosperity for all mankind, particularly the poor. Not without a social bias, he encouraged his audience not to think of the poor as a lazy multitude (*multitude oisive*), but to alleviate their suffering by elevating their standards of living through proper policing which would help civilise them (*les civilisent*).[9] Thinking inclusively about human suffering, Mirabeau also commented on populations in the colonies, offering a biting critique of contemporary practices of slavery, colonisation, and international rivalry. In his view, France should embrace a new stage of colonial empire that dispensed with slavery and monopoly trade.

In his publication, Mirabeau proclaimed that he was influenced by David Hume's *Political Discourses* (1752) and Richard Cantillon's doctrine of *populationnisme* (which took population size to be the indicator of national wealth).[10] A devout Catholic, he also drew inspiration from the divine commandment to populate the earth abundantly and multiply in it (Genesis 9:7). As he announced in the opening section on colonies, 'the entire world is populated only through colonies'.[11] Neither the Bible nor Cantillon nor Hume, however, could have led Mirabeau to draw the controversial conclusions on modern slavery, monopoly trade, and contemporary colonial commerce for which he would become known. The Bible embodies both pro- and anti-slavery arguments while, politically, it was often used as a means to justify European colonisation and slavery.

---

[8] On the fame of *L'Ami des hommes*, see Loménie, *Les Mirabeau*, i, 339.

[9] For examples of these views, see Mirabeau, *L'Ami des hommes*, i, 70, 72, and 84.

[10] Mirabeau stressed his adoption of Cantillon's doctrine in Mirabeau, *L'Ami des hommes*, 238–9. On Hume's impact see Arnaud Diemer, 'David Hume et les économistes français', *Hermès*, May 2005, 15.

[11] 'Le monde entier ne s'est peuplé que par Colonies'. Mirabeau, *L'Ami des hommes*, iii, 555.

With regard to Cantillon, his *Essai sur la nature du commerce en général* highlighted the economic benefits of slavery vis-à-vis free labour with no condemnation of the institution. Like many contemporaries, Cantillon also praised the commercial policies associated with the English Navigation Acts which limited foreign access to British and British colonial markets. Hume did criticise slavery in his work 'Of the Populousness of Ancient Nations', but he focused on the slavery of the ancients and incorporated only a few references to modern slavery and no discussion of its possible eradication.[12] As Michèle Duchet suggested, Mirabeau's forceful rebuke of the European approach to colonial empire was fuelled not by his engagement with intellectual peers, but by his extended conversation with his brother about colonial life during the latter's stint in the Îles du Vent.[13]

In *L'Ami des hommes*, Mirabeau opened by celebrating colonisation as an art form (*l'art des colonies*), but noted with regret that it was still in its infancy. Delineating three historical ages of colonisation, he stated that the first lingered only in fables; the second pertained to ancient times; and the third had opened with the discovery of the New World. The latter and still ongoing age, according to Mirabeau, was no improvement upon the former two but was fuelled by a greedy search for gold. From it ensued conquest, exploitation, the submission of indigenous populations, and the jealousy of trade between colonising nations. As one of the European powers expanding since Columbus' voyage, France was building and maintaining its colonial empire in accordance with principles geared towards war rather than peace – principles that were informed by a spirit of domination, of commerce, and of population.[14]

Weighing the consequences of each of these principles, Mirabeau charged that the spirit of domination was the direct culprit of France's strained relationship with its colonies. France was trying to dominate the colonies but should instead have approached them in less restrictive ways, which would have made the colonies think of France as their protector and not as their despot. Responding to possible detractors of this proposal, he noted that 'people will say that this system . . . in practice will precisely

[12] Richard Cantillon, *Essay on the Nature of Trade in General*, ed. Richard van den Berg (London: Routledge, 2015), 103 and 375–7. David Hume, *Political Discourses* (Edinburgh: R. Fleming, 1752), Chapter X.

[13] Duchet, *Anthropologie et histoire*, 161.

[14] Mirabeau, *L'Ami des hommes*, iii, 359. The jealousy of trade was a topic of intense debate in the mid eighteenth century. See Istvan Hont, *Jealousy of Trade: International Competition and the Nation-State in Historical Perspective* (Cambridge, MA: The Belknap Press of Harvard University Press, 2005).

be the means to relax all the links that attach the distant parts to the mass, to dismiss the affinity between the provinces and the capital, and to turn these colonies [*plantations*], cultivated with such care, into distinct states and separated from the metropole'. Fearing that the colonists (*colons*) would become independent, France had kept its colonies 'feeble and poor'. Continuing such a policy would only precipitate their loss. Repeating to his European audiences what he had heard from his brother in letter after letter only a few years earlier, Mirabeau warned that without reform the colonies would 'either accept coming under the English Crown or cease to exist'.[15]

Prophesying the future loss of colonies through colonial independence or colonial disloyalty was an important part of *L'Ami des hommes'* critique of France's colonial system. Like in letters to Jean-Antoine, Mirabeau argued in his book that secession was ultimately inescapable since it was in the nature of colonies to break from the metropole like 'children' from a 'mother'. Secession 'will start with the strongest colonies', he stressed, 'but once one has made the jump all the others will follow'.[16] This metaphor of the family for colonial-metropolitan relations was a common trope in ancient and early modern political thought. In *Leviathan*, Hobbes stated that 'the Procreation, or children of a Common-wealth, are those we call Plantations, or Colonies'. Hobbes further explained that such colonies would often obtain independence from their metropolis upon being settled, at which point they would owe their 'mother' nothing but honour and friendship.[17] Following such logic, and to benefit from the French colonies for as long as possible, Mirabeau advised releasing the colonies from their chains through an implementation of full liberty within the interior contours of the colonial empire. From such measures, colonies would thrive and 'the *colons*' patriotic spirit' would develop and attach colonies to the mother country without force. France would win 'powerful brothers who would always be ready to support her'.[18]

If the spirit of domination corrupted the development of colonisation, so too did the spirit of commerce in its current form. To Mirabeau, this spirit was imbued with malignant qualities since commerce had become the unique object of French ambitions in America. By making it so, France had 'put first what by nature should follow'. It was futile to trade with the colonies before they were properly on the road to prosperity. As Canada's

---

[15] Mirabeau, *L'Ami des hommes*, iii, 368, and 370–71.   [16] Ibid.

[17] Thomas Hobbes, *Leviathan* (London: Penguin Classics, 1985), 301. On English debates on the future independence of colonies, see J. M. Bumsted, '"Things in the Womb of Time": Ideas of American Independence, 1633 to 1763', *The William and Mary quarterly*, 31, 4 (1974), 533–64.

[18] Mirabeau, *L'Ami des hommes*, iii, 369, and 372.

fishing and fur trade revealed, France had committed a grave error in its attempt to maintain an exclusive privilege to this trade. A restrictive commercial policy had kept Canada weak and an easy prey for the British. Aware of Canadians' poor purchasing power, French merchants preferred trading with the more successful Caribbean islands where they found a ready market for French grain and luxury goods and obtained commodities in exchange that could be re-exported to the rest of Europe at a profit. Yet the Exclusif was lucrative to only a few and ruinous to many. It rendered the French population accustomed to exchanging the necessary for the superfluous and the *créoles* to having only a precarious and very expensive subsistence. For these reasons, Mirabeau recommended preserving flour and wine for the domestic market where the destitute had a dire need for them. French commerce could instead supply the colonies with French luxury goods and allow the colonies to obtain essential provision from foreigners. If France followed such trade policies, he proclaimed, 'no nation in the universe, however economical and vigilant it may be, will be able to prevail over us when it comes to prices'.[19]

Mirabeau's push for a liberalisation of colonial commerce as a means to forge a patriotic bond between the colonies and the metropole and his advice to admit foreign merchants in the colonies were unconventional among metropolitan political economists but would, as we saw in the previous chapter, also inform Le Mercier's report to Choiseul in 1762. Most contemporaries in the metropole with intellectual gravitas, however, promoted views that echoed the Exclusif. In *L'Esprit des loix*, Montesquieu observed that 'a commerce established between the mother countries, does not include a permission to trade in the colonies; for these always continue in a state of prohibition'. He further observed that the 'disadvantage of a colony that loses the liberty of commerce is visibly compensated by the protection of the mother country, which defends it by her arms, or supports it by her laws'.[20] Montesquieu's statement could be read as a mere description of an existing commercial system, but many perceived it as an endorsement of the French Letters Patent of 1717 and 1727. A more overt support for the Exclusif appeared in the *Encyclopédie* in Forbonnais's article 'Colonies' (1753). Forbonnais contended in accordance with his typology of colonies that since the colonies in the Americas (his fifth type) 'were founded only for

[19] Ibid., 374–5, 379, and 385.
[20] Charles-Louis de Secondat, Baron de Montesquieu, *De l'esprit des loix ou du Rapport que les loix doivent avoir avec la constitution de chaque gouvernement, les mœurs, le climat, la religion, le commerce, &c à quoi l'auteur a ajouté des recherches Nouvelles sur les loix romaines touchant les successions, sur les loix françoises, & sur les loix féodales*, 2 vols. (Genève: Barrillot & fils, 1748), ii, 72.

the benefit of the metropole', it followed that they should remain dependent on the metropole and under its protection and that its founders had 'an exclusive right to its commerce'. Free trade in this type of colonies, Forbonnais underlined, was nothing short of 'theft'.[21] What to Forbonnais classified as theft, however, was what Mirabeau encouraged.

The final component of Mirabeau's critique pertained to the spirit of population. This spirit, he argued, had been compromised given its current association with slavery and the slave trade. Slavery was 'to put last art and labour which ought to come first in the esteem of man'. Drawing an analogy to antiquity Mirabeau alleged that once Rome had covered its lands with slaves 'thenceforth masters earned nothing, and Africa had to nourish Italy'. The lesson to be derived from Rome was that slavery pushed the master towards idleness and put the state on a path towards decline. Though focusing on the ancients, this view closely resembled his brother's critique of idle white slaveholders in the Îles du Vent. Continuing to echo his brother, the marquis de Mirabeau proclaimed that there was nonetheless a difference between the slavery of the ancients and that of the moderns. Slaves of the ancients resembled their masters, whereas those in the Americas were 'of a different race' (une race d'hommes à part), separated from their masters along colour lines. Modern slaves were acquired in Africa (la barbarie) and shipped to the sugar islands where 'they arrive[d] as brutes or [were] gifted with an instinct that is foreign to us'. They were then thrown into 'a cowshed together with their kind' and worked as hard as possible. In this way, 'within the law of fraternity and in a century which sees itself as enlightened' was born 'the hardest' and 'most ungodly servitude'. The mere fact that the African slave trade was still ongoing proved that the slave system was malfunctioning. Manifestly, Mirabeau concluded, slaves shipped to the colonies did not reproduce themselves but had to be constantly replaced by fresh blood.[22]

Although blending his outcries against the enslavement of Africans with polygenist views, Mirabeau's critique of the enslavement of Africans was

---

[21] François Véron Duverger de Forbonnais, 'Colonies', Encyclopédie, ou dictionnaire raisonné des sciences, des arts et des métiers, ed. Denis Diderot and Jean le Rond d'Alembert, Chicago: University of Chicago ARTFL Encyclopédie Projet (Winter 2008 Edition), ed. Robert Morrissey, http://encycopedie.uchicago.edu/.

Forbonnais embraced a softer stand once the Seven Years War erupted, arguing that the French colonies should be permitted to trade with neutral powers. However, he maintained that the Exclusif should be restored in full upon the arrival of peace. See Antonella Alimento, 'Competition, true patriotism and colonial interest: Forbonnais's vision of neutrality and trade', in Trade and War: The Neutrality of Commerce in the Inter-State System, ed. Koen Stapelbroek (Helsinki, 2011), 61–94.

[22] Mirabeau, L'Ami des hommes, iii, 390, and 392.

a step forward for French anti-slavery protests.[23] The condemnations of slavery in mid eighteenth-century France was near-inaudible and none among the *philosophes* and political economists had yet called for its eradication. Montesquieu, who insisted that slavery was 'unnatural' but in certain parts of the world founded on 'natural reason', had formulated 'the first vigorous and concentrated attack on slavery in the eighteenth century', yet had not called for its termination.[24] Rousseau, in turn, virulently condemned inequality in his *Discours sur l'origine et les fondements de l'inégalité parmi les hommes* (1755) and later rejected slavery in his *Du contrat social* (1762), but he never made explicit references to the enslavement of Africans in the French colonies except in his fictional work, *La nouvelle Héloïse* (1761). In contrast, Mirabeau condemned plantation slavery and promoted ways to eradicate it. As he said: 'will you limit [slavery] and soon render it useless? Encourage the cultivation of land in the colonies. You can only do that by making the colonies prosperous, and I have demonstrated that you can only make them so by an entire liberty in the importation and exportation [of goods]'. With rich agricultural production would come urbanisation. Slowly European artisans would be drawn to settle in the colonies and '[t]hese artisans will train others and quickly one will prefer labourers and salaried agricultural workers to slaves who have to be purchased at a high price' and who often proved 'unfaithful'.[25]

Mirabeau's proposal on how to move from slave to free labour was thus infused with an economic rationale that looked at the quality, costs, and policing of labour. These views differed quite notably from the views he had shared with his younger brother only the previous year. In a letter to his brother from 1755, he had recommended the immediate though conditional abolition of slavery. The letter is worth quoting at length not just for its early abolitionist sentiments, but also because it reveals more clearly than his published work how easily he – like his brother – combined anti-slavery views with a colour prejudice. As he wrote:

> if I were Minister of the Marine tomorrow, I would pass an edict which would declare all negroes free once they had been baptised and attached themselves to a section of the glebe [*glèbe* indicated land serfs or slaves were attached to and had to cultivate], from which they would pay royalty to the former property owner, if there were any, and to the state if this terrain had still not been conceded. I would divide into fiefdoms all colonial territory,

[23] On Mirabeau's polygenist views, see Andrew S. Curran, *The Anatomy of Blackness Science & Slavery in an Age of Enlightenment* (Baltimore: Johns Hopkins University Press, 2011), 179–81.
[24] Seeber, *Anti-Slavery Opinion in France*, 15.   [25] Mirabeau, *L'Ami des hommes*, iii, 395–6.

with the same seigniorial rights as those applied in France. I would declare a maroon and a convict of the state, all those Negroes deserting from his village. But the only distinction that I would apply between the different skins would be that only whites of origin would be able to own fiefdoms as well as hold municipal and military offices.[26]

In the letter, Mirabeau did not elaborate further on why only whites could hold such offices. Nevertheless, his statement highlights how even critics of plantation slavery grappled with skin colour as a barrier to social and political equality.

Contrary to his private letters, Mirabeau's take on abolition in his published work led him to imagine two possible futures for the Americas. One scenario was one in which industrious Europeans inhabited and laboured to build up a prosperous economy. Another was a future in which the failure to move beyond African slavery would steadily push the colonies into the hands of slaves and their descendants. Slave masters' debauchery, Mirabeau said, had opened households to slaves and 'established a race of people of mixed race [*une race de métis*]'. Together with the most industrious slaves who had acquired skills in the arts and crafts, these people were steadily beginning to take over. One day, 'work and activity' would be theirs, while only 'indolence and pride' would be left for slave masters to enjoy. The plantocracy was accelerating this process, Mirabeau claimed, by employing their slaves in navigation and in the local militias, thereby giving slaves a taste for freedom. In fact, several among the coloured population believe that 'God ha[d] first given this land to the red race, and thereafter to the whites, and finally to the blacks'. Noting that there were already areas on the sugar islands where the coloured population had stopped obeying, Mirabeau warned that far from 'sensing the danger of this kind of revolution', planters seemed 'to run towards it'. Flagging the possibility of a Haitian Revolution in what would soon become a widely distributed publication, Mirabeau hoped that his warning would encourage France to perfect *l'art des colonies*.[27]

Quesnay's 'Gouvernement Œconomique'

In contrast to Mirabeau, Doctor François Quesnay had paid no more attention to the needs for colonial reform than did the royal household that

---

[26] MM to CM, 7 April 1755, FM, vol. 23. The first half of this quotation appears in Loménie, *Les Mirabeau*, i, 203. He leaves out the part on fiefdoms.

[27] Mirabeau, *L'Ami des hommes*, iii, 394. The theme of slave revolts gained attention through Antoine François Prévost *Le Pour et Contre* which carried information about a slave revolt and maroon society in Jamaica in 1730s. See Duchet, *Anthropologie et histoire*, 140–42.

he served. Born in 1694 at Méré, not far from Versailles, Quesnay had studied medicine and surgery before becoming physician in ordinary to the King. In that position, he settled in an apartment near the queen's bed-chambers. He also quickly earned the support of the formidable Madame de Pompadour, mistress to Louis XV and renowned for her ability to forge or destroy the career of political elites. While attending to the health of the royals, Quesnay started cultivating an interest in agrarian political economy, drawing inspiration from earlier political economists, such as François de Salignac de la Mothe Fénelon, Pierre Le Pesant, sieur de Boisguilbert, and Charles-Paul Hurault de l'Hospital, seigneur de Belesbat, all of whom had sought to replace Louis XIV and Colbert's antagonistic commercial policies with a Christian agrarianism. Taking his cues from their preferences for agricultural production and promotion of free trade, and with his analytic eye fixed on France's domestic rather than colonial agricultural potential, Quesnay hoped to cast agrarian political economy as a cure for the Crown's financial ills and to convince his peers that his political economy was a new science.[28]

Pursuing both goals in 'fermiers' and 'grains', Quesnay argued for a form of government that understood how to optimise a state's natural resources and productive forces, a 'gouvernement œconomique'. Speaking admir-ingly of Sully's supposed agrarian policies during the reign of Henri IV, he projected that prosperity would emerge if the Crown guaranteed private property rights, gave preference to the cultivation of land instead of commerce and manufacture, and facilitated agricultural growth by permit-ting free trade. He argued in 'grains' that it was Colbert's efforts to favour manufacturing above agriculture and monopoly trade over free trade that had proven counterproductive to the French economy and caused its current crisis. To him, agriculture, not industry, was the real source of riches. As he said: 'it is agriculture which provides the material for labour and commerce and which pays for the one and the other; but these two branches restore their earnings to agriculture which renews the riches spent and consumed each year'. Based on this insight, Quesnay argued that France should embrace its identity as an agricultural kingdom (*royaume agricole*). Without mentioning the Dutch, he noted that a kingdom with

---

[28] On Quesnay's background and education, see Fox-Genovese, *The Origins of Physiocracy*, 78–93. On Quesnay's turn to political economy, see François Quesnay, *Œuvres Économiques Complètes et Autres Textes*, ed. Christine Théré, Loïc Charles, and Jean-Claude Perrot, 2 vols. (Paris: L'Institut National d'Etudes Démographiques, 2005), ii, 1375–8. On Fénelon, Boisguilbert, and Belesbat's critique of Louis XIV and Colbert and the resemblance of their proposals to Quesnay's ideas, see Rothkrug, *Opposition to Louis XIV*, 249.

the ability to base its financial prosperity on agricultural production and its foreign commerce on the export of raw food products (*denrées du cru*) would be more stable than a commercial republic (*république commerçante*) which centred its riches on commerce in manufactured goods. Only smaller states could thrive based on such commerce, Quesnay believed, although they would never be as secure as a state whose commerce rested on agricultural production.[29]

Quesnay's faith in the superior quality of French grain also led him to promote free trade and comprehensive fiscal reform. Free trade, he argued, would lead to the best price and make France the champion of the grain trade on the international market. Moreover, it had the added advantage of turning commercial rivals into friends. Trying to hurt a neighbour through trade prohibitions was to ultimately hurt oneself. More obscurely, Quesnay claimed that free trade would help bring France closer to the *natural order* – an order also referred to in the writings of Boisguilbert – which Quesnay believed would emerge once the governance of human society followed those laws intended for it and which could be derived from the physical laws of nature.[30] With respect to fiscal reform, he borrowed the notion of a single tax (*impôt unique*) from Vauban's *La Dîme Royale* (1707) to argue that the Crown should abolish its obscure tax policies, which he believed impeded production, and replace them with a single land tax drawn from the net product (*produit net*) of agricultural produce. If the government followed such a policy, the monarchy would divest itself of a ruinous fiscal system and find a reliable and lavish source of revenue. To illustrate how his economic ideas would work, Quesnay began circulating his now famous scientific model, the *Tableau économique,* in late 1758.

Quesnay's glorification of France's agricultural potential stopped at its domestic border. Neither 'grains' nor 'fermiers' accounted for the French colonies. The only colony he considered in these articles was the British colony of Pennsylvania. He mentioned it twice in 'fermiers', discussing its high export of corn and its role in regulating corn prices in England. In 'grains', he mentioned grain-producing colonies to quell the anxieties of free trade sceptics, claiming that at no given time would a society regulated by free trade jeopardise national interests. Competition between an

---

[29] Quesnay, 'grains', in *Œuvres économique et philosophique*, ed. Auguste Oncken (Paris: Jules Peelman & Cie, 1888), 208, 216, and 220.

[30] Ibid., 239. Quesnay, 'Le Droit Naturel', in *Œuvres économique et philosophique*, ed. Auguste Oncken (Paris: Jules Peelman & Cie, 1888), 374. On Boisguilbert and the natural order, see Meyssonnier, *La balance et l'horloge*, Chapter 2.

agricultural colony and its mother country, he said, would always tilt in France's favour, 'the quality of French grain being superior to grain from [the colonies] and all other places'.[31] If at all, Quesnay thus seemed to think of colonies as in competition with the metropole, rather than as entities whose relationship to the mother country could be mutually beneficial.

The Physiocratic Colonial Reform Programme
in *Philosophie Rurale*

Quesnay's lacking attention to the agricultural potential of the French colonies subsided once he started collaborating with Mirabeau. The two would combine their belief in the value of free trade and agricultural development as a source of wealth to articulate a poignant critique of the Exclusif. They would also break with the view of a 'colony' as a territory subjected to the commercial interests of the metropole and instead conceive of them as 'overseas provinces'. Their collaboration, however, replaced Mirabeau's plea to end the enslavement of Africans in the French colonies with an abstract critique of slavery. The colonial reform programme that they proposed in *Philosophie rurale* – the first of their publications to present the physiocratic doctrine in a comprehensive manner – reads like an attempt to shoehorn Mirabeau's preoccupation with the 'art of colonies' into Quesnay's recipe for domestic reform in 'fermiers' and 'grains'.

Philosophie rurale, with the second and longer title *Économie générale et politique de l'agriculture, réduite à l'ordre immuable des loix physique & morales, qui assurent la prospérité des empires*, was published in November 1763 in Mirabeau's name. A milder version of their *Théorie de l'impôt* (1760) (which led to Mirabeau's brief imprisonment), *Philosophie rurale* was a bid to restore French finances and put the monarchy (and other empires) on a path to prosperity. As such, it was a timely publication. The War of the Austrian Succession had absorbed 1–1.2 billion livres tournois in five to six years and the Seven Years War cost another 1.8 billion. Excessive borrowing to finance French military adventures in Europe and overseas had pushed the Crown to its financial limits, with a total debt in 1764 perhaps as high as 2.2 billion livres tournois (which constituted more than seven years of revenues). Without a complete overhaul of the Crown's fiscal and financial systems, many believed that the kingdom could expect a deluge of biblical proportions. Proposing that a single land tax on the

---

[31] Quesnay, 'fermier', in *Œuvres économique et philosophique*, ed. Auguste Oncken (Paris: Jules Peelman & Cie, 1888), 173 and 183. Quesnay, 'grains', 232.

agricultural surplus would provide a generous and sufficient source of fiscal income if agriculture were allowed to flourish, *Philosophie rurale* laid bare the principal concepts pertaining to Physiocracy and presented free international trade as offering the best commercial conditions for agricultural growth.[32]

Positioning the physiocratic doctrine in opposition to what they baptised the 'mercantile system' (*système mercantile*), their section on colonies opened with a direct attack on the Exclusif. Nothing was more 'contradictory to the natural order', they argued, than a system in which European powers combated each other to enrich their merchants and pretended to grant their colonies a right to protection and sovereignty but instead exploited them. The gloss of paternal protectionism used to defend the Exclusif distorted the colonies and the nation's general interests. Taking great pains to clarify why this was so, Mirabeau and Quesnay explained that because the colonies were protected markets, French merchants could sell their goods to them at an excessively high price, which led planters in the colonies to sell their raw goods at an equally elevated price. Merchants – whom Quesnay and Mirabeau referred to as 'cumbersome, helpless, and fearful' people who pretended to serve the monarchy – happily engaged in such an exchange knowing that they could return to France and dump the additional costs on domestic and foreign consumers.[33]

This was not the first time that Mirabeau and Quesnay raised the problem of elevated costs of commodities in the colonies. Mirabeau, as we have seen, had done so in the first edition of *L'Ami des hommes* and Quesnay had spoken on the issue in his *Questions intéressantes*, published in the third edition of Mirabeau's *L'Ami des hommes* (1758).[34] In these questions, Quesnay had asked if it was really advantageous for the planters that foreigners had to overpay merchants with a monopoly and whether it would not be more profitable if colonial goods were sold at their proper value by means of a free and open trade where merchants of all nations would compete for planters' crops. Exhibiting a belief in the benefits of a universal application of free trade, he had pondered whether this would not be the greatest way to 'make the colonies and all other territories in the

[32] On the cost of war, see Butel, *L'économie française*, 244. On the public debt by 1764, see Joël Félix, *Finances et politique au siècle des Lumières: Le ministère L'Averdy, 1763–1768* (Paris: Comité pour l'histoire économique et financière, 1999), 142. On the fear of deluge, see Sononscher, *Before the Deluge*.

[33] Mirabeau, *Philosophie rurale*, iii, 195–96, 197, and 213.

[34] Quesnay, 'Questions Intéressantes', *Œuvre économique et philosophique*, 292–3.

world prosper'.[35] Left unanswered in *L'Ami des hommes*, Quesnay's questions were given a methodical reply in *Philosophie rurale*.

Their response rested on a crucial re-conceptualisation of what was meant by a 'colony' and how it related to the metropole. 'What is a colony', Mirabeau asked, 'if not a province which, like the other provinces of the same state, should enjoy the same prerogatives in order to prosper, build up its riches, its population, and its [fiscal] contribution?'[36] The term 'province', with its roots in roman imperial vocabulary, signified in early modern France territories that had been folded into the royal domain. In the eighteenth century, there were approximately fifty-eight provinces in France, sub-divided into circa 300 pays, each of which enjoyed local privileges. In Quesnay and Mirabeau's view, it was these provinces that generated the agricultural surplus on which their proposed single land tax should fall and which would suffice as source of fiscal income. They should therefore enjoy the best conditions within which to produce, namely free trade and the dismantling of tariff barriers and commercial monopoly. It was these same 'prerogatives' that France's overseas provinces would come to thrive under as sources of production and of state revenue.

In their discussion of domestic France, Quesnay and Mirabeau had appropriated particular concepts to help secure the implementation of their ideas. They had asserted that the sovereign would be the *copropriétaire* (co-owner) of the *produit net* of all French land and that his revenues should depend solely on it (the single land tax).[37] They had thereby made provincial interests and the interests of the sovereign inseparable. If government revenues came solely from a tax on agriculture, the sovereign would want to provide the best possible system for agriculture to prosper (e.g. free trade). It was this same configuration that should apply to the colonies:

> The progress of the colonies depends on the progress of the cultivation of territory; & from such progress comes the successive development of the colony & of its contribution, meaning its population, its consumption, its reproduction, & net product, of which the sovereign is co-owner together with the owner of the cultivated land.

In the same breath, Mirabeau and Quesnay reminded the sovereign that he should not begin to tax the colonies before each plantation owner had

---

[35] Mirabeau, *Philosophie rurale*, iii, 202–3.   [36] Ibid., iii, 203–4.

[37] This use of the term 'copropriétaire' appears as physiocratic termonology from *Philosophie rurale* onwards. It is applied in several articles in the *Éphémérides du citoyen* from 1767 and by Le Mercier de la Rivière in *l'Ordre naturel* from 1767.

started to generate a profit.[38] Once the plantations were profitable, their prosperity would ensure a reliable fiscal contribution from an increasingly affluent population, whose purchasing power would benefit industry as well as other agricultural sectors.

Mirabeau and Quesnay's rebranding of a colony as a province might not appear innovative at first. After all, Hobbes, in the section from *Leviathan* cited above, had mentioned that colonies that did not obtain independence would remain subject to the metropolis 'and then they are no Common-wealths themselves, but Provinces, and parts of the Common-wealth that sent them'.[39] But being part of the same commonwealth did not necessarily mean being subject to the same commercial laws and privileges. In France, disparate commercial policies conditioned trade at the local and regional level. Such myriad privileges and legal exceptions were precisely what Quesnay and Mirabeau were trying to dismantle and replace with a simple and universal set of policies. If a colony could be seen as a province, it would follow logically that its ability to generate a profit should be conditioned by the same set of rules that the two advocated for the metropole, particularly in relation to the free circulation of goods.

Looking at a draft of *Philosophie rurale*, we see that it was Quesnay who insisted on this re-conceptualisation. In the margin next to the answer to the second question, he had scribbled the following: 'Are the colonies then only defeated foreign nations to be treated as enemies. But if they are regarded as provinces of the same empire'.[40] The draft had left the remark pending. Yet the insistence upon a colony as a province in the finished draft highlights not only Quesnay's interest in this question but also that he fully understood that words are normative acts and carry social and economic baggage. Were he and Mirabeau to convince their readers of the need to break with the Exclusif and truly transform the hierarchical nature of colonial-metropolitan relations, they would have to help their readers think of colonies in terms that were not immediately associated with the dominant view that colonies were farms of the metropole.

Mirabeau and Quesnay's re-conceptualisation of colonies in the Americas referenced the French state but did not redefine it. In their critique of French practices in the Indian Ocean, however, it was how people misinterpreted the very essence of the state rather than French

---

[38] Mirabeau, *Philosophie rurale*, iii, 204–5. On provinces, see Roland Mousnier, *Les Institutions de la France sous la monarchie absolue* (Paris: Presses Universitaires de France, 1974), i, 470–71.

[39] Hobbes, *Leviathan*, 302.

[40] Draft of *Philosophie rurale*, Chapter 11, Archives Nationales, Paris, Mirabeau Papers (hereinafter ANPMP), M799, bobine 3.

holdings in the Indian Ocean that drove their analysis. In trading with the East, they charged, France had followed the example of smaller nations whose associations of merchants with an exclusive privilege had successfully created small trade stations far away to purchase exotic goods of great interest to Europeans. Yet whereas an association such as the Vereenigde Oostindische Compagnie made sense for the Dutch because 'the profit of these merchants was the profit of the state since the state was only an association of merchants', the same could not be said about France. France was an agricultural kingdom and its merchants were only a part of the state. To give them a monopoly on trade with the East Indies, such as the one enjoyed by the Compagnie des Indes, was to create a state within the state whose monopoly went directly against the broader interests of the French nation.[41]

In line with their critique of trade privileges and prohibition, Mirabeau and Quesnay's attack on the Compagnie des Indes reflects their proximity to contemporary concerns within the government where the company was under growing scrutiny. Gournay had criticised the company already in 1755 finding its imports of Indian textiles a threat to the domestic textile industry. The Seven Years War fostered further objections. The company accumulated a considerable debt in these years to pay for its military operations in Africa and in the Indian Ocean. To relaunch its commerce, it therefore required a new injection of money. The question was whether efforts to bolster the company was worthwhile? Supporters of the company believed it was, if the company were released from the burden of paying for the maintenance of forts and if the Crown stopped meddling in its affairs. The Crown, however, was having doubts. It appointed the company's directors and handled its finances as 'an appendix to the office of the Controller General of Finance' and its ships as a branch of the Ministry of the Marine, but it also guaranteed a big part of the company's revenues, furnishing the company 9 million livres in rents annually from the royal monopoly on tobacco sales that the General Farm administered. Was the continuation of a chartered company still the best financial solution in the East Indies? Choiseul had already transferred the administration of the company's holdings in Africa to the Crown and opened trade to all French merchants. Yet its continued role remained unclear. Not until 1769, on the heels of years of fierce debate, did the Crown decide to wholly suspend the activities of the company.[42]

---

[41] Mirabeau, *Philosophie rurale*, iii, 214–15.

[42] On the company being a branch of the Ministry of the Marine, see Herbert Luthy, 'Necker et la Compagnie des Indes', *Annales. Economies, sociétés, civilisations*, 15, 5 (1960), 852–81, 861. On debates leading to its suspension, see Kenneth Margerison, 'The Shareholders' Revolt at the Compagnie des Indes: Commerce and Political Culture in Old Regime France', *French History*, 22 (2006), 27.

While writing *Philosophie rurale*, Mirabeau and Quesnay were unquestionably alert to the deliberations unfolding between the shareholders, the Contrôle Général, and the General Farm regarding the Compagnie des Indes. With their eyes fixed on how to generate the greatest fiscal revenues to the benefit of the greater good, they firmly believed that it was time to abandon monopoly trade both in the East and West Indies as well as the many local privileges that undergirded France's domestic economy. To overcome fiscal crisis, and to best benefit from an increasingly interconnected global economy, France should acknowledge its natural strength – agricultural production – and embrace free and unfettered trade as a key condition for its prosperity. If it did, Mirabeau and Quesnay proclaimed, all of the New World would become importers of French agricultural produce because 'no Nation will have as abundant a harvest and at a constant and reasonable price and of the best quality'.[43] France and its colonies, in other words, could become the farmhouse of the world. Whether grain from France or sugar and coffee from the colonies, cash crops should constitute the commodities with which France approached the world market. Thus, Mirabeau and Quesnay's understanding of France as an agricultural monarchy and their espousal of free trade hinged on the same idea of competitive strength on the international market that would later inspire Britain's free trade imperialism and its efforts to cast itself as the workshop of the world.[44]

With their attack on the Exclusif and re-conceptualisation of colonies, Mirabeau and Quesnay's proposals laid the groundwork for a complete reinvention of the French colonial empire. Their ideas, therefore, should not be confused with an anti-colonial stance. Some scholars contend that the co-founders of Physiocracy were against colonies, an interpretation that hinges on a passage in *Philosophie rurale* stating that a country that possessed much fallow land should not think about founding colonies in faraway lands.[45] As the draft of the publication reveals, it was Quesnay who had inserted this remark. It harked back to his complaint in 'fermiers' and 'grains' that one-quarter of French land was still left uncultivated.[46]

---

[43] Mirabeau, *Philosophie rurale*, iii, 212.

[44] On British free trade imperialism, see Bernard Semmel, *The Rise of Free Trade Imperialism – Classical Political Economy the Empire of Free Trade and Imperialism 1750–1850* (Cambridge: Cambridge University Press, 1970).

[45] Those who group the Physiocrats under anticolonialism include Liauzu, *Histoire de l'anticolonialism*, 43, and Marcel Merle, 'L'Anticolonialisme', 815–61; and Das, *Myths and Realities*, 28–9.

[46] There may be a flaw in Quesnay's reasoning here. It had long been recognised that colonies, as markets for French agricultural produce, served to bring more and more French land into cultivation. Quesnay himself seemed to have noticed this in 1759. In the *Questions intéressantes*, he had specified that commerce with the colonies only merited attention as long as it contributed to the

Quesnay could therefore appear to be opposed to French colonisation. A closer look at the draft of *Philosophie rurale* goes against such a view. In the margins, Quesnay had jotted down that newly created colonies should be exempt from taxation until they had developed a sustainable agriculture; he had mentioned that companies with monopolies were 'enemies of the state' and continuously pointed to the importance of free trade. All these arguments remained in the published version of *Philosophie rurale*. They reflect a strong critique of the prohibitive laws and monopolistic structures of the Ancien Régime colonial empire, but not of colonial empire as such.[47]

Quesnay, in fact, was quite willing to speak in favour of colonial empire as long as it entailed its reform. In the mid-1760s, when the debate over whether to permanently liberalise the Exclusif was at its highest (a topic to which we shall return in the next chapter), he penned a rebuke of the status quo in the *Journal d'agriculture, du commerce et des finances*. Entitling it 'Remarks on the opinion of the author of the *Spirit of the Laws* concerning the colonies', he used Montesquieu's well-known defence of the Exclusif and his and Mirabeau's critique of it from *Philosophie rurale* as a means to combat its supporters. This was a clever tactic, since many of the port cities who defended the Exclusif used Montesquieu as 'their best authority'. Against these montesquieuan arguments, Quesnay responded with an emphatic restatement of the ideas presented in *Philosophie rurale* although this time he cast France, not as an agricultural monarchy as he had done earlier, but as an 'agricultural empire' (*empire agricole*).[48]

An Abstract Critique of Slavery

As Mirabeau had done in his pre-physiocratic days in *L'Ami des hommes*, so he and Quesnay set out to develop *l'art des colonies* in *Philosophie rurale*. Yet there was one noticeable omission: *Philosophie rurale* did not include more than an abstract critique of slavery and it was not to be found in the section on colonies. Instead, it appeared in a passage on the three classes into which Quesnay divided society: the propertied, the productive, and the sterile classes (the propertied classes were the landowners, the productive classes were those engaged in agricultural production, and the sterile classes were people such as artisans and merchants – those not directly

---

augmentation of cultivation and the 'débit des denrées du cru'. Quesnay, 'fermiers', *Œuvres économique et philosophique*, 171 and 'Questions Interessantes', ibid., 294n.

[47] On his comment on the draft, see draft of *Philosophie rurale*, Chapter 11. ANPMP, M799, bobine 3.

[48] Quesnay, 'Remarques sur l'opinion de l'auteur de *l'Esprit des lois* concernant les colonies', in *Œuvres économique et philosophique*, ed. Auguste Oncken (Paris: Jules Peelman & Cie, 1888), 428. On Montesquieu as an authority, see Cheney, *Revolutionary Commerce*, 179.

involved in agricultural production). In their discussion of the productive classes, Mirabeau and Quesnay stated that 'slavery is a perversion of the natural order'. They explained that man worked better when he obtained the fruits of his labour and when he 'worked for others while believing he was working for himself'. Slavery could therefore 'only subsist in a grand kingdom to the disadvantage of the nation and at the expense of the state'. Referencing older types of slavery in Europe, *Philosophie rurale* fell silent when it came to African slavery in the French colonies which fuelled the most profitable sector of French foreign commerce.[49]

Why this retreat from historical references and emotional pleas? Experts of Physiocracy ascribe the doctrine's broadly theoretical tone to ontological causes. According to Georges Weulersse, Quesnay did not think that moral sentiments could help change man; only the physical laws intended for society could fix the moral order. This interpretation is echoed by Elizabeth Fox-Genovese, who argues that in collaborating, Mirabeau would have to 'convince Quesnay of the importance of the social dimension of any political economy, whereas Quesnay would have to convince Mirabeau that his specific social commitment could only be realized by the sacrifice of its historical form and the translation of its moral force into a new economic language'. One could argue, therefore, that Quesnay found no room for Mirabeau's impassioned outcries against African slave labour in the colonies, striving as he did to keep his political economy as scientific as possible.[50]

Such an answer is nonetheless unsatisfactory since colonial slavery did make an appearance in *Philosophie rurale*, though in passing. It came up in a critique of the inability of French merchants to supply planters with enough food to feed the slave population and served to censure the Exclusif. The statement offered implicit sympathy with the plight of plantation owners, the masters of African slaves who, according to *Philosophie rurale*'s abstract critique of slavery, daily perverted the natural order. It is likely that such sympathy was rooted in Quesnay's general partiality to big landowners. Coming from the Paris basin, he knew that big landowners produced the agricultural surplus and therefore held the key to domestic growth. In contrast to small landowners, whose meagre means permitted either no or only small profits, big landowners had the

---

[49] Mirabeau, *Philosophie rurale*, i, 116–17.

[50] Weulersse, *Le mouvement physiocratique*, ii, 107–8. Fox-Genovese, *The Origins of Physiocracy*, 166. Quesnay would edit many of the key physiocratic texts produced in the doctor's writing workshop. See Christine Théré and Loïc Charles, 'The Writing Workshop of François Quesnay and the Making of Physiocracy', *History of Political Economy*, 40 (2008), 1–42; Francois Quesnay, *Oeuvres Économique Complètes*, xxii.

capital to employ cattle, horses, and fertiliser. They could therefore end up with a substantial net product. Since the King's finances should be based on a single land tax on the net product of agricultural production according to Quesnay, his view was that big landowners should enjoy the best political, economic, and social conditions within which to thrive.[51] In the colonies, it was the plantation owners who were in charge of *la grande culture*. In Physiocracy, their fiscal role was therefore identical to large landowners in France, although their capital was invested in human 'cattle' and sugar mills. It is not unthinkable that Quesnay was willing to suspend any discussion of how the use of African slaves went against the natural order, believing that France would gain a generous fiscal contribution from the plantation complex if the government decided to adopt his tax reforms.

The first stab at formulating a physiocratic colonial doctrine was therefore a watered-down attack on the plantation complex compared to Mirabeau's diatribe in *L'Ami des hommes*. *Philosophie rurale* carried no discussion of the use of African slave labour, nor did Mirabeau's predictions of the inevitable independence of the New World feature in the work. The absence of a number of Mirabeau's initial attacks on the French colonial system, however, did not mean that only Mirabeau had been affected by his and Quesnay's collaboration. Quesnay had endorsed Mirabeau's critique of the Exclusif and his advocacy of free trade in the colonies. He had incorporated the colonies into his political economic doctrine and introduced an original recasting of them as overseas provinces. As other political economists started collaborating with Quesnay and Mirabeau, the physiocratic response to colonial empire would be further enriched, in part through a re-engagement with Mirabeau's earliest ideas in *L'Ami des hommes*.

Foes and Followers

Quesnay and Mirabeau's political economic doctrine would gain a following both in France and throughout Europe. Le Mercier de la Rivière developed an interest in their ideas already during the Seven Years War and his colonial correspondence from Martinique carries traits of both Mirabeau and Quesnay's earliest ideas. It is unclear, though, to what degree he embraced them in full prior to his final return from Martinique in

---

[51] Mirabeau, *Philosophie rurale*, iii, 209. On big landowners in physiocratic thought see Weulersse, *Le mouvement physiocratique*, i, 268, 323–24, and 333.

1764.[52] The journalist, Du Pont de Nemours, who was substantially younger than the co-founders, embraced the doctrine in 1763. Abbé Pierre-Joseph-André Roubaud and Abbé Nicolas Baudeau joined in the second half of the 1760s. When Baudeau adopted the doctrine in June 1766, his journal, *Ephémérides du citoyen*, became the group's official organ from January 1767. Abbé Roubaud joined in 1768. His connections to a range of journals proved equally beneficial, particularly after the *Ephémérides* was suppressed in 1772. These four people pertained to the inner circle of the group. Others became students attending weekly meetings at Mirabeau's Paris abode. Their 'school' attracted prominent pupils such as Maréchal de Broglie, le duc de la Rochefoucauld, and La Duchesse de la Rochefoucauld d'Anville. Turgot, Diderot, Morellet, and Raynal were sympathetic critics. Leaders of Europe took an interest as well. Le Mercier was in Russia in 1767–8 at the invitation of Catherine the Great and Baudeau was invited to bring Physiocracy to Poland in 1768. A letter between the Mirabeau brothers notes that the King of Denmark was interested in Physiocracy and wished to meet Mirabeau during his stay in Paris in 1768.[53]

With their doctrinaire emphasis on the primacy of agriculture over commerce and industry, Mirabeau and Quesnay's views did not sit well with all contemporaries. Initially, it was their identification with the liberalisation of the grain trade after the Seven Years War that stoked the fire of critics. In May 1763 and July 1764, Controller General Henri Léonard Jean-Baptiste Bertin and his successor Clément Charles François de Laverdy liberalised the grain trade, a policy some believed was guided by Quesnay's political economy. When bread riots broke out throughout France in the aftermath of reform, such association was unfortunate. One historian has noted that 'royal legislation of 1763–4 contributed more to *économiste* notoriety than all their apothegms, paradigms and preciosities'.[54] Yet apothegms and paradigms did not help matters either. The Physiocrats claimed that their doctrine was rooted in the physical laws

---

[52] For a full discussion, see Bernard Herencia, 'Enquête sur l'entrée de Lemercier de la Rivière dans le cercle de Quesnay', *Cahiers d'économie politique*, 64 (2013), 25–45. See also Florence Gauthier, 'Le Mercier de la Rivière et les colonies d'Amérique', *Revue française d'histoire des idées politique*, 20, 2 (2004), 37–59.

[53] On elite interest in Physicoracy, see Weulersse, *Le Mouvement Physiocratique*, i, 128–42. On the King of Denmark, see M.M. to C.M., Paris, 22 November 1768, FM, vol. 26. On its European influences see Bernard Delmas, Thierry Demals, and Philippe Steiner (eds.), *La diffusion internationale de la Physiocratie* (Grenoble: Presses Universitaires de Grenoble, 1995).

[54] Steven L. Kaplan, *Bread, Politics and Political Economy in the Reign of Louis XV*, 2 vols. (The Hague: Martinus Nijhoff, 1976), i, 117, and on these bread riots, 190.

of nature and that an application of their ideas would align society with 'the natural and essential order'. A top down implementation of them, in turn, would constitute 'legal despotism'. With such jargon, detractors started portraying the Physiocrats as a 'secte' and François Quesnay as a leader whose acolytes followed him blindly. Friedrich Melchior, Baron von Grimm was particularly fond of ridiculing the Physiocrats in his famous *Correspondance littéraire, philosophique et critique*. The merchant community, and especially those of maritime commerce, did not passively accept the punches thrown at them either. The *Gazette du commerce de l'agriculture et des finances* criticised Mirabeau and Quesnay in 1766 for being builders of systems, for creating distinctions between 'productive and sterile classes', for placing agriculture above commerce, for claiming that France was 'a purely agricultural nation', and for having no real interest in or understanding of the role of commerce.[55]

The sharpest critique, however, came from Forbonnais in his *Principes et observations économiques* published in 1767.[56] In it, Forbonnais primarily focused his criticisms on Quesnay's economic model, the *Tableau Oeconomique*, and the way in which the Physiocrats claimed to have found the key to fiscal reform. Yet he also took issue with Mirabeau and Quesnay's colonial ideas. To counter their attack on the Exclusif he underlined that accepting foreign trade in the colonies was to freely give up a portion of the metropole's harvest 'and an infallible means to goad the colonies toward independence'. But he clearly worried about the implications of Quesnay and Mirabeau's re-conceptualisation of a 'colony'. In a long footnote, he added that the desire of 'honest and excellent citizens' to see the colonies prosper that had spread on the heels of the Seven Years War had given rise to the erroneous idea that 'a colony should be perceived as another province' of the monarchy. This was not how modern colonies should be viewed. Their sole object was to 'augment the revenues of the countries who had established them [*païs qui les fonde*]' by importing metropolitan goods in exchange for cash crops, the surplus of which the metropole could re-export to foreigners with no colonies of their own.

---

[55] The attack came together with an excerpt from a memorandum written by M. de Montaudouin, read at the Academy of La Rochelle. See 13 September 1766, *Gazette du commerce de l'agriculture et des finances* (Paris, 1766), 642. On critics, see also Gérard Klotz, Philippe Minard, and Arnaud Orain (eds.), *Les voies de la richesses?*

[56] Forbonnais had initially stayed silent, possibly due to his connections to Jean-Antoine de Mirabeau, whose help he had sought while assisting Étienne de Silhouette in the Contrôle Géneral clear up a scandal surrounding Jean-Antoine's nemesis, the then *premier commis*, Arnauld de la Porte. See Forbonnais to CM, Versailles, 22 May 1759, FM, vol. 25, 41.

A firmer restatement of the status quo, and a clearer rejection of Quesnay and Mirabeau's bid for colonial reform, could not be made.[57]

Despite such attack on Quesnay and Mirabeau' proposals for domestic and colonial reform, the injection of fresh blood helped broaden the platform from which they launched their ideas. It also enlarged the contours of the physiocratic colonial doctrine. As Baudeau, Du Pont, and Roubaud added their own views to Physiocracy, they moved the discussion of colonies and slavery outside of the confines of *Philosophie rurale*. In so doing, they not only returned to some of Mirabeau's ideas in *L'Ami des hommes*, they also embraced historical specificity, exploring the growing literature on natural history to educate themselves about lands, plants, and peoples beyond the Americas. In the process, they transformed Physiocracy into an arm for a new form of French imperialism compatible with their celebration of free trade and free labour.

A Renewed Critique of Slavery

In the years after the publication of *Philosophie rurale*, the only physiocratic attack on slavery appeared in Quesnay's 'droit naturel', published in the *Journal d'agriculture, commerce et finance* in September 1765. In it, Quesnay stressed in characteristically abstract terms that man had a natural right to the fruits of his labour.[58] Mirabeau, in contrast, was conspicuously silent on the topic. Le Mercier de la Rivière, who had witnessed slavery in the colonies during his intendancy, also had nothing to add in his physiocratic publications upon his return to the metropole. Had he spoken up, he might also have exposed himself to unnecessary charges of hypocrisy given his advice to Choiseul to augment the slave population of Martinique with an additional 80,000 slaves. Only his vague statement to Choiseul in his 1762 memorandum, in which he mentioned that he preferred that whites should cultivate the land of Martinique but that this was unfortunately 'impossible for several reasons that are too long to list in detail', registers a moral, if not economic, opposition to the institution.[59] In *L'ordre naturel et essentiel des sociétés politiques*, Le Mercier's celebrated masterpiece from 1767 which sent the term 'legal despotism' into circulation, neither slavery nor colonies received a single reference from the former intendant. Thus, after the Seven Years War, the three political economists who were

---

[57] François Véron Duverger de Forbonnais, *Principes et observations oeconomiques,* 2 vols. (Amsterdam, 1767), i, 68–9.
[58] Quesnay, 'Le droit naturel', 371.
[59] Le Mercier de la Rivière, 'Mémoire sur la Martinique' (1762), ANOM C[8A] 64.

celebrated as the most important Physiocrats by their peers – Quesnay, Mirabeau, and Le Mercier de la Rivière – all circumvented what was beginning to be a prominent topic of debate among educated elites throughout the Atlantic World.

Baudeau, in contrast, was an outspoken advocate of slave-free colonial empire even before he joined the Physiocrats. In 1763, he suggested settling colonies by means of a large immigration of Africans and Asians who would work under a form of indenture for a fixed period and then be turned into French citizens. More explicitly, he encouraged French colonial agents to '[b]uy men, women, and children of both sexes, wherever they are up for sale, but refrain from enslaving them. Instead, after having civilized and disciplined them at the very centre of your power, transform them into citizens of your colonies, into cultivators, into artisans'.[60] Once he launched the *Ephémérides du citoyen*, Baudeau returned to this idea on 11 and 18 July 1766. Branding slavery a 'system so gruesome to humanity, so contrary to Christianity and to the mores of our Europe', he proposed joining Spain and Sicily in a 'pacte familial' to create a Compagnie Tripartite that would purchase slaves in Africa and Asia, liberate them, and transform them 'into free men and women, into industrious cultivators, into real citizens of Louisiana'. Such a project, he stressed, would be both honourable and profitable which he could prove by 'simple and sound calculation'. By imposing a perpetual annual fee of a fifth or a sixth of the produce grown by the freed slaves-turned-landowners, it would be possible to cover the cost of purchasing and then freeing a whole slave family.[61]

Baudeau's proposal to create a colonial company was inconsistent with the colonial ideas laid down by Mirabeau and Quesnay. Once he converted to Physiocracy, he therefore offered an upgraded attack on slavery that aligned with the political economy to which he now adhered. This intervention came in a series he ran from 29 September to 10 October 1766, entitled 'Explanation on the slavery of Negroes'. It opened with a letter Baudeau had received from an 'American' from the colonies who had been provoked by Baudeau's previous arguments against slavery. The American had found the proposal to transport Africans and Asians to Louisiana and employ them as cultivators and free citizens 'dangerous and quixotic'. Claiming that he was unable to reply to Baudeau's philosophic attacks on slavery, the American said that he would use the recent work of

---

[60] Nicolas Baudeau, *Idées d'un citoyen sur la puissance du roi et le commerce de la nation dans l'Orient* (Amsterdam [Paris]: François-Ambroise Didot, 1763), 25–6.
[61] *Ephémérides du citoyen*, 18 July 1766, 66–8. On the compagnie tripartite, see *Ephémérides du citoyen*, 11 July 1766, 34–9.

Rousselot de Surgy to argue his case, which offered 'the most complete refutation of your system'.[62]

To help his readers follow the controversy, Baudeau summarised Surgy's pro-slavery argument which had recently appeared in *Mélanges intéressants et curieux, ou Abrégé d'histoire naturelle, morale, civile et politique de l'Asie, l'Afrique, l'Amérique, et des terres polaires* (1763–5). Surgy had argued that Africans shipped to the colonies were already slaves or prisoners of war who, had they stayed in Africa, would have been massacred. The slave trade therefore saved the lives of those already doomed by transporting them to the colonies where they would lead happier lives than in Africa and still live in a climate similar to their own. If this argument did not suffice, Surgy further justified slavery by de-humanising Africans in coarse terms. He claimed that: 'all sense of honour & humanity is unknown to these barbarians: [they have] no ideas, no knowledge … If they had not had the gift of speech, they would only have had the form of man [. . .] they have no heart, & consequently they lack the seed of virtue. Brutality, cruelty, ingratitude, that is what forms their character'.[63]

Surgy, who had never been to Africa, declared in his *Mélanges* that he was drawing on English, French, and Danish writers such as Labat, Bosman, Snelgrave, Dapper, Adanson, and Romer. His reading of these sources was highly selective as contemporaries who had read them would know. Père Labat, who based his *Nouvelle relation de l'Afrique occidentale* on reports received from André Brüe, director general of the French holdings in Senegal between 1697 and 1702, noted both positive and negative encounters between Brüe and local populations in Senegambia. Highlighting the cultural difference among them, he depicted encounters where Brüe was received with 'all of the honour and cordiality that Negroes [*les Nègres*] [were] capable of', but also one where the locals were 'cruel against their enemies' and, when under the influence of alcohol, willing to 'sell their children' to European traders. Adanson's *Histoire Naturelle du Sénégal* (1757), in turn, offered a differentiated yet generally positive portrayal of African peoples. Of the men and women in Senegal, he commented on their beauty and 'gentle [*doux*], sociable, and obliging' manners.[64]

---

[62] *Ephémérides du citoyen*, 29 September 1766, 130.

[63] Ibid., 140–41. And Jacques-Philibert Rousselot de Surgy, *Mélanges intéressants et curieux, ou Abrégé d'histoire naturelle, morale, civile et politique de l'Asie, l'Afrique, l'Amérique, et des terres polaires, par M. R. D. S.*, 10 vols. (Paris: Lacombe, 1766), x, 164–7.

[64] Ibid., x, 76–8. For Brüe's portrayal, see Jean-Baptiste Labat, *Nouvelle relation de l'Afrique occidentale: contenant une description exacte du Sénégal et des païs situés entre le Cap-Blanc et la rivière de Serrelienne*, 5 vols. (Paris: G. Cavelier, 1728), ii, 275 and v, 169. On Adanson's descriptions, see

To counter Surgy's assessment of Africans, Baudeau did not try to point out such inconsistencies in the former's reading of his sources. Instead, Baudeau specified that he would simply follow the laws of nature which ruled over 'the laws of civil society & even *religious* maxims' (appropriating parts of the extended title of *Philosophie rurale*). As part of humanity, Baudeau began, the savage man enjoyed two rights. These were, 'the property of his own person ... which ensures the freedom to work ... and the property of the fruits of his labour, from which is born the freedom to own/enjoy'.[65] Therefore, the only thing that could stand as a reply to his refutation of slavery was Surgy's statement that 'the Blacks of Africa are not *men*'.[66] To disprove this view, Baudeau reminded the American that he was daily surrounded by proofs of the opposite. Thousands of mulattoes, children of a white man and a black woman, inhabited the Americas, and several slave owners freed their slaves who subsequently became good citizens. The Code Noir, moreover, policed slaves in the colonies, and legal codes were only drawn up for human beings, a view reminiscent of Rousseau's views as much as those of Quesnay and Mirabeau.

In response to Surgy's claim that Africans were without virtue, Baudeau countered by underlining that similar traits could be found within Europe as well. In his view, superstition and vice ruled among serfs all over the European countryside. It was the lack of liberty that maintained serfs and slaves in a state of savagery, not any innate traits.[67] But while serfs across Europe might be ignorant, superstitious, and without virtue, Baudeau saved his harshest critique for educated Europeans who, despite their instruction, supported slavery. As he said, if a man could declare himself in favour of slavery – whether in Europe or in the colonies – he 'has not yet left infancy or the state of brutes, regardless of his real age' and would need to 'enlighten himself, when he has not yet acquired the knowledge of the natural and essential order'.[68] In this elaborate rejoinder, which echoed not just Quesnay's economic rationale but also Rousseau's and Mirabeau's charges against European elites, Baudeau turned the notion of the savage black man and the civilised white man on its head. With his reference to 'the natural and essential order', he implied in addition that Physiocracy was itself a tool with which to civilise the white man.[69]

Michel Adanson, *Histoire Naturelle du Sénégal: Avec la Relation abrégée d'un Voyage fait en ce pays, pendant les années 1749, 50, 51, 52 & 53* (Paris: Claude-Jean-Baptiste Bauche, 1757), 22–3.

[65] *Ephémérides du citoyen*, 3 October 1766, 159.

[66] 'les Noirs de l'Afrique ne sont pas des *hommes*'. Ibid., 6 October 1766.   [67] Ibid., 171.

[68] Ibid.

[69] The ambiguities of a 'civilised Europe' are explored in Anthony Pagden, *European Encounters with the New World* (New Haven, CT: Yale University Press, 1993).

After Baudeau's elaborate critique, the Physiocrats would scale down their attack on the institution and only condemn it in reference to other people's publications rather than further their own critique of it. Du Pont de Nemours, who took over the editorship of the *Ephémérides du citoyen* in 1768 when Baudeau went to Poland, adopted this strategy on a number of occasions. For example, in 1768, when Du Pont reviewed Pierre Poivre's *Voyages d'un philosophe*, he chided the role of Europeans in perpetuating war in Africa. Yet there was no direct attack on slavery although Poivre's work had offered references to the superiority of free labour over slave labour and the ability of free labourers to produce twice the amount produced by slaves.[70] Similarly, in 1769, Du Pont published a letter by Benjamin Rush, furnished by Jacques Barbeu du Bourg (friend and French translator of Benjamin Franklin), in which Rush announced that the Quakers of Pennsylvania had agreed 'to liberate all of their Negro slaves'. Celebrating the abolitionist act of the Quakers, Du Pont predicted that the profit that these Quakers would draw from free active workers would soon inspire neighbouring states to abolish slavery on their own lands. Instead of moving to discuss the enslavement of Africans in the French colonies, Du Pont turned to deplore the daily toils of serfs who lived in a 'terrible misery' in large parts of Europe.[71] Shortly after, a similar lack of engagement occurred when Turgot suggested that Du Pont publish extracts from Saint-Lambert's *Saison*, *Ziméo*, and *Chinki* and from Turgot's own *Sur les richesses*. The following day Turgot sent Du Pont his *Sur les richesses* and an extract from *Ziméo* with a celebration of the Quakers who had liberated their slaves.[72] Still, Du Pont did not personally attack French plantation slavery but expressed a critique through references to other people's work.

Using other authors to attack slavery came to a head when Du Pont reviewed Turgot's own *Sur les richesses*, in which Turgot weighed the pros and cons of slavery. In his review, Du Pont altered the original text, including Turgot's argument that slavery could be profitable at times. Upset about the changes, Turgot charged Du Pont to admit officially to the alterations in the journal. Turgot regretted the tone of his letter a few days later, but reasserted his belief in the economic value of colonial

[70] *Ephémérides du citoyen*, vi, 1768, 166–215 and Pierre Poivre, *Œuvres complettes de P. Poivre*, ed. Du Pont de Nemours (Paris: Chez Fuchs, 1797), 157–9.
[71] *Ephémérides du citoyen*, vol ix, part iii, 1769, 172–5.
[72] Turgot to Du Pont, 1 December 1769, in Anne-Robert-Jacques Turgot, *Œuvres de Turgot*, ed. Gustave Schelle, 5 vols. (Paris: F. Alcan, 1913–23), iii, 72. Turgot to Du Pont, 2 December 1769, ibid., iii, 73. On the role of *Ziméo* in French anti-slavery see Miller, *The French Atlantic Triangle*, 103–4.

slavery: 'I still think that in our islands it is advantageous to have slaves, not for the colony itself, but for the owner who seeks to have goods of a great market value to make a quick profit by means of commerce'. Again, Du Pont did not see Turgot's assertion as an invitation to disprove him. A year later, in May 1771, Turgot therefore reproached Du Pont for his and other Physiocrats' failure to enter the debate on the value of slave labour and their propensity only to elaborate on the themes launched by Quesnay.[73] This time, Turgot's provocation worked. Five years after Baudeau's intervention, Du Pont finally used the journal to give his now famous calculation of the profitability of free labour over slave labour.

The assessment appeared in 1771 in volumes VI and VIII following a review of Saint-Lambert's *Ziméo*. Proclaiming that he would disprove the profitability of slavery, Du Pont based his calculations on the purchasing price of slaves, their expected lifespan, cost of their maintenance, and opportunity costs. Setting the price of a slave at 1200 livres tournois, he estimated that a slave lived ten years in the colonies on average. The direct cost of a slave annually was thus 120 livres tournois. However, as the capital invested in the slave would not generate a profit and would be lost upon the death of the slave, there was a further cost based on the missed profits of 10 per cent that such investment could have generated elsewhere. This increased the annual cost to 240 livres. But the slave would also need to be fed and dressed which added another 100 livres, elevating the annual cost of a slave to 340 livres. Moreover, a slave driver would have to be paid, further adding to annual costs and creating an annual loss from profits that could have been made on such outlay. Finally, the planter could expect expenses associated with the use of slave labour, such as the cost towards militias, the dangers and expenses associated with maroons, the cost of burnt down plantations, all of which elevated the final annual cost of a slave to 420 livres per year, or 28 sols per day. In Europe, Du Pont claimed, over 25 million poor lived on less than 30 livres per year and would happily go to the colonies to work for a daily wage of 28 sols.[74]

In making this argument, Du Pont explicitly rejected the claim often made by plantation owners that whites could not survive if subjected to hard labour in the damp colonial climate. As he said, such an argument was ridiculous since it was white Europeans – the *flibustiers* and the

---

[73] In his publication of Turgot's work, Schelle attached a long footnote to Turgot's original text in which he highlighted the changes Du Pont de Nemours had made. See *Œuvres de Turgot*, ii, 544, footnote a. Turgot to Du Pont, 2 February 1770, in ibid., iii, 374; Turgot to Du Pont, 6 February 1770, in ibid., iii, 375; Turgot to Du Pont, 7 May 1771, ibid., iii, 484.

[74] *Ephémérides du citoyen*, vi, 1771, 233–5.

boucaniers – who had founded the colonies in the first place. Exhibiting the same preference for European labourers over African labourers as Mirabeau in *L'Ami des hommes*, he noted that 'the European white man', when exposed to physical labour, is 'one of the most lively and robust species the heavens have place on earth' – more so than the 'Negro, the Asian Indian, and the natives of America'.[75]

Despite considerable errors in Du Pont's calculations (his exaggerated return on investments or miscalculation of the cost of living among European poor for instance), scholars of French anti-slavery have celebrated Baudeau and Du Pont's interventions as key turning points in the history of French abolitionism. Yves Benot has argued that during the years 1766–7, the Physiocrats lifted arguments against slavery from the realm of religion or morality into the world of economics. Caroline Oudin-Bastide and Philippe Steiner have made the same observation, though they clarify that Du Pont did not disqualify moral arguments when turning to calculations. Madeleine Dobie goes further, maintaining that whereas the question of slavery was generally avoided prior to the late 1760s, a discourse thereafter started to evolve, associated principally with the rise of liberal economic theory.[76]

The Physiocrats' role in boosting the sparse though budding French Enlightenment critique of slavery should of course be recognised. Yet it is necessary to acknowledge that they were far less forceful in their attacks on slavery than they were in their relentless efforts to liberalise commerce. Quesnay, Mirabeau, and Le Mercier de la Rivière remained curiously quiet on the question of slavery in these years. Moreover, while he scolded Du Pont for not addressing the topic, Turgot did not manage to initiate policies against slavery during his tenure as Minister of the Marine and Controller General of Finance between 1774 and 1776. Although a rumour circulated in 1776 that Turgot was about to abolish the slave trade, Tarrade notes that it was likely a rumour set in circulation by enemies of Turgot to discredit him, rather than a reflection of reality. His colleague in the Ministry of the Marine, Antoine de Sartine, diligently crushed the charges against Turgot as unfounded gossip.[77] Unmistakably, the plantation complex held a tenacious grip on the minds of French policy makers and

---

[75] Ibid., 237. For Du Pont de Nemours's economic attack on slavery in the context of eighteenth- and ninteenth-century economic debates about slave labour, see Oudin-Bastide and Steiner, *Calcul et Morale*.

[76] Benot, *La Révolution française*, 31; Oudin-Bastide and Steiner, *Calcul et Morale*, 38; Dobie, *Trading Places*, 200.

[77] Tarrade, *Le commerce colonial*, i, 435.

reformers in the eighteenth century. Even those who opposed slavery struggled to wholly commit to its abrogation as long as no alternative option to colonial empire in the Americas seemed credible.

A New Approach to Africa

Could a credible solution be found? This was a question that the Abbé Roubaud, a French journalist turned political economist, began to explore in the late 1750s. Born in 1730 in Avignon, Roubaud moved to Paris at a young age and started writing for the *Journal de commerce* in 1759. Later, he became the editor of a range of journals, including the *Gazette du commerce*, the *Journal de l'agriculture, du commerce et des finances*, and the *Gazette d'agriculture, commerce, arts et finances*, while also writing for the *Ephémérides du citoyen* and the *Nouvelles ephémérides économique*.[78] As editor, Roubaud digested a voluminous European literature on themes ranging from slavery and colonisation to commerce, taxation, population growth, travel, and law and accumulated an extensive knowledge on such matters. Going back over his journalist career, one discovers that Roubaud – like Baudeau – was already committed to colonial reform years before he joined the Physiocrats.

The *Journal de commerce* was a review journal based in Brussels with an audience in Amsterdam, Paris, Liège, and other major cities in France and the Low Countries. During his time with the journal, Roubaud discussed the African slave trade on several occasions. In May 1759, he penned an important review that allowed him to elaborate for the first time what would become a sustained campaign to promote slave-free colonisation in Africa to replace the French plantation complex in the Americas. This germinal piece was predicated on an appraisal of Malachy Postlethwayt's *Importance of the African Expedition Considered* (1758) and an anonymous English text translated as *Histoire du commerce des anglois*. As discussed in the previous chapter, Postlethwayt's view was that the capture of France's Senegalese possessions would strike a lethal blow to French commerce. While Roubaud did not applaud Postlethwayt's pro-position, he appreciated how Postlethwayt had exposed the fragility of French colonialism in the Americas and the ease with which the French

---

[78] See the entry 'Roubaud (Pierre-Joseph-André)', in *Nouvelle biographie générale depuis les temps les plus reculés jusqu'à 1850–60*, 46 vols., ed. M. le Dr Hoefer (Copenhagen: Rosenkilde & Bagger, 1968), and the entry 'Roubaud (Pierre-Joseph-André)', in *Biographie universelle ancienne et moderne*, new edn., 45 vols., ed. J. Fr. Michaud (Bad Feilnback: Schmidt Periodicals, 1998), xxxvi.

colonial enterprise could be destroyed by blocking access to the African slave trade.[79]

In contrast to Postlethwayt's publication, the author of *Histoire du commerce des anglois* advocated what Roubaud termed a peaceful, legitimate African project. This author's aim was to investigate whether there were more lucrative ways to benefit commercially from Africa than the way England had benefitted thus far (i.e. slave trading). The author observed that Africa was a populous and fertile country where all manner of desirable and exotic commodities could be cultivated. If industry and the arts were introduced among its inhabitants, the greater part of Britain's manufactured goods could be exported to Africa more advantageously and in greater quantity than to any other region.[80] The compelling aspect of this idea, to Roubaud, was its attempt to unite philanthropy and economic rationality. Midway into the review, he therefore paused to reflect on the feasibility of such a proposal if applied by France. He reminded his readers that the English proposal had a French equivalent in the marquis de Mirabeau's *L'Ami des hommes*, recently reviewed in the same journal. Quoting from Mirabeau's work, Roubaud noted:

> It is certain that if Africa had on its own coasts, as the Friend of Mankind has said, numerous flourishing towns with settlers and industry, on the one hand its production would increase a hundredfold to the benefit of humanity; on the other hand, its needs will multiply proportionately and the most industrious nations in commerce will profit from it.[81]

After citing *L'Ami des hommes*, Roubaud referred to André Brüe, who in 1701 had suggested founding a colony on the island of Bolama (Boulam) that formed part of the Bissagot Islands. Brüe had noted that 'nothing is easier than to establish sugar production [*sucreries*] in this country' where 'slaves, so expensive in America, can be purchased very cheaply'. Leaving out Brüe's reference to slave labour, Roubaud added that it would be possible to cultivate sugar, indigo, and cotton on this island in exchange for European industrial commodities. The most arresting feature of the

---

[79] *Journal de commerce*, May 1759, 63–99. On this journal and its founder, see Hervé Hasquin, 'Jacques Accarias de Serionne économiste et publiciste français au service des Pays-Bas autrichiens', *Études sur le XVIIIe siècle*, 1 (1974), 159–70.

[80] *Journal de commerce*, May 1759, 75, and 90. William A. Pettigrew has shown that Postlethwayt started publishing anti-slavery views and proposals to civilise Africa in 1759, so the anonymous publication may in fact have been by Postlethwayt as well. See William A. Pettigrew, *Freedom's Debt: The Royal African Company and the Politics of the Atlantic Slave Trade, 1672–1752* (Chapel Hill: University of North Carolina Press, 2013), 206–7.

[81] *Journal de commerce*, May 1759, 90–91. The quote was taken from Mirabeau, *L'Ami des hommes*, iii, 9–10. The *Journal de commerce* had reviewed Mirabeau's book in January, February, and March 1759.

review, therefore, was Roubaud's effort to link the development of Africa to the abrogation of the transatlantic slave trade:

> Will it not be more humane to introduce Christian Religion, commerce, and the Arts to the inhabitants of Africa & provide them with a taste for commodities & the pleasures of life, than to buy them to turn them into slaves & leave uncultivated such a beautiful region only to continue a commerce so contrary to all Christian doctrines & to common notions of conscience?[82]

As Philip Curtin and Christopher Leslie Brown have shown, these ideas immediately generated a response in Britain and inspired future abolitionists like Henry Smeathman, Granville Sharp, and William Wilberforce in their preparations for a slave-free colony in Sierra Leone.[83] In the *Journal de commerce*, Roubaud added a French flavour, merging them with Mirabeau's moral economics and Brüe's colonial recommendations.

Once Roubaud joined the Physiocrats, he, Du Pont, and Baudeau grafted Roubaud's African colonial programme onto the physiocratic doctrine. It appeared in its most elaborate form in Baudeau's *Histoire générale de l'Asie, de l'Afrique et de l'Amérique*, a multi-volume history produced over a five-year period and written in accordance with physiocratic political economy. Although left in the shadow of Raynal's *Histoire des deux Indes*, published slightly later, Roubaud's work is nonetheless far more innovative and consistent in its overall message.[84] His discussion on the relocation of the plantation system in the Americas to Africa featured in volumes X, XI, and XII on Africa, published in 1771, and volumes XIII, XIV, and XV on the Americas, published in 1775. In volumes X and XI, he criticised Africans for selling their population to European traders and admonished Europeans for perpetuating the state of barbarism in Africa. In volume XII, he echoed Baudeau's earlier intervention against the 'American' and stressed that the black skin of an African did not make him any less of a man than had his skin been white (to Roubaud it was the heat that had made the skin of Africans dark). He also employed Rousseau and Quesnay's abstract critique of slavery, stressing that man had a natural right to his own person and to the fruits of his labour.

---

[82] *Journal de commerce*, May 1759, 93–4, and 97–8. Brüe is cited in Labat, *Nouvelle relation de l'Afrique occidentale*, v, 153.

[83] Philip D. Curtin, *The Image of Africa – British Ideas and Action, 1780–1850* (London: Macmillan, 1965), 70 and 96–8. Christopher Leslie Brown, *Moral Capital – Foundations of British Abolitionism* (Chapel Hill: University of North Carolina Press, 2006), Chapter 5.

[84] Roubaud's work was advertised in the *Gazette d'agriculture, commerce, arts et finances*, 11 August 1770, 591.

In volume XII Roubaud presented his elaborate programme to develop Africa. Echoing his 1759 review, he informed his readers that 'you could find in Africa alone with the greatest advantage ... all that which you obtain from Africa and America together, while benefitting all as well as yourself'.[85] This time, he no longer drew merely on the writings of Bruë. Roubaud announced that the recent publications by Michel Adanson, the *Histoire naturelle du Sénégal* (1757), and the *Nouvelle histoire de l'Afrique française* (1767) by Abbé Demanet (to whose colonial schemes we shall return in Chapter 4), were his key reference points.[86] Based on the broadly positive anthropological representations of Africans in Adanson and Demanet's work, Roubaud noted that Africans were dexterous and had lively, incisive minds. Most of their vices were consequences of ignorance, superstition, and misery, with only the sin of excessive lust (*luxure*) to obstruct development.

Dropping the names of connoisseurs of Africa to collect ammunition for or against slavery and the slave trade was part of a growing trend among abolitionists and pro-slavers. Rousselot de Surgy used Labat and Adanson's publications to support the slave trade, as we have seen. The French-born Anthony Benezet, who spearheaded early abolition across the Atlantic and later inspired the *Société des amis des noirs*, dipped into Brüe and Adanson's writings in the same period to demonstrate the humanity of African populations.[87] To Roubaud, moreover, Adanson and Demanet's writings did not only speak to Africans' humanity but further revealed expansionist opportunities in the region. In his view, these texts demonstrated that Africans were easy to educate if approached with pedagogical tact and that African lands were immensely fertile. Europeans should simply go to Africa, settle and embark on agricultural development, set a good example, start trading with Africans, teach them how to exploit their land, and win their confidence. Capitalising on Africa's natural assets, he underscored the continent's proximity to Europe, which would reduce the costs of long-distance trade across the Atlantic. As he said, 'Africa can entirely and abundantly replace America in our commerce'.[88]

---

[85] M.L.A.R. [Abbé Roubaud], *Histoire générale de l'Asie, de l'Afrique et de l'Amerique*, 15 vols. (Paris: Desventes de la Doué, 1770–75), x, 417–20; xi, 302–3; ibid., xii, 198, and 206–7.

[86] As they were to many writers in the 1760s. Duchet, *Anthropologie et histoire*, 48–9. On knowledge of Africa, see also Catherine Gallouët, David Diop, Michèle Bocquillon, and Gérard Lahouati (eds.), *L'Afrique du siècles des Lumières: savoirs et représentations* (Oxford: SVEC, 2009).

[87] On Benezet's use of Brüe and Adanson and his later impact on French abolitionism, see Maurice Jackson, *Let This Voice Be Heard: Anthony Benezet, Father of Atlantic Abolition* (Philadelphia: University of Pennsylvania Press, 2009), Chapters 4 and 7.

[88] Roubaud, *Histoire générale*, xii, 208–9 and 215–16.

The need to find a substitute for France's colonial project in the Americas was further heightened to readers of Roubaud's multi-volume work once he published the volumes on the Americas in 1775. Like Mirabeau and Quesnay, he argued that commerce in its current form would continuously cause wars despite momentary declarations of peace since trade prohibitions fostered hostilities. Britain may have captured Canada, he stated, but had not been able to enjoy its victory. Instead, it was being crushed under the weight of debt accrued to defeat its enemy and now stood to lose what it had struggled so hard to conquer. Echoing the Mirabeau brothers (and increasingly also many other observers throughout the Atlantic World), Roubaud noted that the New World was on the brink of independence. Despite zealous efforts to prevent the colonies from producing commodities other than sugar, coffee, or mining gold and diamonds, the thirteen colonies had managed to produce 'grain and other necessary and useful products' and thereby steadily built a path to freedom. Depicting America as a near-physiocratic paradise with fertile lands and a happy expanding population, he charged that the thirteen colonies 'will become independent whenever they want to be ... And when they achieve independence, all the rest of America will follow because it is in their interest to do so; they will be able to achieve [independence] with North America's help'.[89] Thus, it was not only the British whose days in the Americas were numbered; other European colonial empires were equally vulnerable.

Roubaud's suggestion to replace an American-based empire on a trajectory to independence with what he believed to be an economically sound and humanitarian form of colonisation in Africa instantly became a staple among the Physiocrats. Du Pont recycled the idea in the *Ephémérides* in 1771 alongside his calculations on slave labour versus free labour. In pedantic fashion, he stressed that 'it suffices only to create a few peaceful settlements on the coast of Africa and send artisans and builders of mills and boilers there and then say to the negroes; *friends, you see that cane, cut it, pass it between the two rolls that we offer you, make the juice boil in the boiler like this, and we shall pay you well for the syrup that results from it*'. Similarly, the Abbé Baudeau wrote in his physiocratic manifesto, *Première introduction à la philosophie économique* (1771) that rather than having goaded Africans to sell their population, European merchants should have asked them to cultivate sugar. The latter could then purchase such cash crops in exchange for brandy, iron, and other European merchandise. Baudeau returned to this suggestion in 1783 in his three-volume entry on

[89] Ibid., xiii, 344–5, and 348–9. Roubaud's thoughts on the future of North America has been analysed by Cheney, *Revolutionary Commerce*, 161–2.

'commerce' for the *Encyclopédie méthodique*, in both the 'Discours préliminaire' and in the article 'Nègres'.[90]

With this blend of economic and humanitarian proclamations, the Physiocrats' colonial doctrine was pregnant with imperialist proclamations that would be far more common in the nineteenth century. In part, they advocated an approach to West Africa that would resemble the period of 'legitimate commerce' after the abolition of the slave trade. Their ideas also seemed to be precursors of later arguments in support of 'informal empire' supported by French liberals in the first half of the nineteenth century. Particularly within Roubaud's writings, we also discern basic features of what France would refer to as its *mission civilisatrice* in Africa in the nineteenth and twentieth centuries. Roubaud insisted that he had no intention of promulgating a civilising mission, yet he clearly believed that Europe was superior to Africa and therefore in a position to help Africans progress. As he avowed: 'I am not saying that it is in Europeans' power to civilize Africa'. Yet he continued:

> it is in their power to assist them, & if they are not as barbarian as the Africans themselves, they will understand that it is in their supreme interest to do so. Between nations as between individuals, good is the price of good. The civilised nations have started out as barbarian; civilisation can pass to [Africa] just as it has passed to Europe.[91]

The concept of 'civilisation' that Roubaud drew on was newly intro-duced into European discourse and its meaning was still unstable. It first appeared in the writings of the marquis de Mirabeau and his deployment of it was somewhat equivocal. Using it twice in *L'Ami des hommes*, he introduced it in a reference to the devastating impact of 'l'esprit exclusif', which he argued had a negative impact on 'civilisation and liberty'.[92] The second mention came in the section 'travail et argent', in which he evoked the concept differently, claiming that 'religion is without a doubt the first and most useful brake on humanity: it is the first spring of civilisation'.[93] Scholars rightly tend to argue that 'civilisation', to its French inventor, signalled a 'process of the perfecting of social relations

---

[90] Emphasis in the original. *Ephémérides du citoyen*, 1771, vi, 243. Nicolas Baudeau, *Première introduc-tion à la philosophie économique* (1771), 739–40. Nicolas Baudeau, *Commerce*, 3 vols., *Encyclopédie méthodique*, vols. 78–80 (Paris: Chez Panckoucke, 1783), I, xxvi, and iii, 322.

[91] Roubaud, *Histoire générale*, x, 419–20. On nineteenth-century French liberal support for 'informal empire' and 'formal empire', see David Todd, 'Transnational Projects of Empire in France, c. 1815–c. 1870', *Modern Intellectual History*, 12, 2 (2015), 265–93.

[92] Mirabeau, *L'Ami des hommes*, iii, 238.   [93] Ibid., i, 377.

and material resources' and thus announced an 'ideal'.[94] Yet they do not link Mirabeau's use of it to French and European colonial activities. They might as well have done so, however. In a letter to his brother in Guadeloupe from 1754, Mirabeau momentarily mulled over the impact of missionaries on native American peoples, claiming that he had heard from an eyewitness that neither the French troops nor the colonial administrators were as successful in civilising native Americans as missionaries, who in times of peace 'make continuous conquests with respect to *la police et de la civilisation*'.[95] 'La Police', in the eighteenth century, signified a well-ordered and well-regulated community, and while 'civilisation' was not yet in use, the term 'civiliser' implied a process of 'polishing the mores' of someone or making a person or a people 'civil, honest, and sociable'.[96] In his letter to his younger brother, Mirabeau turned the verb, 'civiliser', into a noun to describe the positive effects he believed missionaries had on native peoples, tying the concept of civilisation explicitly to the civilising missions of French religious proselytisers in the New World.

Mirabeau, however, did not connect the word to the positive, civilising, effects of commerce that many eighteenth-century political economists celebrated as 'doux commerce'. Stemming from Montesquieu's understanding of commerce as a cushion between conflicting mores and values of trading peoples, this vision of commerce was popular in the writings of Gournay and Forbonnais.[97] Mirabeau echoed such ideas in *L'Ami des hommes* in a passage on the profits to be made if free trade and an appreciation for good government and labour were exported to Africa (the passage Roubaud quoted in his 1759 review).[98] It embodied the notion of a possible African progression towards a more civilised stage in European eyes, yet Mirabeau chose not to employ 'civilisation' in this section. Cathrine Larrère has suggested that it is possible that this omission

[94] Jean Starobinski, *Le remède dans le mal – Critique et légitimation de l'artifice à l'âge des Lumière* (Paris: Gallimard, 1989), 20–21; Catherine Larrère, 'Mirabeau et les Physiocrates – L'origine agrarienne de la civilisation', in *Les équivoques de la civilisation*, ed. Bertrand Binoche (Seyssel: Éditions Champ Vallon, 2005), 83–105, 91. For a general discussion, see Bruce Mazlish, 'Civilization in a Historical and Global Perspective', *International Sociology*, 16 (2001), 293–300.

[95] MM to CM, Paris, 9 December 1754, FM, vol. 23, 273.

[96] 'Policer', Dictionnaire de l'Académie française, 4th edn. (1762), *Dictionnaires d'autrefois*, www .portail.atilf.fr. Norbert Elias sees 'policer' and 'civiliser' as synonyms. See Norbert Elias, *The Civilizing Process*, Rev. edn. (Oxford: Blackwell, 2000), 34–5.

[97] On Montesquieu and his idea of 'Doux Commerce', see Albert O. Hirschman, *The Passions and the Interests – Political Arguments for Capitalism before Its Triumph* (Princeton, NJ: Princeton University Press, 1977), 60. On the dubious qualities of commerce in eighteenth-century political thought, see Anoush Fraser Terjanian, *Commerce and Its Discontents in Eighteenth-Century French Political Thought* (Cambridge: Cambridge University Press, 2013).

[98] Mirabeau, *L'Ami des hommes*, iii, 13.

stemmed from the fact that Mirabeau's political economy was agrarian, rather than commercial. He might not have wanted his appraisal of free trade to be seen as a full support for the 'douceur' of commerce, but instead as an account of the best conditions within which industry and agriculture could prosper.[99] In Roubaud's hands, however, the concept of civilisation merged the alleged civilising qualities of religion, commerce, and agriculture. In fact, his insistence that civilisation could pass to Africa indicates that he believed 'civilisation' to have exportable qualities. His comment that Europe was now in possession of civilisation and could help spread it to Africa further reflects that he had a developmental trajectory in mind, a view that many Europeans would begin to share in the following decades.

The Afterlife of the Physiocratic Colonial Reform Programme

By the time Roubaud published his last volumes of *Histoire générale* in 1775, the Physiocrats' dominant intellectual authority, François Quesnay, had died and with him the quest for doctrinaire rigour. To some historians, it is not even possible to speak of Physiocracy proper after Quesnay's death in 1774, but only of physiocratic influences. Even though Mirabeau, Du Pont, and to some extent Le Mercier continued to disseminate their ideas, it seems that apart from a short revival during the ministry of Turgot, between 1774 and 1776, when several of the Physiocrats obtained advisory positions within the royal administration, Physiocracy was in decline. Nevertheless, as Georges Weulersse noted when he followed up on his initial two-volume study of the Physiocrats, 'a school is not without a future, when the ideas it has launched, and whose promoters are progressively forgotten, continue to spread down obscure yet profound paths, diffusing anonymously'.[100] Of these, the physiocratic ideas on colonisation and slavery saw a swift and fulgent future.

The most famous work that acted as a vehicle for physiocratic colonial ideas was Abbé Raynal's Enlightenment bestseller, the *Histoire des deux Indes*. Like the *Encyclopédie*, the *Histoire des deux Indes* was the product of the collective efforts of several men, of whom Raynal and Diderot remained the two most important. Yet the ideas that they presented were not necessarily original, neither in the first version (6 volumes, print date 1770 though published in 1772), nor in its 1774 or 1780 versions. Ann

---

[99] Larrère, 'Mirabeau et les Physiocrates', 98 and 101.
[100] Georges Weulersse, *La Physiocratie à la fin du règne de Louis XV (1770–1774)* (Paris: Presses Universitaires de France, 1959), 12.

Thomson has skilfully pointed to the lifting of Roubaud's arguments on Africans' skin colour from the *Histoire générale* into the *Histoire des deux Indes*. To support her claim, Thomson juxtaposes quotations from Roubaud's *Histoire générale* and Diderot's passages written in 1780 in the *Histoire des deux Indes* and demonstrates how Diderot borrowed from Roubaud in his discussion. Diderot's passages echoed, almost word for word, those of Roubaud.[101]

The same lifting of passages occurred with respect to the idea of cultivation in Africa. In the first edition of the *Histoire des deux Indes*, there is no mention of the possibility of cultivating the colonial commodities of the Antilles in Africa by means of free African labour. As a solution to slavery, Raynal only advocated proper treatment of slaves in the colonies with the prospect of future emancipation.[102] In the 1780 edition, however, the paragraph had been vastly extended and incorporated a section on the possibility of replacing American colonialism with an African venture. Ending slavery in the Americas, it read, would not have to put an end to the lucrative sugar, coffee, cotton, and indigo trade. As its authors broadcasted: 'You can get it from Africa. The most important [goods] grow there naturally, & it will be easy to naturalise the others. Who can doubt that the populations who sell their children to satisfy fleeting fantasies, will not resolve to cultivate their lands to habitually enjoy the advantages of a virtuous and well-ordered society?'[103] Other ideas developed in the physiocratic literature also found their way into the *Histoire des deux Indes*, such as Quesnay and Mirabeau's insistence that colonies should be left to develop before being hit with taxation and Mirabeau's term 'civilisation'. Raynal and Diderot's work would have a profound impact on discussions of colonial empire across Europe and its colonies and ensured that many of the Physiocrats' ideas on colonial empire continued to circulate, even as the group itself started to decline.[104]

Between the Seven Years War and the outbreak of the American Revolution, the Physiocrats were among the few French political economists who rigorously attacked colonial and commercial policies as part of what drove

---

[101] Thomson, 'Diderot, Roubaud; l'Esclavage', 74.

[102] Guillaume Thomas Raynal, *Histoire philosophique et politique des établissemens et du commerce des européens dans les deux Indes*, 6 vols. (Amsterdam, 1770), iv, 165–75.

[103] Guillaume Thomas Raynal, *Histoire philosophique et politique des établissemens et du commerce des européens dans les deux Indes*, 4 vols. (Geneva, 1780), iii, 201.

[104] On the impact of Raynal's *L'histoire des deux Indes* beyond France, see Cecile Courtney and Jenny Mander (eds.), *Raynal's 'Histoire des deux Indes': Colonialism, Networks and Global Exchange* (Oxford: Voltaire Foundation, 2015).

France towards crisis. Although the lion's share of their writings focused on domestic France, their recipe for the regeneration of state finances and French prosperity included a critical rethinking of the monarchy's colonial interests. Pushing for free trade and the cultivation of land by means of free labour, they exhibited an acute awareness of the fragility of the plantation complex in the Americas. In their view, any hope of a prolonged relationship between the mother country and the American colonies could only happen with the help of an immediate recognition of the colonies' equal right to prosperity. In the developmental phase of Physiocracy, however, Quesnay's influence obfuscated the central role of slaves within that equation. Though Mirabeau had initially been attuned to the problem of African slavery in the Americas, not least because his brother had helped him attain a better understanding of life in the colonies, it was recruits to Quesnay and Mirabeau's political economic doctrines who would tackle the issue of plantation slavery rather than the co-founders themselves. Encouraging a redressing of French ties to the Americas, they promoted a new approach to the continent of Africa. Mirabeau had fleetingly speculated about a happier state for Africa in *L'Ami des hommes*, but it was in the hands of Roubaud that a possible French colonial future in Africa, linked to agricultural development and the spread of civilisation, received its fullest articulation. Along the way, as we shall see in the next chapter, the Physiocrats' colonial designs intersected with debates on colonial reform and innovation in the French Îles du Vent – the region which had been so formative in shaping the marquis de Mirabeau's ideas.

CHAPTER 3

Between Enslaved Territories and Overseas Provinces

> I did not fear that the enemy would take all of the island because the planters would surely want to defend themselves, their wives and their possessions.
>
> Beauharnois, Governor-General of Martinique to the
> Minister of the Marine, 27 January 1759[1]

> [T]he way in which the inhabitants have abandoned me, by illegally capitulating to your Excellency, demonstrates only too well that they believe themselves a distinct power. The authority of the King, my master, will look in vain for the sentiments that subjects owe their sovereign . . . all these reasons lead me to propose a capitulation.
>
> Le Vassor de la Touche, Governor-General of Martinique,
> to General Monkton, Commander of the British fleet,
> 12 February 1762[2]

The Seven Years War painfully confirmed the French Crown's fragile hold on its Caribbean colonies. The superiority of the British Navy left little doubt that colonies such as Guadeloupe, Martinique, and Saint-Domingue were in jeopardy. Yet the meagre resistance that Guadeloupe offered once English forces anchored off of the island troubled the local and central governments. To avert further losses and to appease resentful planters, the Crown therefore scrambled in late 1759 to implement reform, founding three Chambres mi-parties d'agriculture et de commerce in the Caribbean, two on Saint-Domingue and one on Martinique for the Îles du Vent.[3] The commission of these chambers was to deliberate on the means and obstacles to colonial prosperity and advise the local and central administration on how to meet local needs. Each chamber would also enjoy representation on the Council of

---

[1] 'Relation de ce qui s'est passé à la Martinique à l'ocasion de l'attaque faite par les anglois le 15. Janvier 1759', 27 January 1759. ANOM C^{8A} 62 f. 1.
[2] Pierre-Franois-Régis Dessalles, *Les annales du conseil souverain de Martinique* (1786), ed. Bernard Vonglis, 2 vols. (Paris: L'Harmattan, 2005), Google Books, ii, 135.
[3] Tarrade, 'L'administration coloniale', 103–22.

Commerce in Paris alongside deputies of the French urban and maritime centres. With an immediate implementation, the Crown hoped that reform could inspire a sense of common purpose between metropolitan merchants and planters in the colonies on whose collaboration France's money-spinning sugar business relied. Although the reform failed to prevent Martinique from capitulating to the British in 1762, the Ministry of the Marine continued its reformist agenda upon the arrival of peace, transforming existing chambers into Chambres d'agriculture, and establishing a new chamber on Guadeloupe. From within these chambers, prominent planters participated in debates on colonial empire and were, for the first time in history, able to influence French colonial policy through institutional means on a level parallel to that of French commercial interests.

Studying the founding and activities of Martinique's Chambre mi-partie d'agriculture et de commerce and its successor institutions, the Chambre d'agriculture (1763–87) and the Assemblée coloniale (established in 1787), allows us to elucidate the linkages among reform, warfare, and political economic debates at the imperial and local levels. For the Crown, war and the fear of colonial loss forced it to break with existing approaches to, and perceptions of, colonies. Integrating elite planters of the Caribbean colonies into the communicative circuit of decision-making processes, the Crown acknowledged colonies' right to prosperity and tacitly started to elevate their territorial status. During the last decades of the Ancien Régime, the French Caribbean colonies therefore began to vacillate between the status of an 'enslaves territory' (*sol esclave*) and an 'overseas province', two designations that mediated much of the debates on the nature and future of French colonial relations in these years.

At the local level, the reform enabled Martinique's planter elite to push against the commercial and imperial regimes to which the Crown subjected them and to participate in their restructuring. Scholars who have dealt with the Chambres mi-parties d'agriculture et de commerce and the Chambres d'agriculture have not paid much attention to their local activities, focusing instead on the founding royal decrees or on the appointment of Martinique's representative to Paris, Jean Dubuc, to the position of *premier commis* during the Choiseul administration.[4] Yet as I show in this chapter, their activities were important to the evolution of colonial-

---

[4] To my knowledge, only four works analyse the colonial chambers of agriculture in some detail. Jean Tarrade focuses on the metropolitan side of this history. See Tarrade, *Le commerce*. Dessalles' study of the *Conseil Souverain* of Martinique and Henri Joucla's study of the history of the *Conseil Supérieur* in the colonies discuss the decrees that founded the chambers. Dessalles, *Les annales du conseil souverain*, ii, especially 93–102. Joucla, *Le Conseil Supérieur*, esp. 20–23 and 38–43. Céline Mélisson offers an

metropolitan relations. Tensions between Martinique's Chambre mi-partie d'agriculture et de commerce and local administrators tested the Crown's willingness to accommodate planters' complaints. In turn, members of Martinique's Chambre d'agriculture produced a flurry of memoranda on planter debt, provisioning, slavery, and taxes, many of which served as proposals for reform in their own right. Exploring their rejoinders to central and local representatives and metropolitan commercial communities bring into view the ways in which members of this second chamber articulated a powerful 'creole' political economic discourse with which to defend their interests. Echoing whenever convenient concepts and political economic ideas that buoyed conversations on empire in the metropole, they steadily gained experience in negotiating their economic and political position within the French colonial empire, a lesson that would serve them well during the early stages of the French Revolution.

The Chambre Mi-Partie d'Agriculture et de Commerce

The founding of the Chambres mi-parties d'agriculture et de commerce in 1759 came in response to Guadeloupe's surrender to British forces in May 1759. With immediate reform, Nicolas René Berryer, Minister of the Marine from 1758 to 1761, hoped that the chambers could serve the dual purpose of calming planters' feelings of metropolitan neglect and help the Crown find ways to boost production. Planters on Martinique, however, found that reform offered too little too late. The members of Martinique's Chambre mi-partie d'agriculture et de commerce spent the war attacking colonial governance and French commerce, causing neither of the Crown's hopes to transpire. Instead, the chamber's activities aggravated relations among local planters, merchants at Saint-Pierre, and royal officials on the ground, fuelling planters' desire to come under English rule.

The Arrêt du conseil d'état of 10 December 1759 that instituted Martinique's Chambre mi-partie d'agriculture et de commerce, instructed Martinique's intendant, Le Mercier de la Rivière, on how to plan the chamber's composition, organisation, and financing. It stipulated that the island's Superior Council should be put in charge of organising the election by ballot of four plantation owners (*habitants*), four merchants (*négociants*), and one secretary, each possessing a 'perfect knowledge' of 'the veritable

overview in 'Les chambres d'agriculture coloniales: entre résistances et contestations de l'impérialisme français au XVIIIème siècle', *Études Canadiennes/Canadian Studies* 76 (2014), 89–102.

interests of the colony and its commerce'.[5] Once elected, these members should nominate three candidates, one of whom the King would pick to serve as a deputy to lobby for planter needs in the Council of Commerce in Paris. While members of the chamber held only advisory positions and remained subject to the local administration – indeed the intendant would preside over the chamber's meetings – their choice of deputy would open a direct avenue to the centre of power. Despite clear instructions, however, the founding of Martinique's chamber was mired in a conflict between agricultural and commercial interests on the island. Leaving it in the hands of Martinique's Superior Council to elect members to the new chamber turned the latter into a vehicle for the political and economic interests of the island's plantocracy.

When the Superior Council met on 19 May 1760 to elect eight members, it orchestrated a string of nominations that superficially adhered to the guidelines of the *arrêt* but which in reality ensured that all members would be either directly or indirectly connected to the planter community.[6] The nominations of planter representatives – Thomazeau, Pierre Dubuc de Sainte Preuve, De Cely, and Arnauld – all aligned with the *arrêt*'s stipulations. According to Le Mercier and governor-general, François de Beauharnois who reported on the election, these four were well-established plantation owners. Thomazeau was a 'brave' and 'gallant' former officer of the French troops and a Knight of St Louis, who had lived on Martinique for six years. Thomazeau had followed the well-trodden path to planter status by marrying a local widow with means. Dubuc de Sainte Preuve was born into the island's powerful Dubuc family and was known as an *homme d'esprit* who had established himself as a plantation owner six years previously. De Cely had lived on Martinique for ten years and had married a widow who brought two sugar plantations to the union both of which were not yet paid off. He was indebted, particularly to the royal treasury on the island, the *caisse de domaine*. Arnauld, finally, had arrived on the island as *pilotin de navire* twenty-five years earlier. Rumoured to be in debt to several on the island, Arnauld had worked as a commissioner at Saint-Pierre before marrying his way to planter status.

---

[5] *Arrêt du conseil d'Etat du Roi Portant établissement d'une Chambre Mi-Partie d'Agriculture et de Commerce aux Isles du Vent, avec faculté d'avoir à Paris un Député à la suite du Conseil. Du 10. Décembre 1759*, in Joucla, *Le Conseil Supérieur des Colonies*, 21 and Article 1.

[6] Beauharnois and Le Mercier to the minister, 7 June 1760. ANOM C^8A 62 400. See also 'Mémoire instructif concernant les nominations des membres de la Chambre mi-partie d'agriculture et de commerce', 7 June 1760. ANOM C^8A 62. Internet reference: ark:/61561/zn40iwxyvys. On the Superior Council, see Laurie M. Wood, 'The Martinican Model: Colonial Magistrates and the Origins of a Global Judicial Elite', in *The Torrid Zone: Colonization and Cultural Interaction in the Seventeenth-Century Caribbean*, ed. Louis H. Roper (Columbia: University of South Carolina Press, 2018), 149–61.

While there was nothing suspicious about the nomination of these four, the profile of the four nominated merchants, Chapelle, Beraud, Clauzel, and Marias, differed little from the above and exhibited only tenuous links to the commercial sector. Chapelle had moved from Guadeloupe to Martinique and married a widowed plantation owner. He too was 'said to be an honest man' despite owing debts to several people on the island. Clauzel, a retiree whose wife owned a shop, was the previous owner of a big sugar plantation and the father-in-law and uncle to two of the *conseillers* in the Superior Council. Marias was involved in commissions and owned a large sugar plantation. Only Beraud seemed to have genuine links to commercial interests. He had lived on the island for twelve years and worked for a merchant house, prior to which he had been involved in commerce in Marseille. Nonetheless, what should have been the creation of a well-balanced chamber, capable of offering unbiased advice on the means to prosperity, instead was instituted as a lobby pushing the agenda of Martinique's planter elite.

The local administrators, from whose reports these brief biographies derive, immediately acknowledged the privileging of agricultural interests among the chamber's members. What Beauharnois and Le Mercier found most problematic was the Superior Council's successful exclusion of merchants from Martinique's principal commercial hub, Saint-Pierre (see Figure 3.1). This port was the largest town on the island with merchant houses, shops, bars, and cabarets serving a third of the island's free population. The exclusion of any representative from Saint-Pierre, Beauharnois, and Le Mercier therefore warned, was bound to raise complaints from the metropolitan chambers of commerce. They further disclosed that when they had brought their reservations to the Superior Council, it had brazenly admitted to the skewed result, alleging that anybody with solely commercial interests on Martinique would not be able to inform Versailles about colonial needs, since the colony's commercial interests were inextricably tied to 'French Commerce'.[7]

The Superior Council's inflammatory position was symptomatic of the socio-economic cleavages that the plantation complex fostered. The divide between free and unfree inhabitants carved out additional lines of demarcation based on colour, socio-economic position, and occupational status. Among the free whites, the elite comprised the more successful plantation owners residing in the countryside, who were interchangeably referred to as *habitants, colons*, or *planteurs*. Wealthy merchants constituted another segment of the top tier, most of whom lived in Saint-Pierre and worked as *négociants* or *commissionnaires*. As we saw in Chapter 1, the latter

---

[7] Beauharnois and Le Mercier de la Rivière to the minister 7 June 1760. ANOM C⁸ᴬ 62 400.

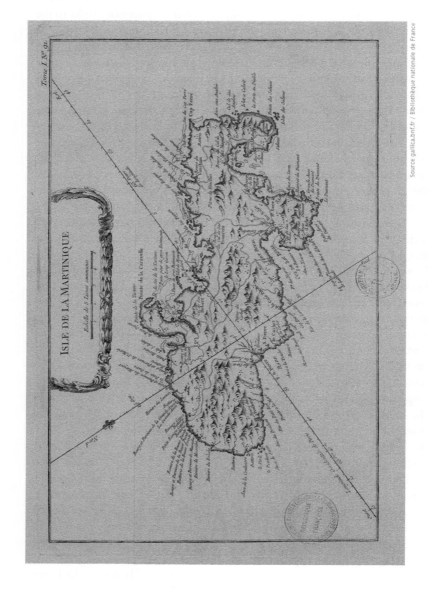

Figure 3.1 Isle de la Martinique par Jacques-Nicolas Bellin, 1754
Source: Bibliothèque nationale de France, département Cartes et plans, GE DD-2987 (9113)

mediated sales between planters and metropolitan merchants and obtained their name from the commission they charged on transactions. Their ready cash flows enabled them to serve as moneylenders to insolvent planters, often leaving the latter in a crippling debt-bondage. Though both groups formed the upper crust of society and enjoyed a shared interest in preserving the plantation complex, the Exclusif, debt, and a lack of specie drove the island's agricultural and commercial elites into opposing camps.[8]

The undercurrent of planter-merchant conflict that characterised the election of members to the chamber carried over into the nomination for a deputy to Paris. The newly elected members nominated three candidates, as the *arrêt* prescribed, but made it clear that Jean Dubuc (sometimes spelled Dubuq or Dubucq or Du Buc) was their preferred choice. Dubuc was one of the most successful planters on the island and the future principal clerk (*premier commis*) in the Ministry of the Marine. In their report, the members described him as a savvy planter whose ability to shed light on agriculture and commerce was unrivalled on the island. In less glowing terms, the local administrators reported that Dubuc was a wealthy, intelligent planter, with 'some experience of colonial commerce'.[9]

Curiously neither the chamber, nor the administrators, mentioned perhaps the most noteworthy feature of this nomination. Dubuc was the brother of Pierre Dubuc de Sainte Preuve who had been elected to the Chambres mi-partie d'agriculture et de commerce and the son of Jean Pierre Dubuc Duferret (born 1692), who participated in the 1717 planter revolt on Martinique, the Gaoulé, which ringleader was their grandfather, Jean Dubuc (born 1672). Dubuc had studied law in Paris and even been a lawyer with the Paris Parliament when the death of his father took him back to Martinique where he married Marie Anne de Fébvrier, the daughter of a wealthy *conseiller* in Martinique's Superior Council (François Lambert de Fébvrier). The Dubuc family extended along various branches throughout the Îles du Vent. We know from their numerous attempts to reclaim the noble status that the family had lost in 1715 (when the Crown purged recently ennobled families of their titles) that Dubuc de Sainte Preuve and Jean Dubuc had two additional brothers on the island – Félix André Dubuc d'Enneville and Julien Antoine Dubuc Duferret – as well as numerous second and third cousins with plantations spread across

---

[8] On social hierarchies, see Liliane Chauleau, *Dans les Îles du Vent La Martinique XVIIe–XIXe siècle* (Paris: L'Harmattan, 1993), 77–83, 87–9, 102; Elisabeth, *La société martiniquaise*, Chapter 1.

[9] 'Extrait des registres des délibérations de la Chambre mi-partie d'agriculture et de commerce', 4 Juin 1760 ANOM C^{8A} 62, f. 512. Beauharnois and Mercier de la Rivière to Berryer, 7 June 1760. ANOM C^{8A} 62.

Martinique an St Lucia. An anonymous author therefore warned Versailles that Jean Dubuc should be excluded as a candidate for the role of deputy, not least due to his family's association with 1717. Versailles ignored the warning, however, honouring instead the chamber's preferences.[10]

The Crown's acceptance of planter domination within Martinique's new chamber reflected its hopes that reform could sooth the colonial-metropolitan rift. In contrast, officials on the ground had little faith that reform could ameliorate matters. Even before the chamber had held its first meeting, Beauharnois and Le Mercier reported that a plethora of obstacles impeded the likelihood of success. As they explained, warfare exacerbated risks of widespread famine because it made the arrival of provisions from the metropole extremely difficult. Additionally, Guadeloupe's economic upturn under British rule exacerbated planters' frustrations with French commerce. The two administrators therefore warned the Minister of the Marine of the utter absence in the colony of any understanding of the reciprocal need that metropolitan ports and the colony had for each other and assessed that this absence was bound to colour the chamber's deliberations as it set about discussing the obstacles and means to colonial success.[11]

These gloomy projections were surely those of Le Mercier, whose role as intendant charged him to mediate between the Crown and the chamber. Under different circumstances the task of overseeing debates on agriculture and commerce might have appealed to him. From Saumur, Pierre Paul Le Mercier de la Rivière was a son of Paul-Philippe Le Mercier de la Rivière de Saint Médard Ecuyer, an Intendant of Finance in the generality (*généralité*) of Tours, and of Marie Claude le Bigot de la Chouanière. While a young magistrate with the Parlement of Paris, Pierre Paul had encountered Madame de Pompadour, François Quesnay, and other elites and subsequently become attached to the Ministry of the Marine. According to an internal report within the Ministry, Le Mercier had been picked for the position of intendant partly because of 'his knowledge of commerce, which he ha[d] studied while fulfilling his duties as a magistrate'. Bringing his

[10] On Dubuc's father's and grandfather's involvement in the Gaoulé, see letter from marquis de Feuquière addressed to the 'Conseil [de marine Marine]', 5 December 1717, ANOM C⁸ᴬ 23, ff. 33–8. On the Dubuc family (Dubuq), see 'Genealogie de Dubuq', marked 'vers 1748', f. 3–6 and 'Lettres de confirmation des lettres de noblesse', 1769, f. 4bis., both in Dossier of the Dubuc family, ANOM E 143. On objections to Dubuc, see 'Observations sur l'exécution de l'arrêt du conseil du 10 Decembre 1759', 6 June 1760 ANOM C⁸ᴬ 62, f. 504. On the Gaoulé and its repercussions, see Sidney Daney de Marcillac, *Histoire de la Martinique, depuis la colonisation jusqu'en 1815*, 5 vols. (Fort-Royal: E. Ruelle, 1846), iii, 32–7.

[11] Beauharnois and Mercier de la Rivière to Berryer, 7 June 1760. ANOM C⁸ᴬ 62, f. 400.

interests in agrarian political economy to bear on his engagements with Martinique's chamber, his letters to Versailles nonetheless reflect a lack of faith in his and the Crown's power to repair colonial-metropolitan bonds in the midst of war.[12]

In his opening speech to Martinique's Chambres mi-partie d'agriculture et de commerce, Le Mercier tried his best to align central and colonial expectations, laying out an agenda that reflected his administrative talents and interest in political economy. Deploying the metaphor of the body to illustrate the nature of the state, he proclaimed that the colonies and the provinces were its essential body parts. Referencing the 'natural order' of things, he stressed that the members of the chamber should keep in mind that the particular interests of each limb were always subordinate to the general interests of the entire body. 'So, Gentlemen', he continued, 'when we consider here the propositions for the good of the colony, our considerations should include the other provinces; we should take the general interests of the state to be the same as those of the colony and each of the provinces'. Stopping short of calling colonies 'overseas provinces', he counselled that a sentiment of shared interests should guide the members of the chamber as they set out to instruct the Crown on the means to attain colonial prosperity. Expressing similar views to those Quesnay and Mirabeau were producing at Versailles, Le Mercier even suggested that free trade in the colonies would be permissible if it were congenial to the overall interests of the state, a suggestion that clearly transgressed the existing limitations on foreign trade, even when including the wartime policy of admitting neutral powers to trade with the colonies.[13]

Like the reform of which it was a product, Le Mercier's speech was a call for unity within a French colonial empire whose distant fragments the the Exclusif and the Seven Years War pushed apart. Unlike his superiors back in France, he was under no illusions that the founding of a chamber could successfully relax colonial-metropolitan tensions in the short term. As he informed his superior, he would work to pass his 'principles onto all the members of this chamber', yet he was sure that the local elite would

---

[12] 'Report', December 1757, Dossier Mercier de la Rivière, ANOM E 276, f. 3. On Le Mercier's family and connections, see Louis Philippe May, *Le Mercier de la Rivière (1719–1801) aux origines de la dcience économique* (Paris: Centre national de la recherche scientifique, 1975), 16–17 and 150–53.

[13] Le Mercier de la Rivière, 'Discours d'Ouverture de la Chambre Mi-Partie d'Agriculture et de Commerce', in *Le Mercier de la Rivière (1719–1801): Mémoires et textes inédits sur le gouvernement économique des Antilles*, ed. L. P. May (Paris: CNRS, 1978), 93–6. The archival version of Le Mercier de la Rivière's speech is in ANOM F³ 126, ff. 144–63.

hear nothing of it and see the founding of the new chamber as a first step towards 'rendering the colony absolutely independent of the metropole'.[14]

Undermining Local Authority

Le Mercier's misgivings were not far off the mark; as soon as Martinique's Chambre mi-partie d'agriculture et de commerce set to work it started attacking central and local officials. After their first extensive deliberations on 17 October 1760, the very first memorandum that they produced was a jeremiad against colonial rule from beginning to end. It opened with an appeal to the King's own experience as sovereign, proclaiming with Aristotelian undertones that good governance was to support each individual while ensuring that all members of society fulfilled their intended duty. While this observation was true in general, the chamber underlined, it was indispensable in a place such as Martinique where most of the population was 'a class inferior to all other people'. Since slaves did most of the work in the colonies, it required singular efforts to ensure that they remained within the bounds of their condition. To the chamber, however, Martinique's urban communities and the colony's administrators completely neglected this task. Local authorities were negligent and corrupt. They failed to uphold Articles 15–20 of the Code Noir that forbade slaves from carrying arms, assembling in and beyond the plantation, and selling sugarcane, or any other goods without written permission from their master. In turn, local cabaret and tavern owners offered slaves and maroons a place to hide and to gamble, acting as 'asylums both day and night'. The admiralty, who were supposed to uphold the law, hosted Negro balls (*des bals de Nègres*) and gambling in their private homes. Such carousing, the chamber continued, took place alongside the all-pervasive suffering of the general population. People were starving, sailors deserted, corsairs swarmed around the port of Saint-Pierre, and innocent people ended up in jail. The price of flour brought from France was excessively high, possibly due to smuggling or hoarding. Without an immediate redressing of all these nuisances, the chamber scolded, France would lose the colony.[15]

Duly forwarding this scathing information to Versailles, Le Mercier was also asked to submit his commentary on the chamber's report and respond to it directly. In his commentary, he gave each of the chamber's complaints

---

[14] Le Mercier de la Rivière to Berryer, Martinique 5 June 1760. ANOM F³ 126, ff. 160–63.

[15] 'Extrait du registre des délibérations de la chambre mi-partie d'agriculture et de commerce établie en l'isle Martinique par Arrêt du Conseil d'Etat du Roy du 10 Xbre, 1759'. Martinique, 17 October 1760. ANOM F³ 126, ff. 182–7. On Articles 15–20, see Sala-Molins, *Le Code Noir*, 120–29.

a meticulous answer but also conveyed his disappointment with its lack of effort to seek solutions rather than merely pointing to errors. He also stressed that it had gone beyond its commission by addressing issues unrelated to agriculture and commerce.[16] In their own letter to Berryer, members of the chamber retorted that their 'astonishment' had been great when learning that the intendant 'reproached it for having meddled in matters which were beyond its competence' when the abuses that they had listed were all directly relevant to commerce and agriculture.[17] Such mud-slinging continued to build over the following months. On 1 February 1761, Le Mercier wrote to the minister about 'some memoranda which the chamber had written at the instigation of the Superior Council against the government of this colony'. Three weeks later, he mentioned another three such memoranda. Soon, the newly appointed governor-general, Louis-Charles Le Vassor de la Touche, chimed in. Echoing Le Mercier's annoyance, he underlined that the chamber did not discuss agriculture and commerce but instead interfered in government and administrative affairs, penning reports that were 'vicious, in essence, form, tone, and style'.[18]

As these snippets reveal, deep-seated frustrations – aggravated by warfare – undermined the ability of Martinique's chamber to function as Versailles had intended it. Rather than focus on agricultural and commercial improvements, the chamber kept its critical gaze fixed on the what its members saw as the defects of French colonial governance. A comparison with the activities of its sibling institution on Saint-Domingue, the Chambre mi-partie d'agriculture et de commerce at Cap, throws the tense situation on Martinique into even greater relief. Within the first two years of its existence, the chamber at Cap wrote at least twenty-five memoranda on topics such as the improvement of public roads, the building of fire-driven mills, the importation of mules and horses, the purchasing of a printing press, and trade with the English colonies in North America.[19] In contrast, Martinique's chamber had no time for such issues, focusing all its energies on decrying what it saw as the utter mismanagement of the French colonies.

---

[16] 'Extrait des archives de la chambre d'agriculture et de commerce établie en l'Isle Martinique', Martinique, 10 November 1760. ANOM F³ 126, ff. 188–91.

[17] 'Extrait des registres des délibérations de la chambre mi-partie d'agriculture et de commerce établie en l'Isle Martinique', 15 January, 1761, ANOM F³ 126, ff. 192–203.

[18] Le Mercier de la Rivière to Choiseul, Martinique 1 February 1761, ANOM C⁸ᴬ 63, f. 143; Le Mercier de la Rivière to Choiseul, Martinique 23 February 1761, ANOM C⁸ᴬ 63, f. 155; Vassor de la Touche to Choiseul, Martinique 20 May 1761, C⁸ᴬ 63, f. 79.

[19] See the list of memoranda and the entire collection in ANOM F³ 124.

In this climate of fury and despair, white colonial resistance during Britain's second attack on Martinique in 1762 evaporated quickly. The inhabitants of Lamentin, a town just south of the capital of Fort-Royal, surrendered to General Robert Monckton, commander of the British fleet, without the consent of the governor-general. Eight other boroughs soon followed. The bigger towns of Trinité and Saint-Pierre held out a little longer but with no assistance from France in sight, their inhabitants pressured Le Vassor de la Touche to capitulate on 13 February 1762. In his report to Versailles, Le Vassor unequivocally blamed defeat on the population's lack of patriotism. He explained that 'the bad example of Guadeloupe' had convinced the inhabitants of Lamentin that 'they had the right to negotiate for themselves'.[20] In the short term, wartime reform had done nothing to abate planter disloyalty.

The British Occupation

The British occupation of Martinique did not prove as liberating as the local planter elite had hoped for. Lasting from February 1762 to July 1763, Martinique's free population received a larger say in fiscal decisions but never attained the rights and concessions that the British had offered Guadeloupe capitulants. Once Monckton had conquered the island, he left the governorship to William Rufane. One of Rufane's earliest tasks was to raise local taxes to pay for the lodging and maintenance of British troops – no easy task given the deplorable state of Martinique. He therefore appointed *commissaires* from each of the island's parishes to include the local population in deliberations on how to levy the tax. Once they met, the assembly used the locales of the Chambre mi-partie d'agriculture et de commerce and consulted with its members as well as Martinique's Superior Council. Rufane did not object to their inclusion into discussions on taxation, but his subsequent refusal to accept the assembly's request to dispense with the tax impaired his ability to administer the island. Forced to comply, Martinique's planters started to retaliate as they knew best: challenge the governor's authority.

Over the course of the occupation, the Superior Council spearheaded a relentless attack on Rufane's administration, sending remonstrances to George III and continuing their illicit trading with the Dutch. In their communication with London, they asked the King to grant the Council

[20] 'Copie de ma lettre à M. Le duc de Choiseul en lui rendans compte de l'opérations du siège de la Martinique', Le Vassor de la Touche to Choiseul, 14 May 1762, ANOM C⁸ᴬ 64, ff. 16–27bis.

the right to oversee some of the tasks formerly in the hands of the French intendant, a position they argued had been left vacant after the occupation. They also conveyed that they had elected Asselin de Vély to go to England to render homage to Martinique's new sovereign and to act as 'deputy to the court of the King' and asked for permission to prepare his departure.[21] When Charles Wyndham, second Earl of Egremont, Secretary of State for the Southern Department, showed no interest in either request, the Superior Council scribbled a second remonstrance, complaining about the decision. It warned Egremont of Rufane's pretentions to 'unite in his own person the authority of both the general and the intendant'. Rufane retaliated that 'the gentlemen of the Superior Council want to assume a share in the government, beyond even what they had under their own governors'. Three months later, he reported that the Superior Council was still seeking 'a greater share of power'. To explain the Council's disruptive behaviour, Rufane noted at the end of the year that the less favourable terms of capitulation that planters of Martinique had received compared to 'their neighbours of Guadeloupe may [have been] the foundation of some uneasiness to many of them'.[22]

Aside from wrestling with a recalcitrant planter community over local governance, the British occupiers also fought in vain to reduce the island's ongoing contraband trade.[23] The receiver general and tax collector on the island, MacLeane, wrote to Rufane that he was unable to 'crush' the illicit trade. The 'coasts, the creeks and harbours of the island' were so numerous that it was simply 'impossible for the officers of the customs, though ever so diligent, to prevent an illicit importation and exportation'. MacLean further conveyed that 'the French have for several years past been entirely supplied from Sint Eustatius with Dutch East India goods, and ... continue to be so to the very great detriment of the fair trade of England and His Majesty's revenue'.[24] That Martinique systematically relied on trade with foreigners was further underlined by a petition from 'the merchants

[21] 'Mémoire du conseil supérieur de la Martinique sur les objets énoncés dans ses très humbles et très respectueuses remontrances faites à sa Majesté', 22 May 1762, National Archives, Kew (hereinafter NAK), Colonial Office, Foreign and Commonwealth Offices (hereinafter CO), 166/2 ff. 115–20; and letter to Rufane from the deputy *commissaires* of the parishes of this island, NAK CO 166/2, f. 121.

[22] 'Très humbles et très respectueuses remontrances que présent au Roy nôtre très honoré & souverain seigneur les gens tenant son conseil supérieur de la Martinique', Martinique, 12 July 1762, NAK CO, ff. 136–8. Rufane to Egremont, Martinique 19 July 1762, NAK CO, f. 127–8. Rufane to Egremont, 2 October 1762, Martinique, NAK CO, f. 124. Rufane to Egremont, Martinique, 1 December 1762, NAK CO, ff. 147–8.

[23] Rufane to Egremont, Martinique, St Peters, 2 June 1762, NAK CO, ff. 99–101.

[24] MacCleane to Rufane, Martinique St Peters, 19 July 1762, NAK CO, f. 130.

and others trading from North America to Martinique', in which they complained without a whiff of embarrassment that Rufane's restrictions preventing 'merchants and seafaring people trading from North America' from provisioning Martinique with the commodities upon which they depended, including flour, staves, sloops, and lumber.[25]

The British occupation therefore did not produce the result that Martinique's plantocracy had hoped for. Unlike on Guadeloupe, which found itself 'in a better position than any other slave owners in the West Indies, whether English or French', Martinican planters had only been able to modestly expand their participation in local governance during the British occupation.[26] Worse, the economic boom they had hoped for never materialised. Whereas the British supplied Guadeloupe with an estimate of 20,400 slaves between 1759 and 1763, they brought only about 7,200 to Martinique in the same period.[27] Guadeloupe could also boast an increase in sugar plantations, whereas the number on Martinique shrunk from 374 in 1752 to 299 in 1762. In fact, the war had completely reversed the economic importance of the two islands.[28] Ongoing frustrations and unfulfilled aspirations would therefore weigh on relations between France and the Îles du Vent, once the latter were back in French hands.

The Chambre d'Agriculture and the Dubuc Family

In a less agitated age, the clashes between the Chambre mi-partie d'agriculture et de commerce and the French local administration on Martinique might have led to the dismantlement of the chamber. However, in an era of crisis, where a large share of royal finances and domestic economic interests rested on trade with the Caribbean colonies, the Crown chose to turn a blind eye. On the heels of the Seven Years War, it pushed ahead with what increasingly looked like royal courtship of planter fidelity. When Guadeloupe and Martinique were restored to France in 1763, Versailles adjusted its initial reform of 1759 to accommodate its colonial plantocracy. An arrêt of 9 April 1763 stipulated that His Majesty recognised that the current composition of the chamber gave rise to unnecessary debate. Since

---

[25] 'To William Rufane from the merchants and others trading from North America to Martinique', St Peters, Martinique, 16 June 1762. NAK CO, f. 132. On the British occupation, see also Pierre-Franois -Régis Dessalles, *Les Annales du conseil*, ii, 164, 174–85.

[26] Richard Pares, *War and Trade in the West Indies, 1739–1763* (London: Frank Cass, 1963), 187.

[27] *Voyages: The Trans-Atlantic Slave Trade Database*, www.slavevoyages.com.

[28] For slave estimates, see *Voyages: The Trans-Atlantic Slave Trade Database*, www.slavevoyages.com. On the number of plantations, see 'Récapitulation des Articles du Recensement général de l'Isle Martinique pour l'année 1762', NAK CO 166/2, f. 149 and Blérald, *Histoire économique*, 28.

the chambers of commerce in the metropole already represented merchant interests, the colonial chamber should be made up purely of plantation owners (*colons*) and renamed the Chambre d'agriculture. Moreover, the intendant was no longer allowed to participate in meetings; instead, the Crown asked the chamber to appraise the performance of the local administration each time a governor-general or an intendant was recalled, turning the chamber into a watchdog for the central government.[29]

Perhaps the most impressive shift was the notable expansion of power of the Dubuc family. Choiseul elevated Jean Dubuc, Martinique's representative in Paris, to the position of *premier commis* of the Bureau of Colonies. As one historian points out, this appointment 'could not have been a more symbolic demonstration of the Marine's desire to learn from past mistakes and integrate colonial voices and experience into the highest echelons'.[30] To replace Jean Dubuc as deputy in Paris, the chamber brought in Julien Antoine Dubuc Duferret, brother of the two Dubucs already in the chamber. Like his older brother Jean, Julien had studied law in Paris and had returned to Martinique to marry the daughter of his distant uncle, Dubuc Dugalion. Pierre Dubuc de Sainte Preuve, member of the Chambre mi-partie d'agriculture et de commerce, had also spent years in Paris. After finishing his studies, he had joined the French Oratorians. Teaching rhetoric for some years, he then became a professor of mathematics at the College of Juilly, a Catholic teaching establishment in the city of Juilly, north-east of Paris, but had returned to Martinique around 1754 as Le Mercier and Beauharnois indicated.[31]

The rise of the Dubuc Family was a thorn in the side of the local administration. The new Governor-General of Martinique, François Louis de Salignac, marquis de la Mothe Fénelon, who arrived in Martinique in 1763 together with the reappointed intendant, Le Mercier de la Rivière, spent much of his time worrying about 'la tribu des Dubucs' (as he called them). He recognised that their lands were admirably cultivated, their roads well-maintained, and their slaves 'healthy well-fed and happy', all of which made them eminently qualified for their positions, yet he worried about their loyalty and commitment to French rule. In his view, the brothers had 'an English heart' and an '*archirepublican* spirit' which they spread across the island. He was particularly critical of Dubuc de Sainte Preuve, with

---

[29] 'Arrêt du Conseil d'Etat du Roi, portant suppression de la Chambre Mi-partie d'Agriculture et Commerce, et Création de la Chambre d'Agriculture du 9 avril 1763', *Code de la Martinique*, 8 vols. (Fort-de-France, 1865), iv, 186.

[30] Banks, *Chasing Empire*, 207.

[31] 'Genealogie de Dubuq', marked 'vers 1748', Dossier of the Dubuc family, ANOM E 143, fols. 3–6.

whom he repeatedly clashed. With disdain floating from his pen, Fénelon told Choiseul that Sainte Preuve was a 'systematic, abstract, anatomical, and metaphysical worker who pretends to have dissected the colony with the same precision as the dissection of a corpse'. Sainte Preuve was the 'soul' of the Chambre d'agriculture, Fénelon charged, a not entirely unfounded assumption since Sainte Preuve was the only member of the initial chamber that continued onto the new Chambre d'agriculture (the new members being Pelletier, Leyritz, Le Jeune, Croquet fils ainé, Girardin, and Désgrottes).[32]

Dubuc de Sainte Preuve was equally unimpressed by Fénelon. The latter was an irreproachable representative of the Ancien Régime aristocracy, whose family were long-time servants of the Crown. His father, François Louis de Salignac, marquis de la Mothe-Fénelon, had been lieutenant general of the King's army and had served as ambassador extraordinary to Holland in 1725. Another illustrious relative was François de Salignac de la Mothe-Fénelon, the famous author of *Les Aventures de Télémaque* (1699). Yet according to Dubuc de Sainte Preuve and the members of the Chambre d'agriculture, Fénelon's attachment to the reputation that his name carried controlled his outlook on life and made him treat 'the island as his fiefdom'. While his arrival 'should have been like the sunset of a beautiful day', it instead brought 'clouds', ruining the hopes of the local population. The chamber observed that Fénelon loved exercising authority but did not understand its purpose. In spite of his fine education and pedigree, he showed himself incapable of intellectual growth. As it noted, it was as 'with exotic plants that are forced to grow on land which is not naturally destined for it. The plant will appear but it will carry no fruit'.[33]

Despite periodical clashes between the Chambre d'agriculture and the local colonial administration, the members of the new chamber met regularly over the years and tended to focus their deliberations on topics pertaining to their commission. Common issues included the lack of provisions, planter debt, the enslaved population, and taxes. As the chamber explored how to improve each of these, they appropriated a variety of

---

[32] Fénelon to Choiseul, Martinique 10 November 1763. ANOM C[8A] 65, f. 187; and Fénelon to Choiseul, St Pierre, 27 November 1763, ANOM C[8A] 65, f. 209. The new members are named in Dessalles, *Les annales du conseil souverain de Martinique*, ii, 96.

[33] 'Administration de M. le M. de Fénelon Gouverneur Général. Extrait des registres des délibérations de la chambre d'agriculture en l'Isle Martinique', 2 August 1765, ANOM C[8A] 67 F380. The planter committee who had signed off of the report included Dubuc de Sainte Preuve, Désgrottes, Le Pelletier, Le Jeune, Leyritz, Croquet fils, and Marraud, which suggests that the latter had replaced Girardin at this point.

political economic arguments in circulation, though often with no concern for potential doctrinal tensions. Like a lawyer's plaidoyer constructed from a variety of arguments favouring a client, so Martinique's plantocracy – several of whom had studied law in Paris – blended conflicting strands of thought with selective interpretations of legal traditions and commercial data to combate colonial regulations and practices that limited their autonomy. Along the way, they steadily built up an arsenal of arguments with which to advocate for their particular interests. Able to rehearse their position over the years, the chamber became an excellent training ground for participatory politics. Both these outcomes would turn planters into a formidable lobby for colonial slavery, separate laws for the colonies, and free trade once the Revolution erupted.

From the Exclusif to the Exclusif mitigé

One of the first opportunities Martinique's new Chambre d'agriculture and its deputy in Paris seized to render the colonial system more amenable to their needs concerned the liberalisation of colonial commerce, known as the transition from the Exclusif to the Exclusif mitigé. The metropolitan side of this debate and the subsequent shift in policy have been detailed by Jean Tarrade who ascribes the relaxing of the Exclusif to the political clout of Jean Dubuc during his years as Choiseul's *premier commis* for the colonies.[34] Dubuc's role in engineering this shift was perhaps not as authoritative as Tarrade suggests, however. As we shall see, Dubuc's later disavowal of the widely circulated document, the famous 'Memorandum on the extent and the limits of the prohibitive laws of foreign commerce in the colonies', in which he initially presented the case for reform to the Council of Commerce in Paris, suggests that the rationale for the proposed policy change in that document was Choiseul's rather than that of Dubuc. Aside from revealing these discrepancies in outlook between Choiseul and Dubuc, a return to the debates on the reform of the Exclusif from the perspective of Dubuc and Martinican planters sheds light on the latter's eclectic appropriation of available arguments in play to forge their own powerful ripostes to the metropole.

Jean Dubuc had taken his seat alongside metropolitan deputies in the Council of Commerce in Paris on 19 November 1761.[35] His wit allowed

---

[34] Tarrade, *Le Commerce Coloniale*, i, 165.
[35] Pierre Bonnassieux, *Conseil de Commerce et Bureau du commerce 1700–1791 Inventaire Analytique des procès-verbaux* (Paris: Imprimerie Nationale, 1900), 411.

him to quickly ingratiate himself with the intellectual elites and become a respected voice among *philosophes* and political economists. The latter seemed to follow his elevation to *premier commis* with interest and admiration. The marquis de Mirabeau mentioned Dubuc's appointment in a letter to his brother in 1764. A little over a year later, François Quesnay referred to Dubuc as 'a citizen of a rare merit' (*un citoyen d'un rare mérite*), whose writings exhibited 'a superior genius' (*un génie supérieur*). Diderot, in turn, considered Dubuc a well-mannered man 'of courage, philosophy, stature, integrity, knowledge, eloquence, and a lot of imagination'.[36] As *premier commis,* Dubuc's task was to help Choiseul balance the scales between commercial interest in the French ports and planter interests in the colonies in a manner conducive to the general prosperity of the French colonial empire. This was not an easy task, and Dubuc struggled to shed his initial identity as deputy for Martinique, both under Choiseul's administration, but also under the administration of Choiseul's cousin, César Gabriel de Choiseul-Chevigny, duc de Praslin (1766–70). The fact that he was now chief clerk placed uncomfortable restraints on his ability to advance the colonial vision he personally endorsed. As he later told Diderot in 1771, being Choiseul's *premier commis* had prevented him from telling 'the truth' in the debate on the Exclusif.[37]

It was the repeal in 1763 of the wartime policy of admitting neutral powers into colonial ports that prompted the lengthy dispute over the Exclusif. Following peace negotiations, French ports had successfully convinced the Crown of their ability to satisfy colonial needs, yet administrators in the Îles du Vent soon testified to the opposite. The Crown therefore drew up a memorandum on 18 April 1763 in which it permitted the colonies to purchase salted fish from foreigners in exchange for rum and molasses. Le Mercier went even further and opened Martinican ports to British slave traders, a decision he believed to be in line with Choiseul's oral instructions but which instead led to his and Fénelon's dismissal. Their successors, Victor Thérèse Charpentier d'Ennery and Louis de Thomassin de Peynier, nonetheless continued to admit foreign ships in the colonies, a choice Dubuc and Choiseul tacitly endorsed in their instructions to them.[38]

---

[36] On these comments on Dubuc, see MM to CM, Paris, 24 November 1764, F.M. vol. 26, 524; François Quesnay, 'Remarques sur l'opinion de l'auteur de l'*Esprit des lois concernant les colonies*' *Œuvres économique et philosophique*, 435. Denis Diderot, *Œuvres complètes de Diderot*, ed. J. Assézat, 20 vols. (Paris: Garnier Frères, Libraires-Éditeurs, 1875), vi, 417.

[37] Diderot, *Œuvres complètes de Diderot*, vi, Letter form 1771, 417.

[38] On Choiseul's recalling of Le Mercier, see letter from Choiseul to Le Mercier de la Rivière, 30 March 1764, ANOM, B 119. On 25 March 1765, Ennery and Peynier decreed that foreigners were permitted in the ports of Fort-Royal, Saint-Pierre, and La Trinité, to which was added the town

Ennery and Peynier's instruction from 1765 predated the 'Memorandum on the extent and the limits of the prohibitive laws of foreign commerce in the colonies' by several months. The instructions signalled to Martinique's administrators that a shift in policy was under way. As *premier commis*, Dubuc is likely to have drafted them in accordance with Choiseul's stated wishes, but notable phrases and tensions in the document indicate that Choiseul and Dubuc's policy agendas did not easily align. Profoundly self-congratulatory in tone, the instructions celebrated the French colonial system as being the only one to operate according to sound principles. Spanish colonisation, they noted, had merely contributed to the rise of foreign powers, while Portugal was nothing but 'an English colony'. The English, in turn, had permitted their colonies in America to produce commodities identical to those of the mother country, which meant that their colonies were marching 'rapidly toward their grand future ... of independence'. The only right way to view colonies, the instructions under-lined, was to understand that they were there to 'facilitate the consumption and outlet of metropolitan products'.[39]

The instructions even went out of their way to divest colonial admin-istrators of possible physiocratic leanings. As they explicated:

> one would be gravely mistaken to think that our colonies are like French provinces separated only by sea from our national territory [*sol national*]. They are as different from French provinces as the means are to an end. They are absolutely only commercial holdings [*des établissements de com-merce*], and to demonstrate this truth it suffices to see that in the kingdom, the administration strives to obtain a greater degree of consumption in favour of its national territory; in contrast, in the colonies, interests in their lands only arises from the consumption they give rise to. Such consumption is the unique object of these holdings, all of whom we would be wise to abandon should they cease to fulfil this purpose.

Thus, the Ministry of the Marine actively combated the Physiocrats' redefinition of colonies that circulated in the metropole and strove to block administrators in the colonies from following their ideas. According to the instructions, colonies should help generate prosperity at home by satisfying domestic consumer desires and stimulating domestic production, all the while helping the Crown enhance its power to satisfy broader

---

of Le Marin on 15 June. Tarrade, *Le commerce colonial*, i, 224, 230, 231, and 237. The decree was revoked by the duc de Praslin on 22 September 1766.

[39] 'Mémoire du Roy pour server d'Instruction au S. Cte d'Ennery Marechal de Camp, Gouverneur Lieutenant General et de Peynier Intendant de la Martinique', Versailles, 25 January 1765. ANOM B121.

European consumer demands and generate a trade surplus. As Ennery and Peynier's instructions further stated, the French Antilles were perfect colonies because they had none of the goods that French commerce offered, and they produced commodities that France itself lacked but foreigners purchased from it to the annual value of between 60 and 80 million livres, stimulating a favourable 'balance of commerce'.[40]

After this emphatic confirmation of the view of colonies as 'farms of the metropole', the instructions moved on to endorse the Exclusif, or so it seemed. Ennery and Peynier were told that to ensure that colonies continued to serve their purpose, 'they should be kept in the greatest state of riches possible and subjected to the most austere prohibitive law in favour of the metropole'. Yet they then immediately offered a rationale for the possible suspension of such prohibitive law: 'there might be circumstances', they noted, 'where colonial riches and colonial prohibition appear to be incompatible'. In those cases, 'the prohibitive law, as essential as it is ... must take a backseat'. Echoing here the advice offered by Quesnay and Mirabeau in *Philosophie rurale* (and Mirabeau's *L'Ami des hommes* before that), they noted that 'one has to found, one has to preserve, before one can enjoy'. The instructions, in fact, asserted that the metropole owed planters a softening of prohibition because the Exclusif stifled their freedom. As they said: 'a *colon* is nothing but a free planter on an enslaved territory [*un planteur libre sur un sol esclave*]', surely a statement inserted by the *premier commis* rather than Choiseul, since Dubuc would go on to repeat it again during the French Revolution. Because colonies were enslaved territories, Ennery and Peyniers should infuse their government 'with sweetness and charity', for instance by reinstating the decree of 18 April 1763, until the King had come up with a more definitive policy.[41]

When the content of Ennery and Peynier's instructions became known to the ports the high-pitched debate on the liberalisation of colonial commerce erupted. It mobilised some of the most prominent political economists of the day as well as representatives of commercial and colonial interests. In response to the complaints of the ports, Dubuc (and Choiseul) penned the widely circulated 'Memorandum on the extent and the limits of the prohibitive laws of foreign commerce in the colonies' based on the rationale that he and Choiseul had offered Ennery and Peynier. The 'Memorandum' was a masterful blend of political economy theory and

---

[40] On the rise of consumption in colonial commodities in Europe, see Vries, *The Industrious Revolution*, 154–64.
[41] 'Mémoire du Roy pour server d'Instruction au S. Cte d'Ennery Marechal de Camp, Gouverneur Lieutenant General et de Peynier Intendant de la Martinique'.

relevant data on patterns of trade which Dubuc submitted to the Council of Commerce on 18 April 1765. Although written by Dubuc, the 'Memorandum' nonetheless did not reflect his views. As Dubuc let Diderot know, Choiseul had read Dubuc's draft with delight, remarking 'Yes, this is what I asked for', to which Dubuc had replied that the memorandum was an expression of 'his obedience', not his opinions. Dubuc had then presented Choiseul with a second memorandum in which he went back on the initial one and, according to the *premier commis*, instead exposed 'the truth'. When Choiseul rejected the content of the second memorandum, Dubuc had merely responded *'servavi animam meam, j'ai sauvé mon âme'* – I have preserved my soul.[42]

Partial to the protests of French merchants, whose representatives outnumbered those of the colonies, the Council of Commerce in Paris rejected the proposal on 9 September 1765.[43] Supporters of liberalisation, however, quickly breathed new life into Dubuc and Choiseul's plans, not least Dubuc's colleagues in Martinique. Meeting on 21 November 1765 to compose a response to the ports' successful dismissal of the 'Memorandum', Martinique's Chambre d'agriculture let the Crown know that it had received numerous reports by chambers of commerce in France announcing a 'great trial' between domestic merchants and colonial inhabitants. It insisted that those whose very existence was at stake should be heard before a final decision was made. As it said: 'here [on Martinique], it is not only a matter of doctrine and opinion. It is a matter of facts of which we are the actual witnesses'. Seeking to support a softening of the Exclusif, the chamber haughtily pushed aside political economic doctrine, proclaiming that it refused to examine 'doctrine, the definition of colonies, their nature and their ties to the body of the state', and insisted that the administration of colonies was 'a practical science' that 'only tolerated definitions and principles that were born from observation, inspection, and analysis'.[44]

The chamber's embrace of empiricism took its members to a step-by-step rejection of the merchant memoranda in which the ports avowed that they were able to sufficiently provision the colonies. Nantes, the chamber noted, had listed that they had furnished the colonies with 22,000 slaves

---

[42] Diderot, *Œuvres complètes de Diderot*, vi, Letter form 1771, 417–18.

[43] The content of the memorandum is analysed in Tarrade, *Le commerce colonial*, Chapter 8; and Cheney, *Revolutionary Commerce*, 178–83.

[44] 'Observations de la Chambre d'Agriculture de la Martinique sur les mémoires des chambres de commerce du royaume', Martinique, 21 November 1765. Signed by Dubuq de Ste Preuve, Marraud, Désgrottes, Leyritz, Pelletier, Surirey, Crocquét fils. (Girardin and Le Jeune were absents), ANOM, C^{8B} 11 N57.

since the arrival of peace and another port listed a total of 30,000. Of these, the chamber reported that Martinique received only 1,710, or – in case the digits did not bring home their point – 'one thousand seven hundred and ten blacks, small and large, healthy and sick'. According to the voyages listed in the Trans-Atlantic Slave Trade Database, this number is largely correct. Martinique received 1,773 captives between 1763 and 1765, while Guadeloupe received 1,923 and Saint-Domingue 25,585 from French slave traders, thus confirming the unequal distribution of slaves in the French colonies.[45]

French slave traders justified this unevenness arguing that planters in the Îles du Vent did not purchase the slaves they brought, an accusation against which the chamber mustered a somewhat feeble response. Its members retorted that their inability to buy the captives brought to Martinique by French slave traders resulted from the policy of exporting manufactured goods of little value (*des pacotilles*) to the colonies for the *colons* to buy on credit. Planters developed debts to French merchant houses from such transactions, the chamber noted, which meant that they had no readily available cash with which to purchase the necessary slaves on the rare occasions that French slave traders did show up. Without slaves, however, plantations could not survive. To corroborate this latter point, the chamber supplied a list of fifty-one destroyed sugar plantations from the parishes of Saint-Pierre, Fort-Royal, Lamentin, and Rivière Salée, concluding with a plea to the government to look beyond the interests of the ports and listen to the voice of the colonies.

As this intervention shows, the chamber readily refused to embrace the terms with which much of the debate over the Exclusif was conducted in the metropole. In so doing, it echoed a parallel trend in France which set out to attack particularly the *économistes* as 'builders of systems' and emphasised the value of scientific empiricism. Yet in furnishing its rejoinder, its members also lent support to the view that planters were feckless consumers who carelessly dug themselves into a hole of debt to maintain an extravagant lifestyle with no intentions of climbing out again. Their eager to blame their financial troubles on French commerce led them to reference their own debilitating consumer habits as a primary cause for their want of slaves, although it is of course entirely possible that they felt pressured into purchasing *pacotilles* from their supplier-creditors.[46]

[45] Ibid. and *Voyages: The Trans-Atlantic Slave Trade Database*, www.slavevoyages.org.
[46] On the critique of builders of systems in Enlightenment debates, see Jessica Riskin, *Science in the Age of Sensibility: The Sentimental Empiricists of the French Enlightenment* (Chicago: University of Chicago Press, 2002), Chapter 4.

In contrast to the Chambre d'agriculture's critique of doctrine and definition in this debate, its erstwhile representative in France, Jean Dubuc, had no problem collaborating with 'builders of systems' to secure reform. Just how the Physiocrats got a hold of the 'Memorandum' submitted to the Council of Commerce is unclear, but in December 1765, they published it *in extensor* in the *Journal d'agriculture, du commerce et des finances,* edited by Du Pont de Nemours. The memorandum, in its published form, closely replicated the instructions to Ennery and Peynier, but also included new sections, including Forbonnais's 1753 phrase from his entry on colonies in the *Encyclopédie* that foreign trade in the colonies was an act of 'theft' against the metropole. However, it omitted the long critique of the physiocratic view of colonies as overseas provinces (whether or not it was Dubuc or the Physiocrats who had taken it out). Otherwise, it followed the strategy of affirming the principles of the Exclusif, only to problematise its ability to help colonies serve their intended purpose.[47] In the next six months, the *Journal d'agriculture, du commerce et des finances* carried articles on colonial regulation, all of which ultimately served to educate the reading public on the beatitude of free international trade – not just a softening of commercial prohibition. It was in this context that Quesnay penned his forceful rejection of Montesquieu's defence of the Exclusif discussed in Chapter 2.

With the sustained push by Dubuc, French Caribbean planters, and the Physiocrats to relax the Exclusif, the Crown moved ahead with its plans. In an *arrêt* of 29 July 1767, the new Minister of the Marine, duc de Praslin, authorised the opening of two free ports in the Caribbean, one at Môle Saint-Nicolas on the northern-western corner of Saint-Domingue, and one on St Lucia, a small island in the Îles du Vent. These free ports enabled French planters to go to St Lucia or Môle Saint-Nicolas to purchase wood, animals, and hides from foreigners in exchange for syrup and rum, thus giving planters access to a circumscribed list of goods that French commerce failed to supply. At the same time, the carefully enumerated list of goods was there to ensure that the French sugar, coffee, cotton, indigo, and slave trades remained exclusively in French hands.[48]

The policy shift was the outcome of Choiseul and Praslin's determination to relax the Exclusif, Dubuc's ability to articulate a convincing rationale for such change, pressure from the colonies, and the concerted

---

[47] 'Mémoire sur l'étendue & les bornes des Loix prohibitives du Commerce étranger dans nos colonies', in *Journal d'agriculture, du commerce et des finances*, December 1765, 87–22, 87–9, 92.

[48] Tarrade, *Le commerce colonial,* i, 358.

efforts of the Physiocrats to massage public opinion. Yet two other factors played a role as well. The first was the mushrooming of free ports within the Caribbean in the 1760s. The founding of free ports at St Lucia and Môle Saint-Nicolas followed on the heels of the British Free Port Act of 1 November 1766, in which the Dominican ports of Port Roseau and Prince Rupert's Bay were opened to foreign ships. After restoring Martinique and Guadeloupe to France, the British hoped that establishing two adjacent free ports on Dominica – conveniently sandwiched between Martinique and Guadeloupe – would allow British merchants to continue trading with the French islands, since planters on Guadeloupe and Martinique were eager to preserve their ties to Britain and access to its goods. Free ports, in this way, could serve as an economic weapon again France. If France created its own free port at St Lucia, it would obstruct such plans. Similarly, a French free port on Saint-Domingue would help stifle the trade that the Spanish had generated on their side of the island from its free port of Monte Christi, established in 1760. All these French and British free ports, moreover, might also challenge the Dutch free ports at Curaçao and Sint Eustatius and the Danish free port of Charlotte Amalie on St Thomas. Thus, while catering to planter interests in France and in the colonies as well as free trade doctrines en vogue among political economists, the founding of free ports at St Lucia and Môle Saint-Nicolas conveniently served to negate Britain's imperial agenda while also challenging the existence of Dutch, Danish, and Spanish free ports.[49]

It is conspicuous, moreover, that the policy shift succeeded during the administration of Praslin. Often portrayed as merely executing the policies of his cousin who had moved to the Ministry of Foreign Affairs in 1766, Praslin used his years as head of the Ministry of the Marine furthering his family's investments in and around the colony of Saint-Domingue. As Trevor Burnard and John Garrigus have pointed out, in the aftermath of the Seven Years War, Saint-Domingue 'attracted investments from leading figures at court'. Beyond Praslin, Jean-Joseph de Laborde, one of Louis XV's financiers and former receiver general, acquired a plantation in Saint-Domingue in 1768. The following year, Rohan-Montbazon,

---

[49] Dorothy Burne Goebel, 'The "New England Trade" and the French West Indies, 1763–1774: A Study in Trade Policies', *The William and Mary Quarterly*, 20, 3 (1963), 355. On the British free ports, see Frances Armytage, *The Free Port System in the British West Indies: A Study in Commercial Policy, 1766–1822* (London: Longmans, Green, 1953). On the Danish, Dutch, and Swedish ports, see Jardaan and Wilson, 'The Eighteenth-Century Danish, Dutch and Swedish Free Ports in Northeastern Caribbean'.

governor-general of Saint-Domingue, purchased a plantation outside Port-au-Prince, explaining to Praslin that 'Your example and that of several persons at court who own property in the colony led me to believe that I was equally allowed to acquire one'.[50] Jean Dubuc also owned plantations in the French Caribbean colonies, and so did other clerks within the Ministry of the Marine, such as François Beudet of whom we shall hear more in the next chapter. That office holders and policy makers were privately joining the ranks of absentee planters in Paris in the aftermath of the Seven Years War to make 'a quick profit' (as Turgot had noted) surely made the Crown further amenable to a softening of the Exclusif.

What Is a Colony?

In the debate over the Exclusif, Martinique's Chambre d'agriculture went out of its way to deride economic theory in favour of facts. Nonetheless, their refusal to engage in the debate over doctrine and definition was transient. For instance, with the renewed outbreak of warfare between France, Spain, the Dutch, and the British during the American Revolution, the chamber eyed an opportunity to make additional gains from an administration seemingly open to liberalisation. It did so through a redefinition of colonies and alongside other Martinican planters who were equally resourceful in their efforts to rethink and redefine colonies at this crucial juncture.

For the Chambre d'agriculture, the vehicle for a redefinition was the Treaty of Amity of 6 February 1778, that granted France and the new United States access to each other's ports during the war. With this treaty, and unlike existing descriptions of colonies in circulation – be it as 'farms of the metropole', 'enslaved territories', or 'overseas provinces' – the members of Martinique's Chambre d'agriculture promoted a vision of Martinique as a 'node of commerce'. Presenting this view in a proposal that the chamber wrote to Versailles on 22 January 1780, the chamber asked the administration to cast aside all prejudice and 'think in new ways about an entirely new state of affairs'. To set up its proposal, the chamber dived into a dispassionate analysis of Britain's relationship with its thirteen colonies drawing parallels to a sterile same-sex marriage. It argued that the similarity of climate between the metropole and the colonies was

---

[50] Quoted in Trevor Burnard and John Garrigus, *The Plantation Machine: Atlantic Capitalism in French Saint-Domingue and British Jamaica* (Philadelphia: University of Pennsylvania Press, 2016), 165.

a direct cause of the current Anglo-American war. As an ally of the thirteen colonies, France should therefore strive not to replace England, which would only reproduce commercial sterility. Instead, it should invite the Îles du Vent into the mix, like a *ménage à trois* (to continue the chamber's metaphor).[51]

Concretely, the chamber wanted American merchants to furnish the French colonies with commodities such as wood, barrels, horses, cattle, manioc, and potatoes in exchange for Martinican molasses and rum, which Americans coveted but for which French metropolitan merchants had no enthusiasm. To further entice American merchants, the colonies should also offer Americans French manufactured goods brought to the island by French merchants. Such a scenario, the chamber reminded Versailles, was not unlike that which had been seen previously on Martinique when French commerce had used the island as a point of departure for its illegal trade with the Spanish Coast of the Americas. While a Spanish ban had made the Franco-Spanish trade a risky endeavour, a legal and open trade among France, its Caribbean islands, and mainland America would be not only risk-free, but also hugely profitable, in that it would allow the French colonists to free up more territory for cultivation. With their hinterlands entirely devoted to sugar, coffee, cotton, or indigo production and its ports booming with French manufactured goods, the French Caribbean islands would become a commercial nodal point – a *noeud de commerce* – between France and America.

The chamber even claimed that the arrangement they proposed would offer France an edge in the international race for industrialisation. It pointed out that the voluminous trade England currently enjoyed with their North American colonies would fall into French hands, which in turn would help secure the American Revolution and the Franco-American alliance. Just as importantly, by replacing American importation of British manufactured goods with French ones, France would retard the development of manufacture in America. In so doing, it would build up its own industry while guiding this new nation towards agriculture and navigation instead. America would easily identify the advantages of purchasing French manufactured goods in the French colonies rather than in the French metropole. Navigation would be shorter and American merchants would receive a faster return on their invested capital, 'finding in the colonies all the [French] provinces gathered together'. In a wonderful mixing of metaphors, the chamber noted that the thirteen colonies were

---

[51] Chambre d'agriculture to Sartine, 22 January 1780. ANOM C[8A] 79, f. 268.

'a fruit detached from its mother'. Given that they did not have a natural link to France, one should be forged based on commercial interests.

Subsequent changes in commercial policy demonstrate the degree to which the Crown was willing to accept such a proposal. After the war, the Council of State drew up the *arrêt* of 30 August 1784, which transferred the status of free ports to Saint-Pierre on Martinique, Pointe-à Pitre on Guadeloupe, Carénage on Sainte-Lucie, Scarborough on Tabago, and to Cap Français, Port-au-Prince, Les Cayes-Saint-Louis on Saint-Domingue. Goods admitted in the 1767 decree were reaffirmed together with new ones such as rice, corn, vegetables, salted fish, salted beef, and – for the Îles du Vent – slaves, all of which foreigners, and particularly Americans, could supply in exchange for molasses, rum, and French manufactured goods. With such changes in place, the Îles du Vent, like a new *noeud de commerce* and to the tune of domestic protest, started bouncing back from their mid-century economic low. In 1788, Martinique's slave population had increased to 71,438 and its sugar plantations to 324, up from 299 in 1762 (as well as 937 coffee plantations, 123 cacao plantations, and 260 cotton plantations). That same year, Guadeloupe counted 85,461 slaves (more than double the number in 1752) and 362 sugar plantations.[52]

The decree of 30 August 1784 reignited a pamphlet war between port merchants, political economists, and representatives in the colonies. Inevitably, it also buoyed discussions of the definition and role of a colony. It was while this debate raged that Jean Dubuc, no longer *premier commis*, eyed an opportunity to put forth his own views on the matter rather than those of Choiseul. Published as *Le Pour et le Contre*, his take on colonies appeared as a rejoinder to a publication by Jacques Risteau, former director of the Compagnie des Indes and trader at Bordeaux, in which the latter charged that colonies were created by and for the metropole and that their commerce therefore belonged to it.[53] In *Le Pour et le Contre*, Dubuc introduced a new definition of colonies to combat Risteau's views. He insisted that colonies were nothing but 'the sum of their agricultural production', and as such they were neither created by nor for the metropole. Slaves were the creators of the agricultural produce, Dubuc underlined, and they had been furnished as much by foreign merchants as by French ones. Rather than stressing that that colonies therefore belonged to

---

[52] Blérald, *Histoire économique*, 28. Tarrade, *Le commerce colonial*, 531–2. On data on coffee, cacao, and cotton plantations, see 'Observations des commissaires du commerce de la Martinique sur le procès-verbal de l'Assemblée colonial de cette îles. Imprimé à Saint-Vincent par Joseph Berrow', 14 January 1788, ANOM C⁸ᴮ 16. Internet reference: ark:/61561/zn401g45zj.

[53] On Jacques Risteau, see Saugera, *Bordeaux port négrier*, 93.

slaves, Dubuc's point was that colonies were created by numerous peoples from a variety of nations. Nor were colonies created for the metropole. They should, however, 'exist to be as useful as possible to it' by improving French national commerce beyond its domestic means – an aim achieved 'by converting goods produced in the metropole into other more useful and more sellable commodities'. To Dubuc, the Exclusif was a policy that obstructed rather than enable this ultimate goal. Writing against 'the inflexible professors of prohibitive laws' – an obvious stab at Montesquieu, Forbonnais, and their followers – Dubuc charged that the Exclusif followed 'the mercantile spirit', strove towards 'monopoly', and 'had been dictated by merchants'. Like Quesnay and Mirabeau before him, he underlined that catering only to merchant interests hampered national interests.[54]

The crossfire that followed Dubuc's publication emboldened proponents of the colonies to assert in stronger terms their refusal to be subservient to metropolitan commercial interests. Against the many ripostes he incited from merchant communities, he found support for his agenda and vision from old friends and the growing lobby of Caribbean planters residing in Paris. As the author of the *Mémoires secrets* reported, the Physiocrat Abbé Baudeau was preparing a rebuttal of the ports' critique of Dubuc in which 'the principles of the economists should serve as base'. So was the group of members belonging to the *club Américains* (absentee planters in Paris).[55] Of these, Hilliard d'Auberteil's intervention is the most famous, though it merely replicated Dubuc's *Le Pour et le Contre*.[56] A more radical response came from Pierre-Ulric Dubuisson, son of a doctor and slave owner on Martinique. Like Dubuc, Dubuisson supported the 30 August decree but he also wholly embraced the idea that colonies were nothing but provinces like those of the metropole:

> The French American colonies are agricultural settlements . . . they are provinces of the French kingdom, like Normandy, Brittany, and Guyenne; and if it were a question of the pre-eminence between the integral parts of the empire, I would not hesitate for one moment to assign greater importance to the colonies.[57]

---

[54] Jean Dubuc, *Le Pour et le Contre sur un objet de grande discorde et d'importance majeure. Convient-il à l'administration de céder aux Étrangers dans le Commerce de la Métropole avec ses Colonies* (London, 1784), 8 and 18–19.

[55] *Mémoires secrets pour servir à l'histoire de la République des Lettres en France depuis 1762 jusqu'à nos jours*, 36 vols. (London: John Adams, 1786), 24 March 1785, xxviii, 201–2.

[56] Hilliard d'Auberteuil, *Commerce des colonies, ses principes & ses loix. La paix est le temps de régler & d'agrandir le commerce* (1785).

[57] Pierre-Ulric Dubuisson, *Lettres critiques et politiques, sur les colonies et le commerce des villes maritimes de France, adressées à G. T. Raynal par M.* *** (Geneva, 1785), 20. On Dubuisson, see *Commission*

The view that colonies were equal to provinces if not of superior importance to the prosperity of the French colonial empire could thus be a pillar
of planter political economy. When convenient, physiocratic ideas and
vocabulary, helped fuel an increasingly bold creole political economic
discourse with which planters inserted themselves in the broader debate
on French colonial commerce.

The Debt Monster

Planters' advocacy of the admission of foreign merchants in colonial ports
can be construed as a quest for legal parity with the domestic provinces – if
the latter could trade with foreigners then so could 'overseas provinces'.
That, for sure, was the premise upon which the Physiocrats had promoted
free trade and colonial integration. Planters, however, were only interested
in supporting legal universalism at specific moments. More often, they
fiercely promoted special laws in the colonies based on a rationale that
echoed Montesquieu's climate theory. This predilection for special laws
comes out particularly clearly in discussions over the endemic problem of
colonial debt. Planters' discussions on how to redress this issue allowed
them to rehearse arguments about the inappropriate application of the
French legal system in the colonies that would feature prominently in the
debates on colonies during the French Revolution.

Along with the Exclusif, the indebtedness of the French Caribbean sugar
planters was the principal cause of tension between commercial and
agricultural interests in France and the colonies. In the metropole and in
towns such as Saint-Pierre, complaints of planters' *mauvaise volonté* (lack of
goodwill) circulated among creditors, while planters constantly talked
about the *monstre des dettes*. In the immediate aftermath of the Seven
Years War, the issue was becoming a major concern to Martinique's local
administration who complained that private funds to help planters rebuild
the colony were no longer forthcoming. During their administration,
Fénelon and Le Mercier had therefore tried to restore trust by proposing
a new means to punish delinquent debtors. The traditional mode of
punishment was imprisonment, but according to Fénelon it was proving
counterproductive, because no payment came of it and because the
incarceration of whites sent a wrong signal to the enslaved population.
Consequently, he and Le Mercier collaborated with Martinique's Superior

Historique et Archélogique de la Mayenne (Laval: Imprimerie-Librairie V A. Gouphil, 1905), xxi,
257–71.

Council to craft a decree that authorised the seizing of plantation slaves belonging to the indebted party. Enforcing this decree required an annulment of Article 48 of the Code Noirs which stipulated that plantation slaves were bound to the territory and could not be seized to pay off a planter's debt (*l'immobilisation des esclaves de culture*).[58] Neither Fénelon nor Le Mercier had the power to annul it. For the proposed decree to be legally binding, Versailles would have to ratify it, yet no such ratification was forthcoming.

With no change on the horizon, the issue reappeared in 1774 during the administration of Pierre Étienne Bourgeois de Boynes (Minister of the Marine from 1771 to 1774). Like in 1763, it was local officials who insisted on the need to act. Referencing Fénelon and Le Mercier's proposal, the new governor-general and intendant, Vital Auguste, marquis de Grégoire, comte de Nozières and Philippe-Athanase de Tascher, observed that 'years had passed without the court being able to sanction this decree'. They further informed that Martinique's Superior Council continued to support the seizure of plantation slaves. Unlike their predecessors, however, Nozières and Tascher cautioned against the adoption of this approach. Instead, they recommended looking at a solution offered by the Chambre d'agriculture, a proposal that aimed to solve the cause of debt and help remedy existing debts.[59]

Opening with a commitment 'to fight the debt monster', the chamber's proposal hinged on a rejection of the appropriateness of applying the Coutume de Paris in the colonies. This system, sculpted according to the needs and customs of the broader Paris region, insisted upon equality among all heirs. Perhaps unaware that the Coutume had already been adjusted in the colonies to have children share only the *value* of the plantation, not its concrete components, the chamber argued that the Coutume de Paris was unsuitable for the colonies because it made the heir who agreed to take over the plantation indebted to his or her siblings. The solution to this problem, the chamber argued, was therefore 'in the hands of

---

[58] Fénelon and Le Mercier de la Rivière to Choiseul, 25 September 1763, ANOM C⁸ᴬ 65, f. 37. And 'Extrait des registres du Conseil Supérieur', 6 September 1763, ANOM C⁸ᴬ 65, f. 89. Article 48 of the *Code Noir* stated: 'Ne pourront aussi les esclaves travaillant actuellement dans les sucreries, indigoteries et habitations, âgées de quatorze ans et au-dessus jusqu'à soixante ans, être saisis pour dettes, sinon pour ce qui sera dû du prix de leur achat, ou que la sucrerie ou indigoterie, ou habitation dans laquelle ils travaillent, soient saisies réellement; défendons, à peine de nullité, de procéder par saisie réelle et adjudication par décret sur les sucreries, indigoteries ni habitations, sans y comprendre les esclaves de l'âge susdit et y travaillant actuellement', in *Le Code Noir*, 186.

[59] 'Question mue sur la saisie des negres de culture', St Pierre, Martinique 3 March 1774, Noziere and Tascher, ANOM C⁸ᴬ 73, f. 15 N101.

the legislator'. Offering a statement that could have come straight from Quesnay or Mirabeau, it asserted that 'agriculture is the mother of laws; she gave birth to them and made them necessary. The goddess Ceres was called Legifera. The state of agriculture thus leads to laws by a necessary chain'. The chamber then diverged from this physiocratic tenor towards a montesquieuan view, arguing that particular climates needed particular legal systems, including particular inheritance laws. While the Coutume de Paris might work in the metropole and during the early stages of colonisation in the Caribbean, current needs in Martinique required a new tailor-made legal code.[60]

In their argument against equality among heirs, the chamber mischaracterised metropolitan practices. The Coutume de Paris did not pertain to the metropole in its entirety but to Paris and its hinterlands. Their proposal to let a father appoint an heir at the expense of other siblings (*droit du père de famille de faire un aîné*), was also already in existence in France (particularly among the nobility in a number of provinces) and had already been proposed as a solution to planter debt by Le Mercier in his memorandum to Choiseul in 1762. Echoing Le Mercier's suggestion, the chamber nonetheless offered a unique rationale for their proposal, claiming that the Martinican climate's impact on men's reproductive abilities necessitated a particular inheritance law for the colonies. As it explained, since Martinique's 'healthy climate' (*la salubrité du climat*) increased a planter's virility he often had more heirs than fathers did elsewhere. A shift away from 'the law of an equal share', which contradicted 'the nature of these colonies', and towards a law that allowed the father to appoint an heir would better suit the colony. Though this remained implicit, the chamber's proposal implied that they wished to be treated as nobles, a status numerous planters (including the Dubuc family) strove to obtain. To further goad the Crown towards reform, the chamber underlined that an adoption of their proposed laws would create colonial subjects whose allegiance would naturally align with the political constitution of the French colonial empire. As it said: 'a subordination of a family under one person, would make the family appropriate subjects of a monarchical state'. Thus, 'a simple scribble with the legislator's pen' could cure the root cause of debt in the colonies and help turn planters' into amenable subjects.

---

[60] 'Extrait des registres des délibérations de la chambre d'agriculture en l'Isle Martinique', 12 February 1775, ANON C⁸ᴬ 74, f. 67. On modifications to the *Coutume de Paris* in the colonies, see Géraud-Llorca, 'La Coutume de paris outre-mer', 239.

In their proposal on how to solve the liquidation of existing debt, the chamber exhibited for the first time a real effort to incorporate merchant interests into its deliberations. They suggested creating a land registry in which all debts could be registered and which would function as a pseudo stock exchange: the clerk registering the debt would divide it into shares, with the value of each not surpassing 500 livres. As shareholders, the moneylenders would then be allowed part of the fruits of production – the only means with which a planter's debt should be repaid – and to sell their shares should they so desire. To better explain their proposed idea, the chamber compared the indebted plantation to a merchant ship, where 'one single ship often has several owners, but which is administered by one single outfitter'. Similarly to a ship, a plantation could have several 'co-propriétaires' and still be administered by one person. To the chamber this suggestion would have two positive outcomes: the indebted planter would be free of his debt and be able to turn his attention and energy towards production without fearing his creditors who were now co-owners; second, the creditor would be able to either sell his shares in the plantation and free up his capital, or remain a shareholder and participate in discussions on how to manage the plantation and divide up revenues. In this way, debt could be redeemed in a gentle (*doux*) and liberating manner, while uniting the interests of the indebted planter and his merchant creditor.[61]

Despite their genuine effort to tackle planter debt, the chamber and the local administration's wishes for legal reform fell into oblivion. Neither the suggestion to alter inheritance laws nor the proposal on how to liquidate debt led to any immediate change in the Îles du Vent. The reasons for this are unknown. Edith Géraud-Llorca has pointed out that seizing plantation slaves would go against the very constitution of these colonies and the way in which the application of the Coutume de Paris had evolved around the privileging of plantations and their ability to produce rare commodities for the metropole. Taking their slaves would negate their purpose. Another problem was that the regulation of property in France was usually in local hands. The King, however absolute he claimed to be, was generally reluctant to meddle in questions of property law. It is possible that the Crown was equally reluctant to intervene in the regulation of colonial property as well.[62]

---

[61] 'Extrait des registres des délibérations de la chambre d'agriculture en l'Isle Martinique', 12 February 1775, ANON C^8A 74, f. 67.

[62] Fénelon to Choiseul, Martinique St Pierre 12 February 1764. ANOM C^8A 66, f. 9. Géraud-Llorca, 'La Coutume de paris outre-mer', 248. On royal reluctance, see David Parker, 'Absolutism, Feudalism and Property Rights in the France of Louis XIV', *Past & Present*, 179 (2003), 73.

A lack of royal interference therefore prompted French creditors to take matters into their own hands. Albane Forestier's study of the Nantes merchants, Honoré and Louis Chaurand, shows that in the 1780s, money lenders were increasingly able to oversee how their debtor in the colonies managed their plantation. Loan contracts began to include 'the mortgaging of the estate to the creditor', giving 'merchants controlling rights over the estates of planters who could not replay their debts'.[63] It is unclear whether these strategies spread to the Îles du Vent prior to the French Revolution. What we do see, is a willingness on behalf of Martinique's Chambre d'agriculture and the Superior Council to seek a solution to the problem of debt. Proposing an alteration of inheritance laws in montesquieuan terms, they lobbied for a law particular to the colonies. Offering advice of what such a law should be, they further implied that planters – with their better understanding of the colonies, their climate, and the particular society the ensued from it – should act as Legifera Ceres.[64]

Slaves – the 'Domestic Enemy'

The debate on seizing plantation slaves to force planters to pay their debt was but one of many times that Martinique's Chambre d'agriculture commented on slavery in the colony. As could be expected, slavery was braided into their concerns for food supplies, debt, local order, and revolt. Yet unlike in the metropole, where a growing number of *philosophes* and political economists started to question the utility and morality of slavery, the chamber never expressed an ounce of regret about the colonies' exploitative labour system. Only in moments of scarcity did the suffering of slaves become an issue and in those instances the chamber used slaves' misery as a vehicle to scold French commerce for its failure to provision the islands. Nevertheless, there was one concern on which the chamber and the growing number of critics of slavery in the metropole saw eye to eye, namely that the slave population constituted an imminent threat to the very plantation complex of which they were an essential part.

With their focus on mono-crop cultivation, plantation owners often struggled to obtain adequate food supplies for their slaves. Article XXII

---

[63] Albane Forestier, 'A "considerable credit" in the late eighteenth-century French West Indian Trade: the Chaurands of Nantes', *French History*, 25, 1 (2011), 60–61.

[64] On Saint-Domingue, creole jurists in these years also adopted a selective reading of Montesquieu to argue that an understanding of the particular mores of the island was 'a prerequisite for the very ability to speak about colonial law', let alone compose it. See Malick W. Ghachem, 'Montesquieu in the Caribbean: The Colonial Enlightenment between *Code Noir* and *Code Civil*', *Historical Reflections/Réflexions Historiques* 25, 2 (1999), 191–3.

of the Code Noir charged planters to feed their enslaved labourers, stipulating in detail the amount of beef, fish, and manioc flour planters had to distribute to their slaves each week. Even so, directives were regularly ignored, and malnourishment among slaves was widespread. Only the minority could boast, like the Dubuc family, of having 'well-fed' slaves. The members of the Chambre d'agriculture played on this common knowledge, conveying in their letters to the Ministry of the Marine that many owners no longer honoured the Code, but instead gave slaves Saturdays off to find their own food. Among those who continued to respect the law, according to the chamber, few had the means to feed their slaves. Most were forced to purchase food on credit but as the discussion on planter debt revealed, credit was increasingly hard to come by.[65]

During times of war, food provisioning was even harder. In 1776, the chamber repeated its usual complaint against an absent French commerce before it requested access to the royal storage houses. Admitting that such food was supposed to go to troops on the island, they avowed that there would be no island left to protect if the slaves starved to death.[66] As the American Revolution progressed, the chamber found wanting food provisions a ticking bomb under their feed. It even blamed some of the Ministry of the Marine's initiatives to strengthen its colonial commerce for their current distress. As they noted, French naval build-up after the Seven Years War, may have ensured that a large number of warships were now patrolling Caribbean waters to protect its colonies but its presence increased the number of mouths the island had to feed. Similarly, they complained that the now one-year-old Franco-American alliance treaty which allowed Americans to trade with the French colonies had not carried fruit. Only those provisions that the French were able to obtain from the Dutch island of Sint Eustatius alleviated the colony yet this option had also come to an end. The British had depleted this island of goods to nourish its own colonies and were blocking other powers from gaining access. For all of those reasons, the chamber concluded, Martinique might be safe from the external foe, but faced a great threat from 'the domestic enemy'.[67]

---

[65] The Code Noir, Articles XXII and XXIV. On the nourishment of slaves in the French Caribbean colonies, see Gabriel Debien, 'La Nourriture des esclaves sur les plantations des Antilles Françaises aux XVIIe et XVIIIe siècles', *Caribbean Studies*, 4, 2 (1964), 8. See also Bertie Mandelblatt, 'A Transatlantic Commodity: Irish Salt Beef in the French Atlantic World', *History Workshop Journal*, 63, 1 (2008), 18–47.

[66] Letter from the *chambre d'agriculture* to the local administration, 15 June 1776. ANOM C^{8A} 75, f. 66.

[67] 'Mémoire sur l'état actuel de la colonie', May 1779, ANON C^{8A} 78 F261. Planters' emphasis on the starvation of slaves has been seen as part of their scheme to push for free trade in the colonies.

For the members of the chamber, starving slaves was a threat not only to colonial production but also to planters and their families. As the chamber lamented 'who can act as a master over the slave he does not feed?' How to 'contain a desperate starving multitude?' In its view, the most dangerous slaves were those working in towns who had no way of cultivating their own food and therefore turned to theft and violence. There were already examples of decapitated cattle on the grazing fields, testifying to the horrors following on the heels of slave starvation. Emphasising the particular dangers of famine in times of war, the chamber warned that 'if the slave is difficult to contain when he is left unnourished, if this multitude who create the riches of the colony cause the plantation owner the highest anxiety during periods of famine, what anxiety should it not cause the government as well as the plantation owner in the presence of the enemy!' Over a decade prior to the slave revolt on Saint-Domingue that sparked the Haitian Revolution, Martinican planters imagined the consequences of a large-scale slave revolt. But rather than throwing their weight behind the search for a potentially more profitable, manageable, and less exploitative system within which to procure the desired cash crops for the metropole, planters rigorously clung to the plantation complex instead.

Taxes

The chamber's attention to slavery, provisioning, debt, and commerce allowed its members to appropriate different economic arguments in circulation to craft their responses to the metropole. As owners of large sugar plantations, they seemed to have a predilection for an agrarian political economy that resembled aspects of Physiocracy, which placed faith in the power of agricultural production as a source of wealth and attacked monopoly trade. That this had little to do with a doctrinal commitment but instead stemmed from a partial overlap in outlook is reaffirmed in an analysis of the drawn-out debate on colonial taxes that lasted from 1763 to the French Revolution. Throughout these decades, the chamber's interventions had minimal impact on the Crown's fiscal policies beyond the year 1763 when French rule was restored on the island. Instead, like in debates on debt and legal reform, the Chambre d'agriculture's attention to fiscal policy proved most useful in helping its members articulate and rehearse a strong creole argument for reform.

Joseph Horan, 'The Colonial Famine Plot: Slavery, Free Trade, and Empire in the French Atlantic, 1763–1791', *International Review of Social History*, 55, special issue (2010), 103–21.

Colonies were expected to contribute to the cost of their local administration, a policy implemented with their inclusion in the royal domains
in 1733. Local taxes went into the royal treasury of the island, which the
Crown had taken over from the General Farm in 1732.[68] In the Îles du Vent,
the main source of revenue stemmed from the *capitation* (a tax on slaves
similar to the poll tax), while milder taxes fell on commodities, town houses,
and cabarets. The larger plantation owners, whose plantations sometimes
counted slaves in the hundreds, therefore carried the heaviest fiscal load.
Though this was in itself a cause for planter disgruntlement, the fact that
taxes had to be paid in coin aggravated matters since, as we have already seen,
it tied them to the *commissionnaires* at the port of Saint-Pierre.[69]

Like in metropolitan France, the King and his Council of State fixed the
colony's annual fiscal contribution. It was left to the governor and the
intendant to levy taxes in a manner acceptable to the local population,
although the latter had the final say. More often than not, the Crown failed
to inform the local administration of the amount of tax it expected. In
those instances, local officials followed the most recent set of instructions.
Upon the retrocession of Martinique in 1763, the King requested 750,000
livres for the remaining six months, and 1.5 million livres for the
following year. Because of the deplorable state in which Martinique
found itself after the war, the local administrators managed to reduce the
amount to 1.2 million.[70] Taxation remained at that level until the 1766
fiscal year, at which point the Crown lowered it to 900,000 livres due to the
island's continued struggle to recover. The following year, a hurricane
destroyed large parts of the island, leading to a full tax exemption. Between
1768 and 1771, taxes stayed at 900,000 livres, but then increased to
1.2 million between 1772 and 1778, after which the Crown agreed to
permanently lower the amount to 1 million livres thanks to repeated appeals
by local administrators. This was also the sum requested by the French
Revolutionary government.[71]

---

[68] See the *Arrêt du Conseil d'Etat ordonnant que les droits du domaine d'Occident ne font plus partie du
bail des Fermes*, 5 August 1732. As cited in Gérard Gabriel Marion's detailed account of the financial
administration of old-regime Martinique. Marion, *L'administration des finances*, 202. On colonial
taxes see also Duchêne, *Histoire des Finances Coloniales*.

[69] Marion, *L'administration des finances*, 70–75.

[70] Choiseul to Fénelon and Le Mercier de la Rivière, Versailles 26 February 1764, ANOM B119, ff. 14,
250. They informed Choiseul that if the colony was charged with such a high tax, the Crown would
'lose that which you have worked to preserve'. Fénelon and Le Mercier de la Rivière to Choiseul,
1 September 1763, ANOM C⁸ᴬ 65, f. 92.

[71] Ordonnance de MM. Les Général et Intendant, sur l'Imposition. Number 352, 12 March 1766. In
Code de la Martinique, ii, 464–71. Ordonnance de MM. Les Général et Intendant, concernant
l'Imposition pour l'année 1768, Number 388, 5 February 1768. In *Code de la Martinique*, ii, 554–6.

The stipulation that taxes should be levied in a form 'agreeable' to the local population became a particularly difficult balancing act after the British occupation of the Îles du Vent. As we saw, Rufane had consulted with the local population to lower the risks of revolt. To appease planters upon retrocession, the French Crown followed suit and ordered Fénelon and Le Mercier de la Rivière to call an assembly constituted by the local administration and representatives of the Superior Council (M. Perrinet) and the Chambre d'agriculture (Dubuc de Sainte Preuve) to discuss the King's order to levy 750,000 livres (*argent des isles*) and find the 'most secure, prompt, unbiased, and least painful' way to levy the sum, and double the amount the following years. The plan the assembly came up with enjoyed only short-lived success, because it conformed entirely to the preferences of Martinique's plantocracy. It is worth examining, nonetheless, because it would influence all subsequent debates on taxation down to the calling of the Estates General.[72]

Both Fénelon, Le Mercier de la Rivière, and the plantocracy considered a levy of taxes in 1763 untimely given the post-war state of desolation in the colony. Forced to respect royal demands, the assembly therefore underlined that taxes should be levied only 'on the *produit net*, meaning on what remains of the total production of land once the necessary funds to ensure such production and the livelihood of the cultivator have been deducted'. Any taxation that ate into such '*fonds d'avance*', as a high tax on slaves did, would destroy agricultural production. The best time to levy a tax on the net product, the report highlighted, was therefore when the commodities left the island. The tax on export should be elevated from one to six per cent, a proposition that went against a royal directive not to increase taxes on imports and exports since this could be seen as an attack on French commercial interests.

If the assembly's attempt to shift all taxes away from big plantations and towards commerce in towns was not already obvious, its further recommendations made it blatantly clear. It suggested transferring the

---

Ordonnance de MM. Les Général et Intendant, portant modification sur l'Imposition sur la Martinique, la Guadeloupe et Dépendances, pour l'année 1772. Number 456, 9 March 1772. In *Code de la Martinique*, iii, 115–19. See Ordinances number 527 for 1778, number 558 for 1779, number 568 for 1780, number 600 for 1782, number 615 for 1783, there is no ordinance for 1784, number 654 for 1785, number 678 for 1786 in In *Code de la Martinique*, iii, and ordinances number 694 for 1787, number 719 for 1788, and number 749 for 1789, In *Code de la Martinique*, iv.

[72] 'Procès-Verbal de l'assemblée convoqué à la Martinique en exécution de l'arrêt du conseil d'état du 9 avril dernier', 26 July 1763, ANOM C⁸ᴬ 65, f. 8. The King's order was the Arrêt du Conseil d'Etat of 9 April 1763. See 'Extrait des registres des délibérations de la chambre d'agriculture en l'Isle Martinique', 8 February 1775. ANOM C⁸ᴮ 14, n. 5.

weight of the head tax from plantation slaves onto those slaves working in urban settings as craftsmen or day labourers. This was to punish their owners, it explained, whom ought to have made such town slaves available for planation work. Keeping slaves on plantations would have the added bonus of freeing up employment opportunities for potential white settlers, the assembly noted, thereby referencing the sensitive issue of European migration to the colonies and the poor employment opportunities of the *petits blancs*. The assembly's effort to shield plantations from taxes, moreover, only pertained to the biggest estates. It argued that small rice, manioc, and vegetable-plantations – plantations most likely in the hands of the island's free people of colour – should continue to pay a high tax on their slaves since these plantations currently profited from the widespread scarcity of food. Finally, it suggested introducing a tax on industry and on the houses in towns, most of which belonged to people involved in commerce rather than agriculture.

The assembly's recommendations, which were duly adopted for the rest of the 1763 fiscal year, have been seen as a product of Le Mercier de la Rivière's physiocratic persuasions.[73] Certainly, the proposal echoed strands of Physiocracy which the intendant would have become familiar with during his return to the metropole during the British occupation were he not already. Aside from the use of specific terms such as *fond d'avance* and *produit net*, the report echoed Quesnay and Mirabeau's argument in *Théorie de l'impôt* (1760) that taxes should not be raised without consent.[74] Yet Quesnay and Mirabeau had also said that the French government should replace its complicated tax system with a single land tax levied on the net product of land and be imposed immediately at the source of revenues. This was not what the assembly proposed. It was also not what Le Mercier had originally suggested to the assembly, namely that planters pay only half of the annual taxes and town dwellers the other half. The assembly had pushed aside Le Mercier's suggestion and gone instead with a proposal that benefitted solely the plantocracy.[75] In his correspondence with the government, Le Mercier therefore distanced himself from the assembly, informing Choiseul that 'the assembly members laid down the law, their views were uniform, and in this case, it was laid upon me to comply. I therefore did so because I had to'.[76]

[73] May, *Le Mercier de la Rivière*, 50–53.

[74] Marquis de Mirabeau, *Théorie de l'Impot* (1761), 72, 125, 150, and 160.

[75] 'Précis du mémoire envoyé à M. Le duc de Choiseul concernant l'imposition à établir sur la Martinique' [1763], ANOM C^{8A} 65, f. 44.

[76] Le Mercier de la Rivière to Choiseul, letter number 64, ANOM C^{8}, ff. 332–4. Once the result of the reform was known, he continued to distance himself from it, but he also reminded the Crown of its

Although the assembly rather than Le Mercier had laid down the law in 1763, their fiscal success was transitory. Peynier, Le Mercier's successor, annulled it the following year and reintroduced the poll tax on plantation slaves. In doing so, he countered the views of Martinique's Chambre d'agriculture and the governor-general, all of whom recommended the continuation of the 1763 reform. Peynier found that its continuation would upset commercial interests but also defy the purpose of colonial taxation. As he noted in his letter to the Crown: 'a tax levied on goods leaving the island falls on French commerce, while the intention is to tax the planter [*le colon*]'.[77]

Peynier's return to the poll tax did not end discussions over the 1763 reform; the latter remained a source of contention down to the French Revolution. In 1775, during a campaign to halt taxation on coffee that was orchestrated collectively by the deputies of Guadeloupe, Martinique, and Saint-Domingue in Paris, Dubuc Duferret contacted the Chambre d'agriculture in Martinique requesting its support. The members of the chamber duly added firepower to their deputy's pleadings, stressing in their report to the Crown that the exemption of coffee from taxes in 1764 had boosted coffee production. Coffee, they said, had been the hope of the colony after the loss of cocoa production and the destruction of numerous sugar plantations by ants. Adding a new tax on coffee that would come in addition to the one that had already been introduced in 1771 would reverse this success. Doing their best to support Duferret, the report nonetheless quickly shifted gear, beginning instead to excoriate the suppression of the 1763 reform.[78]

Complaining that it rarely had the opportunity to discuss taxation, the chamber blamed 'the reign of custom' (*l'empire de l'usage*) on the revocation of the 1763 reform. Reminding the government of the series of horrors Martinique had witnessed in recent years – war, hurricanes, fires, and the infestation of sugarcane by ants – it solicited it to 'see the truth', which was 'demonstrated in all of the theories of those who have studied this matter: that colonies are not liable to any tax' since only 'prosperous colonies' were useful to the metropole. Starting with what was a direct reiteration of

decision to tax a population in distress. See 'Mémoire sur les dépenses de la Martinique et sur les fonds assignés pour payer ces mêmes dépenses', Mercier de la Rivière, 25 December [November], 1763, ANOM C⁸ᴬ 65, f. 335.

[77] Peynier to Minister 'Avantages comparés de la capitation et de la taxation des denrées; avis émis par l'intendant de Peynier', 10 December 1765, ANOM C⁸ᴬ 67, f. 110.

[78] 'Extrait des régistres des délibérations de la chambre d'agriculture', 8 February 1775. ANOM C⁸ᴮ 14, n.5.

Mirabeau and Quesnay's insistence in *Philosophie rurale* that colonies should only be taxed once fully developed and only fall on the surplus and not the means of production (slaves), the chamber then tilted towards Forbonnais and emphasised that the role of the colony was to produce for the metropole. But it then added to the initial 1763 reform, that taxation should happen not in the colonies but in the metropole. As it explained in efflorescent terms: 'The hand that reaches out for the means of production in the colonies, harvests the flowers, and deprives itself of the promised fruit. It is the mature fruit, that the state and the individual, should plan to harvest'. The fruit, however, had only matured once it had reached 'the markets in the metropole'. Quoting the *Histoire des deux Indes*, which by then was one of the best-sellers in the Atlantic World, the chamber concluded:

> Far from attacking . . . the cultivation of the colonies through taxation (says the author of *l'Histoire philosophique* (volume 5 p. 221) *et politique des établissements dans le nouveau monde*) it should be encouraged by liberal means, since, by the state of prohibition in which they are kept, these liberal means will necessarily return to the mother country all of the benefits that they will give rise to.

Marshalling the most colourful language and influential political economic doctrines, the efforts of the Chambre d'agriculture to restore the 1763 fiscal programme fell, if not on deaf ears, then ears that were already overly familiar with excuses why a particular town, fiefdom, or province should not pay taxes. Its members fought for decades to shift the weight of taxation onto different shoulders, but whereas it had managed to put a stick in the wheel of French commerce with the reform of the Exclusif, fiscal policy proved as difficult to modify in the colonies as in the metropole. The real result of the chamber's fight against the status quo, therefore, was the formulation of a clear fiscal agenda, which its members could take to the National Assembly once the Revolution broke out.

Fiscal demands were not the only requests that the chamber took to the National Assembly. After three decades of discussing ways to improve the prosperity of the Îles du Vent, members of the chamber and their representatives in Paris had steadily developed a talent for politics and a clear vision of what they wanted as an economically central part of the French colonial empire. Ideally, and not very realistically, they wanted open access to the international market in African slaves and provisioning and have merchants from all corners of the Atlantic compete for their colonial cash crop. Taxation, if at all, should fall on commercial interests in the colonies and the legal code by which they would abide should be tailor-made for their interests. To advance this perspective, the chamber's members eclectically appropriated strands of political economy if useful, but in no doctrinaire manner. The fact that the Crown had offered them an opportunity to express and rehearse their views to suppress creole aspirations for independence or their desire to come under British rule was not lost on the planters either. Nor would they fail to exploit this knowledge as the ambition to integrate colonial voices began to intersect with the fiscal crisis of the early French Revolution.

The Assemblée Coloniale

In 1787, the Crown's inability to implement fiscal reform in the metropole to alleviate its own debt pushed it to accept the calling of an Assembly of Notables. It also agreed to establish assemblies in domestic provinces and in French colonies. Through a measure that Henri Joucla calls 'decentralising assimilation' (*assimilation décentralisatrice*), an ordinance of 17 June 1787 endowed the colonies with their own assemblies.[79] For Martinique, the establishment of an *assemblée coloniale* also addressed a fatigue with the contentious relations among the Chamber d'agriculture, French commercial interests, and local representatives of the Crown. Already in the early 1780s, the Comité de legislation des colonies, created by Charles Eugène Gabriel de La Croix, marquis de Castries to help draw up a proposal for colonial reform (the commission included Le Mercier de la Rivière and had Jean Dubuc as an adviser), had recommended upgrading the chamber to a colonial assembly.[80] In accordance with this recommendation, the 1787 ordinance announced that a local representative body would offer stability within colonial governance in a context where local administrators were coming and going and 'enlighten [the government] by means of the experience of the most accredited *habitants*, in all such matters which concern the tax base and the just tax distribution, commerce, agriculture, [and] interior works'.[81]

Set to convene annually, the colonial assembly was composed of the governor, the intendant, the second in command, the superintendent, two

[79] Joucla, *Le Conseil Supérieur des Colonies*, 43–4.
[80] The members of the *Comité de Législation des colonies*, created by Castries, consisted of Bongard, Guillemain de Vaivre, Le Mercier de la Rivière, de Lamardelle, de Foulquier, de la Coste, d'Izangrenelle. Duchêne, *Histoire des Finances Coloniales*, 119.
[81] Ordonnance du Roi, portant établissement, aux îles de la Martinique et de la Guadeloupe, d'une Assemblée colonial et d'un Comité en dépendant, avec suppression des chambres d'agriculture. Du 17 Juin 1787, Article 1. *Code de la Martinique* 8 vols. (Fort-de-France, 1865), iv, 33.

deputies of the Superior Council, one deputy of each parish, and one deputy of the commercial houses (*propriétaires des maisons*) of the two principal towns of the colony, and a secretary. Parish assemblies elected their own deputies, drawn from plantation owners with at least twelve plantation slaves (*Nègres de culture*). The electable deputies of the towns were those with a business valuing over 40,000 livres. Such a broad group of representatives had not been assembled since the days of the British occupation.[82]

The ordinance also announced the suppression of Martinique and Guadeloupe's Chambres d'agriculture, but stipulated that an 'intermediary committee' should be put in its place to discuss not only the topics addressed by the chamber but a 'wider range' of things. Six plantation owners chosen from among the deputies of the parishes would compose the committee. Like the chamber, the colonial assembly would have a deputy in Paris in the Bureau des députés du commerce de France.[83] The registry of names produced at the first annual meeting of the assembly on 27 December 1787 discloses a clear continuity between the Chambre d'agriculture and the new colonial assembly. The parish of Trinité had elected Jean Dubuc, 'intendant des colonies', who had returned to Martinique in 1786 to handle his growing debts. Several other members of Martinique's former Chambre d'agriculture were elected. The parish of Saint-Pierre elected M. de Massias, the parish of Jean-Baptiste de la Basse-Pointe elected M. Féreol de Leyritz, and the parish of Macouba elected M. Isaïe Désgrottes. These four were also elected to the intermediary committee together with two other planters.[84]

As the assembly set about discussing how to levy local taxes for the fiscal year of 1788, no instructions were forthcoming from Versailles, so the governor and the intendant referred to the 1 million livres (*argent des colonies*) of the previous year. To levy this amount, the assembly immediately returned to the proposal of 1763, and developed a rationale for its applicability in terms that carried the fingerprints of Jean Dubuc. Like his *Pour et Contre*, the assembly began with a definition of a colony and its ultimate purpose. The role of the colony, it stipulated, was 'to convert commodities from the metropole into other more useful or more easily

---

[82] Ibid., Articles 2 and 3.   [83] Ibid., Article 13.
[84] *Procès-Verbal de l'Assemblée coloniale de la Martinique Créée par l'Ordonnance de Sa Majesté du 17 Juin 1787, rédigé par le Comité intermédiare, en vertu de la Délibération de ladite Assemblée* (Saint-Pierre: P. Richard, Imprimeur du Roi & du Conseil Souverain, 1788), 2–4. The full committee included MM. Dubuc, de Massias, de Leyritz, Levassor, de Jorna, and Isaïe Désgrottes. Ibid., 5. On Jean Dubuc's growing debts and return to Martinique, see Castries to Vievigne, Versailles, 10 March 1786, ANOM E 143, ff. 14–15.

sellable commodities'. This service was based on the exchange between the colonies and the metropole, which in turn was based on colonies' agricultural production, itself based on the means of the planter. Taxing the planter meant taxing the means of production, which was against the essential purpose of the colonies. Therefore, 'the purpose of the colonies does not allow taxation to fall on the plantation owner'. Taxes should fall on obstacles to, not what served, the fulfilment of a colony's purpose. Shifting focus from Dubuc's *Pour et Contre* to his 1765 instructions to Ennery and Peynier, the assembly pointed out that plantation owners were 'free planters on an enslaved territory'. He 'is forever condemned to cultivate solely in order to furnish the kingdom with the means of exchange', from which followed 'the severe prohibition of all foreign goods . . . essential supplies which French commerce does not know how to furnish without charging twice the price'. In other words, since the Exclusif enslaved the colony, it should free it from taxation. Only the borough of Saint-Pierre was not an enslaved territory. This town could and should therefore be taxed, particularly those inhabitants with slaves and for whom they had little use.[85]

Like in 1763, the planter majority within the assembly was able to push through its fiscal proposal, which liberated the plantocracy of over half of its customary taxes and threw 'the greater weight principally on French commerce' and people and their slaves in the city of Saint-Pierre. As frustrated representatives of commerce on the island complained, this was to be expected since 'the Assemblée Coloniale, with its thirty-one members' were composed of 'twenty-four owners of sugar plantations, five owners of coffee plantations, and two representatives of merchant houses in Saint-Pierre and in Fort-Royal'. In a step-by-step attack on the rationale presented by the Assemblée coloniale – and particularly its view that 'taxes should fall as much as possible on that which prohibited production in the colony, and the least on the part that served it' – the island's commercial interests decried as 'political blasphemy' the notion that commerce was a nuisance. They also defended the value and service of 3,720 slaves in Saint-Pierre, of which 'there was not a single one too many'. If the plantocracy needed more slaves, the merchants underlined, they were welcome to purchase them from *commissionnaires* in Saint-Pierre who would purchase them in exchange for their produce.[86]

---

[85] Ibid., 8–9 and 11–12.
[86] 'Observations des commissaires du commerce de la Martinique sur le procès-verbal de l'Assemblée colonial de cette îles. Imprimé à Saint-Vincent par Joseph Berrow', 14 January 1788, ANOM C⁸ᴮ 16, n. 82.

To prevent further clashes, the local administration suspended the tax on imported commodities and on industry. With that, the fiscal agenda of the planter elite collapsed once again. By this time, however, the theatre of combat was steadily moving from the colony to the metropole. Learning of the calling of the Estates General, the intermediary committee contacted their deputy in Paris, Dubuc Duferret, on 17 February 1789, asking him to assemble Paris-based Martinican planters and to lobby at court for representation on a par with French domestic provinces in order to better defend their interests in the metropole. Soon after, Jean Dubuc and several other members went to Paris, leaving the Presidency of the Assembleée coloniale in the hands of Louis-François Dubuc, or as he signed his documents – Dubuc *fils*.[87]

Martinican Planters in Revolution Paris

In their quest for representation at the Estates General and subsequently at the National Assembly, Martinique's plantocracy marshalled many of the arguments that they had used over the years to defend their colonial interests. On the same day that the intermediary committee contacted Duferret in Paris, they wrote to both the King and the Minister of the Marine, César Henri de la Luzerne, that they wished to be represented at the Estates General, given that Martinique formed an 'integral part of the State'. They also repeated their pursuit of a full tax exemption for plantation owners and demanded the opening of colonial ports to foreign commerce (using the destruction wrought by a recent hurricane as the principal argument).[88] Neither the King, nor the Minster accommodated the planters' request. In a tardy response to Dubuc Duferret, Luzerne declared that the King did not want to admit colonial representatives into the Estates General this time around, but promised their participation in a subsequent one should they so desire.[89]

By the time Luzerne's response reached Dubuc Duferret, members of the Third Estate had broken away from the Estates General and proclaimed

---

[87] See, for instance, 'Copie d'une letter écrite par MM. Dubuc, président de l'Assemblée colonial, Gallet de Saint-Aurin, vice-président et Rigordy, secrétaire, à M. de Vioménil', 25 March 1790, ANOM C⁸ᴬ 93 f. 115.

[88] Letter to Luzerne from Jorna, Ferreol Leyritz, Massias, Le Vassor, Pothuau Desgatières, Isaïc Désgrottes, 17 February 1789, printed in Procès Verbal de la séance des electeurs de la Martinique, séante à Paris chez Monsieur Dubuc-Duferret, Député de cette Colonie, le 11 juillet 1789, ANOM, F³ 29, 6–10, and 13–14. Letter to the King, 17 February 1789, printed in ibid., 11. See also Marcillac, *Histoire de la Martinique*, iv, 285.

[89] 'Procès Verbal de la séance des électeurs de la Martinique, séante à Paris chez Monsieur Dubuc-Duferret, Député de cette Colonie', le 11 July 1789, ANOM, F³ 29, 18–19.

themselves the National Assembly. Furthermore, during the Tennis Court Oath on 20 June, the Constituent National Assembly had admitted twelve Saint-Domingue representatives into their fold after the latter, in their own letter to the King, emphasized the colony's status as 'the most precious province of France'.[90] Fearing that Martinique would be left behind, Dubuc Duferret called a meeting among Martinican planters in Paris on 11 July 1789 at his address. Once assembled, thirty-eight Martinican planters decided to constitute themselves as an Assembly of Electors for the island. Among the people present were Jean Dubuc, Dubuc Duferret, Tascher (the former intendant of Martinique), de Leyritz, as well as Médéric Louis Élie Moreau de Saint-Méry, a Martinican born planter whose power would rise as the Revolution progressed. At the meeting, they went on to elect Jean Dubuc president of the assembly and Israël Perpigna its secretary. In the following meeting, which took place on 27 July 1789, they agreed to pursue representation in the National Assembly and elected Moreau de Saint-Méry, Tascher, Perpigna, Dubuc, Dubuc Duferret, and Arthur Dillon to draw up a *cahier de doléances*. They further decided to send Perpigna to Versailles to obtain the *cahier* of the deputies of Saint-Domingue to ensure that the two colonies saw eye to eye on issues that concerned them both.[91]

Martinique's *cahier de doléances*, once composed, reflected the agenda that had emerged within the bosom of the Chambre d'agriculture over the past thirty years. Continuing the eclectic use of terminology that might advance their interests, it opened with the planters' wish to be seen as much as possible as a province forming part of the kingdom. It then expressed a desire to abolish all old laws and establish new laws particular to the colonies, which would be drawn up and implemented with the collaboration of the colonial assemblies. The *cahier* further requested that Martinique be exempt from any direct taxes given the particular climate and production of the island. In terms of commerce, it argued that Martinique should obtain the right to trade with foreigners in exchange for molasses, rum, letters of exchange, and merchandise imported from France. The island's sugar, coffee, cotton, and cacao should be the sole preserve of the metropole. The assembly approved the content of the *cahier* on 17 August 1789 and charged its authors with the responsibility of ensuring that the interests of the colony were maintained as events

---

[90] 'Lettre adressée au Roy par les Propriétaires planteurs de la Colonie de Saint-Domingue', Blanche Maurel, *Cahiers de Doléances de la colonie de Saint-Domingue pour les États Généraux de 1789* (Paris: Librairie Ernest Leroux, 1933), 116.

[91] 'Procès-Verbal de la séance des électeurs de la Martinique, séante à Paris chez Monsieur Dubuc-Duferret, Député de cette Colonie', 18–19, 29–31, and 39.

unfolded and in accordance with representatives of Saint-Domingue and Guadeloupe.[92]

At this critical juncture, Jean Dubuc – the person who had been instrumental in formulating and advancing a Martinican agenda since the Seven Years War – suddenly proved unwilling to go along with the rest of the assembled planters. In his view, the quest for integration was starting to undermine the interest of the planter elite. He therefore opposed moving forward with the bid for representation, arguing that it was a violation of the Minster's orders (an argument that he and Tascher had already raised in the meeting of 27 July) and contradicted the spirit of true representation because the Assembly of Electors was formed by absentee planters and not by the colony. Soon, however, the real reason behind Dubuc's opposition became clear. On 6 September, as the Assembly of Electors set about nominating their deputies, he halted the process to read aloud a statement in which he counselled against the appointment of deputies to the National Assembly. Reacting to the passing of the Declaration of the Rights of Man and of the Citizen, he reminded the assembled planters that their goals were to prevent the abolition of slavery, liberalise existing commercial laws, counteract any direct taxes on the colony, and obtain particular laws for the interior of the colony. All of these, he insisted, would be more easily obtained through direct negotiation with the Minister of the Marine than with the National Assembly. As he warned:

> Regarding the emancipation of the blacks, the prohibitive laws, and taxes, it seems that the National Assembly is not favourably disposed; and when it cannot be otherwise, I cannot see how it might be helpful for us to acknowledge a tribunal whose members have no knowledge of our interests. I cannot see how we can usefully play a game in which we would be six, eight, or ten at most against twelve hundred.

Should the Assembly still wish to proceed, Jean Dubuc stressed, he could no longer continue to participate.[93]

Over the years, Martinican planters had celebrated Jean Dubuc's views and taken them as an expression of their own. This time, however, they would not follow him. Expressing their regrets over his decision, they proceeded to elect their deputies, choosing Moreau de Saint-Méry as

---

[92] The *Cahier* was printed in ibid., 41–7.
[93] Ibid., 71. On this problem in a broader context, see Malick W. Ghachem, 'The "Trap" of Representation: Sovereignty, Slavery and the Road to the Haitian Revolution', *Historical Reflections/Réflexions Historiques*, 29, 1 (2003), 123–44.

their first deputy, Dillon as their second, and Perpigna as their third.[94] The Assembly further elected two replacements and appointed an advisory committee of eight members to assist the deputies and to meet with them once a week. In the meeting of 28 October 1789, Moreau de Saint-Méry announced that he and Dillon had been admitted to the National Assembly on 14 October 1789. Joining forces with the plantation owners of Saint-Domingue and Guadeloupe, the deputies of Martinique and the planters they represented could thus feel content with their successful political representation and integration into Revolutionary France. Nevertheless, the forewarnings of Jean Dubuc would begin to haunt the all-white deputies as arguments against slavery and racial discrimination infiltrated debates in the National Assembly. So would their fears of the 'domestic enemy', those many thousands of slaves who were beginning to rise up in the French Caribbean.

In the years between the Seven Years War and the French Revolution, Versailles showed an unprecedented willingness to placate agricultural interests in the Caribbean colonies to preserve its lucrative sugar business. The Crown founded Chambres mi-parties d'agriculture et de commerce in Martinique and Saint-Domingue in 1759, adding a fourth chamber on Guadeloupe in 1763. Because this institutional reform included the appointment of a deputy to represent planter interests on the Council of Commerce in Paris alongside deputies from principal cities, it implicitly moved the colonies closer to the status of domestic provinces. In the long history of colonial integration, the reform represented a shift in perspective, in that the Crown now tacitly recognised its sugar colonies' right to prosperity.

For the Îles de Vent, reform also meant the ability to slowly forge a creole political economic perspective with which to further nuance and sway policy. In deliberations on the island's commercial, fiscal, and provision needs, members of the Chambre d'agriculture demonstrated a talent for the eclectic appropriation of a range of competing political economic doctrines to advance their own interests. They wholly echoed physiocratic views on the centrality of agriculture, the virtues of free trade, aspects of their tax policies, and, at times, the idea of colonies as overseas provinces. They equally skilfully borrowed Montesquieu's theory of climate to press for the need for special laws on Martinique. At times, this included descriptions of themselves as 'slaves of the metropole' and colonies as

---

[94] 'Procès-Verbal de la séance des électeurs de la Martinique, séante à Paris chez Monsieur Dubuc-Duferret, Député de cette Colonie', 76.

'the sum of its production', 'a province', or a 'node of commerce'. At other times, they rejected economic doctrine altogether, claiming instead an empiricist approach. The essence of the creole discourse that developed over the years would equip the Caribbean plantocracy to trumpet their interests during the French Revolution. Before we turn to this event in Chapter 5, the book shifts to focus on West Africa in the aftermath of the Seven Years War, where people on the ground were beginning to explore expansionist opportunities the potential of which could possibly make colonial empire in the Americas altogether redundant.

CHAPTER 4

Supplying or Supplanting the Americas

Today Gorée is the only obstacle that the enemies will face if seeking to eliminate the French from the entire West African coast. I will not go into any detail vis-à-vis all the resulting consequences. The loss of the trade in Negroes will follow and without Negroes the French American islands will not be able to sustain their cultivation. From then on, the Kingdom will be faced with the collapse of the most lucrative and useful branch of its international commerce.[1]

M. de Silhouette, Commissaire du Roi, Paris, 6 October 1758

When the French Crown insisted on the restoration of Gorée during peace negotiations with Britain in the Seven Years War, it was West Africa's role as supplier of slaves to the profitable sugar islands in the Caribbean that was at stake. Retaining control of this small island would allow France to protect its slave traders as they navigated down the West African coast in search of captives and, by extension, safeguard the main artery of the most dynamic sector of French foreign trade. Paradoxically, the metropolitan government's exclusive interest in Africa as a source of slaves ran parallel to a widening panorama of imperial ideological reorientations, some of which hinged on colonial expansion, cash crop cultivation, and economic development in Africa as a possible alternative to the French plantation complex in the Americas. Africa's warm climate, the presence of local cotton and indigo, and the perceived possibilities of Senegambia's unknown hinterland and labour force cast an enticing spell on colonial officials, independent entrepreneurs, and directors of commercial companies who frequented the coast between 1763 and 1789. Amidst efforts to optimise the French transatlantic slave trade, they periodically solicited the Crown to obtain the right to test colonial projects in the region, mapping new colonial ideas in circulation onto African commercial and agricultural realities.

[1] M. de Silhouette, Paris, 6 October 1758, MAE, AD, Afrique 10, f. 138.

Because the slave trade dominated French activities in West Africa between the Seven Years War and the Revolution, only a small number of studies have engaged with parallel efforts to launch agricultural colonies in the region.[2] To be sure, French colonial experimentation in West Africa did not receive sustained attention from official or independent entrepreneurs and was only promoted by a small and disparate group whose interests fluctuated according to the rhythms of global and local geopolitics and shifting preferences within the Ministry of the Marine. Collectively, these experiments nonetheless reveal that more than a handful of physiocratic political economists saw West Africa as the solution to the French imperial crisis in the Americas. From the moment that the Crown took hold of Gorée, colonial agents in Senegambia gave concrete albeit imperfect expression to an expansionist agenda directed towards the African continent.

To bring this history to the fore, I follow in this chapter the ebb and flow of French efforts to launch cash crop cultivation and colonisation in West Africa between 1763 and 1789. Several interweaving factors conditioned the French presence in the region in these years and therefore people's ability to initiate expansion. One was the Crown's wavering between a commercial policy of opening its Africa trade to all French merchants and one of granting companies a partial monopoly to specific trades. Another was the intermittent influences of Franco-British imperial competition. French possessions along the Senegal River came under British rule between 1763 and 1779. They were recaptured by France during the American Revolution while the British occupied Gorée during most of that war. Local dynamics in Senegambia further aggravated such territorial uncertainties. Throughout the eighteenth century, European powers relied on local collaborators to conduct their trading. The purchasing of African captives and attempts at territorial expansion required careful negotiation with, and sustained permission from, African rulers. The climate of Senegambia, diseases, draughts, and local labour regimes influenced agricultural and commercial activities as well. To explore opportunities for agricultural expansion in West Africa, the French Crown's commercial

---

[2] William B. Cohen mentions discussions of the relocation of the plantation system in the Americas to West Africa in Cohen, *The French Encounter with Africans*, 162–4, and more generally Chapter 6. Léonce Jore mentions it briefly. See Jore, *Les établissements français*, 355. Opportunities for agricultural development in Africa based on free labour are most commonly seen as part of the transition from the European slave trade to 'legitimate' commerce in the nineteenth century. On this, see Robin Law, *From Slave Trade to 'Legitimate' Commerce: The Commercial Transition in Nineteenth-Century West Africa* (Cambridge: Cambridge University Press, 1995), and Robin Law, Suzanne Schwartz, and Silke Strickrodt (eds.), *Commercial Agriculture*.

policies, Franco-British imperial rivalry, and endogenous dynamics therefore appear as integral parts of the chapter's analytic framework.[3]

French Holdings in Lower Senegal

When the Crown took charge of the Compagnie des Indes' African holdings in the early months of 1763, it ended a century of company rule and planted the seeds for what would become a deeply unbalanced Franco-African relationship in the early twentieth century. Few in the eighteenth century, however, would have thought of the tiny island of Gorée as a stepping-stone towards France's future empire in Africa. Versailles considered the take-over a costly yet necessary decision that ensured a continued protection of the French slave trade. Though people such as the botanist, Michel Adanson, had underlined to Choiseul that Gorée could serve as a springboard for wide-scale French colonisation in Africa (as we saw in Chapter 1), Choiseul's ambition was to quickly re-establish French commercial networks between the African interior and a handful of trade stations (*comptoirs* or *escales*) and to bolster Gorée's military position as a regional protector of the French slave trade between Sierra Leone and the Cape of Good Hope.

The transfer of Gorée to the Crown occurred when French claims to Senegambia were at a historic low. A century earlier, its influence had expanded after French merchants broke the Portuguese stronghold, captured the island of Saint-Louis at the mouth of the Senegal River, and set out to control trade on the river. Gorée came into French possession in 1677, after the island had slipped from English into Dutch and finally Portuguese hands. Both Saint-Louis and Gorée were advantageously located for the protection of the slave trade in Lower Senegal and further down the West African coast. The two islands therefore evolved into the main French administrative and military centres in the region. Based on commercial synergies with the coastal rulers of Siin, Kayoor, Waalo, and

---

[3] On African traders dictating terms of trade, see John Thornton, *Africa and Africans in the Making of the Atlantic World, 1400–1800,* 2nd edn. (Cambridge: Cambridge University Press, 1998), Part I. On climate, see James Searing, *West African Slavery and Atlantic Commerce: The Senegal river valley, 1700–1860* (Cambridge: Cambridge University Press, 1993). On ecological factures, see Charles Becker, 'Conditions écologiques, crises de subsistance et histoire de la population à l'époque de la traite des esclaves en Sénégambie (17ᵉ–18ᵉ siècle)', *Canadian Journal of African Studies* 20, 3 (1986), 357–76. On local labour regimes, see Boubacar Barry, *The Kingdom of Waalo: Senegal before the Conquest* (New York: Diasporic Africa Press, 2012), and Boubacar Barry, *Senegambia and the Atlantic Slave trade* (Cambridge: Cambridge University Press, 1997).

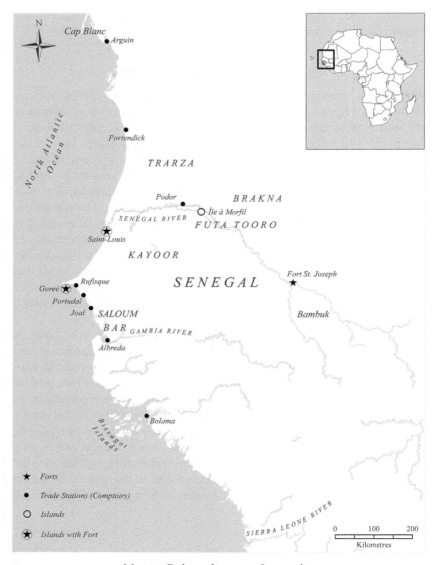

Map 4.1 Eighteenth-century Senegambia
Source: Courtesy Anders Kloch Jeppesen

Baol, the French built a lucrative trade system on leased territories on the mainland. From *comptoirs* such as Fort Saint-Joseph, Arguin, Portendick, Rufisque, Portudal, Joal, and Albreda (see Map 4.1), they tied the capital of

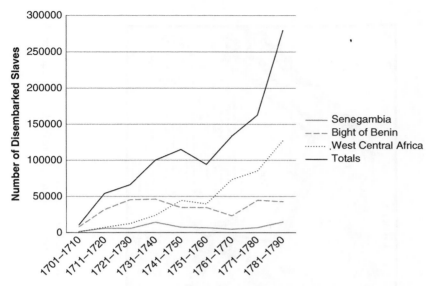

Figure 4.1 French slave trade estimates from Senegambia, Bight of Benin and West
Central Africa, 1700–1790
Source: *Voyages: The Trans-Atlantic Slave Trade Database*, www.slavevoyages.org

their investments to West African commercial networks and international
markets. Senegal's significance as a supplier of slaves to the French colonies
started to decline around 1700, due to the exponential expansion of French
slave trading in West Central Africa and the Bight of Benin (see Figure 4.1),
where the French Compagnie des Indes established a fort at Whydah
(Juda). Nevertheless, Saint-Louis and Gorée remained the administrative
centres for France throughout the transatlantic slave trade.[4]

Between the temporary loss of Saint-Louis to Britain in the Seven Years
War and its reconquest during the American Revolution, Gorée fulfilled
the role of administrative centre singlehandedly. A small island situated
a few kilometres off the shoreline of mainland West Africa, Gorée mea-
sured approximately forty-five acres (900 metres long and 350 metres
wide), not all of which was conducive to human settlement. Adanson,
who resided in Senegal from 1749 to 1753, described the island as a *jambon*
(ham) with a 'tongue-shaped low-lying area' at the one end of which there

---

[4] On seventeenth-century French commercial expansion, see Barry, *Senegambia and the Atlantic Slave
Trade*, 47. On the shift from Senegambia to the Bight of Benin and West Central Africa, see
David Geggus, 'The French Slave Trade: An Overview', *The William and Mary Quarterly*, 58, 1
(2001), 119–38.

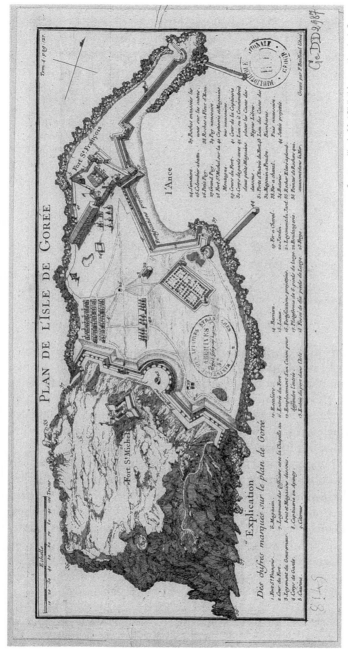

Figure 4.2 Plan of the island of Gorée by François Baillieul l'Aîné, 1754

Source: Bibliothèque national de France, département Arsenal, CPL GE DD-298² (8145), http://catalogue.bnf.fr/ark:/12148/cb40577015h

was a 'very steep mountain' (see Figure 4.2). Small houses built by local inhabitants (*habitants* and *signares*) and the Compagnie des Indes and a fort that in Adanson's view rendered Gorée 'unconquerable' spread across the lowland together with a few gardens and fruit trees that complemented the otherwise 'dry and sterile' island. To survive, Gorée's population therefore lived in close contact with the mainland known as the *grande terre* and regularly sent small boats to the *comptoir* of Portudal to purchase commodities such as 'beef and millet'.[5]

At the moment of Gorée's restoration in 1763, according to Adanson's estimates, the island's population counted approximately 200 inhabitants: 25 women of mixed race (*mulâtresses*), 18 men of mixed race (*mulâtres*), 16 African women (*négresses*), 6 African men (*Nègres*), and 131 captives (*captifs*).[6] Of these, the *mulâtresses* – also known as *signares* – had cultivated mutually beneficial partnerships with employees of the Compagnie des Indes and steadily become powerful agents of Europe's Africa trade. Deftly exploiting their ties to both African and European trade networks, most *signares* were well-to-do. Many owned slaves who lived with them in their households, working as cooks, washerwomen, wet nurses, maids, and confidants if they were women, and as skilled smiths, masons, carpenters, weavers, tailors, and sailors if they were men. The fate of these household slaves, who lived in thatched dwellings within the compounds of their owners, was very different from the on average 220 captives that the island hosted annually while awaiting the Middle Passage and, if they survived it, plantation life in the Americas. Domestic slaves on Gorée were only sold as a punishment for crimes or continued misbehaviour while their children 'were, from infancy, treated as members of the signares' extended families'.[7]

With the royal take-over, the permanent population on Gorée became as integral to the survival of French Crown rule as they had been to the commercial activities of the *Compagnie des Indes*. To establish its authority in a region that in no way depended on it, let alone answered to the Bourbon King, representatives of the Crown needed all the assistance they could get from Gorée's inhabitants and their slaves. African rulers

---

[5] Adanson, *Histoire Naturelle du Sénégal*, 58–9.
[6] Adanson, 'Pièce instructives concernant l'Ile Gorée voisine du Cap-Verd en Afrike, avec un Projet et des vues utiles relativement au Nouvel Établissement de Kaiene – Communikées et présentées à Mr Le duc de Choiseul Ministre de la Guerre et de la marine. Par M. Adanson de l'Academie des Science, de la Société roiale de Londre, Cerveur Roial', May and June 1763, ANOM C[6] 15. See also Searing, *West African slavery*, 107.
[7] E. Brooks, *Eurafricans in Western Africa Commerce, Social Status, Gender, and Religious Observance from the Sixteenth to the Eighteenth Century* (Athens: Ohio University Press, 2003), 206 and 270–71.

on the mainland might desire commercial connections with France and covet the textiles, beads, muskets, and alcoholic beverages that its merchants could furnish, but they were not dependent on the French for these commodities which could be purchased from other European powers, nor would France be able to communicate with African merchants along the coast of Senegambia without local assistance. The Crown was far more reliant on Gorée's population than the other way around.[8]

The Limits of Opportunity

It was within the parameters of these local constraints that France's first official, Pierre François Guillaume Poncet de la Rivière, established French Crown rule at Gorée. Formerly a commander of a voluntary infantry in India, Poncet was an energetic and committed servant whose vigorous embrace of his appointment both expanded and jeopardised French control in the region. He arrived at Gorée in September 1763 with instructions to take possession of the island, ensure the departure of English troops, perform a Te Deum, and 'govern and administer the island like [the] colonies in America'. To assist him, the government provided him with two infantry companies, in addition to soldiers, voluntaries, workers (*ouvriers*), and sailors. The instructions ordered Poncet to lodge those accompanying him and put them to work repairing accommodation, storage houses, and the island's water supply. Another task was to establish good relations with the local rulers and to maintain an upright relationship with the new British governor of Senegal, though Choiseul also ordered Poncet to 'obtain intelligence' from Senegal without 'being discovered'.[9]

The sorry state of post-war Gorée made the execution of the government's wishes a Sisyphean task. Though the Treaty of Paris from 1763 stipulated that the British should return Gorée in the condition in which it was captured,

---

[8] On the relationships between the French and Gorée's and Saint-Louis' populations, see Guillaume Aubert, "'Nègres ou mulâtres nous sommes tous Français" Race, genre et nation à Gorée et à Saint-Louis du Sénégal, fin XVIIᵉ–fin XVIIIᵉ siècle', in *Français? La nation en débat entre colonies et métropole, XVIᵉ–XIXᵉ siècle*, ed. Cécile Vial (Paris: EHESS, 2014), 125–47. The commodities used to trade with African merchants included textiles from India, beads from Amsterdam, muskets from England, and alcoholic beverages from France. See Stein, *The French Sugar Business*, 26, and Olivier Pétré-Grenouilleau, *Nantes au temps de la traite des noirs* (Paris: Pluriel, 2014), 68–9.

[9] Unlike his successors, Poncet de la Rivière's instructions did not consist of one long memorandum, but of a series of letters by Choiseul all dated 2 June 1763. Choiseul to Poncet de la Rivière, Versailles 2 June 1763. ANOM B116.

Poncet and his crew found the colony in dire need of repair. The main port at Gorée needed rebuilding as did the island's water supplies and the Compagnie des Indes' former quarters and storage houses. Workers immediately set about their repair work yet within a brief period of time several had succumbed to the climate. Only with the help of Gorée's local population did the French cement their return. The *signares*, or *metis françaises* as Poncet called them, agreed to rent out lodgings and skilled slaves to assist the new French administration. Local sailors further helped Poncet re-established lifelines to the mainland, enabling an otherwise impossible transition to Crown rule.

Alongside repair work, Poncet had to draw up fresh treaties with African rulers willing to reactivate commercial relations with the French. From the rulers of Siin and Boal, he regained a footing at the *comptoirs* of Joal and Portudal, both of which primarily served as sources of food and livestock. From the ruler of Kayoor (known as the Damel), he re-established ties to Cap Manuel, Cap Bernard, and Rufisque. These three *comptoirs* offered provisions and a modest supply of slaves. Only Albreda in the Gambia River attracted a considerable number of inland slave traders. The British therefore strongly opposed his efforts to raise the French flag there. As Poncet explained to Choiseul, only because the ruler of Bar, 'master of these lands' refused to accept a British bribe to expel the French could he report this victory.[10]

Food, merchandise, building materials, and other essentials were supposed to arrive from the metropole, a responsibility that the Crown had outsourced to the well-known merchant house of the Gradis family in Bordeaux. Nevertheless, provisioning proved as taxing in the West African context as it did in the Îles du Vent. Eight months into his governorship, Poncet reported that not a single ship with provisions had arrived from France, nor did he have any means with which to pay the salary of his military corps. On an island with minimal food production and where European goods were used as currency in trade with African merchants and as salary for employees, a dearth in commodities dangerously destabilised French local order and control. Communicating to the Ministry of the Marine the gravity of the situation, Poncet likened the island of Gorée to 'a vessel in the midst of the sea', infected by scurvy, lacking provisions, and with officers, soldiers, and workers dying in high numbers. If left without supplies, he warned, he would not be able to check growing dissent but would soon have a 'mutiny' on his hands.[11]

---

[10] Poncet de la Rivière to Choiseul, Gorée 25 May 1764, ANOM C⁶ 15.

[11] Ibid. On the Gradis family, see Sylvia Marzagalli, 'Opportunités et contraintes du commerce colonial dans l'Atlantique français au XVIIIᵉ siècle: le cas de la maison Gradis de Bordeaux', *Outre-mers*, 96, 362–3 (2009), 87–110.

Versailles was well-aware of the importance of supplies to its commercial mission in West Africa but also cognisant of the unreliable tempo with which food, building materials, and goods arrived in the colonies. Often, the Ministry of the Marine therefore instructed its local officials to identify local sources to offset risks of starvation. In Senegambia, where local supply networks could be as unreliable as French metropolitan sources, this alone was not a viable remedy. As the Compagnie des Indes discovered in 1757 when a British blockade prevented the French from provisioning Saint-Louis, a drought limited access to local supplies and forced the commander to release 500 captives. Drought and famine plagued Senegambia every decade from the 1710s to the 1750s and again in the 1770s and 1780s, making it difficult for the French to readily rely on local sources of sustenance. When desiccation did not haunt the region, however, the French obtained millet, fruit, fish, cattle, chickens, and palm wine from a number of trade stations on the mainland.[12]

In the period between 1763 and 1789, the general fertility of the mainland opposite Gorée also served as a canvas upon which French colonial agents projected their plans for colonial expansion. As he raised the French flag at the *comptoirs* of Portudal, Joal, and Rufisque, Poncet's eagerness to exploit African agricultural opportunities for commercial gain reverberated across his reports to the Crown. He depicted the area between Cap Manuel and Cap Bernard on the *grande terre* opposite Gorée as a verdant plot ideal for provisioning and the defence of Gorée. The ruler of Kayoor, the Damel, had agreed to transfer this territory to Poncet and 'all of [his] successors' because Poncet had 'bought back from English slavery, one of the King's parents' (a story that would repeat itself under Poncet's successor). To give his superiors a better sense of the land he obtained from the Damel, he included in the letter a map of the territory drawn by the engineer, Lacher de Grandjean (see Figure 4.3). Poncet explained that he had planted 'root vegetables and seeds, such as beans, lentils, peas, potatoes, giromon etc.' on this territory to help nourish the French at Gorée, but he also hoped to 'aggrandise the terrain' to 'make cotton plantations which can easily grow in this country'.

Similarly, Poncet investigated the Bissagot Islands, particularly Bissau and Bolama. As we saw in Chapter 2, Bolama's fertility had led the former director of French commerce in Senegal, André Brüe, to suggest that the island was ripe for sugar production, a suggestion Abbé Roubaud had repeated in 1759.

---

[12] Brooks, *Eurafricans*, 103; on the release of slaves, Curtin, *Economic Change in Pre-colonial Africa*, 110–11.

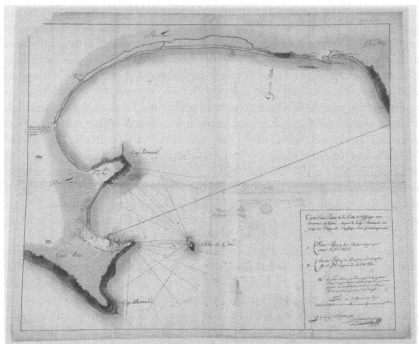

Figure 4.3 Du Cap Manuel au village de Rufisque by Larcher de Grandjean, 1764
Source: Bibliothèque nationale de France, département Cartes et Plan, GE SH 19 PF
III DIV 4 P 10, https://gallica.bnf.fr/ark:/12148/btv1b531537981/f1.item.r=goree.zoom

Whether or not Poncet was aware of these suggestions is impossible to know, but he echoed Brüe's observation. France, he said, already possessed a small territory alongside the Portuguese on Bissau while Bolama was uninhabited but offered an excellent place on which to form 'plantations like those in America'. In his view, the Crown should act immediately on the opportunities Bolama provided – indeed it would be a 'mistake on behalf of the French' to ignore them – since the British already harboured similar ideas, thus foreshadowing the scramble for Africa that would commence over a century later.[13]

Surely aware that gold captivated the Crown in the past, Poncet also showed enthusiasm for the gold mines of Bambuk. The 'lure of Bambuk gold' had a long history in the region with Arab merchants being the first to gain an interest, followed by the Portuguese and then the Dutch, English,

---

[13] Poncet de la Rivière to Choiseul, Gorée 25 May 1764, ANOM C⁶ 15.

and French.[14] To Poncet, the Bambuk gold mines could outrival even the goldmines of Brazil. He therefore drew up a far-fetched plan for how to exploit them which involved an initial phase of trading with local monarchs around Bambuk to gain their confidence. He was convinced that Siratie, the ruler of the Fulbe (*Poules*), would receive the French with open arms since this monarch had rejected British requests for a state visit. In contrast, the rule of Waloo might pose problems. Were that to happened, Poncet would send in an armed expedition of 300 white men and 600 Africans equipped with European armoury. Alternatively, he would 'declare war on [the ruler of Waloo] by means of the Damel', ruler of Kayoor, by giving the Damel, 'gifts of gun powder and ammunition in order to engage him in an attack on the King of Waloo'. If a strategy of divide and conquer did not open access to the mines of Bambuk, Poncet concluded, France could use an army composed of those Africans residing in France and of whom, he said, 'there are a lot of useless ones'.[15]

Poncet did not only draw up elaborate plans for conquest. He also shared his thoughts on what labourers to use in Bambuk's mines. In his view, the best source of labour would be local labour. He estimated that if 10,000 miners worked under European guidance the Crown could obtain a total of 50,000 gros d'or daily, or approximately 191.2 kilograms (thus predicting a result 900 times higher than the volume of gold that Europeans obtained annually from the region in the eighteenth century). Alternatively, he suggested that the Crown could found a penal colony and have prisoners mine the gold. Considering a broad spectrum of labour forms to advance French interests, Poncet alleged that there were no limits to his ambitions for France in Africa other than the King's purse.[16]

Poncet's plans to make the most of the French transition to Crown rule appeared alongside his portrayal of Gorée as a vessel at sea, infected by scurvy and on the verge of a mutiny. How might these diverging messages – one of excitement and another of utter misery – have coloured the *premier commis*' perception within the Ministry of the Marine, let alone the minister? Would they have been enthusiastic at the prospect of adding gold mining and sugar and cotton cultivation to French activities in West

---

[14] Philip D. Curtin, 'The Lure of Bambuk Gold', *Journal of African History*, 14 (1973), 623–31, 624.

[15] Poncet de la Rivière to Choiseul, Gorée 25 May 1764, ANOM C⁶ 15. This was a puzzling comment given modern scholarship's insistence on an upper limit of 5,000 blacks in all of eighteenth-century France. Peabody, '*There Are No Slaves in France*', 4.

[16] Poncet de la Rivière to Choiseul, Gorée 25 May 1764, ANOM C⁶ 15. 1 gros is approximately 1/8 of an old French ounce, or 3.824 g. On the import of gold from Bambuk in the eighteenth century, see Curtin, *Economic Change in Pre-colonial Africa*, 202.

Africa or horrified by the death of Frenchmen at the hands of a merciless climate? Poncet, unlike his successors, would never know the answer to this. His fears of a potential revolt adequately captured local sentiments and therefore shortened his tenure at Gorée. Already in December 1763, the island's population complained to Versailles that the governor prevented them from trading freely and that the island was worse off than during the British occupation. The officer corps were especially upset, accusing Poncet of creating a private slave trading company together with the Gradis family of Bordeaux. This well-founded complaint led to the prohibition act of 1764 which barred governors from any personal involvement in the slave trade. Yet protest continued. Beyond Poncet's troubles with Gorée's population, critics claimed that Poncet had burnt down three local villages in response to a conflict with the monarch at Saloum. The British, in turn, started protesting Poncet's expansionist ambitions. In late 1764, a report from Gorée stressed that if he remained governor, the French would lose the island. This reporter further expressed concern that the King would have to pay a high fee on the land that the Damel had granted Poncet between Cap Manuel and Cap Bernard. The latter threat was a language the financially strained Crown understood; Choiseul recalled Poncet on 22 December 1764.[17]

Each time a governor was replaced, Versailles produced a new set of instructions for his successor. These documents therefore disclose the central government's evolving plans for its activities in Africa as well as its reliance on local information to craft its policies. The instructions of the incoming governor, Jean-Georges, chevalier de Mesnager – which were most likely written by Jean Dubuc and then approved by Choiseul – had incorporated most of the information Poncet had conveyed in his official reports, including his proposal to create a fort at Bambuk to mine its gold. They also pointed out that Poncet had taken possession of Albreda, Rufisque, Portudal and Joal and had obtained the concessions of Cap Manuel and Cap Bernard from the Damel, underlining that of them all Albreda was the most interesting *comptoir* since one could acquire 'negroes, wax, and ivory' from there. The instructions further informed de Mesnager of Bissau and Bolama and repeated Poncet's praise of their potential. With

---

[17] On the local population's complaints, see their letter to Choiseul, 5 December 1763, in Poncet de la Rivière's personal dossier, ANOM E 338, f. 211. On Poncet's personal slave trading, see 'Articles et Conditions d'une société particulière entre Monsieur Poncet de la Rivierre Gouverneur General pour sa Majesté le Roy de France, de l'isle de Gorée et les Sieurs David Gradis et fils negociants armateurs à Bordeaux'. Ibid. 'Report', Gorée, 20 October 1764. Ibid., f. 162. On his recall, see Lettre du Roy à M. Poncet de la Rivière, 22 December 1764, ibid., f. 164.

respect to the latter, the instructions noted with a degree of distance that 'it is said that it would be easy to cultivate all the commodities of America here and that it will be dangerous to let other powers take possession of them'.[18]

Although de Mesnager's instructions revealed the numerous opportunities that Poncet believed were at its feet, the Ministry of the Marine emphatically sought to restrict his successor's potential inclination to act upon them. Charging that the listed establishments seemed 'more costly than useful', de Mesnager's instructions spelled out what would become an integral part of future instructions, namely that 'the point of view from which the chevalier de Mesnager should consider all these in general is commerce, this is the true mine, and it would be to deceive oneself to look for those of Bambuk before having guaranteed the slave trade which is the principle object'. Equating 'commerce' with slave trading in this instance, the instructions highlight the degree to which a positive balance of trade with foreign powers had come to dominate royal ambitions, while its former obsession with bullion had taken a back seat. As the instructions further stipulated, the government had accepted taking control of the holdings to protect and facilitate the slave trade and the profits it generated via the Caribbean. De Mesnager should therefore lower the number of establishments 'not only to reduce expenses' but also because the establishments' proximity to one another and competition between them hindered their individual success.[19]

The Crown's financial calculus was thus a major impediment for the expansionist projects that Poncet had championed. Nonetheless, de Mesnager fell victim to the same temptations as his predecessor, both with respect to his private slave trading as well as his interest in expansionist opportunities. Having frequented colonies in both the East and West Indies prior to his appointment, de Mesnager was intimately familiar with the French colonial empire. Prior to his appointment, Choiseul had brought him to Versailles as an adviser but de Mesnager's appetite for adventure prompted him to request a colonial governorship.[20] Upon arrival at Gorée, and without the slightest whiff of embarrassment, de Mesnager informed Choiseul of his plans to form a commercial society together with the officer corps and employees of the Crown, in the hope that he would obtain an exclusive privilege to the slave trade in the region. In utter disbelief, Choiseul answered the governor that 'all kinds of traffic

---

[18] 'Mémoire du Roy pour server d'Instruction au Chev. Mesnager Brigadier d'Infanterie'. Versailles 22 December 1764. ANOM B119.
[19] Ibid.　　[20] 'Précis des servies de S. Le Baillif de Mesnager', FR ANOM E 310.

were beneath an officer and dangerous in his hands'; they would 'introduce cupidity and the thirst for gain there where only honour and disinterest should reside'. The involvement of the former governor and the entire officer corps in slave trading, Choiseul pointed out, was what had led to the explosive atmosphere under Poncet de la Rivière. He even instructed de Mesnager to read aloud a decree that he had attached, which explicated the ban on slave trading by any official or government employee. If he got wind of any trading by officials, Choiseul threatened de Mesnager that he would be recalled and never again serve under the Crown.[21]

Choiseul's anger exhibits a rather idealistic view of the sentiments that should animate an officer of the Crown, yet his harsh tone may not have been provoked by de Mesnager' slave trading proposal alone. Gorée's new governor was exceptionally skilled at misreading his instructions. In the same letter in which he announced his wish to collaborate in the slave trade, de Mesnager also presented an idea to create a new colony in Lower Senegal. Having learnt about Poncet's project from his instructions, he told Choiseul that he had surveyed the region and concluded that the slave trade would be more successful if the French cultivated the land along the coast off of Gorée and formed 'considerable plantations' there. He proposed creating agricultural colonies from Cap Manuel to Rufisque, claiming that such colonies would increase the demand for European goods and simultaneously solve the issue of food supplies. The colonies should be settled with 'good subjects' from Europe, possibly the King's military personnel, though not 'defectors'.[22]

At first, Choiseul refrained from even responding to his request. De Mesnager therefore wrote again to remind the minister of his plans for a colony, yet to no avail. Silence merely fuelled de Mesnager's excitement. In a long letter dated 13 June 1765, he declared that he would establish a considerable colony, the territory of which would carry the same commodities as those from America. He explained that the Damel had granted him land on which the colony would be founded, measuring 'sixteen or eighteen *lieues de tour*' (between sixty-two and seventy kilometres in circumference), out of gratitude and in exchange for a small annual fee, because de Mesnager had successfully negotiated a return of some of the Damel's family members whom the British had captured to sell into slavery. Before ceding the territory, the Damel had only requested that

---

[21] Choiseul to M. le Chev. de Mesnager, Marly, 22 May 1765, ANOM B121, f. 5.
[22] De Mesnager to Choiseul, Gorée undated. ANOM C⁶ 15, memo 24.

local villagers living on the land would preserve the right to pillage all ships 'which perish along this bay due to the strong current'.[23]

This was the second time within two years that a French governor claimed to have rescued members of the Damel's family from English slave traders and in return received the plot of land between Cap Manuel and Cap Bernard for a small annual fee. Was the Damel's family exceptionally unlucky since Poncet de la Rivière had recounted a story identical to that of de Mesnager's, or was something less conspicuous going on? Poncet had claimed that the Damel had ceded the terrain to him and all of his successors, yet de Mesnager appeared to be receiving it again based on a new treaty. It is not unlikely that the land grant was a way for the Damel to augment his access to European firearms and commodities of which his annual fee consisted. In the late 1750s and 1760s, the ruler of Waloo, the Brak named Naatago Aram, challenged the power of the Damel of Kayoor (Makuudi Kumba Diaring). As part of hostilities, Naatago Aram forced the British at Saint-Louis to pay customs to himself that were customarily due to the Damel. In the military conflict between Kayoor and Waloo that ensued, the Damel gained the upper hand by 1766, but was probably looking for more ways than one to obtain firearms. Leasing out territory off of Gorée would enable him to open a new line of supplies.[24]

To de Mesnager, however, the ceded territory was not about the perpetuation of local warfare. Although warfare helped drive up the numbers of African prisoners of war to be sold into the European slave trade, the territory he received was intended for local provisioning needs and the production of crops such as cotton and indigo. To survey the possibilities of the ceded terrain, de Mesnager solicited the help of Monsieur Le Large, a ship captain, whose knowledge of agricultural opportunities in Senegal impressed the governor. Precise information, de Mesnager told Choiseul, would prevent any disappointment on behalf of incoming settlers who 'arrived with dreams of great fortunes'.[25] In his report, Le Large described the size of the 'excellent' terrain as reaching from the village of Rufisque to the extremity of Cap Verde. He pointed out that cotton and indigo grew naturally and abundantly and that the land was impeccable for husbandry. To harvest millet it was necessary only to 'move up the surface of the land'. Water was readily accessible, and the air was

---

[23] De Mesnager to Choiseul, Gorée 20 March 1765. ANOM C⁶ 15, Letter 44. *Lieue de tours* are an Ancien Régime measure. One *lieue* is approximately four kilometres.
[24] On war between Kayoor and Waloo, see Barry, *The Kingdom of Waalo*, 119–20.
[25] De Mesnager to Choiseul, Gorée undated. ANOM C⁶ 15, memo 24.

fresh. The local population was 'well built', 'robust', and attached to the area, often working as fishermen and farmers. The latter preferred millet production to cotton, 'although cotton would become more profitable if the French took an interest in it'. The area also offered a lot of poultry, rare birds, and palm wine.[26]

While confirming de Mesnager's appraisal of the ceded terrain, Le Large's observation on its population further conveyed an opportunity for future European settlers to draw on local labour to produce cotton and indigo. Le Large's description of 'robust' labourers complemented de Mesnager's marshalling of the emerging rhetoric on the profitability of cheap local labour in Africa that the Physiocrats would embrace and which would become so central to the expansion of capitalism on a global scale in the nineteenth century. The violent struggle over the cost of labour that undergirded the slave-driven production of cash crops in the Americas pushed entrepreneurs such as Le Large to look at land and labour in West Africa as a cheaper and largely untapped region from which to drive up production and consumption of sugar, coffee, cotton, and indigo. As the governor contended in response to Le Large's report, 'one will find for 120 livres per year, food included, as many blacks as will be needed to cultivate the land'. Such labour availability, he emphasised, would be of great use to the French who wished to settle in the colony.[27]

It is not entirely clear who the local population that de Mesnager and Le Large described were, nor if the two Frenchmen had wholly grasped the composition of local labour structures. Possibly, the labourers Le Large described were indeed free peasants of Kayoor. However, they could also have been some of the slaves deployed by local elites. Slavery in Lower Senegal was a commonplace; various forms of unfree labour spread across the region and might not always have been easily distinguishable to French officials. James Searing notes that the Wolof states, of which Kayoor was one, referred to war captives as *jaam sayoor*, slaves for sale, whereas their children, who were born into slavery and treated better, were called *jaam juddu*.[28] These slaves could be rented out or seen serving alongside free labourers, rendering a distinct labour system illegible to Europeans.

Despite de Mesnager's enthusiastic report and Le Large's survey of the ceded terrain, Versailles was unsympathetic to the governor's colonial project. When Choiseul's successor, the duc de Praslin, responded a year

---

[26] Report by Le Large, 14 September 1765, enclosed with letter from De Mesnager to Choiseul, Gorée. ANOM, C⁶ 15, memo 56.
[27] Ibid. [28] Searing, *West African slavery*, 48–9.

after de Mesnager's initial request, he reprimanded de Mesnager for going beyond his instructions and tried to confine his proposed colony to that of food cultivation for local consumption:

> I told the King about the concession of a terrain that the King Damel has granted his Majesty on the *grande terre* for a fee of 600 *livres* annually. His majesty has approved your action and the treaty you have drawn up, but his intention is that you do not create a colony here on his account. You should limit yourself to permit inhabitants to cultivate *menus grains* [peas, lentils, millet], raise cattle and fowl, and even to set up a trade to pay for the cost of living. To that effect you could parcel out land according to their abilities *on the condition that they do not cultivate any commercial commodities such as sugar, cotton, and indigo* [my emphasis] and that you grant them such concession for a period of only ten years if they, in return, preserve the wood for construction and which can be useful for fortification and housing.[29]

As Praslin's response reflects, the Crown supported the plan to create a self-sustaining settler colony in Senegal and agreed that it could alleviate the needs of Gorée's population and French slave traders making a stop to replenish provisions. In fact, Praslin made it clear that 'meeting the needs of the inhabitants of Gorée' should be its only purpose. Yet the Minister of the Marine was unequivocally against the creation of sugar, cotton, and indigo plantations in Africa, though he remained mute as to the reasons why. The only explanation he offered at the time was that royal expenses should be kept at a minimum.

It was not just the French Crown that frowned upon de Mesnager's expansionist ideas. The British administration in Senegal was equally alarmed by the activities of the governor. The Governor of Saint-Louis, Charles O'Hara, protested that de Mesnager's project went against the Treaty of Paris. O'Hara may have made this objection due to his own desire to enlarge British territorial rule in West Africa. In 1766, O'Hara reported to London that he hoped to 'turn Senegambia into a plantation colony' modelled after the British colonies in the Caribbean. Doing so, he believed, would increase the consumption of sugar, cotton, and tobacco in England to the less wealthy parts of the population, and enable Britain to 'dominate the huge markets in Germany and Russia, currently in the hands of the French'.[30] A French attempt to follow a similar plan would infringe on O'Hara's agenda. His complaints drove London and Versailles into a

---

[29] Praslin to M. Le Chev. de Menager, Versailles 4 May 1766, ANOM B123, f. 10.
[30] Matthew P. Dziennik, '"Till these Experiments be Made": Senegambia and British Imperial Policy in the Eighteenth Century', *English Historical Review*, CXXX, 546, 1132–61, 1132.

diplomatic dispute, in which Versailles rallied to the support of de Mesnager. In a letter dated 27 August 1766, Praslin informed de Mesnager that O'Hara's objections were unfounded and advised the governor to act prudently in his communications with O'Hara and only reply 'in vague terms'. Defending de Mesnager's project in its communication with London, the Crown nonetheless used the opportunity to reiterate to de Mesnager in the same letter that 'the intention of the King is that no settlement should be established here at his expense' and that de Mesnager should ensure that the inhabitants did not cultivate 'sugar, cotton, and indigo'.[31]

Multi-layered resistance notwithstanding, de Mesnager managed to found a settler colony on the *grande terre* though a lack of sources makes it difficult to assess how far it developed. Subsequent correspondence with the Crown does not reveal more about his efforts and he was recalled in early 1767. We do obtain some insights from the Crown's instructions to his successor, Claude Le Lardeaux de la Gastière (captain of the Vermandois regiment), which noted that the King had approved de Mesnager's colony but that it had been confined to food production and the raising of cattle and fowl. Inhabitants of the colony had been strictly forbidden from cultivating 'commercial goods such as sugar, cotton, and indigo'. Gastière was also told that the ceded terrain was much too big for what was needed to provide for the livelihood of Gorée's inhabitants. He should therefore limit the size of each plot of land to what one person would be able to cultivate and reserve the rest as a communal space for grazing and wood.[32]

Although Versailles' resistance to cash crop cultivation in Africa had failed to influence Gorée's first two governors, neither Gastière, nor his successor Rastel de Rocheblave (whose appointments straddled the years from 1768 to 1772) expressed an interest in exploiting local agricultural opportunities. The reasons for this silence may not be their obedience to the Crown but local resistance to French territorial expansion. By the time that Gastière was installed at Gorée, the Damel who had granted de Mesnager the sizeable plot of land had been succeeded by a new Damel who was reluctant to honour his predecessor's deal. When the Damel sent an envoy to renew the alliance between the two powers, the envoy conveyed to Gastière that the Damel would not consent to his predecessor's ceding of such a large plot of land, since it went against the rights of his

---

[31] Praslin to de Mesnager, Compiègne 27 August 1766, ANOM B123, f. 19.
[32] 'Mémoire du Roy pour server d'instruction au Sr de la Gastière Capt d'Infanterie', Versailled 22 December 1764. La Gastière ANOM E246.

people to pillage the coast. Gastière was adamant that it was not the new Damel's prerogative to break this treaty but agreed to abandon a section of the territory nonetheless, insisting in his letter to the Ministry of the Marine that he did so only because the French Crown found the establishment too costly.[33]

Exactly how much territory Gastière restored to the Damel is as uncertain as the overall success of de Mesnager's experiment. Although the settlers he deployed may have enjoyed moderate success in the colony's early days, it appears that most of them succumbed to disease. René Claude Geoffroy de Villeneuve, who lived in the region in the mid-1780s during the governorship of the chevalier de Boufflers, mentioned in his publication *L'Afrique, ou histoire, moeurs, usages et coutumes des africains* (1814) that 'an epidemic produced by the fumes of the marches in the near distance has reduced this once considerable village to a couple of families', probably referring to the yellow fever epidemic that had raged in the region.[34] If the first sustained attempt to create a French agricultural colony in Africa after the Seven Years War was stymied by a lack of support from Versailles and resistance from the Damel, it was ultimately mosquitoes and an African climate hostile to European settlers that determined its degree of success.[35]

Expansionist Interests of Private Capitalists

The Crown's firm declaration against the founding of sugar, cotton, coffee, and indigo plantations in West Africa came right as the Physiocrats, led by Roubaud, amplified their advocacy to relocate the plantation system of the Americas to Africa and to base production on free local labour. At that precise moment, the government received a proposal from a M. Saget that echoed the physiocratic agenda. Among the plethora of documents within the Ministry of the Marine and the Ministry of Foreign Affairs, few proposals come as close to advancing physiocratic ideas as Saget's prior to the outbreak of the American Revolution. Only once France had

---

[33] Gastière to Praslin, 14 August 1767, ANOM C⁶15. The new Damel grew increasingly hostile to the French. Joseph-Alexandre Le Brasseur, governor of Gorée in 1777, reported that since the Damel had become sole ruler of Kayoor and Baol in 1773 and had understood 'the extreme need' the French had for him, it was impossible to go to the mainland without 'the risk of becoming a captif'. See Le Brasseur to Sartine, Gorée, 29 April 1777. ANOM C⁶ 17, ff. 2–3.

[34] René Claude Villeneuve, *L'Afrique, ou histoire, moeurs, usages et coutumes des africains*, 4 vols. (Paris: Nepveu, 1814), iii, 56.

[35] On yellow fever as a determining factor in European colonial success, see J. R. McNeill, *Mosquito Empires: Ecology and War in the Greater Caribbean, 1620–1914* (Cambridge: Cambridge University Press, 2010).

recaptured Senegal did other commercial interests and government officials start exercising a similar rhetoric.

Very little is known about Saget. His communication with the Crown
indicates that he was a tax collector to the King of Prussia, an occupation
that many Frenchmen held in this period. How he developed an interest in
colonisation in Africa is uncertain, but his familiarity with Lower Senegal
suggests that he had frequented the region as part of a slave trading crew.
The proposal he submitted was entitled 'Project to establish a plantation
for coffee, cotton, indigo, cocoa, and other products in Africa on the
mainland vis-à-vis the island of Gorée'. In it, he explained that the
French slave trade was no longer as lucrative in the region as it had been
previously, due to increased competition among European merchants and
a decrease in the supply of slaves. Slave traders navigated along the West
African coast for up to eighteen months, Saget said, before acquiring a full
cargo. These prolonged stays had a lethal impact on many sailors, he noted,
having witnessed a good part of a trader's crew perish from disease before
the captain was ready to raise anchor (20 per cent for French slave traders
between 1766 and 1770). He therefore encouraged the Crown to adopt
a new, lucrative approach to Africa based on agricultural development and
underscored that the cultivation of neglected yet immensely fertile territories in the region could offer inexhaustible riches.[36]

With an explicit critique of France's colonial enterprise in the Americas,
Saget challenged Europeans to ask themselves why they went far away to
obtain goods at a high cost, which Africa could offer with little effort. This
region was a mere 900 lieues (approximately 3,600 kilometres) from France
and it took only fifteen to twenty days to reach. Plantations could be
founded on the coast between the island of Gorée and the Gambia River
where France already collaborated with local rulers. As he noted, the
French garrison obtained rice, vegetables, and other foodstuffs from
there and farmers were able to harvest crops twice a year. It would be
easy to produce coffee, sugar and cocoa cheaply on this stretch 'since one
can employ trusted slaves for the clearing of land or free negroes who rent
themselves out one month at a time at little cost'.

To demonstrate the strength of his proposal, Saget offered to go to
Africa and test it at his own expense. He only requested royal protection
and some assistance with shipping the necessary cotton mills, tools, and

---

[36] Saget, 'Projet d'Etablissement en Affrique', ANOM C6 16, f. 38v. On French crew mortality on slave
ships, see Stephen D. Behrendt, 'Crew Mortality in the Transatlantic Slave Trade in the Eighteenth
Century', *Slavery and Abolition*, 18, 1 (1997), 51.

supplies. With the provision of technical equipment, he proposed building storage houses and what he called 'laboratories' on the coast, and to rent land from African allies. He would sell the cultivated commodities to the inhabitants of Gorée and to French traders. To increase the utility of the colony, he would also construct a brewery for the garrison, and cultivate vegetables and raise animals that could nourish the colony and Europeans on arriving ships. Based on such modest beginnings, Saget envisaged a prosperous and thriving future for Africa and its peoples. As he said: 'French ships will find refreshments upon arrival, industry will grow here and bring progress, the cultivator will enrich himself, commerce on the coast reliant on Gorée will flourish more than it currently does and attract merchants from Europe who will come to buy the products of the land in exchange for their manufactured goods'.

Saget's proposal and the way in which it was subsequently processed within the Ministry of the Marine reveal with extraordinary clarity the internal hurdles to radical reform. Saget's proposal was held up in French bureaucratic limbo for two years before it was brought to the attention of the Minister of the Marine, Pierre Étienne Bourgeois de Boynes, in 1772. Reasons for this delay were unaddressed, but Saget's original proposal had evidently alarmed François Beudet, a *commis* – or clerk – to the minister. Saget had had to attach a supplement to his memorandum in which he attempted to fend off claims that his plans for a colony were ill conceived. The supplement had the telling title: 'supplement to the memorandum resubmitted to Monsieur Beudet serving as response to his objections with regard to the difficulty of executing what [the memorandum] proposes because of the proximity to the British [in Senegal] and because of the fear of local inhabitants whom we would need to punish if they dare destroy a plantation established with the permission of the King of France'.[37]

When Saget's memorandum landed on Bourgeois de Boynes' desk, it came not only with these complementary clarifications, but also with an additional report by Beudet. Before listing his recommendations on the matter, Beudet's report reminded Bourgeois de Boynes of de Mesnager's proposal to set up a colony and create plantations on land opposite Gorée. It confirmed that the Crown had approved this proposal but only after laying down numerous restrictions. Listing these in more detail than what materialised in the correspondence between Versailles and de Mesnager,

---

[37] 'Supplémens au Mémoire remit à Monsieur Beudet servant de réponse à ses objections sur la difficulté d'exécuter ce qu'il contient tant à cause du voisinage des Anglois que par la crainte des habitans du Pais dont il faudroit tirer vengeance s'il osoient detruire une habitation etablie avec permission du Roy de France', ANOM C6 16, ff. 42–5.

the report stated that the reason for the restrictions was to prevent the cultivation of a commodity that already enriched the French meridional colonies. Extending production in new regions could only be harmful to these islands, the report noted. As it further stipulated: 'it is important that coffee, indigo, and cotton are always kept at a price that can make up for the expenses of their cultivation'. Evidently voices within the Ministry of the Marine believed that the production of cash crops in Africa might undermine that of the Americas. Cultivating cotton, indigo, sugar, and coffee in a region that France 'cannot defend in times of war', the report concluded, would be too risky.[38]

Opposition to Saget's proposal within the administration is telling. Even if commercial agriculture could happen with no serious investment from the Crown, in a region of Africa where the French trade in slaves was feeble and where it might be possible to substitute slave labour with low-cost wage labour, officials at Versailles rigorously opposed it. Though concerns over the potentially high protection costs formed a part of Beudet's rationale, considerations that Saget's project might be harmful to the investors of the Caribbean sugar islands clearly influenced the formulation of policy at this moment. Among such investors were, of course, Jean Dubuc and the duc de Praslin who had left his post as Minister of the Marine in late December 1770. Yet Praslin's successor Bourgeois de Boynes (after a four-month tenure by Joseph Marie Terray) was equally invested in the Caribbean, having acquired a plantation on Saint-Domingue through his second wife, Charlotte Louise Desgots. Beudet himself had spent eighteen years on Saint-Domingue on his wife's plantation, before becoming an adviser to the Ministry of the Marine between 1762 and 1772. With the Ministry of the Marine staffed with officials whose private investments were anchored in the Caribbean, it is not surprising that Saget's proposal to build up cash crop cultivation in Africa was first delayed and then rejected.[39]

The Role of French West Africa in the Guyana Project

Despite tenacious resistance to cash crop cultivation in Lower Senegal during the administrations of Choiseul, Praslin, and Bourgeois de Boynes, there was one instance in which the Ministry of the Marine expressed an

---

[38] 'Gorée', 20 July 1772. ANOM C6 16, ff. 34–6.
[39] On Bourgeois de Boynes, see Godfroy, *Kourou, 1763*, 196. On Beudet, see Tarrade, *Le commerce colonial*, i, 77 and ii, 302. Another source claims that he resided in Port-au-Prince sixteen years as adviser to the Conseil Superieur. See *Loi relative aux Pensions, Donnée à Paris le 6 Avril 1791* (Paris: L'Imprimerie Royale, 1791), 11.

interest in African plants and crops. Yet this instance confirms the hege-
monic grip of the Caribbean plantation complex on policy makers within
the central administration in this period. In 1763, Gorée and its dependencies came of interest as a source of botanical species for Choiseul's pet
project in French Guiana. It was the botanist Michel Adanson who had
brought Gorée's botanical riches to Choiseul's attention, exemplifying the
inextricable ties between imperial policy and science.[40] At the instigation of
Beudet and E. F. Turgot (the brother of the political economist), both of
whom were instrumental to the Kourou Expedition, Adanson furnished
Choiseul with an elaborate memorandum on potential commercial plants
that he claimed to have purposefully left out of his *Histoire naturelle du
Sénégal* from 1757. For instance, he explained that seeds of the rubber plant
and indigo could be transported to Guiana and cultivated. In Adanson's
words, the object should be to 'let the rock of Gorée, so to speak, serve
as a necessary nursery to the emerging colony of Cayenne'.[41] In the 1763
instructions to Poncet, Choiseul thus instructed the governor to ship grain,
plants, and herbs from Senegal to Guiana. Poncet was also told to find out
the price of horses and all other useful animals that might successfully
survive in Guiana.[42]

Within a few years, it was not merely the agricultural riches of Gorée
that the Crown saw as potential seeds of growth for the colony in Guiana.
In conjunction with the notorious failure to settle Kourou with white
Europeans – an enterprise in which thousands of particularly German-
speaking poor succumbed between 1763 and 1765 – the idea to relocate
parts of Gorée's free and unfree population to Guiana to continue its
colonisation took hold within the Ministry of the Marine. During the
governorship of Gastière, an anonymous report, likely authored by the
former director of the Compagnie des Indes in Africa, Pierre Félix
Barthélémy David, suggested offering the free creole population of Gorée
to relocate to French Guiana at the Crown's expense and in exchange for
territory, if they agreed to bring their slaves. The report depicted successful

[40] On botany and empire, see Drayton, *Nature's Government;* L. Schiebinger and C. Swan (eds.),
Colonial Botany: Science, Commerce, and Politics in the Early Modern World (Philadelphia: University
of Pennsylvania Press, 2005); and McClellan III and Regourd, *The Colonial Machine.*

[41] Michel Adanson, 'Pièce instructives concernant l'Ile Gorée voisine du Cap-Verd en Afrike, avec un
Projet et des vues utiles relativement au Nouvel Établissement de Kaiene', May and June 1763,
ANOM C⁶ 15. For a brief study on Adanson' links to colonisation see Jean-Paul Nicolas, 'Adanson et
le Mouvement Colonial', in *Adanson – The Bicentennial of Michel Adanson's 'Familles des Plantes',* 2
vols., ed. George H. M. Lawrence (Pittsburgh, PA: Hunt Botanical Library Carnegie Institute of
Technology, 1963), ii, 393–449.

[42] Choiseul to Poncet de la Rivière, Versailles, 2 June 1763. ANOM B116.

relocation as a way to destabilise the British hold on Senegal. It estimated that thirty-six to forty free creoles owning approximately 650 slaves lived on Gorée. If they relocated and managed to build successful lives in Guiana, the larger creole population of Saint-Louis might follow and thereby weaken the British on the Senegal River.[43] In a letter dated 24 November 1767, two months after the submitted report, the Minister of the Marine informed Gastière that David had obtained royal approval for his proposition to invite 'the free negroes of Gorée and their captives to move to the new plantations' in Guiana and work as labourers until they had made enough to obtain their own land. The minister asked Gastière to encourage the free Negroes to leave the island, underlining that migration should be voluntary. He further pointed out that in supporting such a project, Gastière's governorship would acquire renewed importance because it would further the goal of the African holdings 'to increase the wellbeing and advancement of the meridional colonies'.[44] This effort to empty Gorée's population to benefit Guiana and the meridional colonies continued under Rocheblave. In June 1769, Rocheblave informed the Crown that there was a high death rate among the King's slaves due to starvation. He therefore encouraged shipping them to Guiana and Saint-Domingue, a proposal the Crown approved.[45]

In the years immediately after the Seven Years War, plants, animals, free creoles, and slaves from Gorée thus travelled across the Atlantic to ensure successful French colonisation in the Americas, while efforts to expand in Africa were blocked from within the colonial administration. Only in the shadows of official policy did local officials and independent agents such as Poncet de la Rivière, de Mesnager, Le Large, and Saget seek to bring the Lower Senegal region into the orbit of colonial experimentation. As they advocated their projects, they tapped into the growing language of the profitability of free labour over slave labour though Poncet, de Mesnager, and Le Large's underlying motivations were squarely centred on how agricultural plantations in Africa would enhance the French imperial enterprise. Only Saget's proposal had a social dimension, hoping as he did that his project would help Africa progress towards industry and

---

[43] Internal report, 7 September 1767, ANOM C[6] 15.

[44] Minister to Gastière, Versailles, 24 November 1767, ANON B126, Letter 41.

[45] 'Extrait de la lettre de M. De Rochelblave du 2 Juin 1769', 9 December 1769, ANOM C[6] 15. Barbara Traver notes that only a total of 20 *habitants* from Gorée and 125 slaves arrived in Guiana since those who arrived managed to write back to Gorée warning others not to follow. See Barbara Traver, '"The Benefits of Their Liberty": Race and the Eurafricans of Gorée in Eighteenth-Century French Guiana', *French Colonial History*, 16 (2016), 5.

prosperity and reduce the high death rate of sailors associated with the transatlantic slave trade.

The Reintroduction of Monopoly Trade

Preventing efforts to launch colonial experiments in Africa was of some concern to the Crown, but it paled in comparison to its troubles covering expenses associated with the shift from company to Crown rule. After the fall of Choiseul and his cousin Praslin in 1770, and prior to the outbreak of the American Revolution, the Ministry of the Marine's ongoing desire to alleviate royal expenses, coupled with a shift in government attitudes towards privileged companies – indeed the two are deeply interconnected – opened up a window for the re-insertion of monopoly trade. Within this context, investors in France, who regretted the recent loss of the French gum trade in Senegal, solicited the Crown for a partial monopoly. Once successful, private and semi-private interests became a new engine for colonial activities in West Africa. Though merchant communities in the French Atlantic ports immediately proclaimed that supporters of a return to monopoly merely used the loss of the gum trade as a pretext to re-monopolise the slave trade, reality was more complex. Just like there were intersecting and sometimes contradicting agendas among officials tied to the Ministry of the Marine, so advocates of a return to monopoly deployed different logics to advance their case and – once their requests were met – to defend their activities on the ground.

The most entrepreneurial agent behind the return to monopoly trade in Africa was Abbé Jean-Baptiste Demanet (sometimes spelled De Manet). Demanet (as well as his brother who went by the same last name) had joined Poncet de la Rivière in Lower Senegal in 1763 as a missionary but had returned to France in the mid-1760s. While in France, he authored the two-volume *Nouvelle histoire de l'Afrique française*, published in 1767, which became a source for *philosophes* and *économistes* in their fashioning of Africans and expansionist opportunities on the continent.[46] Demanet, who did not remain in France to enjoy his literary fame, returned to Africa in 1772 as the director of the Société d'Affrique, a company that he managed to found with the assistance of powerful financiers close to the Crown. This company was the first to earn a set of privileges in Africa after the liquidation of the Compagnie des Indes. In 1777, the Société d'Affrique transformed into the better-known Compagnie de la Guyane française,

---

[46] Duchet, *Anthropologie et histoire*, 105.

which in turn became the Compagnie de la gomme du Sénégal in January 1784 and then the Compagnie du Sénégal in 1786.[47]

Demanet's arguments for a return to monopoly trade played upon French imperial anxieties. In his celebrated book of 1767, he described how France could find in Africa all that it had lost in the Seven Years War. Though France had ceded Senegal to Britain in 1763, Demanet insisted that adjacent rivers and areas could easily restore and further augment previous commercial profits made in 'L'Afrique Française', his moniker for 'the part situated between Cap Blanc ... and the Sierra-Leone River'. Spending most pages describing the availability of gum and slaves and the easy access to provisioning, Demanet also echoed Poncet and de Mesnager's praise for areas such as the island of Bolama which he believed could become the greatest colony Europe had ever seen in Africa. On this island, Demanet proclaimed, the indigenous population was strong and beautiful, and one could cultivate sugar, rum, cocoa, indigo, cotton and 'all that upon which commerce with America is based'.[48]

The enticing depiction of Africa in Demanet's *Nouvelle histoire* rapidly stirred the imagination of French *philosophes* and political economists but also people seeking financial gain. Under the protection of none other than the comte de la Marche, Louis François Joseph de Bourbon-Conti, son of the Prince de Conti and godson of Louis XV, Demanet joined forces with the governor of the Bastille, the comte de Jumilhac, M. de la Porte, and the three *fermiers généraux*, Charles de la Mazière, Jean-Baptiste de Larenc-Borda, and Jacques Paulze. Together, they created the commercial company, the Société d'Affrique, in the summer of 1772. The company's aim was to re-establish French monopoly on the gum trade following the British conquest of Senegal by signing 'treaties with Moors and Arabs of the interior and the sovereign of Arguin and Portendick' who allegedly had awarded France an exclusive right to their goods. Having convinced investors that his missionary work had permitted him to forge strong bonds with the local population, they put Demanet in charge of the company's interests in Africa.[49]

---

[47] Jore, *Les Établissements français*, 329 and 331. On gum and French colonial interests, see James L. A. Webb Jr, 'The Trade in Gum Arabic: Prelude to French Conquest in Senegal', *The Journal of African History*, 26, 2 (1985), 149–68.

[48] Abbé Demanet, *Nouvelle histoire de l'Afrique Françoise, enrichie des cartes & d'observations astronomiques & géographiques, de remarques sur les usages locaux, les mœurs, la religion & la nature du commerce général de cette partie du monde* (Paris: Lacombe, 1767), xix and 114.

[49] 'Rapport au Ministre à l'occasion du détail des opérations de traite par la Société de S. La Roche pour le commerce d'Afrique', 12 August 1773, ANOM C⁶ 16, f. 52; and Lettre à Monseigneur de Boynes de Abbé Demanet, May 1771. ANOM E188, pièce 92.

Once back in Senegambia, Demanet advanced the interests of the Société d'Affrique, though not without causing serious trouble. He drew up treaties with local sovereigns, in which the French King was guaranteed property rights over the forts of Arguin and Portendick and the three gum forests of Sahel, Lebiar, and Alfatak, located north of the Senegal River. The signatories further promised only to trade with France and the Société d'Affrique. It is doubtful, however, that any of them intended to honour this imposition. Though Demanet conveyed his dealings to the minister in triumphant terms, the captain of one of the ships carrying gum back to France noted in his diary that Demanet had been approached by local rulers, each claiming that the other was an impostor and each trying to draw up treaties with Demanet to gain access to European commodities. Looking at the treaties, it does seem peculiar that, whereas one was with Le Roy Alicouri, the ruler of the Emirate of Trarza, another was simply with 'the sovereigns of Africa' (*les souverains d'Affrique*), a hopelessly vague description that suggests that Demanet was signing contracts with break-away rivals of the leading gum traders. To the Abbé, the actual source of supplies made no difference, of course, as long as he obtained his desired cargo.[50]

Although Demanet and his captain portrayed transactions as difficult but ultimately successful, other renditions of the Abbé's commercial strategies bring out the layers of violence that undergirded French commerce in West Africa, even when it was not directly connected to slave trading. Demanet could not speak any of the local languages and, like most European traders, needed translators to facilitate commercial transactions. The gum trade was mostly conducted by the Arab-speaking merchants of the Trarza, Brakna, and Darmankour (in present-day Mauritania). On Gorée, he had therefore tried to force a local African woman with a knowledge of Arabic to join him and his ships. Her great fear of Demanet led the Governor of Gorée, Charles Hippolite Boniface, to ask three Muslim religious teachers (the marabouts) to accept the task instead. The three marabouts, from whose testimony this episode is disclosed, reluctantly agreed out of respect for Boniface. During their days in Demanet's employment, they witnessed the Abbé's behaviour with horror. In one instance, when Demanet failed to negotiate the price he expected to pay, he became aggressive towards hostages that transactions between

---

[50] Treaty 434, 5 May 1775, 'Traité fait entre les souverains d'Affrique et le Sir Abbé Demanet Associé et directeur général de la Société d'Affrique'. And Treaty 435, 8 June 1773 'Treatté entre le sieur abbé Demanet et les princes et souverains de la tribu d'Alicauri'. ANOM Traités, nos. 434 and 435.

a European trader and local gum merchants required to be exchanged on both sides. With a gun in each hand, he threatened to 'burn their brains', after which he threw them into a canoe to return them to their people. Learning that very moment that one of his other ships had successfully traded gum elsewhere, Demanet quickly raised anchor, abandoning without care the French hostages held by the locals.[51]

Complaints also arrived from Gorée's population and Governor Boniface. The free population of Gorée petitioned the Crown conveying their frustrations with the incipient return of monopoly. Broadcasting their commitment to French subjecthood – and critiquing the French for depicting them as 'idle and useless' when in fact they helped mediate trade with the mainland and provided the 'slaves', 'workshops' (*ateliers d'ouvrier*), and 'sailors for provisioning' that secured the French presence in the region – they further denounced merchants' attempts to take their property (their slaves). Boniface, in turn, complained about Demanet's blatant disregard for local authority. The governor also revealed that he feared the powerful commercial interests that Demanet represented. Perhaps to get the Crown on his side, he charged that Demanet was provoking the British in Senegal who considered the Société d'Affrique's activities as a violation of the Treaty of 1763. Demanet countered these allegations by undermining the governor's credibility. He complained that Boniface and his men had helped themselves to the company's private storage houses and cost the company 30,000 livres plus damages and alleged that Boniface tried to discredit him purely because the Société d'Affrique got in the way of the governor's illicit slave trading.[52]

Despite complaints of local disorder, fraud, and misconduct, the Crown was not altogether displeased with the situation. In fact, it shrewdly exploited tensions between the company, the local administration, and the British for its own gain. Hearing about Boniface's concerns, Emmanuel-Armand de Richelieu, duc d'Aiguillon, Minister of Foreign Affairs (1771–4), conveyed to Bourgeois de Boynes, that he did not think that the British had any right to complain about Demanet's activities since France had only given up the right to trade in the Senegal River and not in the region above

---

[51] 'Mémoire du nommé Guiaye Ly marabout traduits de l'arabe en françois (à Portendic)', Gorée, 21 June 1773. ANOM E188, ff. 100–104bis.

[52] On local complaints, see 'Mémoire des habitants de l'isle de Gorée à Monsieur de la Roe, Premier Secrétaire d'Etat au Département de la Marine', 26 December 1773. ANOM C⁶ 16, f. 68. On Boniface's complaints, see Boniface to Bourgeois de Boynes, June 1773, ANOM E188, f. 118. For Demanet's response, see Demanet to Monsieur le Chevalier de Boniface, 6 March 1773, ANOM E188, f. 96.

and below it. Aiguillon also noted that while the Abbé had acted without legitimate powers, 'I do not see why we cannot close our eyes at this point with regard to his actions'. He further indicated that while the exclusive privilege that the Abbé had attempted to obtain for the company was against a policy of free national trade, it might still be useful to let the company enjoy a privilege temporarily if, in exchange, 'the company would pay for the maintenance of the forts' in the region. Independent merchants, Aiguillon stressed, did not have the means required to undertake a project such as this one, and if the Crown tried to recapture the gum trade in such a brazen manner, the British would surely react.[53]

Demanet and the Société d'Affrique could not have asked for a stronger backing than a Crown eager to use the company as a vehicle for its own ambitions. As would soon become evident, moreover, Crown ambitions went far beyond the restoration of the lucrative gum trade. On 4 February 1774, the Société d'Affrique obtained the right to use the royal storage houses and trade stations between Cap Blanc and Sierra-Leone, as long as it did not obstruct national free trade.[54] More importantly, it was allowed to alter its main focus. As the Société d'Affrique applied for a full monopoly on trade in the region around Gorée, its argument that it would enhance the trade in gum arabic and exploit commercial opportunities in Africa was to be expected, but the company also requested an exclusive right to the slave trade in the region and a piece of land in French Guiana. As soon became evident, Guiana was the main focus of the enhanced Société d'Affrique, which transformed into the better-known Compagnie de la Guyane française. Such a bolstering of the company was not the outcome that Boniface and the population of Gorée had hoped for. Yet they did receive a consolation prize; in late 1774, the Société d'Affrique deemed Demanet too much of a troublemaker and ousted him from the company.[55]

The formidable forces backing the transformation of the Société d'Affrique and the launching of the Compagnie de la Guyane française have not gone unnoticed. In his study of the eighteenth-century French nobility, Guy Chaussinand-Nogaret dwells on the fact that the company (like most of its predecessors) was financed exclusively by members of the nobility, the royal officer corps, and the General Farm, with not a single

---

[53] From duc d'Aiguilllon to Bourgeois de Boynes, 27 August 1773, ANOM C⁶ 16, f. 66.
[54] Jore, Les établissements franais, 327. Christian Schefer, Instructions générales données de 1763 à 1870 aux gouverneurs et ordonnateurs des établissements français en Afrique occidentale recueillies et publiées par Christian Schefer, 2 vols. (Paris: E. Champion, 1921), i, 48.
[55] 'Colonies', 12 December 1774, ANOM E188, f. 136.

merchant featuring among shareholders.[56] In papers on Africa, a document of 1777 entitled 'La Compagnie d'Affrique' lists twenty-nine names below a description of the company's privilege, not all of whom conform to the people listed by Chaussinand-Nogaret.[57] The original investors of the Société d'Affrique are listed (Borda, Paulze, Maizière (all three tax farmers), and the Prince de Conti), but so are ministers of the reign of the young Louis XVI, Antoine de Sartine (Minister of the Marine, 1774–80), Charles Gravier comte de Vergennes (Minister of Foreign Affairs, 1774–87), and Jean-Frédéric Phélypeaux comte de Maurepas (Minister of the Marine, 1723–49 and Minister of State 1776–81) as well as former ministers such as, Aiguillon (Minister of Foreign Affairs, 1771–4 and of War, 1774), and Henri Léonard Jean Baptiste Bertin (Controller General of Finance, 1759–63, and of Foreign Affairs for a month in 1774). Others included Emmanuel-Félicité de Durfort duc de Duras, Marshal of France, the tax farmer Antoine-Laurent Lavoisier (sometimes seen as the father of chemistry), and women such as Marie-Philippe Taschereau de Baudry, widow of Abdré Potier de Novion, marquis de Grignon. It may be that the list of twenty-nine names included not just shareholders but also patrons of the company who were willing to support a further expansion of company rule. Either way, the Africa branch of the Compagnie de la Guyane française was backed by powerful investors whose proximity to the Crown had changed little since the days of Colbert's chartered companies.

The combination of a partial monopoly within certain sectors of the economy and open trade among French merchants in others was emblematic of the government's approach to the market in the eighteenth century. Indeed, one scholar argues for its effectiveness and sees it as the engine behind 'the dynamism of state-sponsored economic reform' in this period.[58] Such a policy, however, had to be defended and justified within the ever-expanding arena of public debate to minimise risks of social unrest. The company's high-powered stockholders were eminently attuned to this issue and set out to disarm predictable adversaries among French commercial communities with great intellectual sway. In

---

[56] Guy Chaussinand-Nogaret, *The French Nobility in the Eighteenth Century: From Feudalism to Enlightenment*, trans. William Doyle (Cambridge: Cambridge University Press, 1985), 96–9.

[57] The full list was M. de Sartine, M. de Vergennes, M Taschereau, M. de Maurepas, M d'Aiguillon, M. le duc de Duras, M. le Prince de Conti, M. le Scette de Lamballe, M. le comte de Isles, M. le comte de Tavannes, M. le M. de Renti, M. le comte de Jumilhac, M. Bertin, M. de Beaumanoir, M. Maziere, M. Borda, M. Augeard, M. Paulze, M. de Neubourg, M. Eyriès, M. de Silly fils du S. de Conty, M. le Noir, M. Daligre, M. de Rozambo, M. de Mareuil, M. et M. Lavoisier, M. Dangé, M. de Vermerange, Chante Merle. 'La Compagnie d'Affrique', 1777, MAE, AD, Afrique 10, f. 312.

[58] Horn, *Economic Development in Early Modern France*, 5–6.

the company's memorandum to the merchants of Bordeaux, it used the ports' objections to the recently established French free ports in the Caribbean to squander opposition. It pointed out that the loss of Canada in 1763 had caused the Antilles to lack wood, cattle, and cod. Given the inability of French ports to adequately redress this lack, the Crown had sanctioned the establishment of Môle Saint-Nicolas and St Lucia and thus the entrance of foreigners into the French colonial market. Prodding first the ports' wounded pride, the company then shifted gear and avowed that France needed to close the two free ports. To the company, this could only be achieved by turning Guiana into 'the wet nurse of the islands of the Antilles', which it proclaimed was its primary focus. Acknowledging that people had recently tried to build up Guiana to replace Canada and assist the Antilles, it alleged that this agenda had failed because it was tested 'at a time when one was embarrassed about the means of executing such an interesting project'. Rebuking Choiseul and E. F. Turgot's efforts to turn Guiana into a white settler colony, the company stipulated that only enslaved Africans could be deployed in such a hot climate, thus manufacturing an excuse for the company's request for a monopoly on the slave trade.[59]

The company also informed Bordeaux that it had requested a plot of land in the vicinity of the Oyapock River in Guiana, on which it planned to cultivate commodities identical to those that the sugar islands currently obtained from New England. It was to guarantee the necessary labour for this project that it requested an exclusive privilege to the slave trade in the region from Cap Blanc to the Sierra Leone River, as well as the right to penetrate the interior. This narrow stretch of land was only 'a point on the map' in comparison to the long coastline between Sierra Leone and the Cape of Good Hope where 'all the slave traders do their trading' and obtained the lion's share of France's annual human cargo. With respect to the French gum trade in Senegambia, the company surmised that it would soon be ruined because of the short-term interests of independent merchants who competed with the English and who did not understand that 'this branch of commerce . . . can only be maintained by a reciprocal trade agreement between the company and the Moors'. In contrast, a company with a monopoly on the gum and slave trades would

---

[59] 'Mémoire lû le 13 Juillet 1775', Bordeaux ADG, C4382, f. 11. See also 'Compagnie d'Affrique Mémoire', undated, ANOM C⁶ 16, f. 1 (it is misplaced in a folder marked 'Sénégal 1770').

obtain a much higher profit from this region to the greater benefit of French commerce.[60]

The Minister of the Marine, Antoine de Sartine – who was likely one of the backers of the company – anticipated the resistance that the request for an extended privilege would encounter. Son of a *marchand-banquier* from Lyon and close to Choiseul and Praslin (both of whom signed his marriage contract), he was as skilful as Choiseul at inviting debate in anticipation of policy change, offering the ports to have their say in the matter.[61] On 10 August 1775, the Chamber of Commerce in Bordeaux addressed a long letter to the Crown opposing the company's plans, sending a copy to the merchants of Nantes. Nantes responded with praise, singling out Bordeaux's efforts to go against the 'bad citizens' who were trying to manipulate 'the religion of the Minister of the Marine'.[62] However, it was not only the ports that objected to the return of company rule. The *Ephémérides du citoyen*, edited by Du Pont de Nemours in these years, had written against the ports in 1766–7 on the topic of the Exclusif. Now, it sided with them against the expanding Société d'Affrique. It reminded its readers of Morellet's 1769 attack on the Compagnie des Indes and warned that a new company was about to be founded against the interests of the nation. A copy of this article found its way into the Ministry of Foreign Affairs where it mixed with various memoranda on the Société d'Affrique.[63] Curiously, Du Pont de Nemours did not use the debate over the reintroduction of company rule in Senegambia to repeat the physiocratic argument against the French slave trade and for expansion in Africa based on free labour. Nor did he bring up his and Turgot's alleged attempt to create a slave-free colony in West Africa in 1774, an assertion made during the Revolution, but which is yet to be supported by surviving archival documents.[64]

Foreseeing all these objections, the company's supporters had incorporated into their memorandum a pliant argument for commercial privilege. Stating that they agreed in principle that a monopoly-holding company

---

[60] 'Compagnie d'Affrique Mémoire', undated, ANOM C⁶ 16, f. 1.

[61] Saugera, *Bordeaux port négrier*, 82–3. On Sartine's origins and ties, see Jacques Michel, *Du Paris de Louis XV à La Marine de Louis XVI: L'oeuvre de Monsieur de Sartine*, 2 vols. (Paris: Les éditions de l'Érudit, 1983), i, II, and 29.

[62] 10 August 1775. ADG C4257; 12 August 1775, ADG C4265, f. 25; Nantes to Bordeaux, 26 August 1775, ADG C4336, f. 68.

[63] *Nouvelles Ephémérides Économiques* 1775 – 'Mémoire sur la Compagnie Royale d'Afrique établie à Marseille', Paris, MAE, AD, Afrique 10, f. 248.

[64] On this claim, see Chapter 5, page 227 in this book.

was an offence to national interests and the nation's right to colonial trade, they objected to its universal application. In cases where independent merchants were unable to properly provision a colony, for instance, a company could still be useful. This argument was another clever stab at the ports since it was due to their failure to provision the colonies in the Antilles that the Crown had established free ports. As the company argued its case, it underlined that all it hoped to achieve was 'the reestablishment of the nation's commerce'. The privilege it had obtained on 4 February 1774 to use the royal storage houses and trade stations between Cap Blanc and the Sierra Leone River had already seen a happy development in this direction, it stressed, in that the price of gum arabic had decreased by 50 per cent, to the profit of French manufacture. It further maintained that its requests were only following the tradition that had sustained the rise of the French colonial empire in the first place. As it said, '[i]t is the companies that have founded the colonies, established them with success, and prepared the lustre at which the colonies have since arrived by means of liberty'.[65]

The company's arguments served to refute objections to its privilege from French port cities; yet in so doing, it seized the opportunity to interfere in the debate on the much-contested meaning of the 'liberty of commerce' that also characterised this period. In sharp contrast to ports' understanding of freedom to trade vis-à-vis the colonies, or the view promoted by the Physiocrats, the company stated that: 'from national exclusive privilege emerges the word *liberté*, to which one always gives too extensive a meaning since its definition is little known'. In matters of commerce, the company said, liberty meant the faculty to engage in the sort of commerce which one was permitted to do, 'in this or that manner, and at this or that time, by these or those means'. It was up to the government to assess what should be permitted. In other words, liberty of commerce meant having a right to follow rules freely and without hindrance. The role of the government was to set those rules and protect the rights that they gave rise to.[66] This argument, which echoed in style, tone, and rationale, the arguments developed by Jacques Necker in his 1769 response to Abbé Morellet's attack on the Compagnie des Indes, further suggest that Necker, who had come into office as *directeur general des finances* in late 1777, played a role in concocting the Société d'Affrique's arguments.[67]

[65] Mémoire, Lû le 13 Juillet 1775, ADG C4382, f. 11.
[66] 'Compagnie d'Affrique Mémoire', undated, ANOM C⁶ 16, f. 1.
[67] See Jacques Necker, *Réponse au mémoire de M. l'abbé Morellet sur la Compagnie des Indes, imprimée en exécution de la délibération de Mrs les actionnaires, prise dans l'assemblée générale du 8 août 1769* (Paris: imprimerie royale, 1769).

With sweeping rejoinders to the ports and with the support of a power-ful elite, the company emerged victorious. On 14 August 1777, the Société d'Affrique changed its name to the Compagnie de la Guyane française. The government ceded the territory between the River Oyapock and the River Approuague in Guiana and gave the company rights to the forts of Joal, Rufisque, and Gorée and an exclusive privilege to the slave trade between Cap Verde and the Casamance River. Additionally, the company would receive 300 livres from the Crown for each male slave introduced to Guiana, and 200 livres for each woman and child. Since the company intended to grow tobacco, and later also 'indigo, cotton, coffee, and sugar cane', but could not expect an immediate profit, the King further promised a bonus on tobacco. He also provided the company with three vessels of 450 to 500 tonneaux and expected a profit only on the slave and wood trades.[68]

The French ports immediately castigated the generous privileges offered to the company. On behalf of port merchants, Bordeaux urged Sartine not to sacrifice the general interests of individual merchants for a private company whose veiled agenda was to monopolise the slave trade. In his response, Sartine merely reiterated the company's arguments, but to mol-lify the incensed merchant communities, he insinuated the coming of a reward, a reference to the bonus of 15 livres that independent merchants would begin to receive for each slave purchased east of the Cape of Good Hope and sold to the French West Indies. Dangling pecuniary rewards in front of slave traders, Sartine managed to temporarily appease adversaries of the company.[69]

Considering the strict limitations placed on the colonial projects of de Mesnager on the *grande terre* off of Gorée and the rejection of Saget's self-funded proposal, the conditions that the Crown offered to the company do seem suspiciously favourable. It is remarkable that the territory in Guiana – intended as a 'wet nurse' for the Antilles – could be used for the cultivation of indigo, cotton, coffee, and sugarcane, none of which had anything to do with the provisioning of the plantation islands but would add to the internal competition with the West Indies if successful. The fact that the government was prepared to divert labour supply away from the Antilles

---

[68] 'La Compagnie d'Affrique', 1777, MAE, AD, Afrique 10, f. 312.
[69] On the joint mobilisation of ports, see Le Havre to Bordeaux, 2 October. ADG C4257. Letter from Bordeaux to Sartine, 7 October 1777, ADG C4265 and 'Observations sur l'arrêt du Conseil du 14 Aout 1777' ADG C4383, f. 40. For Sartine's response, see Sartine to Bordeaux, 6 October 1777. ADG C4338, f. 55. On the bonus see Jean Meyer, Jean Tarrade, Annie Rey-Goldzeiguer, and Jacques Thobie, *Histoire de la France coloniale*, 356.

was also striking and stands in contrast to the policies pursued during the administrations of Choiseul, Praslin, and Bourgeois de Boynes.

It appears, moreover, that Sartine diverged from his predecessors in more ways than one. Unlike Choiseul, Praslin, and Bourgeois de Boynes, Sartine seemed more open to the idea of producing colonial cash crops in West Africa. This is evident based on the Ministry of the Marine's response to Pierre Duménil, a trader from Havre de Grace, who had founded a company to create a colony on the island of Bolama south of Gorée for the cultivation of sugar, coffee, cotton, and indigo at the company's expense. Duménil's request echoed the one made by M. Saget earlier in the decade, although the former was wise enough to state that his colony would be subjected to the Exclusif. Duménil further noted that cultivation would be by 'acclamatised Blacks' (*des Noirs acclimates*), avoiding any critique of slavery and the slave trade.[70] The Ministry appeared supportive of Duménil's suggestion. The *commis*, M. de Villeneuve, reported to Sartine that 'the advantages that the state could obtain from a colony founded on this island would be considerable and would come at no expense to it'.[71] Sartine agreed and therefore reached out to Charles Gravier, comte de Vergennes in the Ministry of Foreign Affairs to investigate if the island were part of the Bissagot Islands and therefore under Portuguese control. When neither Sartine nor Vergennes were able to wrestle an answer out of the Portuguese minister, the marquis of Pombal, Duménil's plans faltered, though not because the Crown opposed them.[72]

The first years of Louis XVI's rule which began in 1774 therefore constituted a moment during which the Ministry of the Marine was ready to off-load a sizeable chunk of its administration in West Africa to semi-private forces. It also appeared to be more open to merchants who wished to introduce cash crop cultivation in Africa than it had been during the bureaucratic reign of Dubuc and Beudet under Louis XV. Both of these tendencies would continue into the next decade as French participation in the American Revolutionary Wars on the side of the rebellious thirteen colonies offered France an opportunity to retake Senegal. What this war

---

[70] [Duménil], '2. Mémoire ou eclaircissement pour server de suite au 1er mémoire', ANOM C⁶ 17, f. 8.
[71] 'Cotes d'Afrique: Isle de Boulam', Internal memorandum to Sartine. Marked Villeneuve, ANOM C⁶ 17, f. 1.
[72] This issue is reflected in letter from Sartine to Vergennes, 30 Janury 1776, ANOM C⁶ 17, f. 4; letter from Villeneuve to Duménil, 30 January 1776, ANOM C⁶ 17, f. 5; internal note from Villeneuve to Sartine, 6 February 1776, ANOM C⁶ 17, ff. 6–7; and Letters from Duménil to Sartine, undated, ANOM C⁶ 17, ff. 39 and 40.

also did, of course, was to highlight once again the precariousness of Europe's colonial enterprise in the Americas.

The Recapture of Senegal

Officials within the colonial administration had contemplated ways to retake Senegal since the Treaty of Paris in 1763. In 1764, Poncet de la Rivière designed to stir up trouble for the British government together with the Eurafrican mayor of Saint-Louis, Charles Thevenot, who, as Poncet said, 'is more master of Senegal than the governor'. Based on his connection to Thevenot, Poncet stressed that 'if I had funds for this, I would chase the [British] out of Senegal and the Gambia River without the intervention of a single European'.[73] During the administration of de Mesnager in 1766 and later during the commotion fuelled by the Société d'Affrique, the Crown also happily exploited silences in the Treaty of Paris to reclaim French influence in Upper and Lower Senegal. In 1777, it was Jacques Joseph Eyriès, a 'member and agent of the *compagnie* [de la Guyane française]' and a *lieutenant de port* at Le Havre, who first encouraged the Crown to use the outbreak of war between Britain and its thirteen colonies to recapture Senegal.[74]

In his report to the Crown, Eyriès scolded the public for its lack of interest in Senegambia and praised the latter's limitless promise. He noted that Senegal supplied 2,400 slaves annually, 2 million livres worth of gum, ivory, and 150 to 200 livres of gold (approximately seventy-three to ninety-seven kilograms), totalling trade worth more than 5 million livres each year. To Eyriès, however, it was not what France had acquired from the region until now but what it could expect from it in the future that was of real interest. Marshalling the increasingly familiar argument by enterprising colonial agents, he underlined that with its fertile land on both sides of the river, Senegal offered France an opportunity 'at no expense' to cultivate 'the crops that enriche[d] the planters [*habitants*] of America in spite of the enormous expenses they [were] obliged to make'. The river also led to well-known gold mines, all of which could be reached within twenty to twenty-five days from a French port.[75]

---

[73] Poncet de la Rivière to Choiseul, Gorée 25 May 1764, ANOM C⁶ 15, f. 31v. On Charles Thévenot and his family, see Brooks, *Eurafricans in Western Africa*, 278.

[74] On Eyriès, 'Réponse aux plaintes de M. de Paradis' 1777, ANOM C⁶ 17, f. 131.

[75] 'Mémoire sur la Concession du Sénégal, fort James et Fort de Bense, Projet d'Armement et d'Attaque pour s'en emparer'. Vers 1777, ANOM C⁶ 17, ff. 103–15, f. 103bis.

The former director of the Compagnie des Indes in Africa, David, drummed up support for a reconquest of Senegal the following year. Having proposed to transfer Eurafricans to Guiana to build up this colony only a few years earlier, David now argued that 'one of the greatest advantages France c[ould] draw from the success of the current war against England w[ould] be to take hold of Senegal'. If France took Sierra Leone as well, the only competition left in Africa would be the Portuguese and their trade amounted to little more than one-tenth of the commerce that France could anticipate from the region. The Crown's governor at Gorée, Armény de Paradis, also considered the potential to reconquer Senegal. In a letter to Sartine dated 23 June 1778, Paradis incorporated 'a memorandum on the state of the English in Senegal' which included his 'reflections on the means to take possession of it'. Curiously, papers assembled within the Ministry for Foreign Affairs on the conquest also included Saget's 1770 proposal (though without name or date). Its reappearance suggests that someone had found his arguments for the relocation of the production of sugar and coffee from the Americas to Africa relevant in the context of a possible conquest.[76]

The numerous encouragements to conquer Senegal moved the Crown into action. Based on a comprehensive plan of attack by Eyriès, the Crown assigned a sizeable fleet at Brest to the mission in November 1778. Though nearly bankrupt, the Compagnie de la Guyane française contributed seven to eight smaller ships to carry the troops (totalling 430 men).[77] To head the operation, the Crown chose Armand Louis de Gontaut, duc de Lauzun (also known as the duc de Biron), a court darling whose childhood, according to his biographer, was marked by Enlightenment discussions organised by Madame de Pompadour and her physician, François Quesnay. Lauzun successfully recaptured Saint-Louis on 30 January 1779. In his subsequent communication with the Crown, he stressed with triumphant pride that the reconquest had not seen the loss of a single Frenchman and would 'irreparably wound English commerce' and augment that of the French in equal measure.[78]

---

[76] For David's encouragements, see Letter from David. 14 August 1778, MAE, AD, Afrique 10, f. 343; and 'Mémoire', 15 August 1778, MAE, AD, Afrique 10, f. 344. For Paradis' lettter, see Ar mény de Paradis to Sartine, Gorée 23 June 1778, ANOM C⁶ 17, f. 14. The letter dated Gorée le 20 Juin 1778 contains actual details for the attack. For the copy of Saget's proposal in the Ministry of Foreign Affairs, see 'Projet d'établissement en Afrique', MAE, AD, Afrique 10, f. 317.

[77] Schefer, *Instructions générales*, i, 62–3.

[78] Letter from Lauzun, Senegal 15 February 1779, MAE, AD, Afrique 10, f. 348. Clément C. Velay, *Le duc de Lauzun 1747–1793* (Paris: Éditions Buchet/Chastel, 1983), 20 and 143.

Once Senegal was back in French hands, the new Minister of the Marine, Charles Eugène Gabriel de La Croix, marquis de Castries, was inundated with memoranda on the possible commercial and colonial opportunities Senegal might facilitate. Many regurgitated the familiar registry of arguments on how to enhance French trade in slaves, gum, and gold. On 31 January 1780, David sent the Minister of Foreign Affairs, the comte de Vergennes, two memoranda on the importance of Senegal and how best to benefit from it.[79] Soon after, he forwarded another twenty-two memoranda (approximately 170 pages) on issues pertaining to the Senegalese concession and the goldmines of Bambuk.[80] Jean Dubuc was equally excited about the reconquest, writing to reiterate the role of Africa as a source of slaves to the Caribbean colonies. To Dubuc, it was crucial to augment the number of French trade stations on the coast since France had fewer forts in Africa than any other European colonial power. He encouraged the government to chase the English from the Gambia River and make itself master of the region from Cap Blanc to and including the Sierra Leone River. He further advised establishing forts at Cap Laho, Anamabou, and Porto Novo. If all these areas came under French flag, Dubuc opined, then France would finally be able to meet the labour needs of the sugar plantation without assistance from foreign slave traders.[81]

The most surprising proposal came from the Compagnie de la Guyane française, which appeared to have drastically shifted its position on French opportunities in West Africa during the war. After years of promoting colonisation in French Guiana, the company now joined those who encouraged imperial expansion in Africa. Though it referred to slaves and gold as reasons for maintaining Senegal, it also argued along with Eyriès that the territory on each side of the Senegal River was suitable for cultivation. In its report to Vergennes, it observed that cotton and indigo grew naturally in Senegal and that sugar, coffee, and tobacco could be easily and successfully cultivated there if given due attention. It even dipped into the physiocratic cannon to explain the merits of its proposition. As it stated, it would be possible to 'establish in a few years all along the river the most flourishing of colonies. Immense pastures will be covered with cattle. The first steps towards *civilisation* [my emphasis] will soon

---

[79] David to minister, 31 January, MAE, AD, Afrique 11, f. 5.
[80] 'Inventaire des pieces continues dans le Dossier des mémoires concernant la concession du Sénégal, et les établissements sur les Mines en Bambouk' MAE, AD, Afrique 11, f. 21.
[81] Dubuc to Castries, May 1782, MAE, AD, Afrique 11, f. 119.

open to France the route to Bambuk, Tambaoura, and Naizambana' which were 'the wealthiest mines that existed in the universe'.[82]

Next, the company explained how to implement its proposed project. It noted that 'it is not by force that one can obtain success. The nations of the interior of Africa are sheltered from invasion by a burning climate, immense deserts' and rivers impossible to navigate. Therefore,

> it is by means of persuasion, by the attraction of new pleasures; by an inviolable loyalty to their commitment that one can hope to bind these peoples to France. It is necessary to establish settlements all along the river and with the different nations in the interior. It is essential that those who will be charged to direct these know how to win the affection of these peoples, prevent jealousy and rivalry between nations, that those who will be in charge of defending them refrain from using an apparatus of force or violence . . . and will appear to be occupied with their wellbeing.[83]

Adopting a language of civilisation, agricultural development, and persuasion, the company signalled a clear departure in its thinking about West Africa. Apart from Eyriès' report of 1777, the company and its powerful associates had only ever been interested in trading slaves and gum in West Africa, reserving for the Americas their interest in commercial agriculture. Now, however, it was echoing Poncet, de Mesnager, and Saget and plucking aspects of Roubaud's and Mirabeau's vocabulary to advertise the expansionist opportunities Africa had to offer France. Yet in so doing, the company disassociated proposals for a French civilising mission in West Africa from its erstwhile connection to free trade policies, attaching it instead to the colonising abilities of a privileged commercial company. In fact, it told Vergennes, that only a privileged company would be able to bring such a project to fruition, nominating itself as the ideal candidate to oversee it.[84]

While at war, the French government had no time to digest the Compagnie de la Guyane française's proposal and the arrival of peace precluded its ability to executed it. The company had suffered financial losses during the war and struggled to continue its operations. Moreover, Castries' inclinations were to limit rather than expand company rule. Against the company's request for an exclusive privilege and its claim that it could ensure the progress of commerce in the Senegal River and help 'the Arabs and negroes . . . overcome their ferocity and civilize them', the minister decided to check its operations instead.[85] In recognition of its

---

[82] 'Mémoire', 1782, MAE, AD, Afrique 11, f. 123.
[83] Ibid. On the emphasis on persuasion, see Donath, 'Persuasion's Empire'.
[84] 'Mémoire', 1782, MAE, AD, Afrique 11, f. 123.
[85] 'Mémoire sur le Commerce du Sénégal', 1783, MAE, AD, Afrique 11, f. 191.

ı

assistance during the conquest, the company received an exclusive privilege to the gum trade in the Senegal River and its dependencies on the condition that it change its name to the Compagnie de la gomme du Sénégal. And while it could trade in slaves on an equal footing with independent French merchants, its charter stipulated that it could only purchase captives for the colony of Guiana.[86]

With the Peace Treaty of 1783, France regained control of the European trade up the Senegal River from its mouth to the comptoir of Fort St Joseph at Galam.[87] The reconquest thereby generated opportunities in Africa that the government had steadfastly refused to consider after the Seven Years War. Nevertheless, its approach to the continent shifted only ever so slightly. The instructions the government furnished its French governors in Senegal until the arrival of peace repeated much of the content found within the instructions it had previously composed for its governors on Gorée. Dumontet, the new governor of Senegal in 1782, was instructed that 'the importance of the Senegalese possession consists in what it offers to commerce . . . slaves for cultivation in America, gum, gold, and ivory'. The Crown made no mention of the desire to spread 'civilisation' in West Africa, nor of any wishes to expand into the region and develop agricultural colonies. In fact, Dumontet's instructions insisted that the governor should forge a great relationship with the local populations along the river and never let them think that France was interested in anything but 'a simple commerce' (*un simple commerce*).[88] Dumontet's successor, Louis Legardeur de Repentigny, who arrived in February 1784, received similar instructions. Only during the fêted administration of the chevalier de Boufflers did the Crown convey a nascent support for the cultivation of commercial cash crops in West Africa, though never in terms that evoked civilisation, development, and progress.

Chevalier de Boufflers and the French Administration in Lower Senegal

In 1785, the Crown decided to replace Repentigny with Stanislas Jean, chevalier de Boufflers. Although Boufflers only stayed two years, he remained the official governor of Senegal until 1789, and has often been seen as the most prestigious administrator of the French holdings in

---

[86] 'Arrêt du Conseil d'État du Roi', 11 January 1784, MAE, AD, Afrique 11, f. 202.
[87] On peace negotiations with respect to Senegal see Schefer, *Instructions générales*, i, 103.
[88] 'Mémoire du Roy pour server d'instruction au Sr. Dumontet commandans du Sénégal'. 1 April 1782, ANOM C⁶ 17, f. 2.

Senegambia prior to the French Revolution. A talented poet and friend of renowned men of letters, Stanislas was born on 31 May 1738 to Louis François, marquis de Boufflers and Marie Françoise Catherine de Beauvau-Craon, mistress to the King of Poland and the poet Jean-François de Saint-Lambert (author of *Ziméo*). Boufflers' cousin, Amélie de Boufflers, was the spouse of the duc de Lauzun, who had reconquered Senegal in 1779. Raised at the Court of Lunéville, through which passed leading lights such as Helvétius, Montesquieu, Voltaire, Mme du Châtelet, and Saint-Lambert, Boufflers' worldview was at once tied to the intellectual universe of the *philosophes* and the Physiocrats and deeply embedded in the value system of the high nobility. A military man and member of the Knights of Malta, he had volunteered for the governorship of Senegal to pursue glory and, so he said, to win the hand of his lover, Françoise Eléonore Dejean de Manville, comtesse de Sabran.[89]

Unlike most of his predecessors, Boufflers was seen by his contemporaries in Senegal as a man of great civility. The first director of the Compagnie de la gomme du Sénégal, Jean-Baptiste-Léonard Durand, stated that Boufflers' talents and celebrity generated excitement and hope in the colony. His successor, Jean-Gabriel Pelletan, said that Boufflers 'left a dear and respectable memory which it will be difficult to replace'. Sylvain Meinrad Xavier de Golbérry, a young man who came to Senegal with Boufflers, explained that 'one cannot bring to Africa more liberal intentions, and more noble and pure views than those brought by M. de Boufflers'. René Claude Geoffroy de Villeneuve, a trusted friend of Boufflers in Senegal, stressed that Boufflers had treated him with paternal love. Finally, Lamiral, a former employee of the Compagnie de la Guyane française, wrote in 1789 that Boufflers' was 'too great for such a small colony'. Even foreign visitors lauded Boufflers' administration. The Swedish abolitionist, Carl Bernhard Wadström, recalled that during his, Dr Sparrman's, and Arrhenius's voyage to West Africa, Boufflers received them in 'a manner that need not be explained to those who are acquainted with the amiable character

[89] On Boufflers' childhood at Lunéville, see Gaston Maugras, *Dernières années de la cour de Lunéville – Mme de Boufflers ses enfants et ses amis* (Paris: Plon-Nourrit et Cie, 1906); and Gaston Maugras, *La Marquise de Boufflers et son fils Le Chevalier de Boufflers* (Paris: Plon-Nourrit et Cie, 1907). On his administration in Senegal, see Jore, *Les établissements français*; Schefer, *Instructions générales*; P. Cultru, *Histoire du Sénégal du XVe siècle à 1870* (Paris: E. Larose, 1910), Paul Bouteiller, *Le Chevalier de Boufflers et le Sénégal de son temps 1785–1788* (Paris: Éditions Lettres du Monde, 1995). On his hope to win the hand of Madame de Sabran, see François Bessire, 'Préface', in *Chevalier de Boufflers – Lettres d'Afrique à Madame de Sabran*, 8–10.

and various accomplishments of a man who does real honour to his country, and to civilized society'.[90]

Unanimous praise notwithstanding, Boufflers was not as different from his predecessors as these tributes might suggest. Despite official protocol, he was as engaged in slave trading as Poncet and de Mesnager had been. A mere month into his administration, Boufflers told Sabran that she could let the wife of Louis Philippe comte de Ségur (son of the Minister of War and close friend of Boufflers) know that he awaited Beudet's boat from Bordeaux, on which he would ship fifty 'beautiful Negroes' to Saint-Domingue at a favourable rate to work the countess' plantation. Boufflers' 'liberality', moreover, did not prevent him from buying the Duchesse d'Orléans (Louise Marie Adélaïde de Bourbon, wife of Louis Philippe Joseph, duc d'Orléans from 1785) a 'little Negro girl' aged two or three who, according to Boufflers, was 'pretty, not as the day, but as the night'.[91] Boufflers, in other words, was a typical nobleman of the eighteenth century whose ideas of civility and progress could easily align with the violent tasks associated with the transatlantic slave trade. Nevertheless, his administration stands out from that of his predecessors for two reasons: firstly, the Crown revealed an interest in the cultivation of cotton and indigo in West Africa during Boufflers' administration and, secondly, Boufflers successfully oversaw the execution of precisely such an experiment.

At first, it was not so much the Crown's interest in cash crop cultivation during Boufflers' governorship that merits attention as its more comprehensive commitment to the region. As historian Christian Schefer noted, the instructions that the Crown compiled for Boufflers, encapsulated 'the entire system and policy at which the Ancien Régime finally arrived with regard to the coast of West Africa'.[92] That policy was to enhance the

---

[90] Jean-Baptiste-Léonard Durand, *Voyage au Sénégal ou Mémoires historiques, philosophiques sur les découvertes, les établissemens et le commerce des Européens dans les mers de l'Océan atlantique: depuis le Cap-Blanc jusqu'à la rivière de Serre-Lionne inclusivement; suivis de la Relation d'un voyage par terre de l'île Saint-Louis à Galam; et du texte arabe de Trois traités de commerce faits par l'auteur avec les princes du pays* (Paris: H. Agasse, 1802), xxvii. Jean-Gabriel Pelletan, *Mémoire sur la colonie française du Sénégal: avec quelques considérations historiques et politiques sur la traite des Nègres* (Paris: Panckoucke, 1800), 92. Sylvain Meinrad Xavier de Golbérry, *Fragmens d'un voyage en Afrique: fait pendant les années 1785, 1786 et 1787, dans les contrées occidentales de ce continent, comprises entre le cap Blanc de Barbarie, par 20 degrés, 47 minutes, et le cap de Palmes, par 4 degrés, 30 minutes, latitude boréale* (2 vols. Paris: Treuttel et Würtz, 1802), i, 9. M. Lamiral, *L'Affrique et le people Affriquain* (Paris: Chez Dessenne, Libraire, au Palais Royal, 1789), 80. Carl Bernhard Wadström, *An Essay on Colonization, Particularly applied to the Western Coast of Africa* (London: Darnton and Harvey, 1794), 189–90.

[91] Letter 34, 4 February 1786 and letter 38, 8 February 1786. *Chevalier de Boufflers – Lettres d'Afrique à Madame de Sabran.*

[92] Schefer, *Instructions générales*, 127. Boufflers' instructions were still used during the Restoration by Schmaltz, governor of Senegal 1816–20. On the front of Boufflers' instructions were written 'Il a été fait une copie de cette pièce aux instructions de M. le colonel Schmaltz, commandant et

French trade in gum and slaves. After all, the Crown was a creature of habit. Yet the instructions also reflected the government's greater interest in local populations as well as in the agricultural opportunities Senegal had to offer. They clarified where the slave, gum, and ivory trades were abundant, in what areas to obtain food provisions, and where products of the West Indies could be cultivated. Explaining that Saint-Louis was the French 'chef-lieu' on the River, but also 'absolutely arid' with 'neither trees, nor plants, herbs, or vegetables of any sort', they noted that opposite Saint-Louis was an area known as Saure, which was 'said to be fertile and receptive of tobacco, cotton and even wheat [*froment*] cultivation'. Other smaller islands near Saint-Louis could be used for grazing. Upriver, the former French Compagnie des Indes had constructed the fort of Podor on the Île à Morfil which was 'very fertile' and produced 'a large quantity of millet', had 'lots of cattle', and a natural presence of 'coffee, cotton, and indigo'. Additionally, the instructions stressed that 'sugar can be successfully cultivated there' while tobacco of a quality surpassing that 'of America and Europe' could be found further upriver on the fertile 'land of the independent nation of the Fulbes' (Futa Tooro).

Boufflers' instructions also dwelt at length on the ethnographic features of local populations, no doubt because successful trading on and near the Senegal River required a skilful triangulation of the local geopolitical landscape. Inhabitants of Saint-Louis consisted of predominantly 'Catholic mulattoes' (*mulâtres*) and 'free Negroes' (*Nègres libres*) who earned their living from commerce along the river and from sailing Europeans from trading post to trading post, the instructions stated, further noting that these people were 'vicious', and that the '*signares* in particular ha[d] a multitude of slaves who pass their days doing nothing and who would be more usefully employed in the sugar islands'. The instructions also included assessments on the quality of possible labourers in the region. With stolid reference to the high mortality of slaves in the Antilles, they stated that 'the negroes of Senegal are preferable to all other blacks on the coast of Africa, this type [*espèce*] [being] more beautiful' and 'more laborious and long-lasting when put to work'. When describing the populations adjacent to the gold mines of Natacou and Kelimani (names also found in Durand's publication), a far more pejorative portrayal shone

administrateur pour le Roi au Sénégal'. See 'Mémoire du Roi pour servir d'instructions à Mons. Le Chev de Boufflers. Marechal de Camp gouverneur du Sénégal et dépendances', November 1785. ANOM C⁶ 19, f. 187.

through. Allegedly, they were 'idle, lazy, and in want of ambition' as well as unwilling to exploit the riches around them. The 'negroes and the *maures*' upriver, in turn, with whom the French had to trade, were 'excessively vindictive' and did not 'know how to forgive', a view clerks within the Ministry of the Marine had perhaps gleaned from the reports of French gum traders. Overall, the instructions concluded that the population of Senegal was 'only able to follow the simplest rules, nearly all of which concern[ed] policing'.[93]

Unlike his predecessors, Boufflers was instructed to found new settlements. Since the creation of the Bureau de la station d'Afrique in 1784, which guaranteed that a royal frigate and a corvette patrolled African waters to protect the French slave trade and reconnoitre the region for possible areas to establish additional *comptoirs*, the Crown had obtained a number of land grants from African rulers from which to expand its commercial ties to Africa.[94] This policy was in line with Dubuc's insistence after the reconquest of Senegal that an increase in trade stations along the West African coast would advance the French slave trade, as indeed it did. In the eight years between 1784 and 1791 (when slaves rose up on Saint-Domingue), French slave traders shipped approximately 300,000 men, women, and children to the French colonies in the Americas, nearly as many as the 309,000 captives they loaded onto their ships in the twenty years between 1763 and 1783.[95] From the perspective of investors in the Caribbean plantation complex, the Crown's enhanced commitment to the French slave trade allowed the latter to reach new heights, right before the Crown itself – and the plantation complex – came tumbling down.

Boufflers never expressed concerns that the weight of the transatlantic slave trade and colonial slavery might ultimately crush the production of cash crops in the French Caribbean islands, yet his own experiments with cotton and indigo plantations in Senegambia suggest that he was eager to relocate or extend their production to Africa. He arrived in Senegal with the Rossignol on 15 January 1786. Half a year into his administration, he returned to France to present the colony's numerous needs to his superiors, arriving back in Senegal in mid-January 1787. He stayed only another ten

---

[93] Ibid. On how French gum traders depicted local people on the Senegal River in their communication to the Ministry of the Marine, see Pernille Røge, 'Rethinking Africa in the Age of Revolution: The evolution of Jean-Baptiste-Léonard Durand's *Voyage au Sénégal*', *Atlantic Studies*, 13, 3 (2016), 389–406.

[94] On the *Station d'Afrique*, see Simone Berbain, *Etudes sur la Traite des Noirs au Golfe de Guinée: Le comptoir français de Juda (Ouidah) au XVIIIe siècle* (Paris: Larose, 1942), 37.

[95] *Voyages: The Trans-Atlantic Slave Trade Database*, www.slavevoyages.org.

months, before leaving for good at the end of the year.[96] Despite this brief active service, his tenure was a busy one. He oversaw the relocation of the centre of the government from Saint-Louis to Gorée, where he found the air less dangerous for Europeans. Upon his return from France in January 1787, he and a fresh group of workers constructed a new hospital, a new church, and several new houses and gardens on Gorée.[97] Boufflers also engineered the strengthening of the monopoly of the Compagnie de la gomme du Sénégal. Due to his recommendations and under the new name of the Compagnie du Sénégal, the company obtained a full privilege to trade up and north of the Senegal River in exchange for shouldering the cost of the royal administration in the region, but was barred from the island of Gorée and the region south of Saint-Louis. Later, Boufflers regretted this decision and would bitterly complain about the company's failure to provision the French in Senegambia. He supported its suppression during the French Revolution.[98]

While in Senegal, Boufflers developed several agricultural projects, exaggerated descriptions of which appear in his long-distance tête-à-tête with Sabran. In one of his first letters to Sabran, he depicted Senegal as Sabran's kingdom or empire, he as its King, and Saint-Louis as their capital.[99] After travelling to Gorée, he found the island better suited for such a role. Describing Gorée and its scenery, houses, and gardens to Sabran, he joyfully wrote that 'I have the pleasure of seeing for the first time since my arrival in Africa something which approaches its perfection rather than moves away from it'. He was even more excited about the *grande terre* – the land opposite Gorée which also had enthralled Poncet de la Rivière, de Mesnager, and Saget – commenting on its 'delightful freshness' and 'flowers in a thousand colours, trees in a thousand shapes, and birds of a thousand species'. Declaring his desire to colonise this 'beautiful countryside', he noted that 'by means of a small treaty and a mediocre

---

[96] Boufflers' service is documented in his personal dossier, ANOM E404.

[97] Letter 544, 8 November 1787, *Chevalier de Boufflers – Lettres d'Afrique à Madame de Sabran*. See also letter from Boufflers and d'Aigremont to minister, 22 June 1786, ANOM C⁶ 19, f. 104.

[98] Boufflers, 'Mémoire sur les changemens à faire dans l'exploitation de la colonie de Senegal', 19 September 1786, ANOM C⁶ 19, f. 152; and Boufflers, 'Premier aperçu des frais et des profits de la compagnie du Sénégal dans le cas où elle obtiendroit l'exclusif universel dans tous les cours de la rivière à charge d'acquitter annuellement toutes les dépenses du Roy dans cette partie', 15 October 1786. ANOM C⁶ 19, f. 176. On Boufflers' complaints, see letter to minister from Boufflers and d'Aigremont, 26 March 1786, ANOM C⁶ 19, f. 54. On the company's suppression, see 'Loi Relative au Commerce du Sénégal – Donné à Paris, le 23 Janvier 1791 – Décret de l'Assemblée Nationale du 18 Janvier 1791', in ANOM, Moreau, F3 62, f. 453.

[99] Letter 37, 7 February 1786. Letter 110, 23 April 1786. *Chevalier de Boufflers – Lettres d'Afrique à Madame de Sabran*.

present, I will ensure for the King, and maybe for me, the acquisition of a superb province, a hundred times more sufficient for the provisioning of the French employed in this place'. Indeed, he wanted to attract French and Acadian families and 'found the greatest settlement that will ever have been made outside of France'.[100]

Boufflers' entrepreneurial temperament led him to construct a 'castle of straw' on the *grand terre*. Here, he had his horses, camels, poultry, and a little garden that offered him everything his garden at Gorée could not. Nonetheless, the excitement generated by his straw castle paled in comparison to his descriptions of his dreams of becoming an absentee planter with large fields in Africa. In September 1787, after a walk in the exotic greenery, he confessed to Sabran in a language that echoed, if not mimicked, political economic jargon: 'I feel rising within me a certain spirit of property that I find entirely charming'. On a plot of land, he continued, Villeneuve could execute his *'plan économique'* in return for 'a fifth of the *produit net'*. 'We will learn from time to time about the arrival of a thousand cotton balls and of five hundred quintaux of indigo; and your old husband will share his African riches with his good wife'. A few days after, Boufflers conveyed that he had planted cotton and indigo on all of his land, which 'succeeds remarkably well and which will prepare the future prosperity of the colony because, according to my experiments, there will be nothing of this type which will not succeed, and I can ensure France from here on millions from Africa, whether one asks for it by means of commerce [the slave trade] or by means of cultivation'. Boufflers, it appears, managed to execute what had been the hope of so many of his predecessors.[101]

The governor may have been motivated to develop these plantations through his readings of Diderot, Raynal, or the Physiocrats, but he likely also drew inspiration from French merchants who solicited the Crown to obtain permission to develop plantations in Senegal during his governorship. In the summer of 1786, three merchants by the names of Monsieur Saunier and the Floquets brothers approached the government with a project to create cotton and indigo plantations on a stretch of land along the Senegal River, using slaves of local inhabitants as labourers. This proposal generated serious interest from Castries, the Minister of the Marine. Relating its content to Boufflers, Castries asked the governor

---

[100] On Gorée's beauty, see letter 123, 6 May 1787. For his excitement of the *grande terre*, see letter 126, 9 May 1786. Ibid.

[101] On his little garden, see letter 455, 11 August 1787. On dreams of becoming a planter, see letter 480, September 1787. Ibid., my emphasis. On success of his plantations, see letter 500, 25 September 1787. Ibid.

to 'examine if their project was realisable on the islands neighbouring Saint-Louis'.[102] The enterprise collapsed before Boufflers and the *ordonnateur* (a position similar to that of intendant, but usually found in less important colonies), Aigremont, managed to write up a response. Even so, they decided to express support for the proposal. In a letter written on 27 January 1787, they underlined that 'it is to be desired that other merchants succeed with this project and reveal themselves more consistent in its execution'. To arrive at this point, they continued, it would be necessary to obtain permission from the chiefs of the local villages on whose labour systems they would have to rely. Looking ahead to the future, Boufflers and Aigremont projected that 'if these initial attempts will succeed in a country where there is an abundance of slaves and at a low cost, one can easily imagine that they will soon furnish the manufacturers of the kingdom [of France] with considerable means for growth'. The main issue was to 'establish a gentle enough discipline fairly compatible with the [required] labour to keep the Negroes and prevent revolt and desertion'. 'With this great enterprise', they continued, 'we will try to associate the country's inhabitants with our agriculture, to employ their captives . . . and to share the benefit and work with them'.[103]

In his descriptions of his own cotton plantations, Boufflers never explicitly stated what form of labour he used. Years later, his assistant, Villeneuve, avowed that Boufflers' experiments were rooted in abolitionist desires. Villeneuve's claim appeared in a section in which he promoted creating a free colony in Africa and to spread 'Enlightenment, civilisation, and agriculture . . . for the benefit of its people and for the prosperity of French commerce', a project which 'M. le chevalier de Boufflers had already planned'. Villeneuve's testimony, however, should be read with a great deal of caution since his publication came out in 1814, just as the French prepared to abolish the slave trade. The only thing which can be said with certainty is that the governor successfully demonstrated that cotton could be produced in Africa as an export commodity. In a list of exports that Boufflers and Aigremont drew up for 1787, Boufflers mentioned slaves, gum, ivory, and other familiar African exports, but also the export of 10,500 pounds of cotton. Cotton had not appeared on previous lists recorded for the Ministry of the Marine, nor did the minister seek to

---

[102] Letter to Boufflers and D'Aigremont from Castries, Versailles 27 January 1787, ANOM B192, f. 8.
[103] Boufflers and Aigremont to minister, Senegal, 7 June 1786, ANOM F³ 60, Marked 325. On the social structures and slave systems in the region, see Barry, *The Kingdom of Waalo*, 31–4. On agriculture, see ibid., 23–5.

limit its importation into France once he received Boufflers' and Aigremont's list.[104]

Does this mean that the Ministry of the Marine was beginning to accept the argument that the plantation complex in the Americas was unsustainable in the long run and that France would have to find land and labour elsewhere if it were to preserve its access to cash crop commodities such as sugar, coffee, cotton, indigo, and tobacco? Surely not. In the last few decades of the 1780s, the Crown did everything it could to encourage the French slave trade to the Caribbean. In fact, elsewhere in Africa, it set out to hinder the cultivation of cash crops, even if it was proposed as a means to augment the slave trade. In 1789, the Crown rejected a proposal to cultivate tobacco in the Kingdom of Dahomey made by M. Gourg, the French official at the fort of Whydah. Gourg asserted that the cultivation of tobacco at Whydah would enable French slave traders to compete against the Portuguese who brought tobacco from Brazil and therefore enjoyed a better relationship with local slave traders. In response to Gourg, César Henri Guillaume de La Luzerne, Minister of the Marine from December 1787 to October 1790, replied that he did not think that 'it would be advantageous to introduce the cultivation of tobacco among the Blacks in order to stifle the influence that the Portuguese enjoy because of this commodity'.[105] Gourg did not give up so easily. In the instructions for his successor in 1791, he revealed that he had tested the project and found that his harvest was 'superb, even according to a few Portuguese' and 'of a quality much superior to that of Brazil'. He further noted that 'coffee and cotton' could grow there and probably as successfully as 'in our colonies, and maybe even better' and that sugar could be cultivated near the fort, 'particularly in the low lands where the soil is harder'. While the Crown remained opposed to such opportunities, Gourg's report offers yet an example of a local official eager to expand French colonial activities in Africa. Like several of his colleagues, as we shall see in the next chapter, he would continue to promote the establishment of agricultural colonies in Africa into the French Revolution.[106]

---

[104] On Villeneuve's claims, see Villeneuve, *L'Afrique*, i, 111–13. For the list of export commodities, see list of export commodities from Senegal and Gorée for the year 1787, dated 19 June 1788. ANOM C⁶ 19.

[105] La Luzerne to Gourg, Versailles, 31 July 1789, ANOM B199, f. 21.

[106] M. Gourg, 'Mémoire pour server d'instruction au directeur qui me succedera au comptoir de Juda', 1791, ANOM, Dépôt des fortifications des colonies, XIII, Mémoires, 75, n. 118. For an example of Gourg's proposals for expansion into Africa during the French Revolution, see Gourg, 'Sur l'utilité d'un établissement projetté à Podor dans les Rivières du Sénégal', Paris, 21 Pluviôse, Year 5. ANOM C⁶ 20, ff. 37–40.

Between the Seven Years War and the French Revolution, and against the backdrop of an increasingly uncertain colonial future in the Americas, French colonial agents, whether operating as official representatives of the Crown or as representatives of the commercial sector, argued for, and tacitly experimented with, the founding of colonies and cash crop cultivation in Africa. Very few did so in a language of civilisation, progress, and development that people such as the Physiocrats and increasingly also a number of abolitionists embraced and which would dominate French colonialism in West Africa in the following centuries. Most adopted an economic rationale or turned to Africa for new opportunities for capital investment. While the Crown was aware of these experiments, it generally set out to suppress them since its revenues, as well as the private investments of numerous policy makers, were inextricably linked to the Caribbean sugar business. With the American Revolution, and the geopolitical transformations it brought in its trail, the Crown became slightly more amenable to the cultivation of cotton in Senegal during the governorship of Boufflers, although that was likely a rare exception that confirmed the rule.

In hindsight, Boufflers was not only instrumental in advancing French agricultural colonies in Africa. As this concluding anecdote suggests, he might also have been the first to introduce a notion of how to co-opt locals to help France run a colonial empire in Africa. Upon his return from Senegal, Boufflers wrote a proposal to La Luzerne in which he suggested shipping free black Senegalese children, aged ten to twelve, to Paris, to have them educated in French culture, language, and mores, before sending them back to Senegal to assist French colonial rulers in the management of empire. As Boufflers told La Luzerne: 'It will not take us long to harvest these political fruits and my first attempts in this respect have already proven successful'.[107] What attempts Boufflers referred to are unclear. He had, indeed, brought Senegalese children with him back to France, though not for the reasons he indicated to La Luzerne. His presents to aristocratic friends, as we have seen, included African children, with whom nobles enjoyed sitting for portraits (including Madame du Barry in a portrait by Jean-Baptiste Andrée Gautier-Dogoty, Marie-Antoinette in a painting by Louis-Auguste Brun, and the Prince of Condé in a portrait by Hyacinthe Rigaud). The queen received a parrot, Castries a horse, Sabran rare birds and an African boy, Madame de Blot an African boy called Ziméo (after Saint-Lambert's novel of the same name), and Monsieur de Beauvau an

---

[107] Boufflers to Luzerne, 17 February 1788, ANOM C^6 19, ff. 102–4.

African girl by the name of Ourika.[108] That these children received training to become colonial assistants to the French is unlikely, but Boufflers' proposal was a blueprint for France's future assimilationist policy in West Africa during the twentieth century when the Third Republic used *Evolués*, Africans educated and 'Europeanised' in France and sent back to French colonies in Africa to help with their management. Upon his return, Boufflers also briefly joined the Société des amis des noirs, the first French society to lobby for the abolition of the slave trade and the establishment of new colonies in Africa. It is to the activities of this society and numerous other revolutionaries that the book now turns.

[108] Maugras, *La Marquise de Boufflers et son fils Le Chevalier de Boufflers*, 477–8.

CHAPTER 5

A Revolutionary Crescendo

[T]he old sources of French prosperity are either lost or have dried up. The colonial trade seems destroyed by the Revolution that has just freed the African cultivators and dispersed the plantation managers in our American colonies. This colonial fortune was based on such monstrous foundations that once collapsed it will be very difficult to rebuild it, even had we not adopted our philanthropic principles. The government therefore needs to adopt a new commercial policy in place of this colonial system, which was not the best suited to the interests of France as an agricultural, manufacturing, and maritime power anyway.

Ambroise Marie Arnould, *Système maritime et politique des européens* (1797)[1]

With the outbreak of the French Revolution, concerns about the preservation of colonial empire in the Americas that came to the fore with the Seven Years War gained new heights. The transition from the Estates General to the National Assembly in June 1789 provided revolutionaries with the opportunity to reconstitute the French monarchy and its colonies while committing to the principles inscribed in the first article of the Declaration of the Rights of Man and of the Citizen. The geopolitical context within which they were able to pursue such goals, however, was constantly shifting. Colonial revolt and slave rebellion in the Caribbean in the early years of the Revolution, followed by warfare, blocked traditional avenues of colonial empire and rendered alternative models of colonisation more appealing. People with concrete hopes of shaping French colonial policies and practices moulded their responses to this constantly shifting realm of opportunity with considerable creativity. Capitalising on a purported allegiance to the revolutionary regime, competing factions twisted the Revolution's emphasis on liberty, equality, and the rights

---

[1] Ambroise Marie Arnould, *Système maritime et politique des européens, pendant le dix-huitième siècle; fondé sur leurs traités de paix, de commerce et de navigation* (Paris: Imprimerie d'Antoine Bailleul, 1797), 286.

of man to suit their agendas, all the while tapping into Ancien Régime political economic discourses and experiments.

The forging of a republican imperial agenda becoming of rejuvenated France, I argue in this chapter, continued efforts to reinvent the French colonial system that unfolded in the last decades of the Ancien Régime. Many ideas and discourses in circulation were appropriated and remoulded to speak in new ways to the shifting opportunities generated through revolutionary turmoil. Among the resurging agendas was the bid by the *économistes* to recognise the existing colonies' right to prosperity, to integrate colonies as equals into the metropole, to move beyond a system of slave labour, and to promote colonisation and civilisation in Africa. France's first society for the abolition of slavery, the Société des amis des noirs, appropriated this political economic rationale in their fight against white planter elites and French commercial interests. They and other revolutionaries also infused it with additional political content, transforming an argument originally rooted in an alleged universality of economic laws into one positioned on the universality of constitutional rights.

In the early stages of the Revolution, the continued weight of the slave-driven plantation complex within the French financial and economic sectors precluded a positive response to this abolitionist imperial agenda. Representatives of the Caribbean planter elite joined forces with lobbyists of the French ports and managed to successfully block abolition, in part through their deployment of creole political economic arguments that planters had rehearsed for years through institutional organs such as the Chambre d'agriculture. It took slave revolt and abolition to clear a path for a more radical restructuring of imperial ambitions at the level of national policy. Under the Directory, a commitment to anti-slavery, the integration of the French colonies as overseas departments, and colonial expansion in Africa became a vital albeit precarious part of the French Republic's colonial agenda. Ideas that had reverberated in physiocratic economic writings and found secluded support among anonymous policy makers and capitalist interests thus reached a crescendo during the Revolution. It did not last, however. After the failure of the Egyptian expedition, Napoleon reignited the plantation complex in the Caribbean and left it in the hands of future generations to steer the French colonial enterprise away from it and towards alternative forms of empire.

The Société des Amis des Noirs

The importance of the Société des amis des noirs (hereafter *amis des noirs*) to the debates on slavery and abolition in the French Revolution has been expertly documented by several historians, as has the ability of representatives of France's main urban centres and Caribbean sugar islands to block their agenda from gaining a following in the National Assembly.[2] There is therefore no need to retell this well-known story in great detail, though some engagement is necessary to understand the political events to which the *amis des noirs* were responding. What follows is therefore not intended to be a history of the struggle to abolish slavery between 1789 and 1794 within France, but an analysis of the ways in which physiocratic ideas of colonial empire resurged during the French Revolution through the propaganda of the French abolitionist society.

The founding of the *amis des noirs* was part of a transatlantic 'anti-slavery internationalism' to which the efforts of Quakers such as Benjamin Lay, John Woolman, and Anthony Benezet gave rise. In 1775, the Society for the Relief of Free Negroes Unlawfully Held in Bondage was established in Philadelphia and presided over by Benezet. Similar societies mushroomed in the following decade in New York, Boston, Baltimore, and further in England, where, in May 1787, Thomas Clarkson, Granville Sharp, and others founded the Society for Effecting the Abolition of the Slave Trade. It was as corresponding members and under the encouragement of the English society that Jacques Pierre Brissot de Warville, a lawyer-journalist, and Étienne Clavière, a Swiss financier, established the French abolitionist society in February 1788.[3] They soon started recruiting members to their cause from the upper echelons of society. In the first meeting of the *amis des noirs*, held on 19 February 1788, those present besides the founders included C. Brack, Jean Louis Carra, A. M. Cerisier, A. C. Bellier-Duchesnay, the marquis de Valady, Dufossey de Bréban, and Honoré Gabriel Riqueti comte de Mirabeau. These and subsequent recruits were mostly prominent

---

[2] A far from exhaustive list includes Benot, *La Révolution française*; Jean-Daniel Piquet, *L'émancipation des noirs dans la Révolution française (1789–1795)* (Paris: Karthala, 2002); Dorigny and Gainot (eds.), *La Société des Amis des Noirs*; Manuel Covo, 'Le Comité des colonies Une institution au service de la "famille coloniale"? (1789–1793)', *La Révolution française* 3 (2012), 1–20; David Geggus, 'Racial Equality, Slavery, and Colonial Secession during the Constituent Assembly', *The American Historical Review*, 94 (1989), 1290–1308; Jean Tarrade, 'La Révolution et le commerce coloniale: le régime de l'*Exclusif* de 1789 à 1800', *État, finances et économie pendant la Révolution française* (Paris: Comité pour l'histoire économique et financière de la France, 1991), 553–64; Manuel Covo, 'L'Assemblée constituante face à l'Exclusif colonial', in *Les colonies la Révolution française la loi*, ed. Frédéric Régent, Jean-François Niort and Pierre Serna (Rennes: Presses Universitaires de Rennes, 2014), 69–89; Valerie Quinney, 'The Problem of Civil Rights for Free Men of Color in the Early French Revolution', *French Historical Studies*, 4 (1972), 544–57.

[3] Dorigny and Gainot, *La société des amis des noirs*, 21 and 26. On the radical abolitionism of Benjamin Lay and his ties to Wollman and Benezet, see Marcus Rediker, *The Fearless Benjamin Lay: The Quaker Dwarf who became the first Revolutionary Abolitinist* (Boston: Beacon Press, 2017), 137–9. On Benezet as a driving force for transatlantic abolitionism, see Jackson, *Let This Voice Be Heard*.

journalists, nobles, directors-generals of taxation, *hommes de lettres, censeurs royal*, directors of the Régie générale, and bankers.[4] As the membership expanded, incoming adherents were admitted because of their ability to further the society's agenda through contacts, intellectual prestige, or familiarity with colonisation.

One such was Gilbert du Motier, marquis de Lafayette, whom the society successfully recruited at the request of the English abolitionist society. Lafayette was a critic of slavery and had experimented with its gradual abolition on his own plantation in Guiana. His dedication to political reform, his friendship with the royal family, and his fame in the Anglophone world were all attractive qualities that could serve the agenda of the society.[5] Lafayette soon proved his worth: on 1 April 1788, he presented the duc de la Rochefoucauld-d'Enville to the society. One week later he brought the marquis de Condorcet, who had declared himself against slavery in 1781 under the name of Pastor Schwartz. Another early critic of slavery to join the society, although only briefly, was Louis Sébastien Mercier, whose image of a Black Spartacus gained fame through Diderot's additions to the *Histoire des deux Indes*. Mercier was introduced to the society by the marquis de Valady on 15 April 1788. Other members included François Xavier Lanthenas, Constantin François de Chassebœuf, comte de Volney, and the chevalier de Boufflers, who had just returned from Senegal. Abbé Henri Grégoire joined the society in December 1789 after his impassioned speeches against slavery in the National Assembly.[6]

Though the *amis des noirs* was an abolitionist society lobbying for the end of slavery in the colonies, its broader agenda, as Marcel Dorigny has pointed out, was the total overhaul of the French colonial system.[7] Aside from their campaign to immediately abolish the slave trade and gradually abolish slavery, they advocated for the abrogation of the Exclusif and of monopoly trade. They also pushed for the integration and assimilation of the old colonies into the metropole, and the granting of political rights to all colonial property owners regardless of skin colour. Exactly like Roubaud, Du Pont de Nemours, and Baudeau, they further suggested that France embark on new colonial ventures in West Africa.

---

[4] Dorigny and Gainot, *La société des amis des noirs*, 68–9.
[5] Letter from Brissot to the committee in London, 19 March 1788, ibid., 108–9.
[6] Séance du mardi 29 avril 1788, ibid., 155. After 3 February 1789, Boufflers was no longer present at the meetings of the society.
[7] Dorigny and Gainot (eds.), *La Société des Amis des Noirs*, 38. Jean-Daniel Piquet portrays the society as the first to seriously anticipate political change in the colonies. Piquet, *L'émancipation des noirs dans la Révolution française*, 63.

In its initial phase, the society tried to achieve these goals by enlightening public opinion. To do so, they accumulated a wealth of information with which to combat supporters of slavery and the Exclusif. From their British contacts, they acquired two works by Thomas Clarkson (*Essay on the Slavery and Commerce of Human Species* and *A Summary View of the Slave Trade and the Probable Consequences of Its Abolition*) and Anthony Benezet's *Some Historical Accounts of Guinea*. They also sought information from other sources, including from the Crown. As Brissot noted at one of the society's early meetings: 'the government should have records and memoranda on commerce with Africa and our sugar islands'. He also hoped to consult the records of the Compagnie du Sénégal. Beyond these organs, the society collected data from plantation owners and slave traders. It studied the abolitionist efforts of Quakers in the United States and of the Moravian Church. It also hoped to gain insights into systems of servitude in Russia and Poland, investigated alternatives to sugar, and informed itself about the government's policy of awarding a bonus on slave trading. They even contacted Rome to inquire about black priests. Based on this flow of information, they endeavoured to sway public opinion by projecting an image of Africans as human beings worthy of compassion and the plantation complex as brutal, inhumane, and economically deficient.[8]

Beneath these immediate sources of inspiration, the vision and arguments of the *amis des noirs* owed a great debt to the colonial doctrine developed by the Physiocrats. One of the very few pieces of concrete evidence that demonstrates this is the box of materials that the *amis des noirs* shipped to their English peers. It included the comte de Mirabeau's *Analyse des papiers anglais* (25–8 April 1788), which contained sections from Du Pont de Nemours' article promoting the abolition of slavery and the transplantation of sugar plantations to Africa in the *Ephémérides du citoyen* of 1771.[9] Many of the *amis des noirs*, moreover, were connected to the Physiocrats and well-versed in their writings. Brissot expressed an interest in their colonial ideas, particularly as they appeared in Pierre Poivre's *Voyage d'un philosophe* (1768). The duc de la Rochefoucauld-d'Enville's mother, Louise Elisabeth de La Rochefoucauld, was a follower of the Physiocrats. Condorcet was a trusted friend of Turgot, whose affiliation

[8] On materials from England, see Séance 20 May 1788, hôtel de Lussan rue Croix des Petits Champs, Dorigny and Gainot (eds.), *La Société des Amis des Noirs*, 166. On collecting materials from the Crown, see Séance 4 March 1788, ibid., 81–2. On additional efforts to gather information, see ibid., 82, 108, 220, and 252.

[9] Séance 20 May 1788, hôtel de Lussan rue Croix des Petits Champs, ibid., 166.

with the Physiocrats were well known. Antoine Lavoisier, who joined the *amis des noirs* on 22 April 1788, admired Quesnay and Mirabeau's *Philosophie rurale*. Honoré Gabriel Riqueti, comte de Mirabeau, finally, was the son of Victor Riqueti, marquis de Mirabeau and the nephew of the former governor of Guadeloupe, Jean-Antoine Riqueti, chevalier de Mirabeau. As we know from his father and uncle's correspondence, the comte de Mirabeau had been instructed to read the *Ephémérides du citoyen* and ordered to learn his father's science 'if he wished to carry the name of Mirabeau'.[10] Not only his name during the Revolution, but also his famous speech on abolition and colonies in the Jacobin Club on 26 February 1790, suggest that he did indeed obey his father's instructions despite their notorious confrontations.

The Comte de Mirabeau's Speech in the Jacobin Club

The comte de Mirabeau's speech in the Jacobin Club was an impassioned response to the recent alliance struck between metropolitan ports and colonial planters against the *amis des noirs*. Erstwhile commercial adversaries, port merchants and colonial planters had joined forces after the Declaration of the Rights of Man and of the Citizen in August 1789 flagged the possibility of emancipating slaves in the colonies. Prior to that, debates on the colonial question had focused on the number of deputies the colonies should have in the Assembly, whether colonies could be compared to domestic provinces, and the Exclusif, the latter of which continued to draw a wedge between planters and French port merchants. With the Declaration of the Rights of Man and of the Citizen, of which Mirabeau was a co-author together with the slave owners Lafayette and Thomas Jefferson, slave emancipation was folded into these discussions. Article 1 avowed that 'men are born and remain equal in rights' and could thus be seen as a direct attack on slavery. Article 2 and Article 17, however, underlined the sacred nature of private property. Article 2 stated that property was a 'natural and imprescriptible' right of man while Article 17 stressed that 'no one shall be deprived thereof' unless public necessity demanded it

---

[10] On Brissot's interest in Pierre Poivre, see J. P. Brissot, *Mémoires*, 2 vols. (Paris: Cl. Perroud, 1912). On duc de la Rochefoucauld-d'Enville's links to the Physiocrats see Daniel Vaugelande, *Le salon physiocratique des La Rochefoucauld: animé par Louise Elisabeth de La Rochefoucauld duchesse d'Enville, 1716–1797* (Paris: Editions Publibook, 2001). On Lavoisier, see Georges Weulersse, *La Physiocratie à l'aube de la révolution 1781–1792*, ed. Corinne Beutler (Paris, 1985), 25. On the comte de Mirabeau's reading of physiocratic literature, see Pernille Røge, 'L'économie politique en France et les origines intellectuelles de "la mission civilisatrice" en Afrique', *Dix-Huitième Siècle*, May 2012, 117–30.

and 'then only on condition that the owner shall have been previously and equitably indemnified'. Chances that the financially strained government would offer indemnities to owners of over half a million slaves seem illusory in hindsight, but moved planters to form the infamous Club Massiac on 20 August 1789 to defend a slave-driven colonial enterprise. In early 1790, representatives of the ports joined the Club Massiac to fight a petition for the repression of the French slave trade to the National Assembly by the *amis des noirs*, even as port and planter deputies remained locked in conflict over their opposing views on the Exclusif.[11]

It was this cascade of events that Mirabeau responded to in his speech in the Jacobin Club. As the main centre of revolutionary debates, the club was a podium from which Mirabeau was able to address many of those who were, or would soon become, directly involved in the colonial question. Antoine Barnave and Charles and Alexandre de Lameth, who would sit on the Comité des colonies, had not yet left the Jacobin Club to found their own royalist club, the Feuillants. Brissot, Clavière, Condorcet, and many of the *amis des noirs,* who would later unite as the Girondins or Brissotins (supporters of a Republic), also frequented the Jacobin Club in this period, as did future Montagnards such as Maximilien Robespierre. These listeners were attuned to debates in the National Assembly and would see Mirabeau's speech as a powerful response to the pro-slavery forces that had gained momentum across France, even though historians have now established that the window of opportunity for abolition had probably already passed.[12]

Mirabeau's speech was a proposal to anchor French colonial policy in a new political economy. Opening with an attack on colonial slavery, he referred to the institution as 'the most detestable tyranny' in history and castigated anyone who might object to the inherent rights of an African, since France had just decided that 'all men are born and remain equal and free'. Taking a stab at Caribbean planters who questioned the humanity of Africans with the same level of conviction as Baudeau had done against the 'American' in 1766, Mirabeau thundered that 'it is not on this side of the Atlantic that corrupt sophists dare maintain that the negroes are not men!'[13] But his speech then took an unexpected turn. He asserted that

[11] Déborah Liébart, 'Un groupe de pression contre-révolutionnaire: Le Club Massiac sous la Constituante', *Annales Historiques de la Révolution Française*, 4 (2008), 29–50; Gabriel Debien, *Les colons de Saint-Domingue et la Révolution – Essai sur le club Massiac* (Paris: A. Colin, 1953). On debates on the Exclusif during the Revolution, see Tarrade, 'La Révolution et le commerce coloniale'; Covo, 'L'Assemblée constituante face à l'Exclusif colonial'.

[12] Benot, *La Révolution française*; Geggus, 'Racial Equality, Slavery, and Colonial Secession', 1294.

[13] His speech is printed in Honoré Gabriel Riquetti de Mirabeau, *Mémoires biographiques, littéraires et politiques de Mirabeau*, 8 vols., ed. Lucas de Montigny (Paris: A. Auffray, 1834–5), 122.

the reason why revolutionaries still had not abolished slavery in the French colonies was because slaves were not yet at a level of maturity where they were ready to benefit from the civil rights enjoyed by the revolutionary white man. According to Mirabeau, slavery had perverted the soul of the slaves and they now needed time to 'become free men'. Immediate emancipation would subject them to the tyranny of their passions and 'brutal ignorance'.

In making this observation, Mirabeau echoed the growing tendency to infantilise African slaves that also characterised many other writings by the *amis des noirs* and their peers in Great Britain. For instance, in their petition to the National Assembly requesting the abolition of the slave trade, Brissot and Lepage had debunked any rumour that they wanted immediate abolition, stressing that it would harm the slaves who would become 'like abandoned children' were they to be freed immediately.[14] The paternalistic argument was part of a discursive toolbox used to justify the exclusion of not only slaves, but also women, peasants, and the urban poor from 'active' citizenship. Pinning gradual abolition on an alleged philanthropic rationale, Mirabeau diverged on this issue from the views of his father whose preference for a phasing out of slavery was based on a desire to prevent an immediate lack of labour in the colonies but who also considered Africans *une race d'hommes à part*.[15]

The comte de Mirabeau drew closer to his father on the topic of free men of colour. In his speech, he claimed that the future of the colonies in the New World belonged to them. Unlike white planters, Mirabeau charged, free men of colour considered the colonies their 'terre natale' and were stronger and more numerous. They were also currently outraged by their political exclusion, an insight Mirabeau had gained from the Saint-Domingue property owners and free men of colour Julien Raimond and Vincent Ogé who joined the *amis des noirs* in November 1789. Their anger, Mirabeau noted, contributed to a volatile situation. In a perspicacious remark reminiscent of his father's and uncle's many forewarnings of colonial revolt, Mirabeau predicted that '[t]he most inevitable revolution is threatening our islands; all that is left is to decide whether we should

---

[14] *Archives Parlementaires de 1787 à 1860* (hereinafter AP), French Revolution Digital Archive. University of Stanford, http://frda.stanford.edu. Tome 11: Séance du jeudi 21 janvier 1790, au soir, 273–7.

[15] On such strategies and how women resisted them, see Sara E. Melzer and Leslie W. Rabin (eds.), *Rebel Daughters: Women and the French Revolution* (Oxford: Oxford University Press, 1992). For similar undertones against speakers of regional dialects, see Michel de Certeau, Dominique Julia, and Jacques Revel, *Une politique de la langue: La Révolution française et les patois* (Paris: Gallimard, 1975).

leave it to chance, merely await its coming, however dangerous the explosion, or if it should be the work of our laws and prepared by prudence'.[16]

Speaking directly to slave traders and plantation owners, Mirabeau mocked their revolutionary credentials and charged that they would rather live under despotic rule than compromise their own economic interests. Denouncing their recently formed coalition against the *amis des noirs*, he berated planters' and merchants' underlying hypocrisy:

> Those who provision our islands, the planters, and the slave traders fight each other over how to divide profits which they acquire from the pains, blood, and death of their slaves; but they unite forces against men who declare themselves friends of the Blacks and who seem to focus instead on universal welfare, upon which ties between personal interest and the general interests of society should be formed.[17]

That Mirabeau felt that the *amis des noirs* and not planters and merchants had the interests of society at heart is clear, but his assertion that the agenda of the *amis des noirs* combined personal and general interests with an abolitionist programme required explaining. Many of the maritime ports such as Bordeaux and Nantes owed their prosperity to the slave trade and the plantation complex. How could Mirabeau contend that the slave trade, slavery, and the Exclusif were not as profitable as they appeared?

Like Saget had done two decades earlier (and Clarkson more recently), Mirabeau pointed out that the slave trade was a highly risky business. Large parts of a slave ship's crew died during the voyage and 'profits are so small that the French government feels obliged to support its slave traders through embarrassing bonuses that cost France over 10 million livres between 1784 and 1788'. Mentioning the bonuses explicitly, Mirabeau illustrated how he and his peers used information that they had obtained from the Crown and turned it into ammunition against the slave trade.

Another major defect of the slave trade, Mirabeau continued, was that it contributed to Africa's deplorable state and savage condition. Adopting his father's concept of civilisation, he queried: 'And why does civilisation not make progress prompted by human perfectibility in Africa as on the banks of the Ganges?' The answer, he replied, was that Europeans prompted

---

[16] Mirabeau, *Mémoires biographiques*, vii, 134. On Raimond and Ogé's membership, see Dorigny and Gainot, *La société des amis des noirs*, general assembly 24 November 1789, 244–5. On the fight of free men of colour to obtain representation, see Florence Gauthier, *L'aristocratie de l'épiderme – Le combat de la société des citoyens de couleur 1789–1791* (Paris: CNRS Éditions, 2007).

[17] Mirabeau, *Mémoires biographiques*, vii, 134–5, 136.

Africans to sell their neighbours and brothers into slavery to gain access to European commodities. There were, however, better ways to benefit from such reliance. In an approach reminiscent of Du Pont de Nemours' 1771 suggestion, Mirabeau proclaimed that with the assistance of commercial Europe and America, Africans could start to develop their land and sell its fruits in exchange for those European commodities that they currently obtained when trading away their population.

Shifting to the colonial theatre in the Caribbean, Mirabeau again echoed the Physiocrats. This time it was their attempt to use calculation to undermine the use of slave labour, although he altered it to advocate only for the abolition of the slave trade and not of slavery itself. He argued that the slave trade had a corrupting impact on planters because it made them accustomed to the notion that they could easily purchase more. Its abolition would force planters to treat their current slaves better which would lead to a natural reproduction of the slave population, and a higher quality of labour. According to his calculations, the total cost of a slave under the current system was 8,751 livres, much more than what it would cost to provide for the children of slaves before they were old enough to join the labour force. By abandoning the slave trade and treating the slaves well, Mirabeau argued that planters could save 20 million annually. Such high savings could instead be used to improve plantations and liberate planters of their debts.

Continuing to draw on his arsenal of economic arguments, Mirabeau rejected the claim that the plantation complex generated great profits for France. He acknowledged that sugar, coffee, cotton, and indigo were desirable commodities, yet they were sold at exorbitant prices in France which, to Mirabeau, was because of the high cost of the slave trade. Whereas England, with a population of 10 million, consumed nine-tenths of the 1.4 million quintaux of sugar coming from its colonies, France, with a population of 25 million consumers, only consumed a third of the 1.8 million quintaux of sugar its colonies produced because consumers were too poor to pay the high price of French colonial commodities. What was worse, domestic consumers were deprived of grain, wine, and foodstuffs which French merchants shipped to the colonies to preserve the Exclusif. Exactly like his father, Mirabeau argued that such goods should be kept at home where they were needed. The colonies could receive their essentials from foreign powers while France could export to the colonies 'twenty-five million pieces of cloth, draperies, hosieries and other goods of this kind'. Turning the question of the Exclusif into the very question of the Revolution itself, Mirabeau proclaimed that 'France will not be regenerated as long as monopolies and the monstrous contradictions associated with them have not completely vanished!"[18]

That Mirabeau's response to proponents of the plantation complex was rooted in physiocratic ideas was also evident in the final section of his speech in which he tackled the claim that abolition would cause the French colonies in the Caribbean to secede. This intervention was increasingly important due to a rising concern in the French port cities and in Paris that colonies might end up in the hands of the slaves or, alternatively, fall to the British. After news of a slave revolt on Martinique reached the metropole, fear of secession penetrated the National Assembly. A letter from Saint-Domingue planters to the Assembly expressed concern that revolt would spread to the slaves on Saint-Domingue, while another letter from the maritime provinces noted that if the slave uprising spread to Guadeloupe and Saint-Domingue, France would lose its colonies and the nation would be ruined.[19] These fears allowed planters to threaten to secede from the metropole unless they were allowed to reject the Declaration of the Rights of Man and of the Citizen and draw up particular laws for the colonies. Moreau de Saint-Méry, the deputy of Martinique, took to the tribunal to imply that a white revolt was as much to be feared as a slave revolt. Echoing Jean Dubuc's report from 1765, he noted that the colonies had been nothing but 'enslaved territories' to the metropole and subjected to laws drawn up by people with no idea of life in the colonies. They were now frustrated by their long history of suffering under political despotism and metropolitan trade monopolies and wanted to be allowed to form a colonial committee to discuss what laws would best suit each colony.[20]

To Mirabeau, these anxieties of secession were entirely misplaced. If white planters tried to break away from Revolutionary France upon an abolition of the slave trade and slavery, they would turn the enslaved population into defenders of the metropole. Rejecting the creole argument for legal particularity rooted in montesquieuan climate theory, Mirabeau exclaimed:

> No! The colonies will not secede from the metropole! [. . .] Now that France will see liberty blossom among all its children, why should the colonies tear themselves from their family? Would we deprive them of the benefits of our Constitution? No, we shall not give in to all these political dreams where the imagination, misled by these fallacies of the aristocracy, pretends that

---

[18] Ibid., 161, 175, 191–2, 184, and 186.
[19] AP. Tome 10: Séance du mardi 1 décembre 1789, au soir, 347.   [20] Ibid.

constitutions should be subjected to climates. Liberty and particularly the government of the family are right for all areas inhabited by men.

Underlining the universal validity of the constitution, Mirabeau drew his long speech to a close. The way forward for France, he concluded, would be to convey to the English legislature that the National Assembly wished to join Great Britain in engineering a total ban on the slave trade. He further advised establishing a committee that would restore order in the colonies, prepare the way for the abolition of slavery, and mend the bond between the metropole and the colonies.[21]

Historians focusing on Mirabeau's speech, as well as those of his peers, rarely emphasise the similarities between their colonial ideas and those of physiocratic thinkers such as the marquis de Mirabeau, Du Pont de Nemours, and the Abbés Baudeau and Roubaud. This is not surprising. The *amis des noirs* preferred to link their ideas to the British, something which comes out not only in Mirabeau's recommendation to join Great Britain in the fight against the slave trade but also in their advocacy of creating slave-free colonies in Africa. In 1789, Benjamin-Sigismond Frossard published the two-volume *La cause des esclaves Nègres*, in which he praised England for its attempt to form free establishments in Sierra Leone and suggested that France and England unite in abolishing the slave trade and in civilising Africa to avoid unnecessary competition.[22] The *amis des noirs* also translated and published the *Règlement de l'établissement des noirs libres de Sierra Léona* to bring attention to the British philanthropic experiment. Around the time Mirabeau gave his speech, his colleague, Lanthenas, praised Britain's Sierra Leone project in a publication written against the slave trader M. Lamiral, but encouraged France to embark on philanthropic colonisation in Senegal so as not to fall behind the British.[23] While the *amis des noirs*'s repeated reference to the Sierra Leone project might signal that their influences came from across the Channel, we also know that they were all familiar with Du Pont de Nemours' proposals to cultivate cash crops in Africa using free local labour. Rather than signifying

---

[21] Mirabeau, *Mémoires biographiques*, vii, 202.

[22] Benjamin-Sigismond Frossard, *La cause des esclaves Nègres et des habitans de la guinée, portée au tribunal de la justice, de la réligion, de la politique; ou Histoire de la traite et de l'esclavage des Nègres, preuves de leur illégitimité, moyens de les abolir sans nuire ni aux colonies ni aux colons*, 2 vols. (Lyon: Aimé de la Roche, 1789), ii, 379–86. Marcel Dorigny has suggested that the British inspired the *amis des noirs*' Africa project in Dorigny, 'La Société des amis des noirs et les projects de la colonization en Afrique', 428.

[23] F. X. Lanthenas, *M. Lamiral réfuté par lui-même ou réponse aux opinions de cet auteur sur l'abolition de la traite, suivies de quelques idées sur les établissements libres que la France ne soit pas différer de faire au Sénégal* (Paris: Potier de Lille, 1790), 78.

an intellectual debt, the *amis des noirs*'s mentioning of Britain's so-called philanthropic expansion in Africa could simply be a way for them to instil a sense of competition and urgency in a French audience still focused on the Caribbean.

The Failure of the Amis des Noirs

Despite the growing rhetoric about *liberté, égalité, et fraternité*, Mirabeau and his colleagues failed to steer France towards the abolition of the slave trade, let alone colonial reform. Although Mirabeau's four-hour long speech was met with great applause in the Jacobin Club, and other *amis des noirs* such as La Rochefoucauld, Pétion, and Grégoire pushed the society's agenda in the National Assembly, the united forces of deputies from the maritime centres and the colonies were a formidable buffer against radical change. As the National Assembly received reports of chaos in the colonies, the nation's deputies decided to create a colonial committee to deal with the problem but not in the ways that Mirabeau had suggested. Instead, the committee that came into existence was nothing but a *porte-parole* for planters and slave merchants' shared ambitions to preserve the plantation complex. Not including a single member of the *amis des noirs*, its reporter, Antoine Barnave, advised the National Assembly on 8 March 1790 to write a special constitution for the colonies to reconcile differences over the Exclusif and to preserve slavery and the slave trade.[24]

Bracketing the problem of the Exclusif, the recommendations of the Comité des colonies aligned with the agenda pushed by the planter elite associated with Martinique's former Chambre d'agriculture. The committee recommended not only excluding the colonies from the constitution, but also consulting white *colons* on the type of constitution that might serve them best. It further stressed that the Assembly should reassure the colonies against those who attempted to bring trouble by inciting revolt. Without mentioning the *amis des noirs* directly, the committee argued that while parading as peaceful citizens, these people had perverse motives and could only be considered 'enemies of France and of humanity'. When it was time for the National Assembly to approve its recommendations, members of the *amis des noirs* were prevented from responding, and the committee's report was instantly adopted. With that, planters were ready to commit to

---

[24] AP. Tome 12, Séance du lundi 8 mars 1790, 70–72. For a full discussion of Barnave's views on the colonial question see Cheney, *Revolutionary Commerce*, 218–28.

the Revolution. Upon its adoption, Arthur Dillon, the deputy of Martinique, made a successful motion to instantly inform the colonies of the decree and to ask all *colons* residing in Paris to take the civic oath.[25]

The decision to have a committee handle all questions pertaining to the colonies limited the ability of the *amis des noirs* to advance their programme. When the Constitution was passed in September 1791, it excluded the colonies from its purview, and therefore shielded them from the Declaration of the Rights of Man and of the Citizen. In words echoing the report of the Comité des colonies, Title VII, Article 8 stated that 'the colonies and French possessions in Asia, Africa, and America, although they are part of the French empire, are not included in the present Constitution'.[26] Once the Constituent Assembly gave way to the Legislative Assembly, Brissot, Clavière, and Condorcet were elected deputies. In that capacity, they tried on numerous occasions to advance the agenda of the *amis des noirs*, but with little result. In the months before the closing of the Constituent Assembly, Clavière published a long *Adresse de la société des amis des noirs* dedicated to the Assembly, the maritime provinces, and the colonies in which he offered an elaborate version of the speech that Mirabeau had given in the Jacobin Club. He urged representatives of the nation to abolish the slave trade and prepare for the abolition of slavery, equality among all free people regardless of their colour, free trade, 'and the total destruction of the Ancien Régime'. France should create a liberal empire where colonies were 'not children of the mother country ... but a part of the French empire' that would prosper together and alike (*avec lui, et comme lui*). He pleaded that Africans were not merchandise but consumers of European commodities with needs that 'will give birth to their civilisation' and he encouraged France to forge new bonds with them before the British did, and gain access to their gum, amber, honey, ivory, silver, gold, wood, spices, tobacco, rice, indigo, cotton, and sugar.[27]

Efforts such as the one by Clavière were counterproductive, however. With the outbreak of the slave uprising on Saint-Domingue in August 1791, pro-slavery voices blamed the *amis des noirs* for the massacre of white planters. The Minister of the Marine from October 1791 to March 1792, Bertrand de Molleville, reviewed accusations against the

---

[25] AP. Tome 12, Séance du lundi 8 mars 1790, 73.
[26] See 'Constitution de 1791', Conseil Constitutionnel, www.conseil-constitutionnel.fr.
[27] Étienne Clavière, *Adresse de la société des amis des noirs, à l'Assemblée nationale, a toutes les villes de commerce, à toutes les manufactures, aux colonies, à toutes les sociétés des amis de la constitution – Adresse dans laquelle on approfondit les relations politiques et commerciales entre la métropole et les colonies, etc.* (Paris: Patriote Français, March, 1791), 123–4 and 151–2.

'*philanthropes*' on 19 December 1791, siding with white planters on the matter while undermining the merits of the efforts of the *amis des noirs*. The following year, the *amis des noirs* seemed to make some progress: with the decree of 4 April 1792, revolutionaries extended political rights to all free men of colour in reaction to the now full-blown slave revolt on Saint-Domingue but did not signal a deeper shift in perspective. Little changed during the first period of the Convention. Frossard addressed the Assembly on 23 December 1792 to request the abolition of the slave trade. While applauded by the Assembly, deputies transferred the decision to the colonial committee. When the first French republican constitution was accepted by the Convention on 24 June 1793, it carried no changes to the position of slaves or colonies. The only victory that the *amis des noirs* could cherish was the suppression of the bonus granted to slave traders, which Dominique Joseph Garat, Minister of the Interior, decreed on 27 July 1793.[28]

This decision came only a few months before key members of the *amis des noirs* fell victim to the French Revolution. The radicalisation of events in Paris and in the provinces catapulted some of the *amis des noirs* into powerful positions. Yet differing viewpoints concerning the French declaration of war on Austria and Prussia, and debates over the fate of the King upon the proclamation of the Republic in September 1792, thrust the Girondins, to which many leading *amis des noirs* belonged, into toxic clashes with the Montagnards. In this context, the close affiliation of the *amis des noirs* with England became an Achilles heel. The society's founders were easily targeted as traitors to national interests and spies for the British. As French revolutionaries became increasingly paranoid, such accusations turned lethal.[29] While Mirabeau escaped the horrific fate of his peers – he died from illness in April 1791 – Brissot was guillotined on 31 October 1793. Awaiting a similar fate, Clavière committed suicide in prison on 8 December 1793. Upon his arrest, Condorcet was found dead in his cell in March 1794. Pétion took his own life in June 1794. Of the most outspoken *amis des noirs*, only Abbé Grégoire survived the purge of the

---

[28] On Molleville, see AP. Tome 36: Séance du lundi 19 décembre 1791, 253–6. For a full history of this decree, see Ghachem, *The Old Regime*, Chapter 5. On Frossard's address, see AP. Tome 55, Séance du dimanche 23 décembre 1792, 367–8. On the bonus, see Benot, *La Révolution française*, 94.

[29] On the paranoia of conspiracies in the French Revolution, see John Hardman, 'The Real and Imagined Conspiracies of Louis XVI', in *Conspiracy in the French Revolution*, ed. Peter Robert Campbell, Thomas E. Kaiser, and Marisa Linton (Manchester: University of Manchester, 2007), 63–84.

Girondins and was able to advance their agenda after the Thermidorian Reaction ended the Terror.

Neither of the two founders of the *amis des noirs* therefore lived to see the abolition of slavery. Despite their efforts, it was only due to external pressure that this part of their programme finally materialised. While events in the colonies had played into the hands of planter interests in the early stages of the Revolution, securing them the creation of the colonial committee, further upheaval in the colonies generated results for the *amis des noirs*, some of which were more radical than the society's demands. The combination of slave revolts in the Caribbean (starting with a slave uprising on Martinique in late August 1789, followed by uprisings in Guiana, Guadeloupe, St Lucia, and Marie-Galante, before the slave rebellion on Saint-Domingue erupted on 22–3 August 1791), fears of colonial secession, and the outbreak of war between France and the maritime powers of Spain and Britain in early 1793, led *commissionnaires* Léger-Félicité Sonthonax and Étienne Polverel to abolish slavery on Saint-Domingue in the summer of 1793. In February 1794, the Convention ratified this act and decreed its extension to other French colonies. Though white colonists in Isle Bourbon and Isle de France successfully rebuffed abolition, and Martinique ultimately deserted France and became a British colony, the French Republic of the year II at least nominally honoured the need to extend the principles of Article 1 of the Declaration of the Rights of Man and of the Citizen to the French territories overseas.[30]

The Directory and the Republican Imperial Programme

In the period following the abolitionist decree of 1794 and the collapse of the Convention, France became more amenable to a new colonial system.[31] The outbreak of revolution in the Caribbean, the fall of the monarchy, the birth of the Republic, the declaration of war, and the Terror and its end

---

[30] On this series of events, see Yves Benot, 'La chaîne des insurrections d'esclaves dans les Caraïbes de 1789 à 1791' in *Les abolitions de l'esclavage de L. F. Sonthonax à V. Schœlcher 1793 1794 1848*, ed. Marcel Dorigny (Paris: UNESCO, 1995), 179–86; C. L. R. James, *The Black Jacobins: Toussaint L'Ouverture and the San Domingo Revolution*, 2nd edn. (London: Vintage, 1989); Laurent Dubois, *Avengers of the New World: The Story of the Haitian Revolution* (Cambridge, MA: Belknap Press of Harvard University Press, 2004); Laurent Dubois, *A Colony of Citizens: Revolution and Slave Emancipation in the French Caribbean, 1787–1804* (Chapel Hill: University of North Carolina Press, 2004); Jeremy D. Popkin, *You Are All Free: The Haitian Revolution and the Abolition of Slavery* (Cambridge: Cambridge University Press, 2010).

[31] Carl Ludwig Lokke, 'French Dreams of Colonial Empire under Directory and Consulate', *The Journal of Modern History*, 2 (1930), 238.

shifted perceptions of what was possible and acceptable. Many of the institutional, political, and economic barriers that had prevented thoroughgoing reform of the colonial system had eroded and pro-slavery voices momentarily silenced through imprisonment, death, or migration. In this new climate, what used to be presented as an idealistic alternative to the French plantation complex in the Americas now emerged as a realistic agenda that would enable the French Republic to reconcile its revolutionary principles with colonial empire. The suggestion to elevate colonies to the status of domestic provinces and the proposal to create new colonies in Africa, and to help spread 'civilisation' were moving from the margins and into the mainstream.

The new French Constitution of the year III (22 August 1795) gave concrete expression to the Republic's desire to improve bonds with the Caribbean colonies. It announced the full and equal integration of the colonies into the French Republic, a constitutional shift sometimes described as republican isonomy. The underlying incentive to fold the colonies into the French legal system was the fear of losing them but advocates also avowed that revolutionary self-confidence, the love of liberty and economic aspirations fuelled the process. The legislative Committee of Eleven, appointed by the Convention to write a new constitution in the aftermath of the Thermidorian Reaction, noted as much in its opening comments to the Assembly on 17 Thermidor. Its reporter, Antoine de Boissy d'Anglas, proclaimed that the French Revolution was not just for Europe but for the universe, and that liberty should embrace the entire world 'like rays of morning light'. Revolutionary principles did not belong to only a few but to the entire human race. The committee had therefore set out to find the best foundation upon which to form a sound relationship between the metropole and the colonies, one that would render the latter free and flourishing after their many years of suffering.[32]

The opening was intended to address anxieties that plagued colonial debates after abolition. Summing up two overarching narratives that drove discussions, Boissy d'Anglas pointed out that there were those who thought that the best thing for France would be to abandon the colonies while others feared that they would break away from France and seek their independence. The committee found neither option satisfying. Abandoning the colonies would cause the French navy to dwindle and

---

[32] *Gazette Nationale ou Le Moniteur Universel*, 322, 22 thermidor, year III, 1298. On republican isonomy, see Bernard Gainot, 'The Republican Imagination and Race: The Case of the Haitian Revolution', in *Rethinking the Atlantic World: Europe and America in the Age of Revolutions*, ed. Manuela Albertone and Antonino De Francesco (Basingstoke: Palgrave Macmillan, 2009), 276–93.

national prosperity to collapse. Colonial independence, in turn, was unfeasible. Though the colonies might enjoy a moment of autonomy, their internal economies were unsuited for independence and they would merely end up as subjects of another power. If that other power were England, France's main enemy would obtain all of the commodities that the colonies were capable of producing and sell them at an exorbitant price to French consumers who had acquired a taste for such goods. According to Boissy d'Anglas, the best solution for France and the colonies would therefore be to firmly attach one to the other to the benefit of both.

The way that the committee envisioned attaching the colonies to the metropole was to ensure that the colonies remained 'French rather than only American', 'free though not independent', 'part of the one and indivisible Republic', and 'governed by the same laws and the same government'. Deputies from the colonies should be called to the metropole where they would blend in with the entire population and deliberate on the interests of, and compose laws for, their shared homeland. The committee recommended implementing these principles progressively through temporary particular laws that allowed a strong delegate to represent the government locally. Other than this proviso, they would be administered in a manner identical to French domestic departments. The committee concluded its report with an emphatic endorsement of the abolition of slavery, declaring with no reference to the agency of the thousands of slaves who rose up on Saint-Domingue in 1791 that abolition was the consequence of revolutionary principles and created not only 'free men, but citizens'.

After these inaugural comments, the committee presented the constitutional articles it proposed for the colonies. In these, Article 1 stated that all French colonies formed an integral part of the French Republic and were subject to the same constitutional laws. Article 2 suggested dividing the colonies into departments but left out French territories on the African and Indian continents. Article 3 suggested having public officials appointed directly by the Directory. Article 4 proposed authorising the Directory to send special commissioners to the colonies if need be. Articles 5 and 6 legislated on the powers of these commissioners. Finally, Article 7 suggested letting the legislative body determine the commercial bond between colonies and the metropole as well as their fiscal contributions.

Upon hearing these recommendations, the Convention adopted Article 1 immediately and without discussion. But it then postponed debates of the remaining articles for 25 Thermidor. When these resumed, there were several who raised concerns. One deputy pointed out that Article 2 failed to mention India (it also failed to mention West Africa). Another deputy noted that France was now in possession of the Spanish side of Saint-Domingue as well. The most substantive comment came from M. Pomme who had detected a contradiction in the proposed Articles 1 and 3. As he said, Article 1 gave colonial inhabitants rights equal to French citizens while Article 3 'took them away'. Several others agreed, noting that although Article 3 seemed suitable for troubled colonies (surely thinking of Saint-Domingue), not every French colony was in turmoil. In the end, the Convention sent the remaining articles back for revision and invited the deputies of the colonies to participate in their final articulation.[33]

The consequence of these revisions did not generate the result that some of the protestors might have hoped for. In the final draft of the Constitution, what was now Title 1 Article 6 read that 'The French colonies form an integral part of the Republic and are subject to the same constitutional law'. Article 7 divided the colonies into departments. Saint-Domingue was divided into four; Guadeloupe, Marie-Galante, La Désirade, les Saintes, and the French part of Saint-Martin formed one; Martinique formed one, French Guiana and Cayenne formed one; St Lucia and Tabago formed one; Isle de France, the Seychelles, Rodrigue and settlements on Madagascar formed one; La Réunion (formerly Isle de Bourbon) formed one; and Pondicherry, Chandernagor, Mahé, Karical, and other Indian settlements formed one. The French possessions in West Africa were still left unmentioned. Articles 155 and 156, however, disclosed that Pomme's objections had been ignored. Article 155 stated that until the return of peace, the Directory would appoint all public functionaries in the French colonies. Article 156 gave the Directory the authority to send agents to the colonies for a limited time who were invested with the same powers as the Directory. It is worth nothing, moreover, that Article 314 allowed the legislative body to determine the colonies' fiscal contribution as well as their 'commercial relations to the metropole'.[34]

With the Constitution of the year III, legislators thus granted colonies the same constitutional status as domestic departments in France but included sections that would allow them to overrule such parity if need be. Despite this proviso, historians have identified this constitution as a moment of colonial regeneration. Bernard Gainot notes that its ultimate aim was the 'assimilation of the metropole and its colonies' and the 'unity

[33] *Gazette Nationale ou Le Moniteur Universel*, No. 323, 23 thermidor, year 3 (10 August 1795), 1300 and No. 332, 2 fructidor, year 3 (19 August 1795), 1336–7.

[34] 'Constitution de l'An III', Conseil Constitutionnel, www.conseil-constitutionnel.fr.

of the Republic'.[35] Pierre Serna, in turn, argues that Articles 6 and 7 represent 'a revolution in right which concretely invents a new relation and conception of the geographical space of a republic, affirming the principle of universality'. Emphasising novelty, Serna further stresses that the Constitution was a turn against the principles of Montesquieu.[36] Certainly a turn against montesquieuan principles of climate theory, one might add that it was a turn towards many of the ideas put forth by the Physiocrats. Although departmentalisation was new – provinces were replaced by departments in 1790 – the idea of integrating colonies as 'overseas departments' under the same set of constitutional laws aligned closely with Quesnay's insistence that 'overseas provinces' and 'domestic provinces' would mutually enrich each other when under the same natural and economic laws. Thus, what was 'a new relation and conception of the geographical space of a republic' also carried within it earlier efforts to reinvent the French colonial empire after the Seven Years War.

It is part of the irony of history that the moment colonies were on the road to full integration and assimilation and obtained equal status with domestic land as they had desired during the Ancien Régime, numerous white planters in the colonies rejected it. Because departmentalisation meant slave emancipation, white planters who had called for integration during the Estates General now preferred autonomy or an alliance with Britain. In the French Caribbean, the Constitution was applicable to Guadeloupe and its dependencies, Saint-Domingue, and French Guyana; yet none of these places embraced it without complications.[37] In all three colonies, many of the freed slaves continued to work within a labour regime of 'cultivators' that carried resemblance to slavery and was set up to preserve the plantation economy. Worse, Martinique never adopted the Constitution. The island came under British rule in 1794 as a result of the Whitehall Accord of 1793 signed between Britain and counter-revolutionary planters such as Pierre-Victor Malouet (Saint-Domingue), Louis de Curt (Guadeloupe), and Louis-François Dubuc, the son of Jean-Baptiste Dubuc. Things were no better in the Indian Ocean. In the Mascarene Islands, the local colonial assemblies expelled

---

[35] Bernard Gainot, 'The Constitutionalization of General Freedom under the Directory', in *The Abolitions of Slavery from L. F. Sonthonax to Victor Schoelcher. 1793. 1794. 1848* (Paris: UNESCO Publishing, 2003), 180–96, 182.

[36] Pierre Serna, 'Conclusion générale. Lorsque la loi fait la Révolution aux Colonies . . . ou l'empire des lois républicaines', in *Les colonies la Révolution française la loi*, ed. Frédéric Régent, Jean-François Niort, Pierre Serna (Rennes: Presses Universitaires de Rennes, 2014), 263–82, 274.

[37] Miranda Frances Spieler, 'The Legal Structure of Colonial Rule during the French Revolution', *The William and Mary Quarterly*, 66, 2 (2009), 365–408, 367.

the two *commissionnaires* of the Directory who had been sent to ensure the implementation of the Constitution and the abolition of slavery.[38]

It was not only in the colonies that abolition and departmentalisation met resistance. In the metropole, the Clichy Club – many of whose members were formerly in the Club Massiac – rose to prominence at exactly this time. The principal item on its agenda was to restore the old-regime plantation complex. It nearly succeeded in spring of 1797, when elections sent supporters of the Clichy Club into the Legislative Assembly. The Council of Five Hundred (formed to discuss and vote on resolutions) 'declared null and void' nominations made by an electoral assembly held in Saint-Domingue, a decision the Council of Ancients (charged with turning resolutions into law) confirmed. Shortly after, the Minister of the Marine, Laurent Jean-François Truguet, devout abolitionist and constitutionalist, was dismissed. His successor, Pléville-Lepelley, favoured a restoration of the pre-revolutionary status quo in the colonies. It was only due to the coup d'état of 18 Fructidor year V that pro-slavery forces failed to restore the old colonial order.[39]

A mere week after the coup, supporters of the Republic's new colonial system therefore formed a colonial commission to ensure a speedy implementation of the Constitution of the year III in the colonies.[40] The result was the law of the constitutional organisation of the colonies of 1 January 1798 (Nivôse year VI) that guaranteed the departmentalisation of the colonies and the irreversibility of the decree of 4 February 1794. When the law was discussed in the Council of Five Hundred and the Council of Ancients, a member by the name of Jean-Gérard Lacuée highlighted the main reasons for the need to engineer a terminological shift

---

[38] On the transition to new labour regimes on Saint-Domingue and Guadeloupe, see Dubois, *A Colony of Citizens*, 204–13. On the Whitehall Accord, see Joucla, *Le conseil supérieur des colonies*, 130. On colonies in the Indian Ocean, see Claude Wanquet, 'La tentative de Baco et Burnel d'application de l'abolition aux Mascareignes en 1796 – Analyse d'un échec et de ses conséquences', in *Les abolitions de l'esclavage de L. F. Sonthonax à V. Schœlcher 1793 1794 1848*, ed. Marcel Dorigny (Paris, 1995), 231–40.

[39] Gainot, 'The Constitutionalization of General Freedom under the Directory', 184–5. Although this vote was against the Constitution, only very few objected to it. Joseph Eschassériaux pleaded for an implementation of the Constitution of the year III, Garran-Coulon recalled that Sonthonax had already been approved as deputy, and Quirot stressed that the speeches of the Clichy Club echoed 'the grievances of the white colonists'. 185. See also the report of the sitting of the Council of Five Hundred of 16 Prairial Year V (4 June 1797), and the sitting of 13 Prairial year V (1 June 1797) in *Le moniteur universel*; and Bernard Gainot, 'La députation de Saint-Domingue au corps législative du Directoire', in *Léger-Félicité Sonthonax. La première abolition de l'esclavage, la Révolution française et la révolution de Saint-Domingue*, 2nd edn., ed. Marcel Dorigny (Paris: Société française d'histoire d'outre-mer, 2005), 95–110.

[40] Gainot, 'The Constitutionalization of General Freedom under the Directory', 186.

from 'colonies' to 'overseas departments'. Emphasising the power of language to modify ideas and structure thought, he encouraged inserting a note into the final report formed by the Council of Five Hundred in which they expressed their desire no longer to refer to the departments of the Republic situated in the two Indies as 'colonies'. As he said:

> Indeed, citizens, as long as we will use these expressions, there will remain in some heads, in the words of J. J. Rousseau, a tinge of supremacy, and in some others, a shade of subjection. You want perfect equality of rights to reign over the French from one hemisphere to another. But as long as you use the words 'colonies' or 'colonial' from this platform, you will always awaken the notion of commerce in men and slaves and the equally pernicious ideas of devastation and crime. By changing the signs, you change ideas, and minds will soon adjust to such language.[41]

Jean-Gérard Lacuée's interjection highlights what not only Rousseau but also François Quesnay had understood decades earlier, the power of words to generate or preclude change. By shifting the terminology, by getting rid of the word 'colony' and its derivatives, it would be possible finally to alter French relations with its possessions in the Americas.

Colonial Expansion in Africa

Beyond the corridors of the Councils of Five Hundred and of Ancients, another busy theatre for colonial debates in these years was the Institut National. This institution was 'the spiritual powerhouse' of the republican regime, whose task it was to 'give a central impetus to the minds of the public'.[42] Founded on 25 October 1795, the Institute was organised into three classes focusing on the physical sciences and mathematics, the political and moral sciences, and literature and the fine arts. The class on political and moral sciences was further divided into several sub-sections – the *Analyse des sensations et des idées; Morale; Science sociale et legislation; Economie politique; Histoire; Statistique, géographie et politique;* and *commerciale.* The *Analyse des sensations et des idées* counted among its members Constantin François de Chassebœuf, comte de Volney and journalists such as Garat, Le Breton, and Pierre-Jean-Georges Cabanis. Bernardin de St Pierre, Louis Sébastien Mercier, and the Abbé Grégoire were part of the

---

[41] *Opinion de J. G. Lacuée sur la dénomination qu'il convient de donner aux départements désignés par le nom de colonies.* BN, Le 45 707. On these discussions, see also Bernard Gainot, 'La naissance des départements d'Outre-Mer', *Revue historique des Mascareignes*, 1(1998), 54 and 68.
[42] François Furet, *The French Revolution 1770–1814* (Oxford: Blackwell, 1996), 194.

section *Morale*. *Economie politique* included Abbé Emmanuel Joseph Sieyès, Creuzé-Latouche, Du Pont de Nemours, Talleyrand, and Roederer. *Histoire* had members such as Raynal, Louis Antoine de Bougainville, Reyneval, and Otto.[43] Thus, the second class included some of the key political economists and *amis des noirs* of the Ancien Régime and early revolutionary period. It is therefore not surprising that it was within this institution that discussions about colonisation took place. Nor is it surprising that the content of these discussions often pivoted around the opportunity to create colonies in Africa.

According to the journal *La décade*, edited by Jean-Baptiste Say, Joachim Le Breton, and Pierre-Louis Ginguené, which reported the speeches read at the Institute, it was the Abbé Grégoire and Du Pont de Nemours who initiated discussions about Africa in response to a French attack on the British philanthropist colony in Sierra Leone. In the session of 2 Pluviôse year IV Grégoire condemned the attack and informed the Institute that the Convention had been notified of the British experiment on 29 November 1792, and that deputies of the nation had decreed that France would grant the colony its protection. Unfortunately, a French ship patrolling African waters to destroy the British slave trade had demolished the colony on 28 September 1794, allegedly mistaking it for a British trade station for the slave trade. In conveying this message, Grégoire also encouraged France to emulate the British experiment.[44]

Grégoire had obtained his information from Carl Bernhard Wadström's *Essay on Colonisation* (published in 1794 and translated into French in 1798). Originally from Sweden, Wadström was associated with both the British and French anti-slavery movement and advocated for colonial ventures in Africa. As we saw in the previous chapter, he had travelled in Sierra Leone and visited Senegal during Boufflers' governorship and could therefore speak of such opportunities with authority.[45] Wadström lived in Paris during the Directory and frequented political elites who shared his anti-slavery and colonial agendas. But Wadström's name was not the only one that Grégoire folded into his speech. With reference to Sierra Leone, he conveyed that it had originally been a French project, the mastermind of which was Du Pont de Nemours, whose 1771 article in the *Ephémérides* had

---

[43] *La décade*, viii, 1796, 17–18.
[44] *La décade*, viii, 1796, 405. Dorigny, 'Intégration républicaine des colonies'. Dorigny dates Grégoire's speech to 22 Pluviôse year IV, while *La décade* dates it to 2 Pluviôse.
[45] For a study of Wadström and his attempts to found a colony in Africa, see Ronny Ambjörnsson, 'La République de Dieu – Une utopie suédoise de 1789', *Annales historiques de la Révolution française*, 3 (1989), 244–73.

discussed the facility with which Africa could be colonised. Grégoire noted that Du Pont had offered to oversee such a project in 1774 and that he and Turgot had submitted a ministerial report on the project but which 'suffered the same fate as so many other useful ideas' under the Ancien Régime. Shortly after, Du Pont, who had likely been present during Grégoire's speech, resurrected his old programme in a speech to the Institute on 2 Ventôse year IV (21 February 1796).[46]

It was likely Du Pont de Nemours' and Grégoire's speeches that inspired Talleyrand to offer the most noted speech on colonisation within the Institute. Read on 15 Messidor year V, and subsequently published as *Essai sur les avantages à retirer de colonies nouvelles dans les circonstances presents*, Talleyrand's speech highlights the degree to which slave-free colonisation in West Africa and a better treatment of existing colonies were becoming integral parts of the official republican imperial agenda. Talleyrand had no history as an abolitionist or experience with colonisation but counted among his friends people who were directly involved with France's colonial empire. He was a close friend of the duc de Lauzun, who had been in charge of the reconquest of Senegal, and had also been close with the diseased comte de Mirabeau. The Martinican planter, Moreau de Saint-Méry, whom he had met during his exile in America, was another friend of Talleyrand's. It may have been their inputs over the years that now informed his interest in colonisation, or it may simply have been that he was always guided by his wish to best serve the interests of France, as he underlined time and again in his memoires.[47]

Addressing the Institute only two weeks prior to his appointment to the Ministry of Foreign Affairs, Talleyrand opened his speech proclaiming that perspicacious men had long understood that the American colonies would eventually separate from the metropole. In his view, the French response should therefore be to postpone this moment for as long as possible and to create new colonies whose links to France would be more natural, useful, and sustainable. Having had the strength to reinvent itself as a republic of equal citizens, the French should now reinvent their empire along equally praiseworthy principles.[48] Talleyrand, in fact, claimed that new colonial

---

[46] 'En 1774, il [Du Pont de Nemours] écrivit à Turgot sur cet objet, en s'offrant d'aller lui-même diriger l'entreprise; et de concert, ils firent ensuite un mémoire ministériel qui fut présenté, au conseil, et qui eut le sort de tant d'idées utiles'. *La décade*, viii, 1796, 403. Du Pont's speech was published in the summer of 1798 as *Sur l'esclavage des Nègres, et sur l'utilité de former des établissemens à la côte d'Afrique pour la culture du sucre par des Nègres libres*. See Dorigny, 'Intégration républicaine des colonies', 97.

[47] Charles-Maurice de Talleyrand-Périgord, *Mémoires du Prince de Talleyrand Publiés avec une Préface et des notes par le duc de Broglie*, 5 vols. (Paris: Calmann Lévy, 1891).

[48] Talleyrand, *Essai sur les avantages a retirer de colonies nouvelles*, 3.

ventures would save the Republic because it would serve as an outlet for the current unrest, or surplus energy, that the Revolution had generated but which needed channelling to prevent it from doing harm. Reminding listeners of Montesquieu's words that a free government 'is *always agitated*', he argued that the task before revolutionaries was to cultivate agitation to the benefit of the public good. In his view, the carriers of such surplus energy came from all walks of life. They included those of whom the mother country had become unsupportive, the politically misguided, adventurers, speculators, and 'men burning to associate their name with discoveries, the foundation of cities, and of civilisation; those to whom constitutional France is still too agitated, and those to whom she is too calm'.[49] This, of course, could mean anyone from political prisoners to people such as Napoleon whose star was on the rise on the European battlefield. According to Talleyrand, these restless men should let themselves be guided by the likes of Bougainville – likely among his listeners in the Institute – whose explorations had given them important knowledge of the overseas.

Talleyrand then turned to consider the regions in which these new colonies might be founded. He recommended warm countries because they could offer raw materials to those who intended to promote industry. Founding colonies in areas 'along the coast of Africa, or rather adjacent islands' would be 'easy and convenient'. In making this recommendation, Talleyrand did not reference Grégoire, Du Pont de Nemours, or any of the physiocratic political economists who had advocated such a project. Nor did he mention, Brüe, Adanson, Demanet, Le Large, de Mesnager, Saget, or Boufflers. Instead, he pointed to Charles Leclerc de Montlinot's publication *Essai sur la transportation comme recompense, et la déportation comme peine* (1797), in which Montlinot (who was a director of a poorhouse in Soissons) argued that the French West Indies were lost to France and that it would be necessary to transplant colonial production to Africa. Montlinot therefore suggested creating a penal colony at Bolama and establish agricultural colonies worked by property-less French labourers, a suggestion which Talleyrand claimed that Montlinot had discussed with Dominique Lamiral, a Frenchman who had lived at Saint-Louis in Senegal during Boufflers' governorship.[50]

---

[49] Ibid., 8 and 10.
[50] On Montlinot, see Kate Hodgson, 'French Atlantic Appropriations: Montlinot, Eighteenth-Century Colonial Slavery, and Penal and Forced Labour Schemes between Europe, Africa and the Americas', *Forum for Modern Language Studies*, 51, 2 (2015), 116–32.

Dropping Lamiral's name in his speech, Talleyrand surely intended to show his listeners that his proposal was supported by connoisseurs of West Africa. Nevertheless, it might have caused several in the Institute to lift an eyebrow were they able to recall the shady trajectory of this colonial agent. Hired by the Compagnie de la Guyane française to arrange for the company's slave trade in Senegal, Lamiral had composed a Cahier de doléances to the Estates General in 1789 in the name of the inhabitants of Saint-Louis, requesting the suppression of the monopoly of the Compagnie de Sénégal.[51] In December 1790, he had addressed the Assembly again 'in the name of the inhabitants of Senegal', asking to enjoy the benefits of the new Constitution and be freed from 'arbitrary rule'. A few months later, he had again addressed the Assembly requesting that the inhabitants of Senegal be granted one representative in the National Assembly. However, as Léonce Jore notes, it was clear that none of the actual inhabitants of Saint-Louis or Senegal had been involved in this request and that Lamiral was trying to exploit the ignorance of the National Assembly to obtain a seat for himself within it.[52]

While Talleyrand's listeners may or may not have fastened on Lamiral's name, Talleyrand continued his exploration of colonial opportunities trying to fuel interest by playing on Franco-British rivalry. Like Poncet de la Rivière and the *amis des noirs* before him, he conveyed that the coast of West Africa was an ideal spot for the creation of colonies and reminded his listeners that England had already established new colonies in Sierra Leone and was planning to create more at Bolama. France should be careful not to fall behind in the launching of such projects. But he also added that Egypt was another region that the French might consider colonising. He alleged that Choiseul had already suggested founding colonies in Egypt in the 1760s to substitute for potential colonial losses in the Americas, a claim that seems to exaggerate what the duc de Lauzun, described merely as Choiseul's *rêveries*.

---

[51] Lamiral published a work on Senegal and its surroundings in 1789, entitled *L'Affrique et le Peuple Affriquain*, in which he revealed his desire to suppress the *Compagnie du Sénégal* and his involvement in the slave trade. The publication was subsequently condemned by Lanthenas and the *amis des noirs*, who used it to advocate the creation of philanthropic colonies in West Africa. Jore, *Les établissements français*, 126–31. Lamiral's request had been supported by a deputation from the port of Bordeaux in early 1790. AP. Tome 11: Séance du jeudi 25 février 1790, 696. In November 1790, he again requested the abolition of the exclusive trade privileges associated with trade in Senegal. AP. Tome 20: Séance du mardi 16 novembre 1790, au soir, 472. The requested was sent to the united Comités d'agriculture, de commerce et colonies at the request of Paul Nairac. Ibid., 473.

[52] For Lamiral's requests in the National Assembly, see AP. Tome 21, Séance du dimance 5 décembre 1790, 220 and AP. Tome 24: Séance du samedi 12 mars 1791, 51. Jore, *Les établissements français*, 130. Of Lamiral's many wishes, the National Assembly delivered only on the suppression of the exclusive privilege of the *Compagnie du Sénégal* on 18 January 1791. This decision, however, was a response to the requests of the French ports. AP. Tome 22: Séance du mardi 18 janvier 1791, 321.

In Talleyrand's views, West Africa and Egypt were ideal locations due to their warm climate, but also because they were the sources of the labour that had been used to cultivate plantation crops in the French West Indies prior to abolition. Evidently seeing no difference between the indigenous populations of Egypt and West Africa, Talleyrand encouraged France to cultivate sugar, coffee, indigo, and cotton 'in the places where the cultivators are born'.[53]

Alongside proposals to create new colonies, Talleyrand also suggested modifying the current commercial system that undergirded trade between the metropole and the colonies. Expressing strong opposition to the Exclusif, he urged policy makers to 'leave their state of habit' and found a regime that linked the two parts together through common interests. While the abrogation of monopoly trade, or trade privileges, would go a long way in securing harmonious relations, Talleyrand also praised the cultural *liaisons* among France, Louisiana, and Canada that he found to still thrive and which he claimed continued to stimulate trade relations under the happiest of circumstances, even though both colonies had been ceded to England and Spain in the Seven Years War. Based on these gains and insights, the principles by which the new mode of colonisation should be guided were: 'no domination, no monopoly, always the force that protects, never that which oppresses; justice, benevolence; these are the true calculations for states as for individuals; that is the source of mutual prosperity'.[54]

Given its unashamed call for the creation of new colonies in Africa, some historians have interpreted Talleyrand's speech as a sign of France coming to a crossroad in its colonial policy. Michel Poniatowski, for instance, argued that it marked the passage from 'mercantilist colonialism to the colonialism of empire'.[55] This is an interesting description, though regrettably we are left to ponder its meaning. Poniatowski does not elaborate on the line he draws between his two distinctions, nor why he sees Talleyrand's speech as the crucial moment. In fact, there were hardly any novel features in the speech itself, and it cannot therefore be the actual content that marked a shift. Nevertheless, Poniatowski is right to put his finger on this moment because it captures the increasingly broad appeal of an alternative path to colonial empire that physiocratic political

---

[53] Talleyrand, *Essai sur les avantages à retirer de colonies nouvelles*, 14–15. On early plans to conquer Egypt, including the daydreams of Choiseul, see Michèle Battesti, 'Expédition d'Egypte, un plan de conquête français remontant au milieu du XVIIIe siècle', *Cahiers de la Méditerranée*, 57, 1 (1998), 34.

[54] Talleyrand, *Essai sur les avantages à retirer de colonies nouvelles*, 12–13.

[55] Michel Poniatowski, *Talleyrand et le Directoire, 1796–1800* (Paris: Perrin, 1982), 72.

economists and colonial agents had elaborated and advocated in the last decades of the Ancien Régime. More conventional colonial policies had now become unfeasible given the Republic's affirmation of the abolition of slavery. As revealed in the citation by Ambroise Arnauld with which this chapter opened, the slave-driven colonial system was seen by many at this juncture in the Revolution as unsuitable to the actual agricultural, commercial, and maritime interests of France.

Coupled with this, and perhaps driving it, was France's newfound self-confidence as a 'liberator' of European populations in need. The Edict of Fraternity of 1792 that encouraged European peoples to rise up against their despotic rulers and call for the assistance of the French if need be had turned into a French imperial mission in Europe to establish friendly sister republics around its borders. In the process, French republicans had become convinced that they were at the forefront of civilisation and in a position, or on a mission, to help others enjoy the benefits of French *liberté, égalité,* et *fraternité.* Another relevant factor that constantly emerged in conversations was the fear that Britain would take the lead in colonising a major region still largely left untouched by European colonisers. Combined, these dynamics pushed the door open to French colonisation in Africa.[56]

The call to create colonies in Africa quickly gained support, not least because it came from the impending Minister of Foreign Affairs. In the following months, the Ministry of Foreign Affairs was inundated with proposals reacting to Talleyrand's speech. Five days after its delivery, Dominique Lamiral wrote to the Directory with 'a very detailed memorandum on these interesting lands [Lower Senegal] and on the means to establish with advantage the cultivation of all the commodities of the two Indies by establishing colonies'. Lamiral presented himself as the right Bougainvillean man to advise on the location of such colonies as requested by Talleyrand, given his 'twenty years staying both in Senegal and in other parts of Africa', which had provided him with 'the most profound knowledge of the *naturels* [the indigenous populations] and Africa's nature and climate'.[57]

Another memorandum sent to the Ministry of Foreign Affairs by a M. Ehanuy underlined that the speech Talleyrand had given on the

---

[56] On French imperialism inside Europe, see Michael Broers, 'Cultural Imperialism in a European Context? Political Culture and Cultural Politics in Napoleonic Italy', *Past and Present*, 170, 2 (2001), 152–80.

[57] Lamiral, 'Observations importantes sur les possessions françaises en Affrique' 20 Messidor year V. Paris, MAE, AD, Afrique II, f. 290.

possibilities, utility, and importance of French holdings in Africa was a testimony to the new minister's good heart and his Enlightenment. The author said that he was particularly impressed by the feasibility of the colonial project Talleyrand had outlined because it was not clouded in theories and insurmountable difficulties but was easily realised at a very low cost. Presenting his project as a rupture from Ancien Régime colonialism, Ehanuy underlined that such a venture would be a way to rid the new Republic of its humiliating colonial past. He claimed to be astonished by the lack of interest that the Bourbon monarchy had shown in such a project, despite several agents' reports on Africa's vast colonial opportunities. As he said, the region was capable of growing all of the products essential to French commerce and industry and was 'inhabited by peoples with a coarse but good, simple but industrious character, whose disposition is to imitate'. Echoing the Abbé Roubaud, Abbé Baudeau, and Du Pont de Nemours, he stressed that colonial settlements in Africa would produce more for the Republic than the first colonies in America had ever done. Like Lamiral, Ehanuy noted that he had resided in Saint-Louis for several years, travelled into the interior of Africa, and gained insights useful to the government. It was 'the conformity between his experiences and Talleyrand's proposal' that now prompted him to nominate himself to carry out the project.[58]

Ehanuy also described how he would execute his plans for Africa. As he noted, he would first transplant to Senegal the raw commodities produced in the sugar colonies in America and the sugarcane from Tahiti. According to Ehanuy, Repentigny had successfully done so during his governorship in the early 1780s. He pointed out that cotton and indigo were indigenous to Africa while he assumed that coffee could successfully be cultivated there too. Like Poncet de la Rivière, Ehanuy further suggested exploiting the mines of Bambuk and avowed that he had taken samples of Bambuk gold to Paris, where the *essayeur-general de monnoie de Paris*, had done several tests, with promising results. To realise all these projects in the best possible way, Ehanuy said that it would be necessary to exploit the affection that the native population of the Lower Senegal nurtured for the French. Abolition of slavery had blocked these peoples from obtaining European goods and were forced to find a different export commodity to sustain their trade with

[58] *Apperçu des moyens d'exécuter le projet de fonder des colonies sur les cotes occidentales de l'Afrique, lu à l'institut national, par le citoyen ministre de la relation extérieure* 12 Thermidor year V, MAE AD, Afrique II, f. 291.

Europe. Now was therefore the time to help these people out of their 'inertia', and to have them imitate the French *colons*.

More such proposals abounded within the Ministry of Foreign Affairs and the Ministry of the Marine, yet the impact of Talleyrand's speech was not confined to these government institutions.[59] In this period, Talleyrand regularly communicated with Abbé Grégoire, Wadström, and the political economist and journalist J. B. Say, all of whom were quick to exploit the moment as well. On 17 Frimaire year VI (7 December 1797), Wadström wrote to Talleyrand, encouraging the minister to support Franco-British philanthropic colonies in Africa.[60] Wadström published the letter as a preface to his brochure entitled 'Précis sur les colonies de Sierra Léona et Boulama' (Paris, 1798). *La décade* reviewed Wadström's essay on 20 March 1798, recounting what the essay had said in its review of Grégoire's speech: that this English project was praiseworthy, originated in the writings of Du Pont de Nemours, had been attempted by him and Turgot, and now was the way forward for France. The reviewer further noted that Talleyrand had conveyed these truths in an excellent memorandum read to the Institut National.[61]

In the end, the wish to create colonies in Africa stirred up so much attention that Wadström's essay was discussed in the Council of Five Hundred and referred to a committee for a report. The resulting report, read by Eschasseriaux the Elder, was entitled *Rapport au nom de la commission chargée d'examiner l'ouvrage présenté au conseil par le Citoyen Wadstrom [sic], relatif à l'establissement de Sierra-Léona, et de la colonisation en général, et de quelle utilité peut-être cet établissement pour le commerce français*. When it was presented to the council on 23 Germinal year VI (12 April 1798), discussions transformed into a rallying call for an armed mission to colonise Egypt rather than create new colonies in Lower Senegal. The climate of Lower Senegal and Egypt were deemed very similar by the deputies of the nation. An immediate occupation and colonisation of Egypt, however, had the added advantage that it would stand as a threat

---

[59] A 'secret memorandum', written in response to Talleyrand's speech, suggested that the French government should be in charge of a penal colony in Africa, while a private *compagnie de commerce* should launch a colony of settlers and commerce mirrored on the English colony at Sierra Leone. The aim of this latter colony should be to penetrate deep into Africa from the west and link up with a scientific expedition entering Africa from Tripoli, aiming for the gold mines at the Kingdom of Bomon. 'Mémoire secret', MAE AD, Afrique 11, f. 294. Numerous proposals to create agricultural colonies in West Africa within the Ministry of the Marine can be found in ANOM Col C⁶ 20.

[60] Dorigny and Gainot, *La société des amis des noirs*, 313.

[61] *La décade*, xvi, 1797, 525, and 529. The reviewer signed himself L.B. It was therefore probably by Le Breton.

to England with whom France was at war. General Bonaparte had already written to the Directory on 16 August 1797, underlining that 'the time is not far away that we will feel that, in order truly to destroy England, we must take Egypt'. With Italy being a satellite state of France, and with the British Navy largely excluding the French from the North Atlantic, the Mediterranean should be 'a French lake' and open a route to India via the Red Sea. Napoleon, moreover, had pointed out that sugar, indigo, cotton, and coffee could be cultivated in Egypt. Yet what possibly fixed the Council of Five Hundred on Egypt rather than Senegal was the fear of Napoleon. After his successes in Italy, the general enjoyed immense popularity, and had already demanded to be installed as a director. To several in the Directory, there was therefore a need to redirect Napoleon's hunger for power – or his unruly energy, to use Talleyrand's words – towards projects outside of France. The conquest of what contemporaries celebrated as the 'crib' of civilisation seemed to be a worthy distraction.[62]

The Société des Amis des Noirs et des Colonies

Although France now became involved in a vast mission to merge conquest, science, and colonisation in Egypt, several within the Republic still looked to Lower Senegal as the place for colonisation. The heir to the Société des amis des noirs, the Société des amis des noirs et des colonies (hereafter *amis des noirs et des colonies*) would have the creation of new colonies in Africa as one of its chief agendas. This would not have been of great significance were it not for the role that the society played as a 'superior council or extra-legislative commission to define the general line on matters of colonial policy'.[63] Unlike its predecessor, the *amis des noirs et des colonies* attained the status of adviser to the government. Through their contact with one of the five directors, La Revellière-Lepaux, members of the new society gained the support of the Minister of the Marine, Étienne Eustache Bruix, who promised 'to take all the demands of the society into account'.[64]

Formed after the coup d'état of 18 Fructidor (4 September 1797), the society counted a total of ninety-two members during its sixteen months of existence. The most active of these included survivors from the first group such as Lanthenas, Grégoire, Frossard, and Servan. These four, together

---

[62] On discussions within the Council of Five Hundred, see Lokke, 'French Dreams', 240, 244, 247–8. The *Monitor* also commented on Wadström's work on 2 Ventose year VI. On Napoleon's rationale, see Juan Cole, *Napoleon's Egypt: Invading the Middle East* (New York: Palgrave, 2007), 13, 14, and 16.

[63] Dorigny and Gainot, *La société des amis des noirs*, 309.   [64] Séance 30 Floréal year VI, ibid., 346.

with Wadström, Mentor, Bayard, and Thomany were the society's eight founders.[65] But there were other noteworthy members, including Charles Leclerc de Montlinod, the author referred to by Talleyrand. Geoffroy de Villeneuve, Boufflers' colleague in Senegal, was also a member. Some members – Volney and Cabanis, for example – were members of the Institut National. The political economist J. B. Say, who previously had worked as a secretary for Clavière and a writer for Mirabeau's journal *Courrier de Province,* was also a member. Say was one of the chief editors of *La décade.*[66] Additionally, the society counted eight blacks, one of whom was Jean-Baptiste Belley, and four people of colour. The society further admitted women among its members, including Wadström's wife, Ulrica Westerberg, and Say's wife, Julie Gourdel de Loche.[67]

The objectives of the society lined up with official republican imperial ideology. It was a strong supporter of the Constitution of the year III and the abolitionist decree of February 1794. It also nourished a firm interest in improving sugar cultivation through industry and botanical experimentation, and it was an avid supporter of colonial expansion in Africa and the use of free local labour. To achieve these objectives, members spent their meetings presenting and scrutinising proposals and memoranda, some of which were even furnished by the Ministry of the Marine. Of the proposals focusing on creating new colonies, the society briefly entertained the idea of creating colonies in Louisiana and Madagascar. One member, Daniel Lescallier, who was the former civil commissioner of the French establishments east of the Cape in 1792, also suggested regenerating French Guiana.[68] By far the most important colonial project deliberated, however, was the creation of new colonies in Africa. On the same day that Lescallier became a member of the society, Montlinot donated twenty copies of his *Essai sur la transportation comme recompense, et la déportation comme peine* (1797). Upon receiving Montlinot's donation, Geoffroy de Villeneuve read a memorandum of his travels in Africa (an early draft of *L'Afrique; ou histoire, mœurs, usages et coutumes des Africains; le Sénégal* published in 1814) in which he proposed creating slave-free colonies in Senegambia. After the lecture, the society decided to elect a commission to draw up a proposal for

---

[65] Ibid., 314.
[66] Letter to the *Amis des noirs et des colonies* from J. B. Say, 19 Floreal year 6. Paris, Bibliothèque de Port Royal, Fond Abbé Grégoire. See also Gainot's long footnote on Say, in Dorigny and Gainot, *La société des amis des noirs,* 339.
[67] Séance 30 Brumaire year VII, and Session of 10 Pluviôse year VII, ibid., 350 and 356.
[68] Dorigny and Gainot, *La société des amis des noirs,* 311 and Séance 20 Floréal year VI, ibid., 342, and Séance 30 Floréal year VI, ibid., 345.

a colony at Cap-Vert (the peninsula facing Gorée) based upon the information in Villeneuve's report.[69]

The society's discussion of Villeneuve's proposition came at a time when
Bruix was considering a near-identical proposal by M. Denyau (sometimes
spelled Deniay), director of the former French slave station at Whydah
(Juda). Denyau conveyed to Bruix that he had left Whydah six months
earlier to come to Paris to inform the government of the slave fort's current
distress. He complained that since the abolition of slavery, the government
had abandoned the station even though the area was a little paradise with
immense potential. There was an 800-metre-long garden full of fruit trees
and a local village with 400 inhabitants, whose devotion to the French
nation, Denyau claimed, was well known. Like his predecessor, M. Gourg,
who wrote near-identical proposals to the Ministry of the Marine in 1789
and again in 1795 as we saw in Chapter 4, Denyau could further reveal that
he had experimented with the cultivation of sugar cane and tobacco in the
region, both of which had succeeded perfectly and generated sugar and
cotton of a good quality. Additionally, he noted that cotton, pepper,
indigo, palm oil, and provisions of all sorts were indigenous to the area.
The climate secured two harvests per year, three in the case of nutmeg, and
there was as much land as an individual could wish for.[70]

Denyau's views on how to turn this into a sustainable colonial enterprise
largely echoed those presented to the Ministry of the Marine by the
Compagnie de la Guyane française during the American Revolution.
France should exploit the local demand for French commodities by developing a large colony based on philanthropic principles. Once such a colony
had been 'secured and civilised' it would clear the path to 'penetrate into
a multitude of small peoples well-disposed to receive our principles and our
industry'. He concluded his memorandum by encouraging France not to
fall behind nations who were already undertaking such enterprises, referencing established philanthropic colonies in the regions founded by 'the
English, Swedish, and Danish'. If the Directory so wished, Denyau – like
Ehanuy and Lamiral had offered before him – would happily take charge of
such a venture.[71]

The way in which Denyau's memorandum was subsequently processed
by the government illustrates the high status that the *amis des noirs et des
colonies* enjoyed within the Directory. In an internal report of 6
Pluviôse year VII (25 January 1799), the minister was advised to have the

[69] Séance 30 Floréal year VI, ibid., 346.
[70] Denyau 'Mémoire', Paris 25 Nivose year 7, ANOM, C⁶ 27, f. 106.   [71] Ibid.

proposal analysed by the 'Société des Amis des Noirs who after their examination, would prepare the minister to decide definitively both on the degree to which this holding was important and on the return of the Director'.[72] A few weeks later, on 18 February 1799, Denyau participated in the society's meeting to elaborate on his proposal, the latter of which was subsequently transferred to the society's internal commission on colonisation.[73] This meeting, however, was the penultimate one figuring in the society's register. It is therefore impossible to know if the society ever wrote a report on this proposal. The project does not seem to have taken form. At least, no document in the colonial archives focuses on Whydah until the restoration of slavery in 1802.[74]

Although the *amis des noirs et des colonies* were unable to report back to the minister, it is unclear whether or not Bruix would have supported a proposal for the creation of a colony in Whydah. The scarce communication between the Ministry of the Marine and Blanchot, Governor of Senegal at this time, suggests that Bruix's priorities lay elsewhere. In his instructions to Blanchot from 23 Ventôse year VII (13 March 1799), Bruix underlined that the governor's main focus in Senegal should be to retake Gorée (temporarily abandoned by Blanchot due to a lack of supplies and therefore an easy conquest for the British) and ensure that the colony continued to offer French commerce refreshments and assistance. Blanchot should also aim to protect the trade in gum, gold, ivory, and millet. To do so, the Directory would furnish Blanchot with a 'company of coloured men' (*compagnie d'homme du couleur*) who could 'provide Africans with an idea of the manner in which they would be treated were they to join' the French. Bruix included vague references to projects of colonisation and underlined the need to convey to Africans on all occasions that, according to the Declaration of the Rights of Man and of the Citizen, men could 'not sell themselves nor be sold'. Yet he further encouraged Blanchot to try to recruit cultivators (*cultivateurs*) to go to the colonies in the Antilles to 'revive cultivation' there, though he should accomplish this by means of 'persuasion' if at all possible, and if not then by means of 'ransom'.[75]

These instructions, which echoed similar proposals within the Ministry of the Marine from Saint-Domingue planters, suggest that Bruix had

---

[72] 'Rapport', 6 Pluviose year 7, ANOM C⁶ 27, f. 107.
[73] 30 Pluviôse year VII, Dorigny and Gainot, *La Société des Amis des Noirs*, 361.
[74] 25 Prairial Year X, 14 June 1802, ANOM C⁶ 27, f. 113.
[75] 'Instruction pour le C. Blanchot commandant au Sénégal', 23 Ventose, year 7. 1799, ANOM C⁶ 20, f. 5–6.

become more interested in finding a way to preserve plantations in the Antilles than in creating new agricultural colonies in Africa. They further indicate that conflicting imperial agendas vis-à-vis West Africa separated the Directory's early and later years. Bruix's predecessors, Laurent Jean François Truguet and Georges-René Pléville-Lepelley, supported a policy proposal which Blanchot had developed in communication with Truguet in 1797 centred around the expansion of the French trade in gum arabic and cash crop cultivation in Senegal. Their aim had been to launch 'a new field of industry worthy of the efforts and the means of the French Republic' now that the 'odious' slave trade had been abolished. Franco-British warfare, however, seriously limited any such efforts because the British Navy cut French supply lines to Senegal, preventing Blanchot from receiving the men, commodities, and provisions he requested to embark on agricultural and commercial development. To sustain French presence in Senegal, Blanchot even hinted that pressure from local African slave traders and the need to obtain provisions from neutral powers such as the Danish in the absence of French ships complicated his ability to suppress the slave trade entirely. When Bruix enquired about the feasibility of obtaining labour for the Caribbean islands through means of 'persuasion' or 'ransom', Blanchot therefore promoted the latter option finding the former in conflict with the preferences of local rulers.[76]

In the months following Denyau's presentation, the *amis des noirs et des colonies* fell out of grace. Allegedly, Bruix had been alarmed to discover connections between the society and similar societies in America. Forcing open a drawer in a room provided by the minister for the society's meetings which contained information on its Franco-American ties, Bruix decided to eject the society from its lodging, stating that the information he had found was 'on all matters contrary to the commitment they had made to me'.[77] It is impossible to know what exactly Bruix believed that the *amis des noirs et des colonies* were up to, yet his outburst took place at the peak of the Quasi-War between France and the United States that had evolved when the latter decided to remain neutral in the war between France and Britain.

---

[76] On Blanchot's communication to Truguet, see 'Considérations sur l'organisation du Sénégal par Blanchot', ANOM Col C⁶ 20, ff. 50–54. On Peley de Pléville's focus, see his letter to Blanchot, 29 Germinal year VI, ANOM C⁶ 20, ff. 31–2. On Blanchot's advice to Bruix, see Blanchot to Bruix, 5 Brumaire year 8, ANOM C⁶ 20, f. 25. Not all African rulers wished for the continuation of the slave trade. The ruler of the Fulbe sought to prohibit the enslavement of the Muslims of the Fulbe ethnic group. See Rudolph T. Ware, *The Walking Qur'an: Islamic Education, Embodied Knowledge, and History in West Africa* (Chapel Hill: University of North Carolina Press, 2014), Chapter 3.

[77] Letter from Bruix to Merlin, 1 Pluviose year 7, Paris, Archives Nationales, Paris, Directoire, AF III 206.

Although he may have disapproved of the society's American connections, it is more likely that the society's support of abolition was becoming a thorn in the side of the minister.[78] Expelled from its lodgings, the *amis des noirs et des colonies* relocated to Wadström's home. Its last documented meeting took place on 10 Germinal year 7 (30 March 1799). At that time Wadström was mortally ill and died only a few days later, on 15 Germinal year VII (4 April 1799). Wadström had guaranteed connections to Talleyrand as well as to *La décade* and the Institut National. Grégoire, who enjoyed similar connections, also suffered from illness and could not be there to support the society. In Bernard Gainot's words, the death of Wadström therefore became symbolic of the fate of the society as a whole.[79]

The Ebb and Flow of Modes of Empire

It was not only the Société des amis des noirs et des colonies that was singing its last verse. The days of the Directory were numbered too. The coup d'état of 18 Brumaire year VIII (9 November 1799) transformed the Directory into the Consulat and with that began the steady restoration of the slave-driven French colonial system. Napoleon, who had abandoned the Egyptian expedition before news of the ill-conceived military conquest reached the metropole, had lost interest in testing new forms of colonisation across the Mediterranean. The population of Egypt resisted the influx of French 'civilisation', not least because of the tax Napoleon imposed on them. One of the first things Napoleon did as consul was to replace the Constitution of the year III with the Constitution of the year VIII, which made the colonies separate territories to be governed by special laws once again.[80] Bonaparte and the other two consuls, Cambacérès and Lebrun, explained this shift to the citizens of Saint-Domingue in words reminiscent of the white planters' appropriation of montesquieuan climate theory:

> Citizens, a Constitution that has not been able to protect itself from multiple violations is replaced by a new pact destined to affirm liberty. Article 91

---

[78] On the Quasi-War, see Gordon S. Wood, *Empire of Liberty: A History of the Early Republic, 1789–1815* (Oxford: Oxford University Press, 2010), Chapter 7.

[79] Séance du 30 Pluviôse year VII, Dorigny and Gainot, *La Société des Amis des Noirs*, 326.

[80] As Bénédicte Fortier notes, 'the colonies se trouvent donc tout à fait écartées de l'élaboration des règles qui les concernant. Les dix années de Révolution sont bien achevées'. Bénédicte Fortier, '1799–1830 Ruptures et Continuités du régime législatif des quatre vieilles colonies françaises', in *Rétablissement de l'esclavage dans les colonies françaises aux origines de Haïti*, ed. Yves Bénot and Marcel Dorigny (Paris: Maisonneuve et Larose, 2003), 505–22, 508.

states that the French colonies will be ruled by special laws. This provision derives from the nature of things and the difference of climates. The inhabitants of the French colonies situated in America, in Asia, in Africa cannot be governed by the same law. The difference in habits, mores, and interests, the diversity of the soil, cultivations, and productions requires various modifications.[81]

Though the letter also stressed that the question of abolition was not put in doubt, the new Constitution marked a victory for those who wished to restore slavery in the colonies.

From this moment on, as Yves Benot has demonstrated, the role of abolitionists like Grégoire, Trugues (adviser to Napoleon) and Volney declined, while colonial administrators of the Ancien Régime, such as the Clichy Club-member, Barbé-Marbois, the former intendant of Saint-Domingue, won the ear of the first consul. The result is well known. In December 1801, Napoleon sent Leclerc to Saint-Domingue to suppress the republican regime and reinstate slavery. With the decree of 30 Floréal year X (20 May 1802), Napoleon proclaimed that slavery and the slave trade should be restored in all of France's colonies and conducted in accordance with the laws prior to 1789. The colonial regime, it was further decreed, should be subject to special laws for the next ten years.[82]

Napoleon's restorative efforts easily gained the support of the nation's deputies. Having decreed the colonisation of Egypt with great enthusiasm only a few years earlier, many now felt that with its failure it was time to push colonial innovation to one side and resurrect a colonial system that had proven itself to be extremely profitable. In this way, a full fifty-four deputies in the tribunal voted in favour of the decree to restore slavery while only twenty-seven deputies voted against.[83] In the colonies, news of the decree of 30 Floréal had varying outcomes. On Saint-Domingue, citizens headed by Dessalines repelled the attack by Leclerc and declared their independence in 1804, thus founding the first black republic in the New World. On Guadeloupe, slavery was restored and remained in place for another forty-six years. Martinique had never experienced abolition under British rule. Once the British restored it to France in the Treaty of

---

[81] Aux citoyens de Saint-Domingue, 4 Nivôse an VIII [25 décembre 1799], *Correspondance de Napoléon Ier publiée par ordre de l'empereur Napoléon III*, in Pierre Branda and Thierry Lentz, *Napoléon, l'esclavage et les colonies* (Paris: Fayard, 2006), 48–9.

[82] On influence of Barbé-Marbois, see Yves Benot, *La démence coloniale sous Napoléon* (Paris: La Découverte, 1992), 35.

[83] Among those voting against were Jean-Baptiste Say, Joachim Le Breton, and Joseph Eschassériaux. Bernard Gainot, 'La Décade et la "colonisation nouvelle"', *Annales historiques de la Révolution française*, 339 (2005), 99–116, 103–4.

Amiens in March 1802, it therefore merely continued to function as the slave colony it had been before the Revolution.

The restoration of the plantation complex also saw the return of debates among economists about the eventual secession of colonies in the Americas, the opportunity to preserve them if perceived as provinces, critiques of the Exclusif, and opportunities to expand in Africa. J. B. Say and newcomers such as Jean Charles Léonard de Sismondi and Dominique-Georges-Frédéric Dufour de Pradt, pondered these topics, sometimes in dialogue with each other. In his *Traité d'économie politique* from 1803, Say pointed out that while the sugar colonies might one day become autonomous or independent, there was an easy substitute in Africa where 'sugar and most of the colonial commodities grow much closer to us'. De Pradt and Sismondi, in turn, were in direct dialogue with regard to a possible French colonial future in the Americas. To de Pradt, colonies would necessarily separate from their metropole regardless of metropolitan measures. In response to Pradt's conclusion, Sismondi penned in his *De la richesse commerciale*, that 'we do not agree with him [de Pradt] that their separation is necessary, we even think that a good government can prolong it indefinitely by no longer considering them to be farms destined to produce but as provinces equal in rights to all the other [provinces] and whose growth, wealth, and population is no less interesting to it than that of all the other parts of the nation'.[84]

Debates on the possibilities of colonial expansion in Africa did not die down either. In the years between 1800 and 1802, when Napoleon was restoring the plantation complex, three publications appeared in close succession, penned by Jean-Gabriel Pelletan, Sylvain Meinrad Xavier Golbérry, and Jean-Baptiste-Léonard Durand. All three had worked in Senegal in the 1780s. Durand and Pelletan had each been appointed director of the Compagnie de la gomme du Sénégal and the Compagnie du Sénégal respectively whereas Golbérry had been there at the request of Boufflers to assist the latter during his governorship. In their publications, each of them fused ideas of agricultural development, the transplantation of colonial cash crops to Africa, and the physiocratic concept of 'civilisation' with bids for large-scale territorial conquest but took the infantilisation of Africans to a whole new level.

---

[84] Jean-Baptiste Say, *Traité d'économie politique; ou, Simple exposition de la manière dont se forment, se distribuent, et se consomment les richesses* 2 vols. (Paris: Deterville, Libraire, 1803), i, 226. Dominique-Georges-Frédéric Dufour de Pradt, *Les trois âges des colonies*, 3 vols. (Paris: Chez Giguet et Cie, 1801–2). Sismondi, *De la richesse commerciale ou principe d'économie politique appliqués à la législation du commerce*, 2 vols. (Geneva: J. J. Paschoud, 1803).

The first book to appear was Jean-Gabriel Pelletan's *Mémoire sur la colonie française du Sénégal* (1800). In it, Pelletan argued that it was time to turn to Africa, 'a land still brutish and savage' with 'men thirty centuries behind in the arts and civilisation'. Since the Consul had just 'regenerated Egypt' by introducing the arts and sciences, he should do the same for West Africa. According to Pelletan, this could be achieved by introducing 'the cultivation of the cash crops of America' and 'by employing on their native land and without removal, the hands which avarice every year robbed Africa of'. As he saw it, the Republic deserved to obtain 'without violent means' and 'without any overload of expenses', a 'territory of two hundred *lieues* of coastline', in a country that could carry all sorts of specie and covered with 'the best navigable rivers' and 'where the population, although very debased' would be enough to develop (*mettre en valeur*) this land. He maintained that such a 'new colonial system is preferable to the one we have followed until today' and would greatly benefit both France and the new African colony. Because the French conquest of Egypt was ongoing, he suggested that the 'agricultural colony' in Senegal could serve to connect these two African extremities, which would have the added advantage of stunting Britain's ambition to capture for itself 'the commerce of all of the world'.[85]

Sylvain Meinrad Xavier Golbérry, whose book appeared in 1802, went one step further. In his view, France should colonise an area comprising 'the territory between the fourth and the thirtieth-degree latitude and between the Atlantic Ocean and the thirtieth-degree longitude of the île de Fer. The surface of this part of Africa is more than 375,400 square lieues, the equivalent of more than a fifth of the entire surface of the continent'. He further noted that it would not be enough to introduce this part of the world to 'agriculture and civilisation' – clearly insinuating that they had neither – nor to merely civilise Africans and to teach them not to sell their own population but raw commodities. It would be necessary to ensure that they only entered the class of citizens, 'once they had proven themselves deserving of it', an assessment Golbérry surely intended to be in the hands of the French.[86]

Jean-Baptiste-Léonard Durand echoed Golbérry and Pelletan in his publication, *Voyage au Sénégal*, also published in 1802, underlining the 'ignorance, barbarie, misery, and deplorable state of the inhabitants of Africa' and the need to spread civilisation through colonisation. In a letter

---

[85] Pelletan, *Mémoire sur la colonie française du Sénégal*, iii, vii–viii, xiv, and xv.
[86] Golbérry, *Fragmens d'un voyage en Afrique*, i, 54, and ii, 363–4.

to the Ministry of Foreign Affairs, moreover, Durand merged his plans with an argument for the return of company rule, more specifically, a national Compagnie d'Afrique which would set up colonies in Africa. In one of these memoranda, Durand scolded the Physiocrats for having attempted to destroy French commerce in Africa with their preference for free trade. As he said, 'the freedom of the *Economistes* would have consummated the ruin of our commerce'. Little did he seem to know that, if not their trade policies, he was proposing the same plans to promote the transplantation of civilisation and agricultural development to Africa as the *économistes* had done over four decades earlier.[87]

Ancien Régime colonial agents were not alone in proposing a turn to Africa in 1802. Pierre François Page, former plantation owner on Saint-Domingue and enemy of Sonthonax and Polverel, argued to the Ministry of the Marine that since colonial empire in the Americas was ultimately doomed, France should stay fixed on setting up agricultural colonies in Egypt and Senegal where France could dominate for centuries to come.[88] In the same period, a group of colonial entrepreneurs in Marseille established the Société de l'Afrique intérieure. Very little is known about this society, but it was likely founded by a combination of scientifically engaged business men and scientists interested in the advancement of commerce. Its president, D. P. Azuni, explained in a letter to the Minister of Foreign Affairs, that the society proposed to undertake explorations in Africa to further geography, natural history, astronomy, and commerce and help Africa progress. It conveyed that it had already gained the support of the Ministers of the Interior and of the Marine the previous year.[89] Its prospectus clarified that the society sought to amend the harmful effects of greedy conquerors who had 'exchanged only their vices for Africa's riches'. Animated by 'a generous philanthropy', the Société de l'Afrique intérieure wished not only to perfect the 'physical history of the world', but also 'to work effectively towards the prosperity of these peoples'. As it stated: 'without having as its design the exaggerated pretention to have them adopt in their entirety our mores and our customs, it is evident that time and communication with the civilised nations [Nations policées]

---

[87] Durand, *Voyage au Sénégal*, 164. Durand, 'Commerce du Sénégal', 1802, MAE AD, Afrique II, f. 324.

[88] Pierre François Page, 'Notes sur l'établissement des cultures colonials en Égyptes et au Sénégal', 10 Pluviôse year X, ANOM COL C6 20, ff. 63. On Page's clashes with Sonthonax and Polverel, see biographic note in Benot, *La Révolution française*, 276.

[89] 'Règlement de la Société de l'Afrique intérieure'. The Règlement was sent to the Ministry of Foreign Affairs together with a letter from Azuni and dated 11 Germinal year X. MAE AD, Afrique II, f. 312.

should serve to introduce them to the benefits of civilisation'. A precursor to the Société française de géographie, founded in Paris in 1821, the Société de l'Afrique intérieure, illustrate the degree to which calls to bring 'civilisation' and agricultural development to Africa that a few Physiocrats and colonial agents promoted during the Ancien Régime not only reached a crescendo during the French Revolution in various articulations but continued into the nineteenth century.[90]

The revolutionary decade that ended with the rise of Napoleon was a complex moment in the broader history of French colonial ideology, policy, and practice. The outbreak of revolution gave deputies of the nation and numerous lobbyists an opportunity to reconstitute the French colonial empire, particularly with respect to Africa and the Americas. The Société des amis des noirs welcomed such an opportunity and promoted an agenda reminiscent of proposals by the Physiocrats and a select group of Ancien Régime colonial agents. While they borrowed the Physiocrats' emphasis on the need to reshape metropolitan-colonial relations, move away from slave labour, and transfer colonial cash crop cultivation from the Caribbean to Africa, their responses were not identical to physiocratic political economy. The *amis des noirs* had a notable tendency to infantilise Africans and they repeatedly used colonial expansion in Sierra Leone by British and Swedish abolitionists to encourage French audiences to embark on colonising adventures in Africa. At this early stage in the Revolution, however, deputies of French ports and white Caribbean planters, whose investments were tied up in the Ancien Régime plantation complex, were adamant that the impact of revolution in the colonies should be limited. They were successful at first but not for long. As slave rebellion jumped from one French colony to another, and war severed supply lines, the possibility of perpetuating the Ancien Régime sugar and coffee business eroded. In such a context, ideas to recalibrate the political economic underpinnings of the French colonial empire started to appeal to a greater number of the nation's deputies. What had initially been on the agenda of only French abolitionists – full integration of the old colonies, abolition, and the creation of slave-free colonies in Africa – became a concrete part of the First Republic's imperial agenda. In Egypt, Napoleon's army blended these ambitions with territorial conquest, a project that was met with fierce resistance from British and local forces.

---

[90] Joseph Fournier, 'Une Société de Géographie à Marseille en 1801', *Bulletin de la Société de Géographie de Marseille*, 23, 4 (1899), 375.

As the latter successfully curtailed French advances, Napoleon grew disillusioned with the republican imperial agenda and halted French advances in Africa momentarily. In collusion with proponents of the Caribbean plantation complex, he restored slavery in the remaining French sugar colonies, though again, he could not do so permanently. As the conclusion will discuss, competing modes of colonial empire continued to influence French colonialism and empire-making in the nineteenth and twentieth centuries.

Ancien Régime Legacies

For a book that focuses on the ways in which historical continuity inter-locks with innovation, transformation, and rupture, it seems appropriate to open and close with Citizen Talleyrand: who better embodies continuity in a time of change than a man who had a political career in every regime between the Bourbon and the July monarchies? In his speech to the Institut National on colonial opportunities in 1797, Talleyrand spoke at length on past, current, and future possibilities but he also included a passage which elegantly captured his vision of historical development. Referencing Machiavelli's *The Prince*, he reminded his audience that 'upheaval, Machiavelli says, always leaves the scaffolding for building further change'.[1] Quoting a line from a passage on 'hereditary monarchies' may have seemed facetious to some of his regicide listeners, yet they may also have understood that he was trying to convey a philosophy of history that apprehended the complex ways in which revolutionary upheaval and rupture carried within it older traditions and innovations that were, perhaps, themselves the fruits of distant disruptions. The French Revolution was indeed a cataclysmic moment set within a broader age of transatlantic imperial crisis, upheaval, and revolt. Yet as much as revolu-tionaries then, and historiographies (if not historians) today, depict it as a moment of rupture, we profit intellectually from taking seriously the continuities.

In the history of French colonial empire, the Revolution was a crescendo of imperial processes of innovation and reform that had gestated for decades in response to the colonial debacle of the Seven Years War. This pan-European and global imperial conflict generated unprecedented levels of financial, political, and geostrategic anxiety for the main powers involved and propelled Crown officials, colonial entrepreneurs, political economists, and intellectual elites to endeavour to rectify deficiencies

---

[1] Talleyrand, *Essai sur les avantages à retirer des colonies nouvelles*, 4.

within their colonial empires. For France, the official line became to build a leaner colonial economy, better equipped to harvest the profits to be made from the rising consumption of sugar and coffee in Europe but which production sites came with considerable protection costs. With Choiseul at the helm, and against the backdrop of a cacophony of views on which policies to follow, France sacrificed its unremunerative territories on the North American mainland and set out to bolster its plantation complex in the French Antilles by boosting its slave trade and softening the Exclusif.

Such a strategy of colonial empire made economic sense in the short term. An influx of more slaves could augment production, satisfy investors, merchants, and planters and replenish the treasury. To the Crown, the high protection costs associated with empire was acceptable as long as profits came in fast and abundantly. In the long term, however, betting on the Caribbean plantation complex was unsustainable within the existing structures of the French colonial system. The sugar islands were fragile societies whose vulnerability alternated according to the whims of weather, climate, and European warfare. Internal to metropolitan–colonial relations, the unreliable influx of supplies from France, illicit trade, elevated costs of commodities, a lack of coin in the islands, planter debt, political disloyalty, corruption, violence, slave resistance, and famine further weakened the sugar islands' ability to satisfy metropolitan expectations. Augmenting the colonies' slave populations and opening up trades in food provisions and building materials may briefly drive up production but could not tackle many of these existing problems at a deeper level. To clear-sighted observers such as Jean-Antoine, chevalier de Mirabeau, governor of Guadeloupe, it was obvious already in the early 1750s that the combined forces of metropolitan, colonial, and imperial weaknesses steadily undermined French colonial empire in the Americas.

Mirabeau's forebodings found an audience in his older brother, Victor Riqueti, marquis de Mirabeau. Connected to a myriad of practical-minded political economists that permeated the state apparatus, Mirabeau, Quesnay, and followers such as Le Mercier de la Rivière, Du Pont de Nemours, Roubaud, and Baudeau developed a colonial doctrine in response to the French colonial crisis that sought to move beyond the problems that colonial slavery and commercial prohibition produced. Projecting that Europe's American colonies would inevitably secede from their metropoles, they believed that only a new bond between France and its colonies based on an upgrading of the latter's status to overseas provinces and a repealing of the Exclusif might offer French ambitions in the

Americas a new lease of life. While Quesnay and Le Mercier remained suspiciously silent about the role of plantation slavery in the colonies, Du Pont de Nemours, Roubaud, and Baudeau virulently criticised the exploitation of Africans in the Caribbean colonies and suggested relocating the production of sugar, coffee, indigo, cotton, and other cash crops to Africa where the local population could be taught to cultivate their lands. Such an approach, they predicted, would render an ultimately unsustainable plantation complex in the Americas redundant and allow 'civilisation' and 'progress' to penetrate the African continent, all the while expanding opportunities for European export.

Due to the major profits that state coffers, French ports, colonial investors, and a not insignificant number of Crown officials stood to reap from sugar and coffee plantations in the Caribbean, there was no incentive to follow the physiocratic proposal. In its attempt to redress the soft underbelly of its plantation complex, the Crown tried to mend the system within its existing structures through a process of centralisation and moderate liberalisation of colonial commerce. Creating three Chambres mi-partie d'agriculture et de commerce on Martinique and Saint-Domingue, the Ministry of the Marine offered the colonial elite representation in the Council of Commerce in Paris to alleviate planter resentment. It also took direct control of the administration of French holdings in Senegambia and on the Gold Coast to help protect the slave trade. This did not mean that physiocratic colonial ideas had no resonances within the French colonial empire or failed to influence activities on the ground. Just like their political economic doctrine was informed by colonial officials enmeshed in disparate colonial settings, so colonial officials, policy makers, and private entrepreneurs in France and the colonies echoed aspects of the physiocratic colonial doctrine as they set out to mould the French colonial system in accordance with their particular interests or tried to push French colonial empire in new directions.

In the Îles du Vent, one theatre upon which the Physiocrats fastened their ideas, the Crown's efforts to set up a Chambre mi-partie d'agriculture et de commerce integrated colonial voices into institutions of participatory colonial policy-making. Colonial integration represented a step forward in the longer history of colonial-metropolitan relations in that it recognised colonies' right to prosperity. Planters, however, used the opportunities that reform offered to exercise and develop a creole political economic agenda which would stand them in good stead during the French Revolution. Through intercessions in debates on colonial taxation, provisioning, debt, and slavery, the planter elite on Martinique articulated arguments that supported their political economic interests. They did so incrementally and in dialogue with metropolitan debates, eclectically grabbing concepts and theories developed by the Physiocrats, Montesquieu, Forbonnais, and others to further their case within an expanding discursive universe. In the French African holdings, colonial officials and independent entrepreneurs dipped into such conversations as well, as they set about testing proposals to cultivate cash crops associated with the Americas. Testing alternative models of empire on the margins of the prevailing colonial system, they made sense of their activities and proposed ventures with references to free labour, development, and 'civilisation', a language that would later help imperialists legitimise efforts to integrate African land and peoples into an evolving capitalist world economy on European terms.

When paying attention to these Caribbean and West African developments, the history that emerges of Ancien Régime colonialism between the Seven Years War and the French Revolution is one of complex interplays between more conventional and new experimental approaches to colonial empire. The no-territory policy that dominated the Crown's colonial policies in the decades after the Seven Years War and filled state coffers only to empty them again to protect the colonies from foreign conquest coincided and intermittently intersected with budding alternative paths to empire that grew in response to an underlying concern with the untenable nature of the American colonies. One such path offered the contours for a different mode of empire based on the integration of existing colonies, a transition from slave labour and monopoly trade to free labour and free trade, and the alleged spread of civilisation and progress in Africa by means of French-led agricultural development.

It was these latter efforts that revolutionaries such as the *amis des noirs*, Talleyrand, and others appropriated when seeking to formulate a republican imperial agenda during the French Revolution. As long as the plantation complex appeared intact, the National Assembly remained committed to slavery in the colonies, convinced as the representatives of the nation were that the abrogation of the plantation complex would damage French national interests. It took slave rebellion in the Caribbean and the outbreak of warfare to recast the parameters of colonial possibility and pave the way for a comprehensive shift in policy. Under the Directory, French revolutionaries endorsed a model of empire which sought to preserve France's remaining colonies through integration, abolition, and legal universalism. In the Constitution of the year III, and with the law of the constitutional organisation of the colonies of the year VI, colonies became overseas departments. The Directory also sanctioned the establishment of new colonies in Africa in the name of progress, agricultural development, and civilisation and in the search for cheap labour to reignite the French sugar business. The conquest of Egypt was immediately informed by such ambitions.

The rise of Napoleon, however, pushed aside the Directory's imperial policies, though not before they had been associated with military conquest in Egypt. After failing to stamp out Egyptian and British resistance to the French invasion, Napoleon put the brakes on colonial experimentation and threw his weight behind the restoration of the Ancien Régime sugar business. Stakeholders of the Caribbean plantation complex drew a sigh of relief as Napoleon's forces managed to reinstate slavery in French sugar colonies, though on Saint-Domingue his schemes culminated in Haitian independence in 1804. By that time, Napoleon's ambition to create an overseas empire was declining rapidly. With the sale of Louisiana to the United States, he pivoted to create a substitute for overseas empire in Europe, a project that ended in a humiliating collapse as well. French defeat in Europe and overseas during the Napoleonic reign consolidated Britain's position as Europe's leading global power and permanently relegated France to a less prominent position.[2]

Thus, as France endeavoured to reassert its global presence in the nineteenth and twentieth centuries, it was saddled with a complicated colonial past that included the legacies of a lucrative colonial system based on slave labour and commercial privilege in the Americas, of an alternative imperial agenda based on the integration of existing colonies and the promotion of new ones in Africa, and of the recent memory of Napoleon's military conquests in Europe and Egypt. It is worth concluding the book's explorations of these interlocking developments with a glance into the post-Napoleonic period and return to the Îles du Vent and the French holdings in Senegal to analyse how the competing legacies and modes of empire that characterised the period between the Seven Years War and the rise of Napoleon continued to condition French colonial ambitions and approaches as they developed in new directions and in dialogue with the evolving French nation-state.

The Long, Rugged Road to the DOM-TOM

After the fall of Napoleon, Martinique, and Guadeloupe remained slave societies for another three decades. Yet the broader context within which

---

[2] For a general overview of French colonial history under Napoleon between 1799 and 1804, see Branda and Lentz, *Napoléon, l'esclavage et les colonies*, and for the following period, see Benot, *La démence coloniale.*

supporters of the French sugar complex hoped to reignite success was changing rapidly. The collapse of Saint-Domingue paved the way for the rise of Cuba, Puerto Rico, Brazil, and Java and demoted France's prominence on the international sugar market. Although sugar production in the Îles du Vent boomed in the 1830s, French Caribbean sugar was reoriented towards the domestic market. The Exclusif remained in place until 1861 but was continuously challenged in the colonies due to their ongoing trade with foreign powers such as the United States and at home due to metropolitan importation of foreign sugar. In fact, the tables gradually turned with regard to disputes over the Exclusif. Planters now demanded protection by means of high tariffs against the importation of foreign sugar in France and they lobbied against domestic cultivation of the sugar beet, whereas several French merchants started to agitate for the dismantlement of the Exclusif.[3]

It was not only rising competition that propelled economic anxieties in the Îles du Vent. The abolition of the slave trade in 1815 stood as a formidable challenge to the restoration of the plantation complex. Though an illegal trade in slaves continued, and the slave population reached new heights in the early 1830s, it declined in the following decades.[4] Alongside concerns about labour shortages, planters feared the possibility of another Haiti. The slave uprisings of 1822 and 1831 on Martinique did little to divest the shrinking plantocracy of their qualms. Whites' continuous attempts to oppress the growing population of free people of colour added to an intensifying critique of planter inhumanity. The Bissette affair, in which Cyrille Bissette, a free man of colour, was convicted of conspiring against white planters, was a case in point. Bissette was sentenced to life as a galley slave and deported to Paris in 1824. In Paris, his trial became a cause célèbre and reignited debates over the need for colonial reform and the abolition of slavery. Not until the Revolution of 1848, however, did a non-elected French government re-abolish slavery in the French colonies, an act that did not reach Martinique before another major slave rebellion had broken out.[5]

The French abolition of slavery in 1848 did not bring an end to social and economic injustice among Martinique and Guadeloupe's populations. After abolition, France introduced labour legislation similar to that of the

---

[3] Butel, *Histoire des Antilles françaises*, 325.   [4] Ibid., 340.
[5] Melvin D. Kennedy, 'The Bissette Affair and the French Colonial Question', *The Journal of Negro History*, 45, 1 (1960), 5. On French abolitionism in the post-Napoleonic period, see Lawrence C. Jennings, *The Movement for the Abolition of Slavery in France, 1802–1848* (Cambridge: Cambridge University Press, 2000).

slave system. Many of the former slaves who did not manage to transition to the status of *petits propriétaires* worked under harsh labour contracts or fell into what authorities labelled 'vagabondage'. The islands also saw an influx of Indian, Asian, and African labourers who had been contracted to work under pitiful conditions in the colonies' sugar plantations and new rum and banana industries. Few of these people were more than nominally free and social conditions failed to improve.[6]

Within such a fast-changing national and international context, France and its colonies in the Îles du Vent continued down a long, rugged road towards colonial integration. Along the way, as broader sectors of colonial and metro-politan societies were able to participate, novel arguments for and against integration and assimilation entered the fray and new questions arose. Was integration the same as assimilation? Should the process be limited to legal and political integration or also include cultural, social, and economic assimilation? Were any of these options desirable? Were they inherently racist? Queries such as these characterised the French metropolitan relationship with the Îles du Vent in the nineteenth and twentieth centuries and linger even today. Yet as much as they responded to and were part of historical processes that emerged in the period after the French Revolution, braided into these questions were also Ancien Régime economic and legal discourses.[7]

Perhaps the single most noteworthy area in which such continuities were present is in nineteenth- and twentieth-century constitutions and constitu-tional debates. Resurfacing the moment that the Napoleonic Empire col-lapsed, they initially drew solidly on the montesquieuan argument for special laws and a preference for the concept of colonies over that of provinces or departments. In the Constitutional Charter of 1814 that restored the Bourbon monarchy, Article 73 stated that 'the colonies shall be governed by special laws and regulations'.[8] This article was confirmed during Napoleon's hundred days, and the Charter was reapplied upon the fall of Napoleon in 1815. Fifteen years later, the Constitution of 1830 preserved the status quo, stating in Article 64 that 'the colonies are ruled by means of particular laws'.[9] It took the

---

[6] Nelly Schmidt, 'The Drafting of the 1848 Decrees: Immediate Application and Long-Term Consequences', in Marcel Dorigny (ed.), *The Abolitions of Slavery*, 311. On the influx of migrants, see Laurence Brown, 'The Three Faces of Post-Emancipation Migration in Martinique, 1848–1865', *The Journal of Caribbean History*, 36, 2 (2002), 310–36.

[7] For an introduction to the trajectory to overseas departments, see Robert Aldrich and John Connell, *France's Overseas Frontier: Départements et Territoires d'Outre-Mer* (Cambridge: Cambridge University Press, 1992).

[8] 'Charte constitutionnelle du 4 juin 1814', Conseil Constitutionnel, www.conseil-constitutionnel.fr.

[9] 'Charte constitutionnelle du 14 aout 1830', Conseil Constitutionnel, www.conseil-constitutionnel.fr. On the extensive debate on the phrasing of this law see Archives parlementaires de 1787 à 1860 Serie 2

Revolution of 1848 before colonial integration moved ahead though it once again proved to be circumscribed. In the Constitution of 1848 that established the Second Republic (4 November 1848), Article 109 noted that 'the colonies are declared French territory, and will be ruled by particular laws until a special law places them under the regime of the present Constitution'. Article 21 announced that the French colonies would obtain representation in the National Assembly.[10] An extraparliamentary commission was also established on 3 April 1848 to work on a new set of laws. Napoleon III's Coup of 2 December 1851 blocked these efforts. The regime based on particular laws continued and the emperor withdrew colonial representation for both whites and men of colour in the Corps législatif in 1854.[11]

Despite this emphasis on particular laws, Ancien Régime political ideas about reconceptualising colonies and legal universalism had not been forgotten before 1848. During the July Monarchy, as pressure to abolish slavery mounted, the issue of colonies' status came up within the commission established in 1840 to examine 'questions relating to slavery and the political constitution of the colonies'. Chaired by Victor de Broglie, the commission wrote an elaborate report on the possible impacts that abolition might have on France, its colonies, and their mutual relationship. The commission pointed out that were slavery to be abolished, the colonies would lose 'the physiognomy' and the 'exterior character of colonies' and obtain instead the appearance of 'French departments'. In making this observation, the commission implied that slavery alone was the cause of colonies' distinction from French domestic territory. But commercial trade privileges were clearly also an influential factor in this. The commission noted that the traditional status of colonies reached back to the regulations of Colbert but had been modified after the loss of Canada and Louisiana with the transition to the Exclusif mitigé.[12] In its recommendation, the commission thus implied that without slavery there was no need for the Exclusif, and without either, colonies were nothing but overseas provinces.[13] In spite of its well-researched arguments for

Vol. 63. 1886, 74, 362, 467 (11 September 1830), 679 (25 September 1830). On the legislative evolution see Fortier, '1799–1830 Ruptures et Continuités du régime législatif des quatre vieilles colonies françaises', 505–22.

[10] 'Constitution de 1848'. Conseil Constitutionnel, www.conseil-constitutionnel.fr.

[11] Albert Duchêne, *La Politique Coloniale de la France Le Ministère des colonies depuis Richelieu* (Paris: Payot, 1928), 198–9. Martin, *L'Empire Renaissant*, 169.

[12] *Ministre de la marine et des colonies. Commission instituée par décision royale du 26 mai 1840, pour l'examen des questions relatives à l'esclavage et à la constitution politique des colonies*, 2 vols. (Paris: Impr. Royale, 1840–43), 347–8.

[13] According to the commission, what was really at stake was the supply of sugar. France already relied on foreigners to satisfy demands (two-thirds came from the four old colonies of Martinique, Guadeloupe, Guyane, and Île Bourbon, it noted, and one-third from foreigners). Sugar from

the abolition of slavery, the commission's report failed to convince the majority of policy makers within the French liberal constitutional monarchy, who – like their predecessors in 1791 – were sensitive to the arguments of a pro-slavery lobby.[14]

After the fall of Napoleon III, the Third Republic restored colonial representation in 1871, though only Martinique, Guadeloupe, and Réunion were allowed to elect a senator and a deputy. Moreover, the colonies maintained the name of 'colonies' rather than 'overseas departments'. It was only after World War II that a ministerial report noted that the four old colonies that had been assimilated into the metropole tended 'naturally to become departments'.[15] Supported unanimously by the National Assembly, Article 1 of the law of 19 March 1946 stated that 'the colonies of Guadeloupe, Martinique, Réunion, and French Guiana are elevated to French departments'. Article 2 noted that 'The laws and decrees currently in place in metropolitan France and that are still not applied in these colonies shall be, before 1 January 1947, the object of a decree of application in these new departments'.[16]

As Kristen Stromberg Childers has argued, the reason why the conversion of the *vieilles colonies* into departments in 1946 materialised at this point was because the process promised to solve both metropolitan and colonial problems in the aftermath of the Second World War. For people of colour in the colonies, it was a matter of 'rectifying centuries of inequality' through the adoption and application of citizenship rights equal to those bestowed in the metropole and to address deep economic disparities between the black majority and the local white minority. For the metropolitan officials, departmentalisation served the dual purpose of putting French civilisation in the Americas on display while affirming France's sustained relevance in the Western hemisphere in the post-war period. As Childers points out, in the face of mounting pressure from other former European colonies to seek the path of independence, Martinique, Guadeloupe, Réunion, and French Guiana chose instead to seek 'imperialism's embrace'.[17]

India, Java, and Sumatra was cheaper than sugar from the colonies. Abolishing the French monopoly on trade with the colonies would therefore have little impact on the cost and supply of sugar. Ibid., 349.

[14] Jennings, *The Movement for the Abolition of Slavery in France*.

[15] René Belenus, '19 Mars 1946: Les Quatre "vieilles colonies" sont érigées en departements français d'outre mer'. *60 ans de Départementalisation: Catalogue collectif documents conservés dans les Bibliothèques de Guadeloupe, de guyane, de Martinique et de la Réunion* (CIR, 2006), 9.

[16] Ibid., 16.

[17] Kristen Stromberg Childers, *Seeking Imperialism's Embrace: National Identity, Decolonization, and Assimilation in the French Caribbean* (Oxford: Oxford University Press, 2016), 48.

Aimé Césaire, who represented Martinique in the National Assembly as a member of the French Communist Party in 1945, was one of the chief advocates of departmentalisation. In his speech to the Constituent Assembly on 25 February 1946, which came after the collapse of Vichy France but before the referendum on the constitution of the Fourth Republic, he described departmentalisation as the culmination of a long battle between authoritarian and republican forces. Alleging that colonial integration had begun in 1635, he argued that it had subsequently been conditioned by fluctuations between French authoritarian regimes that had sought to 'exclude Martinique and Guadeloupe from the national community' and liberal regimes who had tried to 'wrest these territories from arbitrary decrees to allow them to enjoy the benefits of the generosity of French law'. He heralded in particular, efforts of the First, Second, and Third Republics to pursue the 'republican doctrine of integration'. In his view, however, full assimilation and integration were still incomplete.[18]

Yet it was clearly not merely a matter of authoritarian versus republican principles but also one of underlying political economic ideas. Césaire explained that the economic and social status of the broader population of workers in the Antilles and in Réunion lagged far behind the political status that they had obtained nearly a century before. Salaries in Martinique were 'abnormally low' whereas the cost of living resembled that of France and there was no guaranteed social security or health care. A wealthy minority lived in the castles of the old slave owners, sought protection from world competition, and exploited the 'local proletariat' while the latter, who constituted the great majority, lived in huts on plots of clay and still needed to escape 'feudal servitude'. Césaire observed that powerful whites had time and again sought shelter in the name of Montesquieu and his famous climate theory to advocate against uniformity and for particular laws. But the time had come to side with the Montesquieu who condemned slavery and 'to free almost one million men of colour from one of the modern forms of slavery'.

The solution Césaire promoted was to adopt a flexible, intelligent, and realistic form of integration and assimilation: one that went beyond that of Boissy d'Anglas, which he found too rigid and idealistic, to embrace a form of 'geometric assimilation' which still took geography into account. This meant that while the French legal regime should be extended in its entirety

---

[18] Aimé Césaire, 'Rapport fait au nom de la commission des territoires d'outre-mer sur les propositions de loi', Annexe au procès-verbal de la séance du 25 février 1946, 520, 3, www.assemblee-nationale.fr /histoire/images/rapport-520.pdf.

to the colonies, the local prefects (representatives of the state in the departments) should be accorded slightly more extensive powers than in France to help them to 'immediately regulate certain affairs that are within the competence of the central government'. This was necessary, he explained to metropolitan deputies, to ensure for the colonies the same great social and economic transformation that had taken place in France by means of nationalisation, and which had organised production to the benefit of the 'general interests and no longer to a few private interests'.[19]

Césaire's reference to the exploited proletariat and the nationalisation of the economy embodied clear Marxist connotations, a sound strategy given the influence of the French Communist Party immediately after the war. Yet Césaire's vision on departmentalisation was also rooted in his under-standing of the French Revolution, the political aims of Toussaint Louverture, and his recent visit to Haiti. His partiality for a certain reading of Montesquieu was also evident. But woven into the deeper textures of his claims, it is also possible to discern ideas for integration articulated by the Physiocrats, particularly the notion that prosperity within the embrace of empire was best attained if all its component parts were perceived as equals and afforded the same opportunity to prosper under the same set of economic laws and to the benefit of general rather than private interests. While Césaire and Quesnay were of different worlds and of different political economic persuasions, they still shared some of the same responses to empire.[20]

From Gorée to l'Afrique Occidentale Française

Like in the Caribbean, the Bourbon monarchy was able to recover the holdings that Britain had conquered in West Africa (Saint-Louis, Gorée, and Albreda) during its wars with Napoleon. Together with other European states, France also committed to the abolition of the slave trade at the Congress of Vienna in 1815. With that, its old possessions in West Africa lost their primary purpose. Except for Senegal's role as a source of gum arabic, French interests in the region would therefore have to be

---

[19] Ibid., 5 and 12.

[20] Césaire soon became disillusioned with departmentalisation, and France and its overseas territories are still locked in battle over the future of the DOM-TOM. For a discussion on this topic, see Yarimar Bonilla, *Non-Sovereign Futures: French Caribbean Politics in the Wake of Disenchantment* (Chicago: Chicago University Press, 2015). On Césaire's multiple influences vis-à-vis his views on departmentalisation, see John Patrick Walsh, 'Césaire Reads Toussaint Louverture: The Haitian Revolution and the Problem of Departmentalization', in *Small Axes*, 15, 1 (2001), 110–24.

reformulated to justify an ongoing investment in these territories. At this juncture, Geoffroy de Villeneuve published his work on Senegal, parts of which he had presented to the Société des amis des noirs et des colonies in the year VI. In a section entitled 'Project for a free and colonial settlement on the African coast', Villeneuve encouraged carrying 'Enlightenment, civilisation, and agriculture' into the very heart of Africa 'for the good of its peoples and for the prosperity of French commerce'. Referencing his time in Senegal under Boufflers' governorship in the 1780s, he underlined that 'I have seen the plantations in Africa and I have seen those of Saint-Domingue'. Based on this experience, he could verify that 'those in Africa are stronger and more vigorous'.[21]

Insisting on the inferiority of Saint-Domingue plantations to those in Africa at a moment when France had not yet relinquished the hope of one day recapturing Haiti was a strategic move. Villeneuve's resurrection of an alternative French path to empire that echoed strands of the physio-cratic colonial doctrine but also claims and experiments by Ancien Régime governors from Poncet de la Rivière to Boufflers and agents of commercial companies came at a time when decision makers were once again receptive to a reorientation of French imperial ambitions. After sixty years of largely ignoring French colonial opportunities in Africa, the steady loss of Canada, Louisiana, and now also Saint-Domingue, as well as the abolition of the slave trade, opened the door to a renewed interest in what the Abbé Demanet had referred to as 'l'Afrique Française'.[22]

Following Villeneuve's recommendations, the restored Bourbon monarchy sent a convoy carrying a thousand settlers to reclaim Senegal and to establish plantations, exploit gold mines, boost the French national economy and spread 'civilisation'. Owing to Théodore Géricault's *Radeau de la Méduse* (1819) we tend to think that the project never bore fruit. The painting depicts survivors from this expedition on a raft after their ship, the *Meduse*, had sunk. Yet many of the settlers made it to Senegal. Under the leadership of Governor Julien Schmaltz, they were able to obtain land grants from the rulers of Waalo, and started experimenting with the cultivation of cotton, tobacco, and sugar. Their efforts only produced meagre results, however, and France ended these experiments in 1831.[23]

[21] Villeneuve, *Le Sénégal*, i, 110–11, and 116.

[22] Demanet, *Nouvelle histoire de l'Afrique Françoise*, xix.

[23] Barry, *Senegambia and the Atlantic Slave Trade*, 137. Martin A. Klein, 'Slaves, Gum, and Peanuts: Adaptation to the End of the Slave Trade in Senegal, 1817–48', *The William and Mary Quarterly*, 66, 4 (2009), 906; Quinn, *The French Overseas Empire*, 154–5. Georges Hardy, *La mise en valeur du Sénégal de 1817 à 1854* (Paris: Émile Larose, Libraire-Éditeur, 1921), 35–40.

According to Boubacar Barry, the abandonment of the initiative to establish agricultural colonies in West Africa was due to successful local resistance. The Trarza, Futa Tooro, and Kayoor States had all feared that these plantations might be a first step towards large-scale French colonial conquest and therefore mobilised to block French attempts.[24] In the years that followed, the French government tried instead to boost the trade in gum, vacillating between monopoly trade and free trade like in the years from 1763 to 1789. It was not until the mid-nineteenth century that France committed to colonial conquest. In stiff competition with Great Britain, and urged on by French merchant houses eager to promote the cultivation of peanuts for the production of industrial lubricants, soap, and in cooking, France firmly established itself as a colonial power in Senegal under the governorship of Louis Faidherbe. From here – and better equipped to withstand African diseases based on European medical advances – France turned to military conquest, pushing deep into the Sudan, the Niger, and down to the Ivory Coast.[25] A confederation of eight colonial territories in Africa (Mauritania, Senegal, French Sudan, French Guinea, Ivory Coast, Upper Volta, Dahomey, and Niger) ended up under French rule, greatly surpassing the territorial size of any claims to colonial empire France had ever had in the Americas.

The policies that undergirded French rule in Africa under the Third Republic were often deeply exploitative and had little to do with the universal application of French law, free trade, or free labour. Except for the four communes of Dakar, Gorée, Saint-Louis, and Rufisque in Senegal, no African colony benefitted from rights to parliamentary representation during the Second and Third Republics. Gregory Mann has argued persuasively that during the Third Republic, the Indigénat – a legal system applied in Algeria in 1881, in Senegal in 1887, and in the AOF in 1904 – served as a 'regime of exception' that was 'based on rule by decree', enacted arbitrarily and 'concerned primarily with asserting administrative power'.[26] When the Indigénat was abolished in 1946, a few Africans from the four communes were elected to the French National Assembly and limited citizenship rights were extended to people in the African colonies with the Loi Lamine Guèye.

---

[24] Barry, *Senegambia and the Atlantic Slave Trade*, 138.
[25] Quinn, *The French Overseas Empire*, 154–5. C. W. Newbury and A. S. Kanya-Forstner, 'French Policy and the Origins of the Scramble for West Africa', *The Journal of African History*, 10 (1969), 253–76. Barry, *Senegambia and the Atlantic Slave Trade*, 142–7. Klein, 'Slaves, Gum, and Peanuts: Adaptation to the End of the Slave Trade in Senegal, 1817–48'.
[26] Gregory Mann, 'What Was the "Indigénat"? The "Empire of Law" in French West Africa', *Journal of African History*, 50, 3 (2009), 331–53, 333, and 351.

The Constitution of the French Fourth Republic folded African colonies into the French Union, but it was not until 1956 that they could enjoy universal suffrage. Meanwhile, power at the local level remained in the hands of a French governor. Under the Fifth Republic of 1958, the French Union transformed into the French Community with local autonomy, but it lasted only shortly. By late 1960, all former French colonies of the AOF had obtained independence.[27]

There are thus profound differences between the French colonial empire in West Africa imagined by eighteenth-century thinkers, colonial officials, independent agents, and French Revolutionaries, and the French empire in Africa that materialised under the Third Republic. But there were also underlying continuities. The ideological justification for French expansion and then empire in Africa manifested itself in a desire to bring agricultural development to Africa (based on a belief that there was none) and in a civilising mission (*mission civilisatrice*). At the origins of this mission, as Alice L. Conklin has pointed out, was the term 'civilisation'.[28] Civilisation became a magnificent tool with which not only France but also many other European powers as well as the United States justified their imperial expansion into Africa and Asia in the nineteenth and twentieth centuries. Although studies highlight the slippery nature of the concept of civilisation and discuss its numerous and constantly evolving meanings, the ways in which it was understood by its originator and the group of political economists that joined him do not seem fundamentally different from some of the ways in which it was understood and attached to justifications for empire in later periods.[29]

When coining the concept, Mirabeau had immediately associated it with colonisation and religion, celebrating the contributions of French missionaries to the advancement of civilisation in the New World. In *L'Amis des hommes*, he further condemned the Exclusif as contrary to civilisation and mentioned that religion was civilisation's first spring. Its meaning tended to be clearer in the hands of the Abbé Roubaud. In his discussions on how France could help spread civilisation on the African continent, Roubaud thought that civilisation denoted French and

---

[27] Quinn, *The French Overseas Empire*, 242–5; Frederick Cooper, *Citizenship between Empire and Nation: Remaking France and French Africa, 1945–1960* (Princeton, NJ: Princeton University Press, 2014).

[28] Conklin, *A Mission to Civilize*, 14–15.

[29] On the meanings and evolutions of the term 'civilisation', see, for instance, Bertrand Binoche (ed.), *Les équivoques de la civilisation* (Seyssel: Éditions Champ Vallon, 2005); and Mazlish, 'Civilization in a Historical and Global Perspective'.

European norms, values, and production and consumption patterns. He was particularly eager to connect it to agricultural development and cash crop cultivation. This understanding also seemed to be the one promoted by the Société des amis des noirs. In the period between the Physiocrats and the rise of Napoleon, there were also differing articulations of how civilisation might spread to Africa. To the Physiocrats, it was through the peaceful means of commerce and settler colonies that France and Europe might aid in the spread of civilisation. Others, such as directors of the Compagnie de la Guyane française, recommended putting a chartered company in charge of developing agricultural settlements along the Senegal River and spread civilisation by winning the affection of local populations without 'using an apparatus of force or violence'. At the turn of the nineteenth century, however, colonial agents such as Durand, Pelletan, and Golbérry, inspired by recent developments in Egypt, tended to propose colonial expansion by means that did not exclude territorial conquest, a preference that could also be found in the writings of Poncet de la Rivière but which was rarely articulated before the revolutionary decade.

These varying understandings of civilisation and how to spread it continued into the nineteenth century. Between the Bourbon restoration and the July Monarchy, liberals such as François Guizot, Alphonse de Lamartine, and Michel Chevalier appropriated the concept of civilisation to promote French global interests without territorial conquest. What David Todd identifies as a French form of 'informal empire' and 'free-trade imperialism' echoed many of the colonial ideas promoted by the Physiocrats, though not their political preference for 'legal despotism'.[30] Curiously, the colonial ideas of physiocratic thinkers also seemed to resonate in liberal promotions of a more formal empire. In 1836 in the *Revue des Deux Mondes*, the French lawyer and liberal journalist, Eugène Lerminier, made a call for a grand new colony in Algeria in a language reminiscent of elements of Mirabeau and Roubaud's writings on civilisation and agricultural development, but also of the *amis des noirs'* infanti-lisation of slaves in the colonies, all the while embracing the legacy of Napoleonic military conquest. Agreeing that colonies would inevitably develop into mature independent states, he noted,

> We should recognise that these children of civilisation, submissive and docile in their crib, will necessarily find their independence once wholly developed. Let us therefore hurry up and make up for what might escape us later. Here is a vast colony without slaves which offers itself to us, do you

[30] Todd, 'Transnational Projects of Empire'.

hear? [In Algeria], we neither need to debase nor torment humanity. There, the planter's whip will not hurt the slave in front of the sugar cane. No, on the African terrain everything can happen nobly; free men will cultivate the land, French and European planters will live from work and under the protection of our arms, and the new colony will bring into bloom three of the most noble human components, liberty, agriculture, and war.[31]

Writing at a time where France remained undecided on what to do with its Algerian conquest, Lerminier clearly appropriated a range of discursive strands on colonial empire that the liberal elite who read the *Revue des Deux Mondes* as well as the French military could rally behind.

It is, of course, mostly the writings of the political economist, Paul Leroy-Beaulieu, that are seen to have offered the roadmap for the French *mission civilisatrice*. In his *De la colonisation chez les peuples modernes*, published for the first time in 1874, Leroy-Beaulieu stated that colonisation was about revitalising the mother country and seeing to the evolution of inferior peoples towards civilisation. Initially a supporter of informal empire, Leroy-Beaulieu developed a growing emphasis on the need to civilise 'barbaric' peoples through conquest, arguing that 'by joining Algeria to Senegal, we shall one day dominate and civilise all the north-west of Africa'.[32] Articulating such a vision in the aftermath of the humiliating Franco-Prussian War, Leroy-Beaulieu spoke at a time when French military might in Europe was called into question. At that moment, he may have appropriated the concept of civilisation formulated by Ancien Régime *économistes*, but merged it with an understanding of how it should mediate Franco-African relations that echoed people such as Durand, Pelletan, and Golbérry.

It may seem paradoxical to suggest that elements of physiocratic colonial ideas in some ways underpinned later arguments for both formal and informal empire in Africa, yet it need not be. Ideas lead curious lives and afterlives. As Bernard Semmel pointed out in his study of British free trade imperialism, once conceived, free trade imperialism could serve the interests of Britain's informal empire building and its 'formal' empire alike. He further argued that both 'conceptions were elaborated in terms of political economy and substantially moulded by struggles over economic principle'

---

[31] 'De la conservation d'Alger', *Revue des Deux Mondes*, vol. 6 (Paris: Bureau de la Revue des Deux Mondes, 1836), 611–12. I am grateful to Françoise Vergès for this reference. Plans for territorial conquest in Algeria would also come to find support among many of those initially favouring informal empire. Guizot was one such figure. Another was Alexis de Tocqueville. See Todd, 'Transnational Projects of Empire', 286 and 289.

[32] Paul Leroy-Beaulieu, *De la colonisation chez les peuples modernes* (Paris: 1874), 355, quoted in Todd, 'Transnational Projects of Empire', 291–2.

and that 'both forms were passed on, in altered form, to the time which saw the fall of the old colonial system, were extended, in the age of "imperialism", into rival party programmes, and, indeed, with further alterations, are present today'.[33] Without seeking to disregard nineteenth and twentieth centuries intellectual innovations that helped legitimise and shape French overseas expansion in the post-Napoleonic period, venturing forward in time illustrates how Ancien Régime political economic ideas and experiments found resonance in these later periods as promoters of empire set out to sway decision makers and political audiences of successive French regimes. Just as scholars have identified the continuity of racial and commercial structures pertaining to the prevailing mode of Ancien Régime colonial empire into the French Revolution and post-Napoleonic periods, so I show how these later periods carry within them elements from initiatives in the second half of the eighteenth century to reinvent colonial empire.[34] As we become more attuned to the ways in which historical continuity interlocks with innovation, change, and rupture, the polyrhythmic qualities of the history of the French colonial empire hopefully becomes more visible in the stories that we tell.

---

[33] Semmel, *The Rise of Free Trade Imperialism*, 8.
[34] Ghachem, *The Old Regime and the Haitian Revolution*; David Todd, 'A French Imperial Meridian, 1814–1870'.

Bibliography

Archival and Manuscript Sources

Archives Nationales d'Outre-Mer, Aix-en-Province, France (ANOM)
Correspondance au départ avec les colonies – Série B

Sénégal 116
119
121
123
126
192

Correspondance à l'arrivée – Sous-série C

Sénégal et Côtes d'Afrique Sous-série C^6
Guadeloupe Sous-série C^{7A}
Martinique et Îles du Vent Sous-série C^8, C^{8A}, C^{8B}

Moreau de Saint-Méry

F^3 29
F^3 60
F^3 62
F^3 124
F^3 126

Personnel colonial ancien   Série E
Abbé Demanet   E188
La Gastière   E246
Poncet de la Rivière   E338
Rocheblave   E355

Boufflers   E404
Dubuc   E143
Mercier de la Rivière   E276

Traités (1687/1911)

Number 409   between Poncet de la Rivière and Roy Damel
Number 434   between Abbé Demanet and sovereigns of Africa
Number 435   between Abbé Demanet and the Alicauri Tribe

Musée Arbaud, Aix-en-Provence

Fonds Mirabeau (FM)

Correspondances des Mirabeau

  Vol. 23
  Vol. 24

Archives départementales de la Gironde (ADG)

Chambre du Commerce de Guienne (C)

  4246
  4257
  4265
  4336
  4338
  4382
  4383

Ministère des affaires étrangères, Paris (MAE)

Archives Diplomatiques (AD)

  Afrique 10
  Afrique 11

Archives Nationales, Paris

Mirabeau Papers

M799

Directoire

AF III 206

National Archives, Kew

Colonial Office, Foreign and Commonwealth Offices

CO 166/2

Printed Primary Sources

Adanson, Michel, *Histoire naturelle du Sénégal: avec la relation abrégée d'un voyage fait en ce pays, pendant les années 1749, 50, 51, 52 & 53* (Paris: Claude-Jean-Baptiste Bauche, 1757)

Arnould, Ambroise Marie, *Système maritime et politique des européens, pendant le dix-huitième siècle; fondé sur leurs traités de paix, de commerce et de navigation* (Paris: Imprimerie d'Antoine Bailleul, 1797)

Baudeau, Nicolas, *Commerce*, 3 vols, Encyclopédie méthodique 78–80 (Paris: Chez Panckoucke, 1783)

Baudeau, Nicolas, *Idées d'un citoyen sur la puissance du roi et le commerce de la nation dans l'Orient* (Amsterdam [Paris, François-Ambroise Didot], 1763)

Baudeau, Nicolas, *Première introduction à la philosophie économique (1767)*, ed. A. Dubois (Paris: P. Geuthner, 1910)

Boufflers, Stanislas de, *Chevalier de Boufflers – lettres d'Afrique à Madame de Sabran*, ed. François Bessire (Arles: Actes-Sud/Babel, 1998)

Brissot, J. P., *Mémoires*, 2 vols. (Paris: Cl. Perroud, 1912)

Cantillon, Richard, *Essay on the Nature of Trade in General*, ed. Richard van den Berg (London: Routledge, 2015)

Césaire, Aimé, 'Rapport fait au nom de la commission des territoires d'outre-mer sur les propositions de loi', Annexe au procès-verbal de la séance du 25 février 1946, n. 520, 3, www.assemblee-nationale.fr/histoire/images/rapport-520.pdf

Choiseul, Étienne-François le duc de, *Mémoire historique sur la négociation de la France & de l'Angleterre, depuis le 26 mars 1761 jusqu'au 20 septembre de la même année, avec les pièces justificatives* (Paris: Imprimerie Royale, 1761)

Clavière, Étienne, *Addresse de la société des amis des noirs, à l'Assemblée nationale, a toutes les villes de commerce, à toutes les manufactures, aux colonies, à toutes les sociétés des amis de la constitution – adresse dans laquelle on approfondit les relations politiques et commerciales entre la métropole et les colonies, etc.* (Paris: Patriote Français, March 1791)

Code de la Martinique, 8 vols. (Fort-de-France, 1865)

d'Auberteuil, Hilliard, *Commerce des colonies, ses principes & ses loix. La paix est le temps de régler & d'agrandir le commerce* (1785)

Demanet, Abbé, *Nouvelle histoire de l'Afrique Françoise, enrichie des cartes & d'observations astronomiques & géographiques, de remarques sur les usages locaux, les mœurs, la religion & la nature du commerce général de cette partie du monde* (Paris: Lacombe, 1767)

Dessalles, Pierre-Franois-Régis, *Les Annales du conseil Souverain de Martinique* (1786), ed. Bernard Vonglis, 2 vols. (Paris: L'Harmattan, 2005). Google Books.

Diderot, Denis, *Œuvres complètes de Diderot*, ed. J. Assézat, 20 vols. (Paris: Garnier Frères, Libraires-Éditeurs, 1875)

Dubuc, Jean, *Le Pour et le Contre sur un objet de grande discorde et d'importance majeure. Convient-il à l'administration de céder aux Étrangers dans le Commerce de la Métropole avec ses Colonies* (London, 1784)

Dubuisson, Pierre-Ulric, *Lettres critiques et politiques, sur les colonies et le commerce des villes maritimes de France, adressées à G. T. Raynal par M. **** (Geneva, 1785)

Durand, Jean-Baptiste-Léonard, *Voyage au Sénégal ou Mémoires historiques, philosophiques sur les découvertes, les établissemens et le commerce des Européens dans les mers de l'Océan atlantique: depuis le Cap-Blanc jusqu'à la rivière de Serre-Lionne inclusivement; suivis de la Relation d'un voyage par terre de l'île Saint-Louis à Galam; et du texte arabe de Trois traités de commerce faits par l'auteur avec les princes du pays* (Paris: H. Agasse, 1802)

Forbonnais, François Véron Duverger de, 'Colonies', *Encyclopédie, ou dictionnaire raisonné des sciences, des arts et des métiers*, ed. Denis Diderot and Jean le Rond D'Alembert, University of Chicago ARTFL Encyclopédie Projet (Winter 2008 edn.), ed. Robert Morrissey, http://encycopedie.uchicago.edu/

Forbonnais, François Véron Duverger de, *Principes et observations oeconomiques*, 2 vols. (Amsterdam, 1767)

Frossard, Benjamin-Sigismond, *La cause des esclaves nègres et des habitans de la guinée, portée au tribunal de la justice, de la réligion, de la politique; ou Histoire de la traite et de l'esclavage des nègres, preuves de leur illégitimité, moyens de les abolir sans nuire ni aux colonies ni aux colons*, 2 vols. (Lyon: Aimé de la Roche, 1789)

Golbérry, Sylvain Meinrad Xavier de, *Fragmens d'un voyage en Afrique: fait pendant les années 1785, 1786 et 1787, dans les contrées occidentales de ce continent, comprises entre le cap Blanc de Barbarie, par 20 degrés, 47 minutes, et le cap de Palmes, par 4 degrés, 30 minutes, latitude boréale*, 2 vols. (Paris: Treuttel et Würtz, 1802)

Hobbes, Thomas, *Leviathan* (London: Penguin Classics, 1985)

Hume, David, *Political Discourses* (Edinburgh: R. Fleming, 1752)

Labat, Jean-Baptiste, *Nouvelle relation de l'Afrique occidentale: contenant une description exacte du Sénégal et des païs situés entre le Cap-Blanc et la rivière de Serrelienne*, 5 vols. (Paris: G. Cavelier, 1728)

Lacuée, *Opinion de J. G. Lacuée sur la dénomination qu'il convient de donner aux départemens désignés par le nom de colonies.* BN, Le 45 707.

Lamiral, M., *L'Affrique et le people Affriquain* (Paris: Chez Dessenne, Libraire, au Palais Royal, 1789)

Lanthenas, F. X., *M. Lamiral réfuté par lui-même ou réponse aux opinions de cet auteur sur l'abolition de la traite, suivies de quelques idées sur les établissements libres que la France ne soit pas différer de faire au Sénégal* (Paris: Potier de Lille, 1790)

Letters Patentes du Roy, Portant Règlement pour le Commerce des Colonies Franoises. Du mois d'Avril 1717. Registrées en Parlement (Paris: Imprimerie Royale, 1717)

Lettres Patentes du Roy en forme d'édit, Concernant le Commerce estranger aux Isles & Colonies de l'Amérique. Fontainebleau, October 1727 (Paris: Imprimerie Royale, 1727)

Loi relative aux Pensions, Donnée à Paris le 6 Avril 1791 (Paris: L'Imprimerie Royale, 1791)

Mémoires secrets pour servir à l'histoire de la République des Lettres en France, by Louis Petit de Bachaumont and Mathieu-François Pidansat de Mairobert, 36 vols. (London: Chez John Adamson, 1783–9)

Ministre de la marine et des colonies. Commission instituée par décision royale du 26 mai 1840, pour l'examen des questions relatives à l'esclavage et à la constitution politique des colonies, 2 vols. (Paris: Impr. Royale, 1840–43)

Mirabeau, Honoré Gabriel de Riquetti, *Mémoires biographiques, littéraires et politiques de Mirabeau*, ed. Lucas de Montigny, 8 vols. (Paris: A. Auffray, 1834–5)

Mirabeau, Victor de Riqueti marquis de, *L'Ami des hommes*, 6 vols. (Haye, 1758)

Mirabeau, Victor de Riqueti, marquis de, *Philosophie rurale, ou économie générale et politique de l'agriculture, réduite à l'ordre immuable des loix physiques et morales, qui assurent la prospérité des empires*, 3 vols. (Amsterdam: Chez les libraires associés, 1763)

Mirabeau, Victor de Riqueti marquis de, *Théorie de l'Impot* (1761)

Montesquieu, Charles Louis de Secondat, Baron de, *De l'esprit des loix ou du Rapport que les loix doivent avoir avec la constitution de chaque gouvernement, les moeurs, le climat, la religion, le commerce, &c à quoi l'auteur a ajouté des recherches Nouvelles sur les loix romaines touchant les successions, sur les loix françoises, & sur les loix féodales*, 2 vols. (Genève: Barrillot & fils, 1748)

Necker, Jacques, *Réponse au mémoire de M. l'abbé Morellet sur la Compagnie des Indes, imprimée en exécution de la délibération de Mrs les actionnaires, prise dans l'assemblée générale du 8 août 1769* (Paris: imprimerie royale, 1769)

Pelletan, Jean-Gabriel, *Mémoire sur la colonie française du Sénégal: avec quelques considérations historiques et politiques sur la traite des nègres* (Paris: Panckoucke, 1800)

Poivre, Pierre, *Œuvres complettes de P. Poivre*, ed. Du Pont de Nemours (Paris: Chez Fuchs, 1797)

Postlethwayt, Malachy, *The Importance of the African Expedition Considered: With Copies of the Memorials, as Drawn up Originally, and Presented to the Ministry; to Induce Them to take Possession of the French Forts and Settlements in the River Senegal, as Well as All Other on the Coast of Africa* (London: C. Say, 1758)

Pradt, Dominique-Georges-Frédéric Dufour de, *Les trois âges des colonies*, 3 vols. (Paris: Chez Giguet et Cie, 1801–2)

Procès-Verbal de l'Assemblée coloniale de la Martinique Créée par l'Ordonnance de Sa Majesté du 17 Juin 1787, rédigé par le Comité intermédiare, en vertu de la

Délibération de ladite Assemblée (Saint-Pierre: P. Richard, Imprimeur du Roi & du Conseil Souverain, 1788)

Quesnay, François, *Œuvres économiques complètes et autres textes*, ed. Christine Théré, Loïc Charles, and Jean-Claude Perrot, 2. vols. (Paris: L'Institut National d'Etudes Démographiques, 2005)

Quesnay, François, *Œuvres économique et philosophique*, ed. Auguste Oncken (Paris: Jules Peelman & Cie, 1888)

Rapport de l'archiviste de la Province de Québec (1924–5) (Ls-A.: Proulx Imprimeur de sa Majesté le Roi, 1925)

Raynal, Guillaume Thomas, Abbé, *Histoire philosophique et politique des établissemens et du commerce des européens dans les deux Indes*, 6 vols. (Amsterdam, 1770)

Raynal, Guillaume Thomas, Abbé, *Histoire philosophique et politique des établissemens et du commerce des européens dans les deux Indes*, 4 vols. (Geneva, 1780)

Roubaud, M. L. A. R., Abbé, *Histoire générale de l'Asie, de l'Afrique et de l'Amerique*, 15 vols. (Paris: Desventes de la Doué, 1770–75)

Rousselot de Surgy, Jacques-Philibert, *Mélanges intéressants et curieux, ou Abrégé d'histoire naturelle, morale, civile et politique de l'Asie, l'Afrique, l'Amérique, et des terres polaires, par M. R. D. S.*, 10 vols. (Paris: Lacombe, 1766)

Say, Jean Baptiste, *Traité d'économie politique; ou, Simple exposition de la manière dont se forment, se distribuent, et se consomment les richesses*, 2 vols. (Paris: Deterville, Libraire, 1803)

Sismondi, Jean Charles Léonard de, *De la richesse commerciale ou principe d'économie politique appliqués à la législation du commerce*, 2 vols. (Geneva: J. J. Paschoud, 1803)

Talleyrand-Perigord, Charles Maurice de, *Essai sur les avantages à retirer de colonies nouvelles dans les circonstances présents* (Paris: Imprimeur de l'Institut National, place du Carrousel, 1797)

Talleyrand-Périgord, Charles-Maurice de, *Mémoires du Prince de Talleyrand Publiés avec une Préface et des notes par le Duc de Broglie*, 5 vols. (Paris: Calmann Lévy, 1891)

Turgot, Anne-Robert-Jacques, *Œuvres de Turgot*, ed. Gustave Schelle, 5 vols. (Paris: F. Alcan, 1913–23)

Villeneuve, René Claude, *L'Afrique, ou histoire, moeurs, usages et coutumes des africains*, 4 vols. (Paris: Nepveu, 1814)

Wadström, Carl Bernhard, *An Essay on Colonization, Particularly Applied to the Western Coast of Africa* (London: Darnton and Harvey, 1794)

Journals and Newspapers

Ephémérides du citoyen (1765, 1766)
Gazette du commerce de l'agriculture et des finances
Gazette d'agriculture, commerce, arts et finances
Gazette Nationale ou Le Moniteur Universel

Journal d'agriculture, du commerce et des finances
Journal de commerce
La décade
Nouvelles Ephémérides économiques
Revue des Deux Mondes

Secondary Sources

Abénon, Lucien, *La Guadeloupe de 1671 à 1759 – Étude politique, économique et sociale*, 2 vols. (Paris: L'Harmattan, 1987)

Adelman, Jeremy, 'An Age of Imperial Revolutions', *The American Historical Review*, 113, 2 (2008), 319–40

Adelman, Jeremy, *Sovereignty and Revolution in the Iberian Atlantic* (Princeton, NJ: Princeton University Press, 2006)

Aldrich, Robert and John Connell, *France's Overseas Frontier: Départements et Territoires d'Outre-Mer* (Cambridge: Cambridge University Press, 1992)

Alimento, Antonella, 'Competition, true patriotism and colonial interest: Forbonnais' vision of neutrality and trade', in Trade and War: The Neutrality of Commerce in the Inter-State System, ed. Koen Stapelbrock (Helsinki: Helsinki Collegium for Advanced Studies, 2011), 61–94

Altman, Ida and James Horn (eds.), *'To Make America': European Emigration in the Early Modern Period* (Berkeley: University of California Press, 1991)

Ambjörnsson, Ronny, 'La République de Dieu – Une utopie suédoise de 1789', *Annales historiques de la Révolution française*, 3 (1989), 244–73

Ames, Glenn J., *Colbert, Mercantilism, and the French Quest for Asian Trade* (DeKalb: Northern Illinois university Press, 1996)

Armitage, David and Sanjay Subrahmanyam, *The Age of Revolutions in Global Context, c. 1760–1840* (Basingstoke: Palgrave Macmillan, 2010)

Armytage, Frances, *The Free Port System in the British West Indies: A Study in Commercial Policy, 1766–1822* (London: Longmans, Green, 1953)

Asher, Eugene L., *The Resistance to the Maritime Classes: The Survival of Feudalism in France of Colbert* (Berkeley: University of California Press, 1960)

Aubert, Guillaume, '"The Blood of France": Race and Purity of Blood in the French Atlantic World', *The William and Mary Quarterly*, 61, 3 (2004), 439–78

Aubert, Guillaume, '"Nègres ou mulâtres nous sommes tous Français" Race, genre et nation à Gorée et à Saint-Louis du Sénégal, fin XVIIe-fin XVIIIe siècle', in *Français? La nation en débat entre colonies et métropole, XVIe–XIXe siècle*, ed. Cécile Vidal (Paris: EHESS, 2014), 125–47

Banks, Kenneth J., *Chasing Empire across the Sea Communications and the State in the French Atlantic, 1713–1763* (Montreal: McGill-Queen's University Press, 2006)

Barry, Boubacar, *The Kingdom of Waalo: Senegal before the Conquest* (New York: Diasporic Africa Press, 2012)

Barry, Boubacar, *Senegambia and the Atlantic Slave Trade* (Cambridge: Cambridge University Press, 1997)

Bassi, Ernesto, *An Aqueous Territory: Sailor Geographies and New Granada's Transimperial Greater Caribbean World* (Durham, NC: Duke University Press, 2016)

Battesti, Michèle, 'Expédition d'Egypte, un plan de conquête français remontant au milieu du XVIIIᵉ siècle', *Cahiers de la Méditerranée*, 57, 1 (1998), 33–8

Baugh, Daniel, *The Global Seven Years War 1754–1763: Britain and France in a Great Power Contest* (New York: Longman, 2011)

Becker, Charles, 'Conditions écologiques, crises de subsistance et histoire de la population à l'époque de la traite des esclaves en Sénégambie (17e-18e siècle)', *Canadian Journal of African Studies*, 20, 3 (1986), 357–76

Behrendt, Stephen D., 'Crew Mortality in the Transatlantic Slave Trade in the Eighteenth Century', *Slavery and Abolition*, 18, 1 (1997), 49–71

Belenus, René, '19 Mars 1946: Les Quatre "vieilles colonies" sont érigées en départements français d'outre mer', in *60 ans de Départementalisation: Catalogue collectif documents conservés dans les Bibliothèques de Guadeloupe, de Guyane, de Martinique et de la Réunion* (CIR, 2006)

Belmessous, Saliha, *Assimilation and Empire: Uniformity in French and British Colonies, 1541–1954* (Oxford: Oxford University Press, 2013)

Benot, Yves, *La démence coloniale sous Napoléon* (Paris: La Découverte, 1992)

Benot, Yves, *La Révolution française et la fin des colonies 1789–1794*, 2nd edn. (Paris: La Découverte, 2004)

Benot, Yves, 'La chaîne des insurrections d'esclaves dans les Caraïbes de 1789 à 1791', in *Les abolitions de l'esclavage de L. F. Sonthonax à V. Schœlcher 1793 1794 1848*, ed. Marcel Dorigny (Paris: UNESCO, 1995), 179–86

Berbain, Simone, *Etudes sur la Traite des Noirs au Golfe de Guinée: Le comptoir français de Juda (Ouidah) au XVIIIe siècle* (Paris: Larose, 1942)

Binoche, Bertrand (ed.), *Les équivoques de la civilisation* (Seyssel: Éditions Champ Vallon, 2005)

Blackburn, Robin, *The Making of New World Slavery from the Baroque to the Modern 1492–1800* (London: Verso, 1997)

Blérald, Alain-Philippe, *Histoire économique de la Guadeloupe et de la Martinique du XVIIᵉ siècle à nos jours* (Paris: Karthala, 1986)

Bonilla, Yarimar, *Non-Sovereign Futures: French Caribbean Politics in the Wake of Disenchantment* (Chicago: Chicago University Press, 2015)

Bonnassieux, Pierre, *Conseil de Commerce et Bureau du commerce 1700–1791 Inventaire Analytique des procès-verbaux* (Paris: Imprimerie Nationale, 1900)

Bosher, J. F., 'Success and Failure in Trade to New France, 1660–1760', *French Historical Studies*, 15, 3 (1988), 444–61

Boulle, Pierre, 'The French Colonies and the Reform of Their Administration During and Following the Seven Years War' (PhD dissertation, University of California, Berkeley, 1968)

Boulle, Pierre H., 'Eighteenth-Century French Policies towards Senegal: The Ministry of Choiseul', *Canadian Journal of African Studies*, 4 (1970), 305–20

Bouteiller, Paul, *Le Chevalier de Boufflers et le Sénégal de son temps 1785–1788* (Paris: Éditions Lettres du Monde, 1995)

Branda, Pierre and Thierry Lentz, *Napoléon, l'esclavage et les colonies* (Paris: Fayard, 2006)

Brennan, Thomas, *Burgundy to Champagne: The Wine Trade in Early Modern France* (Baltimore: Johns Hopkins University Press, 1997)

Broers, Michael, 'Cultural Imperialism in a European Context? Political Culture and Cultural Politics in Napoleonic Italy', *Past and Present*, 170, 2 (2001), 152–80

Brooks, George E., *Eurafricans in Western Africa Commerce, Social Status, Gender, and Religious Observance from the Sixteenth to the Eighteenth Century* (Athens: Ohio University Press, 2003)

Brown, Christopher Leslie, *Moral Capital: Foundations of British Abolitionism* (Chapel Hill: University of North Carolina, 2006)

Brown, Laurence, 'The Three Faces of Post-Emancipation Migration in Martinique, 1848–1865', *The Journal of Caribbean History*, 36, 2 (2002), 310–36

Bumsted, J. M., '"Things in the Womb of Time": Ideas of American Independence, 1633 to 1763', *The William and Mary Quarterly*, 31, 4 (1974), 533–64

Burnard, Trevor and John Garrigus, *The Plantation Machine: Atlantic Capitalism in French Saint-Domingue and British Jamaica* (Philadelphia: University of Pennsylvania Press, 2016)

Butel, Paul, *Les négociants bordelais: l'Europe et les Iles au XVIIIe siècle* (Paris: Aubier, 1974)

Butel, Paul, *L'économie française au XVIIIe siècle* (Paris: SEDES, 1993)

Butel, Paul, *Histoire des Antilles françaises XVIIe–XXe siècle* (Paris: Perrin, 2007)

Certeau, Michel de, Dominique Julia, and Jacques Revel, *Une politique de la langue: La Révolution française et les patois* (Paris: Gallimard, 1975)

Chailley-Bert, Joseph, Les compagnies de colonisation sous l'ancien régime (Paris: A. Colin, 1898)

Charles, Loïc and Paul Cheney, 'The Colonial Machine Dismantled: Knowledge and Empire in the French Atlantic', *Past and Present*, 219, 1 (2013), 127–63

Chauleau, Liliane, *Dans les Îles du Vent la Martinique XVIIe-XIXe siècle* (Paris: L'Harmattan, 1993)

Chaussinand-Nogaret, Guy, *Choiseul – naissance de la gauche* (Paris: Perrin, 1998)

Chaussinand-Nogaret, Guy, *The French Nobility in the Eighteenth Century from Feudalism to Enlightenment* (Cambridge: Cambridge University Press, 1985)

Cheney, Paul B., *Revolutionary Commerce: Globalization and the French Monarchy* (Cambridge, MA: Harvard University Press, 2010)

Cheney, Paul B., *Cul de Sac: Patrimony, Capitalism, and Slavery in French Saint-Domingue* (Chicago: University of Chicago Press, 2017)

Childers, Kristen Stromberg, *Seeking Imperialism's Embrace: National Identity, Decolonization, and Assimilation in the French Caribbean* (Oxford: Oxford University Press, 2016)

Clark, Henry C., *Compass of Society Commerce and Absolutism in Old-Regime France* (Lanham, MD: Lexington Books, 2007)

Clément, Alain, '"Du bon et du mauvais usage des colonies": political colonial et pensée économique française au XVIIIᵉ siècle', *Cahiers D'Économie Politique*, 56 (2009), 101–27

Cohen, William B., *The French Encounter with Africans White Response to Blacks, 1530–1880* (1980; repr., Bloomington: Indiana University Press, 2003)

Cole, Juan, *Napoleon's Egypt: Invading the Middle East* (New York: Palgrave, 2007)

Collins, James B., *The State in Early Modern France*, 2nd ed. (Cambridge: Cambridge University Press, 2009)

Commission Historique et Archélogique de la Mayenne (Laval: Imprimerie-Librairie V A. Gouphil, 1905)

Conklin, Alice, *A Mission to Civilize: The Republican Idea of Empire in France and West Africa, 1895–1930* (Stanford, CA: Stanford University Press, 1997)

Cooper, Frederick, *Citizenship between Empire and Nation: Remaking France and French Africa, 1945–1960* (Princeton, NJ: Princeton University Press, 2014)

Courtney, Cecile and Jenny Mander (eds.), *Raynal's 'Histoire des deux Indes': Colonialism, Networks and Global Exchange* (Oxford: Voltaire Foundation, 2015)

Covo, Manuel, 'L'Assemblée constituante face à l'Exclusif colonial', in *Les colonies la Révolution française la loi*, ed. Frédéric Régent, Jean-François Niort, and Pierre Serna (Rennes: Presses Universitaires de Rennes, 2014), 69–89

Covo, Manuel, 'Le Comité des colonies Une institution au service de la "famille coloniale"? (1789–1793)', *La Révolution française*, 3 (2012), 1–20

Crouzet, François, *La guerre économique franco-anglaise au XVIIIe siècle* (Paris: Fayard, 2008)

Crowston, Clare Haru, *Fabricating Women: The Seamstresses of Old Regime France, 1675–1791* (Durham, NC: Duke University Press, 2001)

Cultru, P., *Histoire du Sénégal du XVe siècle à 1870* (Paris: E. Larose, 1910)

Curran, Andrew S., *The Anatomy of Blackness Science & Slavery in an Age of Enlightenment* (Baltimore: Johns Hopkins University Press, 2011)

Curtin, Philip D., *Economic Change in Precolonial Africa: Senegambia in the Era of the Slave Trade* (Madison: University of Wisconsin Press, 1975)

Curtin, Philip D., *The Image of Africa – British Ideas and Action, 1780–1850* (London: Macmillan, 1965)

Curtin, Philip D., 'The Lure of Bambuk Gold', *Journal of African History*, 14 (1973), 623–31

Curtin, Philip D., *The Rise and Fall of the Plantation Complex: Essays in Atlantic History*, 2nd ed. (Cambridge: Cambridge University Press, 1998)

Das, Sudipta, *Myths and Realities of French Imperialism in India, 1763–1783* (New York: Peter Lang, 1992)

Daubigny, Eugène, *Choiseul et la France d'outre-mer après le traité de Paris: étude sur la politique coloniale au XVIIIᵉ siècle, avec un appendice sur les origines de la question de Terre-Neuve* (Paris: Hachette, 1892)

Daudin, Guillaume, 'Profitability of Slave and Long-Distance Trading in Context: The Case of Eighteenth-Century France', *The Journal of Economic History*, 64 (2004), 144–71

Davis, David Brion, *The Problem of Slavery in Western Culture* (Oxford: Oxford University Press, 1966)

Dawdy, Shannon Lee, *Building the Devil's Empire French Colonial New Orleans* (Chicago: University of Chicago Press, 2009)

Debien, Gabriel, 'La Nourriture des esclaves sur les plantations des Antilles Françaises aux XVIIe et XVIIIe siècles', *Caribbean Studies*, 4, 2 (1964), 3–27

Debien, Gabriel, Les colons de Saint-Domingue et la Révolution – Essai sur le club Massiac (Paris: A. Colin, 1953)

Delcourt, André, *La France et les établissements français au Sénégal entre 1713 et 1763* (Dakar: IFAN, 1952)

Delmas, Bernard, Thierry Demals, and Philippe Steiner (eds.), *La diffusion internationale de la Physiocratie* (Grenoble: Presses Universitaires de Grenoble, 1995)

Desan, Suzanne, Lynn Hunt, and William Max Nelson (eds.), *The French Revolution in Global Perspective* (Ithaca, NY: Cornell University Press, 2013)

Desbarats, Catherine M., 'France in North America: The Net Burden of Empire during the First Half of the Eighteenth Century', *French History*, 11 (2007), 1–28

Dessert, Daniel, *Argent, pouvoir et société au grand siècle* (Paris: Fayard, 1984)

Dessert, Daniel and Jean-Louis Journel, 'Le lobby Colbert: un royaume ou une affaire de famille?', *Annales. Economies, sociétés, civilisation*, 30, 6 (1975), 1303–6

Dewar, Helen, 'Canada or Guadeloupe? French and British Perceptions of Empire, 1760–1763', *Canadian Historical Review*, 91, 4 (2010), 637–60

Diemer, Arnaud, 'David Hume et les économistes français', *Hermès*, May 2005, 1–27

Dobie, Madeleine, *Trading Places: Colonization and Slavery in Eighteenth-Century French Culture* (Ithaca, NY: Cornell University Press, 2010)

Donath, Christian, 'Persuasion's Empire: French Imperial Reformism, 1763–1801' (PhD dissertation, UC San Diego, 2012)

Dorigny, Marcel, 'Intégration républicaine des colonies et projets de colonisation de l'Afrique: civiliser pour émanciper?', in *Grégoire et la cause des noirs (1789–1831)*, ed. Yves Bénot and Marcel Dorigny (Paris: Société française d'histoire d'Outre-mer, 2005), 89–105

Dorigny, Marcel, 'La Société des Amis des noirs et les projets de colonisation en Afrique', *Annales historiques de la Révolution française*, 293–4 (1993), 421–9

Dorigny, Marcel, 'The Question of Slavery in the Physiocratic Texts: A Rereading of an Old Debate', in *Rethinking the Atlantic World: Europe and America in the Age of Democratic Revolutions*, ed. Manuela Albertone and Antonino De Francesco (London: Palgrave Macmillan, 2009), 147–62

Dorigny, Marcel and Bernard Gainot, *La société des amis des noirs, 1788–1799: Contribution à l'histoire de l'abolition de l'esclavage* (Paris: UNESCO, 1998)

Drayton, Richard, 'The globalisation of France: Provincial cities and French expansion c. 1500-1800', *History of European Ideas*, 34, 4 (2008), 424–30

Drayton, Richard, *Nature's Government Science, Imperial Britain, and the 'Improvement' of the World* (New Haven, CT: Yale University Press, 2000)

Drescher, Seymour, *Abolition: A History of Slavery and Antislavery* (New York: Cambridge University Press, 2009)

Dubé, Alexandre, 'Making a Career out of the Atlantic: Louisiana's Plume', in *Louisiana: Crossroads of the Atlantic World*, ed. Cécile Vidal (Philadelphia: University of Pennsylvania Press, 2014), 44–67

Dubois, Laurent, *Avengers of the New World: The Story of the Haitian Revolution* (Cambridge, MA: Belknap Press of Harvard University Press, 2004)

Dubois, Laurent, *A Colony of Citizens: Revolution and Slave Emancipation in the French Caribbean, 1787–1804* (Chapel Hill: University of North Carolina Press, 2004)

Duchêne, Albert, *Histoire des finances coloniales de la France* (Paris: Payot, 1938)

Duchêne, Albert, *La Politique Coloniale de la France Le Ministère des colonies depuis Richelieu* (Paris: Payot, 1928)

Duchet, Michèle, *Anthropologie et histoire au siècle des Lumières*, 2nd ed. (Paris: Albin Michel, 1995)

Dziennik, Matthew P., '"Till These Experiments Be Made": Senegambia and British Imperial Policy in the Eighteenth Century', *English Historical Review*, CXXX, 546 (2015), 1132–61

Ehrard, Jean, *Lumière et Esclavage L'Esclavage colonial et l'opinion publique en France au XVIIIᵉ siècle* (Bruxelle: André Versaille éditeur, 2008)

Elias, Nobert, *The Civilizing Process*, Rev. ed. (Oxford: Blackwell, 2000)

Elisabeth, Léo, *La société martiniquaise aux XVIIᵉ et XVIIIᵉ siècles 1664–1789* (Paris: Karthala, 2003)

Félix, Joël, *Finances et politique au siècle des Lumières: Le ministère L'Averdy, 1763–1768* (Paris: Comité pour l'histoire économique et financière, 1999)

Félix, Joël, 'The Financial Origins of the French Revolution', in *The Origins of the French Revolution*, ed. Peter R. Campbell (Basingstoke, UK: Palgrave Macmillan, 2006), 35–62

Fitzpatrick, Matthew (ed.), *Liberal Imperialism in Europe* (Basingstoke, UK: Palgrave Macmillan, 2012)

Forestier, Albane, 'A "Considerable Credit" in the Late Eighteenth-Century French West Indian Trade: The Chaurands of Nantes', *French History*, 25, 1 (2011), 48–68

Forster, Robert, 'The Noble Wine Producers of the Bordelais in the Eighteenth Century', *The Economic History Review*, 14, 1 (1961), 18–33

Fortier, Bénédicte, '1799–1830 Ruptures et Continuités du régime législatif des quatre vieilles colonies françaises', in *Rétablissement de l'esclavage dans les colonies françaises aux origines de Haïti*, ed. Yves Bénot and Marcel Dorigny (Paris: Maisonneuve et Larose, 2003), 505–22

Fournier, Joseph, 'Une Société de Géographie à Marseille en 1801', *Bulletin de la Société de Géographie de Marseille*, 23, iv (1899), 365–75

Fox-Genovese, Elizabeth, *The Origins of Physiocracy: Economic Revolution and Social Order in Eighteenth-Century France* (Ithaca, NY: Cornell University Press, 1976)

Frostin, Charles, *Les révolte blanches à Saint-Domingue aux XVIIe et XVIIIe siècles*, New ed. (Rennes: Presses Universitaires de Rennes, 2008)

Furet, François, *The French Revolution 1770–1814* (Oxford: Blackwell, 1996)

Gainot, Bernard, 'The Constitutionalization of General Freedom under the Directory', in *The Abolitions of Slavery from L. F. Sonthonax to Victor Schoelcher. 1793. 1794. 1848* (Paris: UNESCO Publishing, 2003), 180–96

Gainot, Bernard, 'La Décade et la « colonisation nouvelle', *Annales historiques de la Révolution française*, 339 (2005), 99–116

Gainot, Bernard, 'La députation de Saint-Domingue au corps législative du Directoire', in *Léger-Félicité Sonthonax. La première abolition de l'esclavage, la Révolution française et la révolution de Saint-Domingue*, 2nd edn., ed. Marcel Dorigny (Paris: Société française d'histoire d'outre-mer, 2005), 95–110

Gainot, Bernard, 'La naissance des départements d'Outre-Mer La loi du 1er janvier 1798', *Revue historique des Mascareignes*, 1 (1998), 51–74

Gainot, Bernard, 'The Republican Imagination and Race: The Case of the Haitian Revolution', in *Rethinking the Atlantic World: Europe and America in the Age of Revolutions*, ed. Manuela Albertone and Antonino De Francesco (Basingstoke, UK: Palgrave Macmillan, 2009), 276–93

Gallouët, Catherine, David Diop, Michèle Bocquillon, and Gérard Lahouati (eds.), *L'Afrique du siècles des Lumières: savoirs et représentations* (Oxford: SVEC, 2009)

Garraway, Doris, *The Libertine Colony: Creolization in the Early French Caribbean* (Durham, NC: Duke University Press, 2005)

Garrigus, John D., *Before Haiti: Race and Citizenship in French Saint-Domingue* (Basingstoke, UK: Palgrave Macmillan, 2006)

Gauthier, Florence, *L'aristocratie de l'épiderme – Le combat de la société des citoyens de couleur 1789–1791* (Paris: CNRS Éditions, 2007)

Gauthier, Florence, 'Le Mercier de la Rivière et les colonies d'Amérique', *Revue française d'histoire des idées politique*, 20, 2 (2004), 37–59

Geggus, David, 'The French Slave Trade: An Overview', *The William and Mary Quarterly*, 58, 1 (2001), 119–38

Geggus, David, 'Racial Equality, Slavery, and Colonial Secession during the Constituent Assembly', *The American Historical Review*, 94 (1989), 1290–1308

Géraud-Llorca, Edith, 'La Coutume de paris outre-mer: l'habitation antillaise sous l'Ancien Régime', *Revue historique de droit français et étranger*, 60 (1982), 207–59.

Ghachem, Malick W., 'Montesquieu in the Caribbean: The Colonial Enlightenment between *Code Noir* and *Code Civil*', *Historical Reflections/Réflexions Historiques* 25, 2 (1999), 183–210

Ghachem, Malick, *The Old Regime and the Haitian Revolution* (Cambridge: Cambridge University Press, 2012)

Ghachem, Malick W., 'The "Trap" of Representation: Sovereignty, Slavery and the Road to the Haitian Revolution', *Historical Reflections/Réflexions Historiques*, 29, 1 (2003), 123–44

Godfroy, Marion F., *Kourou, 1763: Le dernier rêve de l'Amérique française* (Paris: Vendémiaire, 2011)

Goebel, Dorothy Burne, 'The "New England Trade" and the French West Indies, 1763–1774: A Study in Trade Policies', *The William and Mary Quarterly*, 20, 3 (1963), 331–72

Grant, William L., 'Canada versus Guadeloupe: An Episode of the Seven Years' War', *The American Historical Review*, 17 (1912), 735–43

Grove, Richard H., *Green Imperialism – Colonial Expansion, Tropical Island Edens and the Origins of Environmentalism, 1600–1860* (Cambridge: University of Cambridge, 1995)

Hardman, John, 'The Real and Imagined Conspiracies of Louis XVI', in *Conspiracy in the French Revolution*, ed. Peter Robert Campbell, Thomas E. Kaiser, and Marisa Linton (Manchester: University of Manchester, 2007), 63–84

Hardy, Georges, *La mise en valeur du Sénégal de 1817 à 1854* (Paris: Émile Larose, Libraire-Éditeur, 1921)

Hasquin, Hervé, 'Jacques Accarias de Serionne économiste et publiciste français au service des Pays-Bas autrichiens', *Études sur le XVIIIe siècle*, 1 (1974), 159–70

Haudrère, Philippe, *L'empire des rois (1500–1789)* (Paris: Persée, 1997)

Herencia, Bernard, 'Enquête sur l'entrée de Lemercier de la Rivière dans le cercle de Quesnay', *Cahiers d'économie politique*, 64 (2013), 25–45

Hirschman, Albert O., *The Passions and the Interests – Political Arguments for Capitalism Before its Triumph* (Princeton, NJ: Princeton University Press, 1977)

Hodgson, Kate, 'French Atlantic Appropriations: Montlinot, Eighteenth-Century Colonial Slavery, and Penal and Forced Labour Schemes between Europe, Africa and the Americas', *Forum for Modern Language Studies*, 51, 2 (2015), 116–32

Hodson, Christopher, *The Acadian Diaspora: An Eighteenth-Century History* (Oxford: Oxford University Press, 2012)

Hoefer, M. le Dr. (ed.), *Nouvelle biographie générale depuis les temps les plus reculés jusqu'à 1850–60*, 46 vols. (Copenhagen: Rosenkilde & Bagger, 1968)

Hont, Istvan, *Jealousy of Trade International Competition and the Nation-State in Historical Perspective* (Cambridge, MA: The Belknap Press of Harvard University Press, 2005)

Hopkins, Daniel, *Peter Thonning and Denmark's Guinea Commission: A Study in Nineteenth-Century African Colonial Geography* (Leiden: Brill, 2012)

Horan, Joseph, 'The Colonial Famine Plot: Slavery, Free Trade, and Empire in the French Atlantic, 1763-1791', *International Review of Social History*, 55 (2010), 103–21

Horn, Jeff, *Economic Development in Early Modern France: The Privilege of Liberty, 1650–1820* (Cambridge: Cambridge University Press, 2015)

Horton, Donald J., 'Laporte de Lalanne, Jean de', in Dictionary of Canadian Biography, vol. 3 (Toronto: University of Toronto/Université Laval, 2003), www.biographi.ca/en/bio/laporte_de_lalanne_jean_de_3E.html

Houllemare, Marie, 'Le bureau des colonies et ses commis', in *La liasse et la plume: Les bureaux du secrétaiat d'État de la Marine*, ed. Jörg Ulbert and Sylviane Llinares (Rennes: Presses Universitaires de Rennes, 2017), 99–109

Hufton, Olwen H., *The Poor of Eighteenth-Century France, 1750–1789* (Oxford: Clarendon Press, 1974)

Jackson, Maurice, *Let This Voice Be Heard: Anthony Benezet, Father of Atlantic Abolition* (Philadelphia: University of Pennsylvania Press, 2009)

James, Alan, 'The Development of French Naval Policy in the Seventeenth Century: Richelieu's Early Aims and Ambitions', *French History*, 12 (1998), 384–402

James, C. L. R., *The Black Jacobins Toussaint L'Ouverture and the San Domingo Revolution*, 2nd ed. (New York: Vintage Books, 1989)

Jardaan, Han and Victor Wilson, 'The Eighteenth-Century Danish, Dutch and Swedish Free Ports in Northeastern Caribbean: Continuity and Change', in *Dutch Atlantic Connections, 1680–1800: Linking Empires, Bridging Borders* (Leiden: Brill, 2014), 275–308

Jennings, Lawrence C., *The Movement for the Abolition of Slavery in France, 1802–1848* (Cambridge: Cambridge University Press, 2000)

Jore, Léonce, *Les établissements français sur la côte occidentale d'Afrique de 1758 à 1809* (Paris: Société française d'histoire d'outre-mer, 1965)

Joucla, Henri, *Le Conseil Supérieur des Colonies et ses Antécédents avec de nombreux documents inédits et notamment les procès-verbaux du comité colonial de l'assemblée constituante* (Paris: Les Editions du Monde Moderne, 1927)

Kafker, Frank A. and Serena L. Kafker, *The Encyclopedists as Individuals: A Biographical Dictionary of the Authors of the Encyclopédie* (Oxford: Oxford University Press, 1988)

Kapila, Shruti, 'Global Intellectual History and the Indian Political', in *Rethinking Modern European Intellectual History*, ed. Darrin M. McMahon and Samuel Moyn (Oxford: Oxford University Press, 2014), 253–74

Kaplan, Steven L., *Bread, Politics and Political Economy in the Reign of Louis XV*, 2 vols. (The Hague: Martinus Nijhoff, 1976)

Kennedy, Melvin D., 'The Bissette Affair and the French Colonial Question', *The Journal of Negro History*, 45, 1 (1960)

King, Stewart R., *Blue Coat or Powdered Wig: Free People of Color in Pre-Revolutionary Saint Domingue* (Athens: University of Georgia Press, 2001)

Klein, Martin A., 'Slaves, Gum, and Peanuts: Adaptation to the End of the Slave Trade in Senegal, 1817–48', *The William and Mary Quarterly*, 66, 4 (2009), 895–914

Klooster, Wim, 'Inter-Imperial Smuggling in the Americas, 1600–1800', in *Atlantic History: Latent Structures and Intellectual Currents, 1500–1830*, ed. Bernard Bailyn and Patricia L. Denault (Cambridge, MA: Harvard University Press, 2009), 141–80

Klotz, Gérard, Philippe Minard, and Arnaud Orain (eds.), *Les voies de la richesses? La physiocratie en question (1760–1850)* (Rennes: Presses Universitaires de Rennes, 2017)

Kriger, Colleen E., '"Our indico designe": Planting & Processing Indigo for Export, Upper Guinea Coast, 1684–1702', in *Western Africa: Commercial Agriculture, the Slave Trade and Slavery in Atlantic Africa*, ed. Robin Law, Suzanne Schwarz, and Silke Strickrodt (Suffolk, UK: James Currey, 2013), 98–115

Kwass, Michael, *Contraband: Louis Mandrin and the Making of a Global Underground* (Cambridge, MA: Harvard University Press, 2014)

Labrouquère, André, *Les idées coloniales des physiocrates – (documents inédits) thèse pour le doctorat présentée et soutenue le Samedi 12 mars 1927* (Paris: Presses Universitaires de France, 1927)

Lamotte, Mélanie, 'Colour Prejudice in the Early Modern French Atlantic World', in *The Atlantic World*, ed. D'Maris Coffman, Adrian Leonard, and William O'Reilly (London: Routledge, 2015), 151–71

Larrère, Cathrine, *L'Invention de l'Économie au XVIIIᵉ siècle* (Paris: Presses Universitaires de France, 1992)

Larrère, Catherine, 'Mirabeau et les Physiocrates – L'origine agrarienne de la civilisation', in *Les équivoques de la civilisation*, ed. Bertrand Binoche (Seyssel, France: Éditions Champ Vallon, 2005), 83–105

Law, Robin, *From Slave Trade to 'Legitimate' Commerce: The Commercial Transition in Nineteenth-Century West Africa* (Cambridge: Cambridge University Press, 1995)

Law, Robin, '"There's Nothing Grows in the West Indies but Will Grow Here": Dutch and English Projects of Plantation Agriculture on the Gold Coast, 1650–1780s', in *Western Africa: Commercial Agriculture, the Slave Trade and Slavery in Atlantic Africa*, ed. Robin Law, Suzanne Schwarz, and Silke Strickrodt (Suffolk, UK: James Currey, 2013), 116–37

Law, Robin, Suzanne Schwartz, and Silke Strickrodt (eds.), *Commercial Agriculture, the Slave Trade & Slavery in Atlantic Africa* (Rochester, NY: Boydell & Brewer, 2013)

Levasseur, E., *Histoire du commerce de la France* (Paris: Librairie Nouvelle de Droit et de Jurisprudence, 1911)

Liauzu, Claude, *Histoire de l'anticolonialism en France du XVIᵉ siècle à nos jours* (Paris: Fayard/Pluriel, 2010)

Liébart, Déborah, 'Un groupe de pression contre-révolutionnaire: Le Club Massiac sous la Constituante', *Annales Historiques de la Révolution Française*, 4 (2008), 29–50

Livingstone, David N., *Putting Science in Its Place: Geographies of Scientific Knowledge* (Chicago: Chicago University Press, 2003)

Lokke, Carl Ludwig, *France and the Colonial Question: A Study of Contemporary French Opinion 1763–1801* (New York: Columbia University Press, 1932)

Lokke, Carl Ludwig, 'French Dreams of Colonial Empire under Directory and Consulate', *The Journal of Modern History*, 2 (1930), 237–50

Loménie, Louis de, *Les Mirabeau, Nouvelles Études sur La Société Française au XVIIIe siècle*, 5 vols. (Paris: E. Dentu, 1879–91)

Luthy, Herbert, 'Necker et la Compagnie des Indes', *Annales. Economies, sociétés, civilisations*, 15, 5 (1960), 852–81

Mandelblatt, Bertie, 'A Transatlantic Commodity: Irish Salt Beef in the French Atlantic World', *History Workshop Journal*, 63, 1 (2008), 18–47

Mann, Gregory, 'What Was the "Indigénat"? The "Empire of Law" in French West Africa', *Journal of African History*, 50, 3 (2009), 331–53

Marcillac, Sidney Daney de, *Histoire de la Martinique, depuis la colonisation jusqu'en 1815*, 5 vols. (Fort-Royal, Martinique E. Ruelle, 1846)

Margerison, Kenneth, 'The Shareholders Revolt at the Compagnie des Indes: Commerce and Political Culture in Old Regime France', *French History*, 20, 1 (2006), 25–51

Marion, Gérard Gabriel, *L'administration des finances en Martinique 1679–1790* (Paris: L'Harmattan, 2000)

Marion, Gérard Gabriel, 'L'outre-mer français: de la domination à la reconnaissance', *Pouvoirs*, 113 (2005), 233–40

Marshall, P. J., *The Making and Unmaking of Empires: Britain, India, and America c. 1750–1783* (Oxford: Oxford University Press, 2005)

Martin, Jean, *L'empire renaissant (1789–1871)* (Paris: Persée, 1987)

Marzagalli, Sylvia, 'Opportunités et contraintes du commerce colonial dans l'Atlantique français au XVIIIe siècle: le cas de la maison Gradis de Bordeaux', *Outre-mers*, 96 (2009), 87–110

Maugras, Gaston, *Dernières années de la cour de Lunéville – Mme de Boufflers ses enfants et ses amis* (Paris: Plon-Nourrit et Cie, 1906)

Maugras, Gaston, *La Marquise de Boufflers et son fils Le Chevalier de Boufflers* (Paris: Plon-Nourrit et Cie, 1907)

Maurel, Blanche, *Cahiers de Doléances de la colonie de Saint-Domingue pour les États Généraux de 1789* (Paris: Librairie Ernest Leroux, 1933)

May, L. Ph., *Le Mercier de la Rivière (1719–1801) aux origines de la science économique* (Paris: Centre National de la Recherche Scientifique, 1975)

May, L. P. (ed.), *Le Mercier de la Rivière (1719–1801) Mémoires et Textes inédits sur le gouvernement économique des Antilles avec un commentaire et des notes de L. Ph. May* (Paris: Éditions du Centre National de la Recherche Scientifique, 1978)

Mazlish, Bruce, 'Civilization in a Historical and Global Perspective', *International Sociology*, 16 (2001), 293–300

McClellan, James, III, *Colonialism and Science: Saint Domingue in the Old Regime* (Baltimore: Johns Hopkins University Press, 1992)

McClellan, J., III and F. Regourd, *The Colonial Machine: French Science and Overseas Expansion in the Old Regime* (Turnhout, Belgium: Prepols Publishers, 2011)

McNeill, J. R., *Mosquito Empires: Ecology and War in the Greater Caribbean, 1620–1914* (Cambridge: Cambridge University Press, 2010)

Mélisson, Céline, 'Les chambres d'agriculture coloniales: entre résistances et contestations de l'impérialisme français au XVIIIème siècle', *Études Canadiennes/Canadian Studies*, 76 (2014), 89–102

Melzer, Sara E. and Leslie W. Rabin (eds.), *Rebel Daughters: Women and the French Revolution* (Oxford: Oxford University Press, 1992)

Merle, Marcel, 'L'Anticolonialisme', in *Le livre noir du colonialisme: XVIe-XXIe siècle: de l'extermination à la repentance*, ed. Marc Ferro (Paris: Robert Laffont, 2003), 815–61

Meyer, Jean, Jean Tarrade, Annie Rey-Goldzeiguer, and Jacques Thobie, *Histoire de La France Coloniale Des origines à 1914*, 2 vols. (Paris: Armand colin Éditeur, 1991)

Meysonnier, Simone, *La balance et l'horloge. La genèse de la pensée libérale en France au XVIIIe siècle* (Paris: Edition de la Passion, 1989)

Michaud, J. Fr. (ed.), *Biographie universelle ancienne et moderne*, New edn., 45 vols. (Bad Feilnback, Germany: Schmidt Periodicals, 1998)

Michel, Jacques, *Du Paris de Louis XV à La Marine de Louis XVI: L'oeuvre de Monsieur de Sartine*, 2 vols. (Paris: Les éditions de l'Érudit, 1983)

Miller, Christopher L., *The French Atlantic Triangle Literature and Culture of the Slave Trade* (Durham, NC: Duke University Press, 2008)

Mims, Stewart L., *Colbert's West India Policy* (New Haven, CT: Yale University Press, 1912)

Minard, Philippe, *La fortune du colbertisme: État et industrie dans la France des Lumières* (Paris: Fayard, 1998)

Miquelon, Dale, 'Canada's Place in the French Imperial Economy: An Eighteenth-Century Overview', *French Historical Studies*, 15, 3 (1988), 432–43

Moitt, Bernard, *Women and Slavery in the French Antilles 1635–1848* (Bloomington: Indiana University Press, 2001)

Mousnier, Roland, *Les Institutions de la France sous la monarchie absolue* (Paris: Presses Universitaires de France, 1974)

Moyn, Samuel and Andrew Sartori (eds.), *Global Intellectual History* (New York: Columbia University Press, 2013)

Muthu, Sankar, *Enlightenment against Empire* (Princeton, NJ: Princeton University Press, 2003)

Newbury, C. W. and A. S. Kanya-Forstner, 'French Policy and the Origins of the Scramble for West Africa', *The Journal of African History*, 10 (1969), 253–76

Nicolas, Jean-Paul, 'Adanson et le Mouvement Colonial', in *Adanson – The Bicentennial of Michel Adanson's 'Familles des Plantes'*, 2 vols., ed. George H. M. Lawrence (Pittsburgh, PA: Hunt Botanical Library Carnegie Institute of Technology, 1963)

Oostindie, Gert and Jessica V. Roitman, *Dutch Atlantic Connections, 1680–1800: Linking Empires, Bridging Borders* (Leiden: Brill, 2014), 275–308

Oudin-Bastide, Caroline, *Travail, capitalisme et société esclavagiste: Guadeloupe, Martinique (XVIIe–XIXe siècle)* (Paris: Édition La Découverte, 2005)

Oudin-Bastide, Caroline and Philippe Steiner, *Calcul et Moral Coûts de l'esclavage et valeur de l'émancipation (XVIIIe–XIXe siècle)* (Paris: Albin Michel, 2015)

Pagden, Anthony, *European Encounters with the New World* (New Haven, CT: Yale University Press, 1993)

Palm, Franklin Charles, 'Mercantilism as a Factor in Richelieu's Policy of National Interests', *Political Science Quarterly*, 4 (1924), 650–64

Palmer, Vernon Valentine, 'Essai sur les origines et les auteurs du Code Noir', *Revue Internationale de droit comparé* 50, 1 (1998), 111–40

Paquette, Gabriel B., *Enlightenment, Governance, and Reform in Spain and Its Empire, 1759–1808* (Basingstoke, UK: Palgrave Macmillan, 2008)

Pares, Richard, *War and Trade in the West Indies, 1739–1763* (London: Frank Cass, 1963)

Parker, David, 'Absolutism, Feudalism and Property Rights in the France of Louis XIV', *Past & Present*, 179 (2003), 60–96

Peabody, Sue, *'There Are No Slaves in France': The Political Culture of Race and Slavery in the Ancien Régime* (New York: Oxford University Press, 1996)

Perrot, Jean-Claude, *Une Histoire intellectuelle d'économie politique* (Paris: Éditions de l'École des Hautes études en sciences sociales, 1992)

Pétré-Grenouilleau, Olivier, *Nantes au temps de la traite des Noirs* (1998 repr., Paris: Pluriel, 2014)

Pettigrew, William A., *Freedom's Debt: The Royal African Company and the Politics of the Atlantic Slave Trade, 1672–1752* (Chapel Hill: University of North Carolina Press, 2013)

Pincus, Steven, 'Rethinking Mercantilism: Political Economy, the British Empire, and the Atlantic World in the Seventeenth and Eighteenth Centuries', *The William and Mary Quarterly*, 69, 1 (2012), 3–34

Piquet, Jean-Daniel, *L'émancipation des noirs dans la Révolution française (1789–1795)* (Paris: Karthala, 2002)

Pitts, Jennifer, *A Turn to Empire: The Rise of Imperial Liberalism in Britain and France* (Princeton, NJ: Princeton University Press, 2005)

Pluchon, Pierre, *L'histoire de la colonisation française, I: Le premier empire colonial: des origines à la restauration* (Paris: Fayard, 1991)

Pluchon, Pierre, *Nègres et Juifs au XVIIIe siècle: Le racisme au siècle des Lumières* (Paris: Tallandier, 1984)

Poniatowski, Michel, *Talleyrand et le Directoire, 1796–1800* (Paris: Perrin, 1982)

Popkin, Jeremy D., *You Are All Free: The Haitian Revolution and the Abolition of Slavery* (Cambridge: Cambridge University Press, 2010)

Pritchard, James, *In Search of Empire: The French in the Americas, 1670–1730* (Cambridge: Cambridge University Press, 2004)

Pritchard, James, *Louis XV's 1748–1762: A Study of Organization and Administration* (Montreal: McGill-Queen's University Press, 1987)

Quinn, Frederick, *The French Overseas Empire* (Westport, CT: Praeger, 2000)

Quinney, Valerie, 'The Problem of Civil Rights for Free Men of Color in the Early French Revolution', *French Historical Studies*, 4 (1972), 544–57

Rediker, Marcus, *The Fearless Benjamin Lay: The Quaker Dwarf Who Became the First Revolutionary Abolitionist* (Boston: Beacon Press, 2017)

Rediker, Marcus, *The Slave Ship: A Human History* (London: John Murray, 2007)

Régent, Frédéric, Jean-François Niort, and Pierre Serna (eds.), *Les colonies la Révolution française la loi* (Rennes: Presses Universitaires de Rennes, 2014)

Reinert, Sophus A., *Translating Empire Emulation and the Origins of Political Economy* (Cambridge, MA: Harvard University Press, 2011)

Reinert, Sophus and Pernille Røge (eds.), *The Political Economy of Empire in the Early Modern World* (London: Palgrave, 2013)

Richardson, John, *The Language of Empire: Rome and the Idea of Empire from the Third Century B.C. to the Second Century A.D.* (Cambridge: Cambridge University Press, 2008)

Riley, James C., *The Seven Years War and the Old Regime in France: The Economic and Financial Toll* (Princeton, NJ: Princeton University Press, 1987)

Riskin, Jessica, *Science in the Age of Sensibility: The Sentimental Empiricists of the French Enlightenment* (Chicago: University of Chicago Press, 2002)

Røge, Pernille, "'La Clef de Commerce" – The Changing Role of Africa in France's Atlantic empire c. 1760–1797', *History of European Ideas*, 34 (2008), 431–43

Røge, Pernille, 'L'économie politique en France et les origines intellectuelles de "la mission civilisatrice" en Afrique', *Dix-Huitième Siècle*, May 2012, 117–30

Røge, Pernille, '"Legal Despotism" and Enlightened Reform in the Îles du Vent: The Colonial Governments of Chevalier de Mirabeau and Mercier de la Rivière, 1754-1764', in *Enlightened Reform in Southern Europe and Its Atlantic Colonies, c. 1750–1830*, ed. Gabriel Paquette (Farnham, UK: Ashgate, 2009), 167–82

Røge, Pernille, 'A Natural Order of Empire: The Physiocratic Vision of Colonial France after the Seven Years' War', in *The Political Economy of Empire in the Early Modern World*, ed. Sophus Reinert and Pernille Røge (Basingstoke, UK: Palgrave, 2013), 32–52

Røge, Pernille, 'The Question of Slavery in Physiocratic Political Economy', in *L'economia come linguaggio della politica nell'Europa del Settecento*, ed. Manuela Albertone (Milan: Feltrinelli, 2009), 149–69

Røge, Pernille, 'Rethinking Africa in the Age of Revolution: The evolution of Jean-Baptiste-Léonard Durand's Voyage au Sénégal', *Atlantic Studies*, 13, 3 (2016), 389–406

Rothkrug, Lionel, *Opposition to Louis XIV: The Political and Social Origins of the French Enlightenment* (Princeton, NJ: Princeton University Press, 1965)

Rothschild, Emma, 'A Horrible Tragedy in the French Atlantic', *Past & Present*, 192, 1 (2006), 67–108

Ruggiu, François-Joseph, 'Falling into Oblivion? Canada and the French Monarchy, 1759–1783', in *Revisiting 1759: The Conquest of Canada in Historical Perspective*, ed. Phillip Buckner and John G. Reid (Toronto: University of Toronto Press, 2012), 69–94

Ruggiu, François-Joseph, 'India and the Reshaping of the French Colonial Policy (1759–1789)', *Itinerario*, 35, 2 (2011), 25–43

Rushforth, Brett, *Bonds of Alliance: Indigenous and Atlantic Slaveries in New France* (Chapel Hill: University of North Carolina Press, 2012)

Sala-Molins, Louis, *Le Code Noir ou le calvaire de Canaan*, 2nd ed. (Paris: Presses Universitaires de France, 2003)

Saugera, Éric, *Bordeaux port négrier XVIIe–XIXe siècles* (Paris: Karthala, 1995)

Schefer, Christian, *Instructions générales données de 1763 à 1870 aux gouverneurs et ordonnateurs des établissements français en Afrique occidentale recueillies et publiées par Christian Schefer*, 2 vols. (Paris: E. Champion, 1921)

Schiebinger L. and C. Swan (eds.), *Colonial Botany: Science, Commerce, and Politics in the Early Modern World* (Philadelphia: University of Pennsylvania Press, 2005)

Schmidt, Nelly, 'The Drafting of the 1848 Decrees: Immediate Application and Long-Term Consequences', in The Abolitions of Slavery: from Léger Félicité Sonthonax to Victor Schoelcher, 1793, 1794, 1848, ed. Marcel Dorigny (Paris: UNESCO, 2003), 304–13

Schwartz, Stuart B., *Sea of Storms: A History of Hurricanes in the Greater Caribbean from Columbus to Katrina* (Princeton, NJ: Princeton University Press, 2015)

Scott, H. M. (ed.), *Enlightened Absolutism: Reform and Reformers in Later Eighteenth-Century Europe* (London: Macmillan Education, 1990)

Searing, James F., *West African Slavery and Atlantic Commerce: The Senegal River Valley, 1700–1860* (Cambridge: Cambridge University Press, 1993)

Sée, Henri, 'Les Économistes et la Question colonial au XVIIIe siècle', *Revue de l'Histoire des colonies françaises*, 4 (1929), 381–92

Seeber, Edward Derbyshire, *Anti-Slavery Opinion in France during the Second Half of the Eighteenth Century* (London: Oxford University Press, 1937)

Semmel, Bernard, *The Rise of Free Trade Imperialism – Classical Political Economy the Empire of Free Trade and Imperialism 1750–1850* (Cambridge: Cambridge University Press, 1970)

Serna, Pierre, 'Conclusion générale. Lorsque la loi fait la Révolution aux Colonies . . . ou l'empire des lois républicaines', in *Les colonies la Révolution française la loi*, ed. Frédéric Régent, Jean-François Niort, and Pierre Serna (Rennes: Presses Universitaires de Rennes, 2014), 263–82

Sessions, Jennifer E., *By Sword and Plow: France and the Conquest of Algeria* (Ithaca, NY: Cornell University Press, 2011)

Shovlin, John, *The Political Economy of Virtue Luxury, Patriotism, and the Origins of the French Revolution* (Ithaca, NY: Cornell University Press, 2006)

Shovlin, John, 'Selling American Empire on the Eve of the Seven Years War: The French Propaganda Campaign of 1755–1756', *Past and Present*, 206 (2010), 122–49

Smallwood, Stephanie E., *Saltwater Slavery: A Middle Passage from Africa to American Diaspora* (Cambridge, MA: Harvard University Press, 2008)

Smith, David Kammerling, 'Structuring Politics in Early Eighteenth-Century France: The Political Innovations of the French Council of Commerce', *The Journal of Modern History* 74, 3 (2002), 490–537

Soll, Jacob, *The Information Master: Jean-Baptiste Colbert's Secret State Intelligence System* (Ann Arbor: University of Michigan Press, 2009)

Sonenscher, Michael, *Before the Deluge: Public Debt, Inequality, and the Intellectual Origins of the French Revolution* (Princeton, NJ: Princeton University Press, 2007)

Spector, Céline, 'Le concept de mercantilism', *Revue de métaphysique et de morale* 39, 3 (2003), 289–309

Spieler, Miranda Frances, 'The Legal Structure of Colonial Rule during the French Revolution', *The William and Mary Quarterly*, 66, 2 (2009), 365–408

Starobinski, Jean, *Le remède dans le mal – Critique et légitimation de l'artifice à l'âge des Lumière* (Paris: Gallimard, 1989)

Stein, Robert Louis, *The French Sugar Business in the Eighteenth Century* (Baton Rouge: Louisiana State University Press, 1988)

Steiner, Philippe, *La 'science nouvelle' de l'économie politique* (Paris: Presses Universitaires de France, 1998)

Stern, Philip J. and Carl Wennerlind (eds.), *Mercantilism Reimagined: Political Economy in Early Modern Britain and Its Empire* (Oxford: Oxford University Press, 2014)

Tarrade, Jean, 'L'administration coloniale en France à la fin de l'Ancien Régime: Projets de réforme', *Revue Historique*, 229, 1 (1963), 103–22

Tarrade, Jean, 'La Révolution et le commerce coloniale: le régime de l'*Exclusif* de 1789 à 1800', in *État, finances et économie pendant la Révolution française* (Paris: Comité pour l'histoire économique et financière de la France, 1991), 553–64

Tarrade, Jean, *Le commerce colonial de la France à la fin de l'ancien régime: l'évolution du régime de 'l'Exclusif de 1763 à 1789*, 2 vols. (Paris: Presses Universitaires de France, 1972)

Tarrade, Jean, 'Liberté du commerce, individualisme et État. Les conceptions des négociants français au XVIIIe siècle', *Cahiers d'économie politique/Papers in Political Economy*, 27/28 (1996), 175–91

Terjanian, Anoush, Fraser, *Commerce and Its Discontents in Eighteenth-Century French Political Thought* (Cambridge: Cambridge University Press, 2013)

Théré, Christine and Loïc Charles, 'The Writing Workshop of François Quesnay and the Making of Physiocracy', *History of Political Economy*, 40 (2008), 1–42

Thomson, Ann, 'Diderot, Roubaud; l'Esclavage', *Recherches sur Diderot et sur l'Encyclopédie*, 35 (2003), 73–93

Thornton, John, *Africa and Africans in the Making of the Atlantic World, 1400–1800*, 2nd edn. (Cambridge: Cambridge University Press, 1998)

Todd, David, 'A French Imperial Meridian, 1814–1870', *Past & Present*, 210, 1 (2011), 155–86

Todd, David, 'Transnational Projects of Empire in France, c. 1815–c. 1870', *Modern Intellectual History*, 12, 2 (2015), 265–93

Traver, Barbara, '"The Benefits of Their Liberty": Race and the Eurafricans of Gorée in Eighteenth-Century French Guiana', *French Colonial History*, 16 (2016), 1–25

Vardi, Liana, *They Physiocrats and the World of the Enlightenment* (Cambridge: Cambridge University Press, 2012)

Vaugelande, Daniel, *Le salon physiocratique des La Rochefoucauld: animé par Louise Elisabeth de La Rochefoucauld duchesse d'Enville, 1716–1797* (Paris: Editions Publibook, 2001)

Vaughan, Megan, *Creating the Creole Island: Slavery in Eighteenth-Century Mauritius* (Durham, NC: Duke University Press, 2005)

Velay, Clément C., *Le Duc de Lauzun 1747–1793* (Paris: Éditions Buchet/Chastel, 1983)

Vries, Jan de, *The Industrious Revolution: Consumer Behavior and the Household Economy, 1650 to the Present* (Cambridge: Cambridge University Press, 2008)

Walsh, John Patrick, 'Césaire Reads Toussaint Louverture: The Haitian Revolution and the Problem of Departmentalization', *Small Axes*, 15, 1 (2001), 110–24

Wanquet, Claude, 'La tentative de Baco et Burnel d'application de l'abolition aux Mascareignes en 1796 – Analyse d'un échec et de ses conséquences', in *Les abolitions de l'esclavage de L. F. Sonthonax à V. Schœlcher 1793 1794 1848*, ed. Marcel Dorigny (Paris, 1995), 231–40

Ware, Rudolph T., *The Walking Qur'an: Islamic Education, Embodied Knowledge, and History in West Africa* (Chapel Hill: University of North Carolina Press, 2014)

Webb, James L. A., Jr., 'The Trade in Gum Arabic: Prelude to French Conquest in Senegal', *The Journal of African History*, 26, 2 (1985), 149–68

Weulersse, Georges, *La Physiocratie à la fin du règne de Louis XV (1770–1774)* (Paris: Presses Universitaires de France, 1959)

Weulersse, Georges, *La Physiocratie à l'aube de la Révolution 1781–1792*, ed. Corinne Beutler (Paris: Éditions de l'Écoloe des Hautes Études en Sciences Sociales, 1985)

Weulersse, Georges, *Le mouvement physiocratique en France (de 1756 à 1770)*, 2 vols. (Paris: F. Alcan, 1910)

Wood, Gordon S., *Empire of Liberty: A History of the Early Republic, 1789–1815* (Oxford: Oxford University Press, 2010)

Wood, Laurie M., 'The Martinican Model: Colonial Magistrates and the Origins of a Global Judicial Elite', in *The Torrid Zone: Colonization and Cultural Interaction in the Seventeenth-Century Caribbean*, ed. Louis H. Roper (Columbia: University of South Carolina Press, 2018), 149–61

Databases/Websites

Archives Parlementaires de 1787 à 1860, French Revolution Digital Archive, University of Stanford, http://frda.stanford.edu

Conseil Constitutionnel, www.conseil-constitutionnel.fr

The Avalon Project Documents in Law, History, and Diplomacy, http://avalon.law.yale.edu/18th_century/rightsof.asp

Voyages: The Trans-Atlantic Slave Trade Database, www.slavevoyages.org

Dictionnaire de l'Académie française, 4th ed. (1762), *Dictionnaires d'autrefois*, www.portail.atilf.fr

Index

abolition of slave trade, 251, 256

abolition of slavery, 1, 20, 219, 251, *See also Société des amis des noirs*; *Société des amis des noirs et des colonies*

abolitionism, 55, 92, 94, 97, 150, 200, 206

Accaron, Jean-Augustin, 56

Adanson, Michel, 57, 90, 98, 155, 157, 176

Africa

    colonisation of, 2, 15, 57, 153, 225–38, 241–4, *See also* Senegal, agricultural colonies in

    commercial agriculture in, 2, 10, 54, 55, 166, 172, 175, 179, 191, 201, 236, *See also* Physiocracy: relocation of cash crop cultivation to Africa

    French forts in West Africa, 27, 31, 57, 156, *See also* Senegal

    source of slaves, 32, 53, 153, 166, 191, 197

    substitute for Americas, 25, 54–5, 62, 95–102, 153, 174, 179, 197, 213

Afrique française, 179, 257

Afrique occidentale française, 258

Age of Revolutions, 246

agrarian political economy, 9, 75

agriculture, 13, 38, 111, 115, 130, 135, 142, 192, 257

    commercial agriculture in Africa. *See* Africa, commercial agriculture

    in Physiocracy. *See* Physiocracy

Aigremont, Monsieur de (ordonnateur of Senegal), 200

Aiguillon, Emmanuel-Armand de Richelieu, duc de, 181, 183

Albreda, 57, 156, 161, 165, 256

Alembert, Jean-Baptiste le Rond de, 66

Algeria, 19, 20, 258, 260, 261

American Revolution, 8, 129, 130, 138, 172, 188, 193, 202, 236

Americas

    future of, 8, 15, 17, 74, 99, 241, *See also* colonies, independence of

Anamabou, 54, 55, 191

Arguin, 156, 179

Arnould, Ambroise Marie, 204, 231

Arnouville, Jean-Baptiste de Machault de, 45

Arrhenius, Carl Axel, 194

assemblée coloniale, 106, *See also* Martinique, *assemblée coloniale*

assimilation, 20, 145, 203, 207, 223, 252, 254, 255

Auberteil, Hilliard de, 132

Azuni, D. P., 243

balance of commerce, 5, 124

Baltimore, 206

Bambuk, 163–4, 166, 191, 192, 232

bankruptcy, 8, 51, 52

Baol, 156

Bar, ruler of, 161

Barbé-Marbois, François, 240

Barbeu du Bourg, Jacques, 92

Barnave, Antoine, 210

Barry, Boubacar, 258

Barry, Madame du, 202

Basse-Terre, 47

Baudeau, Nicolas, 10, 65, 86, 89–91, 99, 132, 210, 232, 247

Baudry, Marie-Philippe Taschereau de, 183

Beauharnois, François de, 108, 112

Belesbat, Charles-Paul Hurault de l'Hospital, seigneur de, 75

Belley, Jean-Baptiste, 235

Benezet, Anthony, 98, 206, 208

Benot, Yves, 94, 240

Bernardin de St. Pierre, Jacques-Henri, 225

Berryer, Nicolas René, 115

Bertin, Henri Léonard Jean Baptiste, 57, 86, 183

Beudet, François, 129, 174, 175, 176, 195

Bight of Benin, 31, 157

Bissagot Islands, 188

    Bissau, 162, 165

    Bolama, 96, 162, 165, 179, 188, 228

Bissette, Cyrille, 251

Blanchot, François, 237, 238

Blot, Madame de, 202

286